# Cold War Correspondents

# Cold War Correspondents

Soviet and American Reporters
on the Ideological Frontlines

DINA FAINBERG

Johns Hopkins University Press
*Baltimore*

Johns Hopkins University Press
2715 North Charles Street
Baltimore, Maryland 21218-4363
www.press.jhu.edu

Library of Congress Cataloging-in-Publication Data

Names: Fainberg, Dina, author.
Title: Cold War correspondents : Soviet and American reporters on the ideological
frontlines / Dina Fainberg.
Description: Baltimore, MD : Johns Hopkins University Press, 2020. | Includes
bibliographical references and index.
Identifiers: LCCN 2019045848 | ISBN 9781421438443 (hardcover) | ISBN 9781421438450 (ebook)
Subjects: LCSH: Foreign correspondents—United States—History—20th century. |
Foreign correspondents—Soviet Union—History. | Foreign news—United States—History—20th
century. | Foreign news—Soviet Union—History. | Cold War—Press coverage—United States. |
Cold War—Press coverage—Soviet Union. | United States—Foreign public opinion, Soviet. |
Soviet Union—Foreign public opinion, American. | United States—Politics and
government—1945–1989—Press coverage. | Soviet Union—Politics and
government—1945–1991—Press coverage.
Classification: LCC PN4888.F69 F35 2020 | DDC 071.4/332—dc23
LC record available at https://lccn.loc.gov/2019045848

A catalog record for this book is available from the British Library.

*Special discounts are available for bulk purchases of this book. For more information,
please contact Special Sales at specialsales@press.jhu.edu.*

*For my parents, Evgenia Voronova and Boris Feinberg*
*For Zohar and Barak*

CONTENTS

I follow the Library of Congress system of transliteration, with the exception of names that have a common spelling in English, such as Ehrenburg, Mikoyan, Gorky, or Sharansky. I refer to Soviet organizations and institutions either by their Russian names and acronyms (e.g., TASS, Agitprop, *Pravda*, Glavlit) or by their commonly used English-language terms (e.g., Writers Union, Central Committee).

Cold War Correspondents

# A Battle of Words

A few days after arriving in Moscow in 1949, Harrison Salisbury realized that covering the Soviet Union for the *New York Times* would be difficult, even for a seasoned foreign correspondent. Since Salisbury's previous assignment in Moscow during the Second World War, there had been a sea change in Soviet treatment of American journalists. Mysterious men followed him everywhere, and Salisbury was certain that his room and office at the Hotel Metropol were bugged. He could not file a dispatch without getting clearance from Soviet censors, and journeying outside of Moscow required applying for a special permit, which could take months to obtain. In the Soviet press, vicious articles and cartoons accused foreign correspondents of spying for "American aggressors," leading some journalists to fear Soviet entrapment. This sense of anxiety soon caught up with Salisbury. In his letters home, he described living as if "under siege behind enemy lines" and voiced his concern that he or a colleague might become the target of a Soviet spy fabrication.[1]

Ivan Beglov had never been to a foreign country before 1949. That year, however, as he embarked on the long journey from Moscow to New York, Beglov knew how daunting it would be to head the US bureau of TASS (Telegraph Agency of the Soviet Union), the leading Soviet news agency. FBI agents followed Beglov's every step and meticulously inspected his offices, scrutinizing every bill and scrap of correspondence. When Beglov wanted to travel beyond a forty-mile radius of his office, he had to obtain a special permit from the State Department. Opinion columns in American newspapers discussed the specter of Soviet journalist-spies, soon to be expelled from the United States. Soviet correspondents isolated themselves, spending nights and weekends locked inside their apartments and indulging in drink. Reporting back to his superiors in Moscow, Beglov lamented that the atmosphere of suspicion and constant attacks on the agency made it impossible for TASS correspondents to carry out their reporting duties.[2]

Harrison Salisbury, a journalist working for a privately owned, liberal American newspaper, and Ivan Beglov, a correspondent for an official Soviet news agency, are not generally considered side by side. Yet their efforts to navigate an increasingly polarized world make for a striking comparison. Between 1945 and 1991, scores of American and Soviet journalists relocated to the capital cities of Communism and Capitalism to report firsthand on the rival superpower's politics, society, and culture. As they journeyed through distant lands, foreign correspondents confronted hostility and suspicion, made new friends, and struggled to understand a host country that appeared to stand against everything they held dear. Articles written by these journalists reached millions on a daily basis, and their best-selling books flew off library shelves. As gifted storytellers, foreign correspondents related their observations in ways that resonated with readers' interests and sensibilities, combining expertise with an accessible style. In an era of closed borders, foreign correspondents' reports were the nearest readers could get to actually visiting Moscow or New York City. Pundits, policy makers, and ordinary people on both sides of the Cold War divide came to see the Soviet Union and the United States through these journalists' eyes.

This book investigates how foreign correspondents shaped Soviet and American perception of the rival superpower during the Cold War. Over the decades, the adversary's coverage was fashioned through public and private interactions among multiple groups. These included the journalists, their sources, editors, news media executives, government officials, information specialists, propagandists, diplomats, American pundits, Soviet censors, and audiences on both sides. International reporting evolved, sometimes in tandem with and sometimes ahead of changes in international relations, domestic politics, and Soviet and American cultures as generations of correspondents succeeded each other in Moscow, Leningrad, New York, and Washington, DC. Scholarship and the public imagination often cast American correspondents as emissaries of free speech, who challenged the Soviet regime and reported the news objectively, "without fear or favor." Conversely, Soviet journalists are commonly depicted as cynical disseminators of party propaganda, who aided communist elites in concealing the truth about the obvious advantages of Western life.[3] In contrast, this book demonstrates that the main distinction between Soviet and American international reporting was not *whether* ideology informed journalism on each side, but *how*.

I argue that two distinctive Soviet and American sets of truth systems—ideological convictions, professional practices, and political cultures—permeated journalists' reporting and gave meaning to their encounters with the adversary.[4] Foreign correspondents were keen analysts who aspired to understand their host country. At the same time, they were fundamentally shaped by their cultural and institutional backgrounds. As journalists brought the foreign world to the doorsteps of their readers at home, their depictions of the rival superpower were refracted through their own culture's values. International reporting described the other side in readily recognizable, self-referential terms and personalized the differences between the two superpowers with real-life examples. While expanding their compatriots' knowledge about the adversary overseas, foreign correspondents also helped Soviet and American audiences to see themselves as citizens of the socialist or the liberal-capitalist world. In this way, Americans and Soviets who lived through the Cold War fundamentally understood themselves by creating images of each other.[5]

To tell the story of Cold War era international reporting from a comparative perspective, this book draws on Soviet and US government records, the archives of newspapers and news agencies, and individual correspondents' personal papers. These sources reveal the rich tapestry of institutional, professional, and personal dynamics that influenced international reporting, shed light on the relationship between journalists and the foreign policy establishment, and illuminate how foreign correspondents fit into the information universe of the Cold War. Oral history interviews clarified how international reporting worked on the ground and offered precious insights into the journalists' personal experiences. Finally, a great deal of attention is dedicated to the reports that journalists produced between 1945 and 1991, especially the long-form accounts—books or article series—that they wrote after their assignments ended. Readers from all walks of life encountered the rival superpower primarily through these reports, which played a crucial role in shaping the perception of the adversary in the popular imagination. Exploring the reporting and the experiences of American and Soviet correspondents from a comparative perspective illuminates a rich history of private and professional lives at the heart of the superpower conflict.

## News Media, Ideology, and the Cold War

The new historiography of the Cold War recognizes that ideology was an important factor in the superpower standoff.[6] David Engerman has characterized the years between 1945 and 1991 as a "battle of ideas" between American liberal capitalism and Soviet socialism. Both nations associated their ideologies with modernity and universality, each convinced that one nation's special mission could not succeed as long as the other existed.[7] Both nations also understood historical development as an inevitable progression toward a better future—one defined by "the spread of their own influence."[8] During much of the Cold War, both sides sought to mobilize audiences at home and abroad in support of their ideas.[9] According to Melissa Feinberg, the ideological confrontation between Soviet socialism and American liberal capitalism created a political culture dominated by the binary concepts of "truth" and "lies." As Feinberg explains, "Actors on both sides of the Iron Curtain placed truth at the center of politics, making the Cold War a moral contest that pitted right against wrong."[10] Both sides insisted that they were the only custodians of the truth and lambasted the rival's ideas as lies, disinformation, and propaganda. Policy makers and information specialists on both sides became deeply invested in harnessing the power of mass media to expose the rival's lies and to bring their own truth "to the masses" at home and abroad.[11] Unsurprisingly, information and propaganda became a primary site of the competition between the Soviet Union and the United States. Radio stations, books, journals, and television programs intended to disseminate "the truth" about the competing ideologies sprang to life on both sides. Soviet and American governments engaged heavily in this process by commissioning, sponsoring, encouraging, and promoting a wide range of information and propaganda materials. Thus, a diverse cast of state and non-state agencies, as well as individual actors, participated in perpetuating the Cold War's universe of information. In both cases, this process went hand in hand with the expansion of domestic mass media that mobilized audiences to support respective Cold War agendas through entertainment as well as through instruction.[12]

Foreign correspondents actively participated in their nations' projects of disseminating the truth and exposing their adversary's lies. On both sides, foreign correspondents belonged to a specially designated elite cohort of professional journalists entrusted with the task of representing the outside world to domestic audiences and explaining their country's increasingly complicated role in world affairs. On both sides, too, international reporting guided audiences in how to think of themselves in contrast to foreign "others" and ultimately mobilized public opinion to support the superpower standoff. In the global competition for hearts and minds, international reporting mattered considerably because it claimed to offer exclusive access to "the truth" about the rival: eyewitness accounts of what life on the other side was really like. Representations of everyday life functioned as a major platform for the ideological confrontation that defined the Cold War. Soviet and American propaganda often stressed the advantages of their respective ideologies by focusing on such mundane topics as schools, housing, home appliances, and clothing.[13] Similarly, it was through portraying the unhappy conditions of everyday life on the other side that Soviet and American foreign correspondents sought to demonstrate the superiority of their own political systems and the benefits of living under socialism or a liberal democracy. International reporting thus became intensely political and ideological.

What distinguishes international reporting from other sites of Cold War knowledge production is that journalists belonged to a profession in which truth telling was both a mandate and a source of legitimacy. Both Soviet and American journalism claimed to bring truth to the people and to speak truth to power. Both claimed to adhere to professional practices and truth-telling standards, which were independent of and preceded the superpower confrontation.[14] However, journalists' understanding of truth was also shaped by their respective professional and political cultures. The United States had a relativistic notion of truth that allowed for different viewpoints and competing interpretations of the same topic. In the Soviet Union, in contrast, there was what Natalia Roudakova has called "a realist view," whereby the truth of socialism was understood to be "singular," "solid," and "tangible."[15] These different epistemological notions of truth shaped the evolution of ideal journalistic practices on both sides.

Establishing and accurately reporting the facts were central to American journalistic practice, as was a rigid distinction between professional journalism and fiction.[16] The claim to truthfulness in the American press relied on the concept of journalistic objectivity—an ideal in which journalists approached the world as "disinterested realists" and, to the best of their knowledge, provided the public with an unbiased account of reality.[17] This ideal translated into a set of professional practices designed to ensure the objectivity of the press by meticulously presenting multiple sides of an issue, identifying something as "fact" only when supported by independently verified evidence, and distinguishing reporting from interpretive journalism.[18] With time, these practices promoted a dispassionate and professional incarnation of news, cementing faith among both journalists and the American public that the press offered "essentially factual and truthful descriptions of 'the way things are.'"[19]

This emphasis on journalistic objectivity, as well as the growing professionalization of reporting, helped to obscure the ideological constructions permeating news media in the United States and promoted the illusion that the press did not share the interests of those in power. However, a complex set of links bound the news media and the Establishment. On the one hand, owners of large news media enjoyed enormous prestige, unprecedented influence, and the ability to build or destroy reputations in business and politics. On the other hand, the media relied on close relationships with politicians and government officials to gain access to exclusive information and scoops—features that enhanced sales and publicity. Thus, news coverage continued to privilege the elite groups that dominated government, business, and other institutions of power.[20] Compartmentalization of news into different subject sections, or hierarchical organization of information within a single column, created an impression of a "natural" division and obscured editorial intervention. Significantly, these methods suggested that the press separated facts, opinions, and interpretations and thus contributed to an image of responsible media that reflect reality rather than selectively construct it. According to Phyllis Frus, in the American press, ideology worked by concealing and naturalizing the mechanisms that generated it.[21]

In contrast, the Soviet press openly and self-consciously projected socialist ideology and values. Sharing the Soviet writers' aspiration to become the "engineers of human souls," Soviet journalists considered factual accuracy to be secondary in importance to the "moral truth" of socialism.[22] As a result, according to Natalia Roudakova, Soviet journalistic practices often borrowed from literature, featuring techniques such as selective presentation of material, "guesswork and suppositions," "fabrication of details," descriptions of protagonists' inner worlds, and frequent reliance on "epithets and other forms of narrative enhancement."[23] Alongside impersonal statements about party pronouncements and heroic achievements of the Soviet people, newspapers featured journalistic essays (*ocherk*). These essays told "contemplative moral tales based on real events" and used singular stories to convey universal social truths in a concise and accessible form.[24] In these features, Soviet journalists offered their personal assessment of characters and events and frequently reflected on their own processes of gathering material for a story and thinking about it. Soviet journalists saw no contradiction between these practices and being truthful; their profession emphasized "the truth of meaning"—universal values and ideas revealed through an individual story or episodic detail.[25]

Interestingly, owing to this emphasis on moral values and literary techniques, personalized feature stories published in the Soviet press—especially if they exposed official corruption, negligence, or injustice—were often scrutinized for subversive potential. Although Soviet journalists who wrote these pieces always made sure to point out that they were addressing an "isolated occurrence," editors, censors, and vigilant party officials often believed that critical feature essays highlighted larger systemic problems and thus cast a shadow on the Soviet order as a whole. Yet abolishing critical features altogether was impossible because they were central to newspapers' mandate to promote socialist accountability by communicating citizens' grievances to the party-state.[26] By straddling the line between journalism and literature and focusing on "the truth of meaning" as opposed to "the truth of facts," Soviet journalism created space for ambiguity and alternative interpretations.[27]

Information specialists and journalists on both sides believed that their respective professional practices were mutually exclusive and dismissed the other's claim of being custodians of "the truth." Marxist-Leninist interpretations prompted Soviet ideologues to reject the American liberal model of news as false consciousness aimed at concealing the bourgeois bias of the Western press. They positioned the rival press corps squarely within a narrative of class warfare, with Soviet journalists representing the Marxist-Leninist truth and American journalists disseminating lies on behalf of the bourgeoisie. Conversely, American criticism of Soviet international reporting focused on the relationship between the government and the press. Soviet correspondents were perceived first and foremost as government-controlled journalists and were therefore expected to promote enemy propaganda and advance the interests of a hostile power. Convinced that the only way to report the news was the way practiced by the liberal news media, Americans charged that Soviet-style reporting was not journalism at all.

A comparative examination reveals, however, that American and Soviet journalistic practices developed in dialogue with each other.[28] In the United States, as newspapers rallied to combat the threat of Soviet propaganda, the boundaries of journalistic objectivity were redrawn to accommodate and naturalize anti-communist positions. In the Soviet Union, as newspapers grappled with the challenges of foreign radio broadcasting, correspondents turned to interpretive long-form journalism, began to emphasize human interest stories, and thought of themselves not just as journalists, but as writers and experts on international affairs.

Moreover, the seemingly incompatible Soviet and American journalistic practices, in fact, resembled and influenced one another. At the core of Soviet and American international reporting was a form of comparative writing and reading that invited audiences to contrast life on the other side with an ideal image of the home country as either a socialist utopia or the American dream. Glossing over the shortcomings of life at home, foreign correspondents reaffirmed readers' faith in their own country's creed and thus helped to popularize the respective Cold War ideologies. This style of writing has been typically viewed purely as a function of censorship and journalists' lack of faith in their own words—a feature that ostensibly distinguished Soviet totalitarian journalism from its liberal American counterpart.[29] In contrast, this book demonstrates that bias and subjective comparative writing were also central to American journalists' work. Thus, foreign correspondents *on both sides* actively promoted the ideas and values of the Cold War.

Foreign correspondents contributed to their country's Cold War propaganda and personally engaged with the ideological rhetoric they created and reproduced. International reporting combined a projection of Soviet or American culture onto the foreign world and the journalists' own personal interests and convictions. Professional duty demanded that journalists immerse themselves in their nation's ultimate "other" in order to make the rival intelligible to their compatriots. At the same time, they had to resist that "other's" ideological temptations. In this way, foreign correspondents simultaneously occupied the position of insider and outsider as they crossed boundaries of culture, customs, and worldviews on a daily basis. The ideological prism helped the journalists as they struggled to understand the Cold War adversary and to make their experience overseas meaningful. The foundational ideological claims of the period thus became deeply intertwined with the subjectivity of individual journalists. At the most fundamental level, the story of Soviet and American foreign correspondents demonstrates that Cold War ideology was not a fixed constant. Rather, it was a dynamic and adaptive force that helped individuals living in the era of superpower confrontation to make sense of their experiences and understand the world around them. On each side of the Cold War divide, foreign correspondents both contributed to and were shaped by the ideologies of their home countries.

The multifaceted nature of the superpower conflict, as well as the depth of Soviet and American investment in evaluating themselves vis-à-vis each other, offer a unique perspective on the complex relationship between journalism, ideology, and foreign relations. In the Soviet Union, journalism symbolized a belief in propaganda as a vehicle of enlightenment, a tool to help the New Men and Women of socialist society transform themselves into historical actors and builders of socialism. In the United States, journalism represented freedom to express one's opinion, informed participation in the democratic process, and public scrutiny of officeholders. On both sides, journalists were entrusted with the responsibility to monitor those in power, to expose corruption, and to protect citizens from injustice. But while the Soviet press fulfilled this role only in close collaboration with the party-state, the American media's capacity to stand up to power resided in the principle of separation between the press and the government.[30] Even though both journalistic ideals remained unattainable (and were subjects of debate within the profession), they endured as powerful symbols of Soviet and American modernity.

During the Cold War, journalism came to embody the quintessential distinction between socialism and capitalism, totalitarianism and democracy, figuring prominently in explanations for the Soviet-American confrontation. Officials and commentators in the US regarded Soviet information policies as both one of the USSR's defining traits and an important *cause* of the superpower conflict more broadly. Soviet surveillance, restrictions on journalists' mobility, and censorship of domestic and foreign press came to signify the standoff between an oppressive communist dictatorship and American freedom.[31] In addition, many American observers believed that Soviet people would never understand or trust the United States as long as their information came from articles written by loyal party propagandists and the censored Soviet media. In contrast, Soviet officials and propagandists claimed that the primary *manifestation* of the Cold War was the American press's hostility toward the Soviet Union. Negative reporting about the USSR promoted the interests of aggressive capitalism, turned the American public against the Soviet Union, and thus had the potential to bring the countries dangerously close to a real war. These different interpretations of the press's role in the Soviet-American confrontation reveal two competing sets of universal values at work. While American perceptions of the Cold War were predicated on a dichotomy between freedom and oppression, Soviet participants and observers understood the standoff in terms of the opposition between war and peace.

Harrison Salisbury and Ivan Beglov's professional and personal lives remained closely connected to the Cold War at home and abroad. Much to his own amazement, Salisbury remained in Moscow until 1954. After returning to the United States, he won the Pulitzer Prize for a series of articles about Soviet life after Stalin and wrote a highly regarded book about his experiences as an American correspondent in the USSR. In the following decades, Salisbury continued to shape US coverage of the Soviet Union and Eastern Europe, eventually expanding his expertise to include China. In the late 1960s, his reports from North Vietnam stirred up a furor that helped shift the American public's views of the Vietnam War and in the long run inspired journalists to question the Cold War consensus. He went on to write dozens of books and remained a sought-after commentator on Soviet and Chinese affairs until the end of the Cold War. Several generations of journalists at the *New York Times* and elsewhere regarded Harrison Salisbury as their role model.

Ivan Beglov's US assignment lasted until 1960. During the final years of his tour, working in TASS's offices became much more pleasant, thanks to the atmosphere created by Soviet-American dialogue and investment in "peaceful coexistence." After his long-awaited return home, Beglov continued to work for TASS but dedicated every spare minute to his passion project: a scholarly monograph on the US political economy. Meanwhile his son, Spartak Beglov, embarked on a spectacular career as a foreign correspondent and eventually became a leading commentator for the Novosti Press Agency, founded in 1961 to spearhead Soviet cultural diplomacy overseas. Ivan Beglov died on August 21, 1968, the day Soviet troops invaded Czechoslovakia. The invasion, which ended the hope of building "socialism with a human face," sent waves of disappointment throughout the socialist bloc and transformed Soviet international reporting into a lonely bastion of critical reflection on socialism in the world. In the early 1980s, as Soviet-American relations hit their lowest point since 1949, Ivan Beglov's grandson, Mikhail, was appointed as a foreign correspondent in New York, to the same TASS bureau that his grandfather once headed.

Although there was much that distinguished Salisbury and Beglov, they also had much in common. Both hailed from the heartland of their respective countries—Salisbury from the Midwest and Beglov from Siberia. Both developed an in-depth understanding of the other side and sympathy toward its people. And both remained committed to their professional responsibility to help their audiences understand the rival superpower and their own country's unique mission in world history. Their words, their versions of events, their characterizations of daily life, and their ideological principles would ultimately represent two adversarial nations to one another during one of the most significant conflicts of the twentieth century.

# PART ONE

# SPIERS VERSUS LIARS, 1945–1953

Only a few months after the Second World War ended, the relationship between former allies spiraled downward under the weight of mutual mistrust and fear of nuclear weapons. Soviets and Americans began to regard each other with anxiety and suspicion. Fears of foreign enemies quickly evolved into anxieties about domestic fifth columns. On both sides, enemy subversion was imagined as propaganda that aimed to infect the population with enemy ideology. On both sides, these anxieties focused on the press, transforming it into a symbol of the nation's virtue and the rival's vice.

In the first postwar years foreign correspondents found themselves caught in the crossfire between Soviet anti-Americanism and American anti-communism. As journalists whose duty it was to report from the enemy's den, they were deemed especially susceptible to the rival's manipulative propaganda or the seduction of a hostile ideology. In the Soviet Union as well as in the United States, the analytical capacities, professional experience, and allegiances of individual correspondents became the subjects of constant scrutiny and verification. At the same time, the anti-American campaign and the Red Scare singled out the rival's foreign correspondents as symbols of enemy propaganda and deceit. Soviet journalists working in the US and American journalists working in the Soviet Union confronted restrictions on travel and mobility, hostile coverage in the host country's press, and unwelcome attention from government officials and security services. Thus, at home, foreign correspondents faced the unpleasant task of constantly proving their ideological integrity. Abroad, they developed an acute sense of living in hostile encirclement.

International reporting quickly reacted to the rising tensions between the Soviet Union and the United States and to the two countries' growing sense of disadvantage vis-à-vis the rival's propaganda. The United States finished the war with a sizable and experienced international press corps, which represented the nation's major newspapers, magazines, and news agencies across Europe and Asia. Between 1945 and 1948, US news media drastically reduced their presence in the Soviet Union owing to a mixture of political considerations, financial concerns, and the tightening of Soviet censorship. Rather than sending their own correspondents to the Soviet Union, major newspapers, magazines, and news agencies turned to the services of in-house "Russia experts," who wrote international commentary based on Soviet publications, prior (and often dated) knowledge about the USSR, and insights gleaned from conversations with US government officials. In contrast to the United States, the Soviet network of foreign correspondents was patchy at best, and the journalists reporting from overseas often lacked the necessary language and professional skills. In the first postwar years the Soviet Union began to rapidly recruit and train a new cohort of journalists who would specialize in covering foreign affairs and would promote the Soviet viewpoint abroad. Soviet newspapers began to cultivate their own network of in-house experts, who used foreign language publications and institutional insights to write political commentary on international affairs.

Foreign correspondents became important players in the two countries' respective international information initiatives, as policy makers hoped that eyewitness news reports from the US or the USSR would deliver the "truth" about the other side and help battle the "lies" of enemy propaganda. Constant preoccupation with the "truth" and "trustworthiness" of information from overseas eventually turned international reporting into a sort of collective enterprise whereby journalists' reports were subject to intervention by editors, experts, and government officials. The "truths" produced by international reporting became steeped in, and largely dedicated to reiterating, the respective assumptions about the nature of the capitalist or the communist world.

Soviet and American treatment of the rival's correspondents and the ways that each side drew its own journalists into its domestic and international propaganda were shaped by their respective ideologies and political cultures. The Soviet system of government-controlled information relied on a large establishment designed to protect state secrets, and in 1946 this apparatus became responsible for censoring the dispatches of foreign correspondents stationed in the USSR. In the United States, where the First Amendment precluded the establishment of a centralized censoring body, the government circumvented the activities of Soviet correspondents through the application of the 1938 Foreign Agents Registration Act (FARA). The Soviet model of close collaboration between the press and the government ensured that foreign correspondents could be easily incorporated into the state's anti-American propaganda campaigns. Yet Soviet journalists' contribution to anti-American propaganda often was a far cry from a disciplined, coordinated effort, because party officials, editors, and foreign correspondents differed in their vision of what international reporting ought to be like. In the United States, foreign correspondents' contribution to official propaganda depended a great deal on individual journalists' readiness to cross the boundaries separating the government and the fourth estate. Still, the reporting of many American correspondents upheld the major tenets of US international propaganda and the government's policy toward the Soviet Union. Thus, despite the important institutional, political, and cultural differences between the superpowers, there was much similarity in their respective approaches to, and practices of, international reporting.

British and American writers, journalists, and propaganda experts referred to postwar international relations as the "Cold War" starting in 1945, and by the mid-1950s the term had entered wide circulation. Yet American journalists who worked in Moscow during the first postwar decade rarely used it in their coverage of Soviet domestic affairs or international relations. US news reports focused on the Soviet totalitarian dictatorship's manipulative propaganda and repressive practices and defined the American standoff with the USSR as a battle between "freedom" and "oppression." Soviet journalists and political commentators rejected the very idea of the Cold War as a fabrication of American media. They argued that disparaging reports in the American press *were* the "Cold War," which was being waged by the capitalist owners of US news services against the Soviet Union. The "warmongering American press" became an important pillar in the Soviet narrative of postwar international relations, which positioned the USSR as the sole protector of peace from capitalist aggression. On both sides, journalists emphasized that "hearts and minds" were the most important front in the battle between Soviet socialism and American liberal capitalism and volunteered to help their country confront the enemy's lies.

Regardless of their different attitudes to the idea of the Cold War, Soviet and American journalists came to play an important role in constructing its meaning. In their capacity as storytellers, political commentators, symbolic figures, and participants in international drama, foreign correspondents shaped their readers' views of the adversary overseas and demarcated the boundaries between "us" and "them" that became central to Cold War thinking.

# CHAPTER ONE

# Making "Soviet Restons"

Rumor has it that during the war Stalin once said, "We need Soviet Restons."[1] Having mobilized many of the most talented Soviet writers to cover the war effort, it is unlikely that Stalin was interested in the legendary *New York Times* reporter James (Scotty) Reston for his journalistic or literary skills. Rather, Stalin was fascinated by Reston's contribution to American propaganda around the world during his tenure as the head of the London Bureau of the US Office of War Information. As Stalin envisioned the expansion of propaganda at home and abroad, he realized that the success of the Soviet message would depend on those who carried it. As in all other spheres, cadres decided everything.

In the early days of the Cold War, Soviet ideologues, writers, and editors created and institutionalized "Soviet Restons"—professional journalists specializing in writing about international affairs for domestic and foreign audiences. The decision to establish such a press corps was driven by Soviet anxieties about American anti-Soviet propaganda. When Soviet officials imagined this new branch of journalism, they did not seek to create yet another mouthpiece for party slogans. Soviet international correspondents were to be trained in the most elite institutions, intimately familiar with foreign cultures, and proficient in foreign languages. They were expected to produce sharp and beautifully written accounts that would use real-life stories to demonstrate the superiority of Soviet socialism over American capitalism. Soon, however, this ideal clashed with the realities of the Soviet information establishment. The anti-American propaganda campaign generated suspicion of anything foreign and severely circumscribed the journalists' work. The ideals of Soviet propagandists and the literary aspirations of individual journalists turned out to be incompatible with the Soviet institutional hierarchy and the laconic style of the Soviet press. Until Stalin's death, Soviet foreign correspondents would speak with the voice of the Soviet state.

## Three Journalists Go to America

In late 1945, Soviet leaders realized their country faced a new threat: foreign headlines. Only a few months earlier, these headlines had praised Stalin's acumen and the achievements of the Red Army. Now, newspapers in Great Britain, France, and the United States took a decidedly negative view of the USSR's positions and interests.[2] Clippings from the international press landed on the desks of Politburo members once a week, thanks to the efforts of the Soviet news agency TASS (Telegraph Agency of the Soviet Union). TASS had representatives in thirty countries, and one of their duties was to collect every important article published about the Soviet Union overseas. The articles were translated, assembled into bound volumes, and dispatched to Moscow, where they were available only to senior Politburo members. By the end of 1945, the compendiums of press reports, particularly from the United States, became thicker and the articles they contained more acrimonious.[3] American newspapers accused the USSR of aggression and the violation of wartime agreements, and they frequently expressed fears of, or a readiness for, a new war, this time against the Russians. The way in which TASS bound these press selections into volumes made it impossible for readers to determine how important any given article was relative to other news items of that day. The format of presentation—a single binder containing only reports about the USSR—gave the impression that the American press did nothing but criticize the Soviet Union and report on its affairs. This impression was amplified by other reports from Soviet representatives in foreign countries, who told of growing animosity toward Soviet policies in Eastern Europe.[4] Still others warned of the "bourgeois propaganda offensive" against the USSR and urged the leadership to "counter with offensive tactics of our own."[5]

In March 1946, Winston Churchill delivered his "Sinews of Peace" speech in Fulton, Missouri, and accused the Soviet Union of building an "iron curtain" in Europe. Stalin personally rebuffed Churchill's remarks and accused him of "slander" and of "sowing the seeds of dissension" between former allies.[6] Stalin then gave a series of interviews in which he stressed that the only aim of Soviet foreign policy was to preserve peace.[7] Soviet officials concluded that they must take decisive action against the USSR's negative image in the foreign press and reinforce their message of peace.[8] As they had done during the war years, Soviet ideologues enlisted renowned writers and journalists for the task.[9]

*Figure 1.1.* Soviet journalists on their North American tour, visiting Canada to address a meeting sponsored by the National Council of Soviet-Canadian Friendship. June 13, 1946. *Left to right,* Mikhail Galaktionov, Ilya Ehrenburg, and Konstantin Simonov. (Photo: Powley W. Gordon/Toronto Star via Getty Images.)

In April 1946, Konstantin Simonov, Ilya Ehrenburg, and Mikhail Galaktionov left the Soviet Union for a two-and-a-half-month tour of the United States. It would have been difficult to come up with a more distinguished group to represent the Soviet viewpoint, for all three were well-known figures at home and abroad. Ehrenburg—a cosmopolitan Jewish intellectual and renowned writer—achieved notoriety during the war with his fiery articles calling on Red Army soldiers to kill the German enemy. Simonov, a dashing celebrity writer, became famous thanks to his intrepid frontline reporting, his lyrical poetry, and his international bestseller about the battle of Stalingrad, *Days and Nights.* Galaktionov, a talented propagandist and historian, obtained distinction writing for the army's popular newspaper, the *Red Star,* during the war and now headed the military department of *Pravda*—the official newspaper of the Communist Party of the Soviet Union.

The delegation was scheduled to attend a conference of newspaper editors at the Overseas Press Club and to remain in the US as guests of the State Department. Soviet foreign minister Vyacheslav Molotov briefed Simonov for the trip and instructed him and his colleagues to travel as much as possible after the conference and meet as many people as they could. The objective of the trip was "to impress upon all the people we meet [. . .] that establishing and strengthening peace is of utmost importance for us."[10] Although Molotov never said so explicitly, Simonov had the impression that these instructions came directly from Stalin.[11] The writers were expected to rebuff the accusations of the foreign press and to reinforce the Soviet message with the personal authority and international renown they had gained through years of war reporting.

The delegation arrived in Washington, DC, on April 19 and immediately assumed the task of publicizing Soviet peaceful intentions. In countless public appearances and interviews that the visitors gave in Washington, New York, and Boston, they stressed the importance of dialogue and collaboration between journalists and intellectuals in the two countries. Ehrenburg, the dominant voice of the delegation, frequently reminded his hosts that fascism was defeated by the strength of Soviet-American friendship and ridiculed the idea that the war-ravaged Soviet Union was planning another military campaign overseas. The guests urged their US colleagues to cease misrepresenting the Soviet Union and insisted that the future of Soviet-American relations depended on the efforts of American journalists.[12]

Yet the trip failed either to mend the growing estrangement between the former allies or to change American public opinion in the Soviets' favor. Even worse, the writers' experiences seemed to provide definitive proof that the American press was waging an organized anti-Soviet propaganda campaign. Several American commentators remained skeptical of Ehrenburg's calls for mutual understanding and predicted that when the Soviet journalists returned home, their reports about the United States would not challenge their communist masters' propaganda.[13] Nor did it help the Soviet case that while Ehrenburg was inviting foreign journalists to visit his country and learn firsthand about its peaceful intentions, Soviet authorities at home intensified the censorship of foreign correspondents and subjected their work to new restrictions. American reporters took Ehrenburg to task for ignoring these restrictions and accused him of hypocrisy.[14] Ehrenburg later recalled in his memoir that it was the antagonism of American newspapers that thwarted his mission. As the trip progressed, he wrote, attitudes toward the "Red journalists" and the

Soviet Union steadily deteriorated: "The newspapers expressed hostility more and more often; the people we met became more watchful. [. . .] The mood of regular Americans was changing in front of our very eyes. I was particularly struck by journalists writing for Hearst newspapers: they concocted improbable tales about us, even though we were right in front of their eyes."[15]

Ultimately, Ehrenburg's unhappy experiences with the American press colored the series of articles about the United States that he would publish in *Izvestiia*. The last installment of the series explained that American capitalists and "fascists" feared that the Soviet triumph in the war would inspire progressive forces in the US to rise up against domestic racism and inequality. Enlisted by reactionary forces, fear-mongering American newspapers smeared the Soviet Union's reputation and concealed its peaceful intentions from American readers: "Americans often speak about the 'iron curtain' that the Soviet Union is supposedly hiding behind from the rest of the world. I must admit that the iron curtain indeed exists and that it prevents the average American from seeing what is happening in our country. This curtain is manufactured in America—in the editorial rooms of newspapers, on radio stations, and in the offices of filmmakers and film distributors. Many American newspapers, aided by their foreign correspondents, deceive readers on a daily basis."[16] Although the series concluded with the hope that the American people might learn to cut through the belligerent noise of their newspapers, Ehrenburg ultimately sided with official Soviet analyses of the foreign press. He accused American newspapers of deliberately trying to undermine the friendship between the two countries by propagating the idea of an "iron curtain." He charged that US politicians were using sensationalistic rhetoric and prophesying an imminent war to advance their own political ends. According to Ehrenburg and others, smear reporting in the American press, funded by "reactionary forces," *was* the iron curtain and accounted for the growing rift between the Soviet Union and the United States.

The conclusion to Ehrenburg's American series demonstrates how Soviet actors used ideology to interpret the changing relations with their former allies. Many Soviets observed a reactionary capitalist response to the triumph of the socialist state and socialist ideas in the postwar world.[17] In the evolving struggle between socialism and capitalism, the American press appeared as an important strategic asset in establishing geopolitical supremacy and international prestige. Soviet leaders believed the press to be the official voice of the state, and they assumed that publications in American newspapers reflected the existence of an organized and officially sanctioned propaganda campaign against the USSR.[18] Ehrenburg's articles also make visible how Soviet actors used the language of war to articulate their concerns with international propaganda. Unfriendly reporting in the rival's press represented an act of aggression. Public opinion at home and abroad became a battlefield that had to be conquered. "Fascists" and "revanchists" lurked behind every publication that took an adversarial view of the Soviet Union and undermined the hard-won peace. This rhetoric linked the recent war to ongoing international tensions and created the impression that foreign propaganda threatened the very existence of the Soviet Union.

## Fighting Enemy Propaganda at Home and Abroad

Whereas the American press seemed to be a well-calibrated weapon in the developing ideological war, its Soviet counterpart appeared unprepared to meet the challenges of postwar information.[19] In 1946 and 1947, two reports commissioned by the Central Committee, one for the Agitation and Propaganda Department (Agitprop) and the other for the International Department, revealed that Soviet newspapers and news agencies suffered from severe shortages of cadres qualified to work with international information. Employees lacked sufficient understanding of Marxism-Leninism, knew close to nothing about foreign countries, and had poor command of foreign languages. Many were not members of the Communist Party, had no higher education, and came from the ranks of "the non-leading nationalities of the USSR" (read: Jews).[20] The reports made clear that the Soviet press corps overseas was in dire straits and routinely "failed to fulfill the most important goals of Soviet propaganda."[21] Often foreign correspondents' duties were performed by "simply strange people" with no journalistic training whatsoever.[22] For example, the TASS correspondent in Stockholm, one Luniakov, was a machine gun technician who had happened to drift into TASS's Vilnius bureau during the war. The TASS correspondent in Rio de Janeiro, Kalugin (nicknamed "the cyclist"), was a professional rowing instructor.[23] Correspondents overseas were mostly left to their own devices and rarely received guidance or instructions from their home offices. In contrast to the impressive international infrastructure of the US news media, the reports noted, the Soviet network of foreign correspondents was perpetually understaffed. Although the central papers, *Pravda* and *Izvestiia*, were allowed to run bureaus in fourteen countries, neither paper had any foreign correspondents at all. TASS's overseas operations often relied on foreign nationals, exclusively so in some countries.[24] One report estimated that the Soviet international press corps was about 120 correspondents short.[25] Both reports concluded that the Soviet higher education system had failed to train enough specialists in journalism; meanwhile, capitalist countries, especially the United States, had entire university programs and other institutions devoted to journalistic training.[26]

Soviet officials began to overhaul domestic and international propaganda and to scrutinize the people and institutions responsible for shaping hearts and minds. It was in this context that the Central Committee issued its famous resolution condemning the "ideologically harmful" journals *Zvezda* and *Leningrad*, and that chief Communist Party ideologue Andrei Zhdanov launched his eponymous campaign (the "Zhdanovshchina") attacking Soviet intellectuals for "kowtowing to bourgeois culture."[27] The premise of the campaign was that the party should take it upon itself to raise the standards of work on "the ideological front" and increase its supervision over writers and the press—the custodians of the nation's ideological purity.[28]

To make propaganda better coordinated and more effective, Agitprop launched its own newspaper, *Culture and Life*, which focused on elucidating the tasks and criticizing the shortcomings of "ideological work." From its establishment in 1946 until its sudden dissolution in 1951, *Culture and Life* spearheaded every propaganda campaign of the Cold War, signaling the dos and don'ts in the press, literature, and the arts.[29] The front page of *Culture and Life*'s first issue rallied Soviet elites for a new battle for the communist consciousness of the people. The editors warned journalists, writers, and artists against indulging in "light entertainment" or "bourgeois themes" and stressed that Soviet culture must inspire ideas of "creative Soviet patriotism."[30]

*Pravda* editorials linked the domestic and international aspects of the ideological battle and explained that the Soviet triumph over foreign propaganda depended first and foremost on the unwavering communist consciousness of the Soviet people. In October 1946 a front-page editorial entitled "We Must Increase the Role of the Press in Our Economic and Political Life" explained that "reactionary bourgeois ideology" threatened the Soviet people and sought to "poison them with worldviews alien to Soviet society."[31] Therefore, it was the duty of the Soviet press to protect Soviet people's consciousness and launch an international offensive against "bourgeois ideology." A month later *Pravda* featured Simonov's article "Dramaturgy, Theatre, and Life," which explained that Soviet culture played a crucial role in the international "battle for world peace."[32] Simonov urged fellow members of the cultural elite to focus on the international challenges facing the Soviet state and to mobilize for "an active unstoppable offensive" against its "ideological enemies."

Now more than ever, it was the duty of Soviet writers and artists to demonstrate the "prominence of the Soviet Man in international affairs and world history" and to declare that "communism was the only true path for the future of humankind."[33] Militaristic language and references to "ideological war" or the "ideological front" increasingly dominated the Soviet press and mobilized the engineers of souls for a full-fledged campaign against the bourgeois enemy.

In February 1947, the Voice of America launched Russian-language broadcasts, delivering another blow on behalf of bourgeois propaganda. Initially, the US government had planned to dispense with the station after the end of the war. However, just as Soviet propagandists worried about the effectiveness of their own international message, US policy makers decided to reinvigorate the Voice of America with new funding, mainly as a response to Soviet anti-American propaganda.[34] In particular, Americans observed with alarm the increased standing of European communist parties, along with the struggles by the French, the Dutch, and the British to contain revolutionary movements in their South Asian colonies during the winter of 1946–1947. State Department analysis of the situation concluded that Soviet anti-American propaganda was responsible for the international ferment.[35] Like their Soviet counterparts, American policymakers feared losing the propaganda battle and escalated their efforts in response. The broadcasts of Voice of America were designed to neutralize Soviet propaganda and promote a positive image of the United States.[36]

The Soviet response to the Voice of America was to double down on its attacks on American media and to launch an information offensive against the "bourgeois press." In April 1947, Ilya Ehrenburg wrote two articles for *Culture and Life* in which he accused the Voice of America of fearmongering and condemned it for undermining Soviet-American relations.[37] In other publications, the term "bourgeois press" began to replace "reactionary forces" as the main culprit behind the mounting tensions between the Soviet Union and the United States. References to the foreign press as "bourgeois" had been prominent in prewar newspapers, but at that time the term had most often been used to describe non-communist or non-socialist newspapers. By 1947, the "bourgeois press" appeared in articles as an *acting subject*, depicted as persistently undermining the cause of peace. These articles explicitly identified the American press with the worst excesses of capitalist mass media and invariably described it as "slanderous," "deceitful," or "warmongering."[38]

Eye-catching cartoons in the popular satirical journal *Krokodil* helped personify the term "bourgeois press" and endow it with vivid images.[39] The June 1947 issue featured a comic strip entitled "Illustrations to the Notes of a Foreign Correspondent's Visit to Moscow." The comic depicts a foreign journalist who misrepresents his Soviet experiences with evidently "true" comments that cast the USSR in a negative light. While visiting a beach, for instance, the journalist scribbles in his notebook, "I was able to observe that the people surrounding me had nothing to wear." As the campaign progressed, *Krokodil's* representations of the "bourgeois press" grew more and more threatening, depicting foreign journalists as sinister figures, spiders, or snakes, busily constructing malignant lies about the Soviet Union.[40]

A preoccupation with the "bourgeois press" was also evident in the flagship of Soviet Cold War propaganda at home and abroad: Simonov's 1947 play *The Russian Question*, which was, according to the author, based on his experiences in the United States.[41] Stalin personally endorsed the play and instructed that it be widely publicized. *The Russian Question*, which won the prestigious Stalin Prize in Drama, was staged simultaneously in thirty Soviet theaters, including five in Moscow and three in Leningrad.[42] In 1948 Mikhail Romm's film adaptation also received the Stalin Prize and thus reinforced the importance of its political message.[43]

The play tells the story of Harry Smith, an American journalist and Second World War veteran who had visited the USSR during the war. Smith's boss, the news magnate McPherson (whose character was modeled after William Randolph Hearst Jr.) feels threatened by the towering reputation of the Soviet Union and seeks to undermine it. McPherson sends Smith on another trip to the Soviet Union and expects him to write a book showing that the Soviets are planning a war against the United States. Upon his return, however, Smith refuses to produce the slanderous account and writes a different book, which explains to Americans that they have been misled by anti-Soviet propaganda. McPherson and his capitalist friends on Wall Street are incensed. Smith loses his job, his girlfriend, and his house, but he maintains his dignity and resolve and sticks to his story. At the end of the play, Smith realizes that he does not belong in "Hearst's America" and hopes, instead, to find a place in the "America of Lincoln and Roosevelt."[44]

Although it is considered a classic example of Soviet anti-American propaganda, *The Russian Question* differed substantially from many subsequent works in this genre. Simonov did not denounce the capitalist press in unqualified

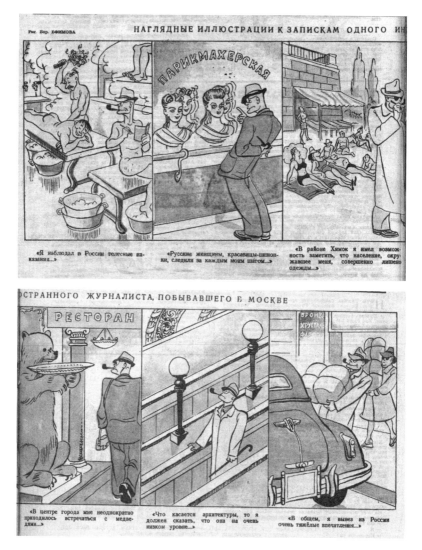

*Figure 1.2.* Boris Efimov, "Illustrations for the notes of a foreign journalist who visited Moscow." Originally published in *Krokodil* no. 17, June 20, 1947. (Image courtesy of Neboltai.org collection. Published by permission of Viktor Aleksandrovich Fradkin.)
Captions, *top row, left to right*:
I saw corporal punishment administered in Russia.
Beautiful Russian female spies followed my every move (sign on the window reads "hair salon").
In the Khimki area, I was surrounded by a population that had nothing to wear.
Captions, *bottom row, left to right*:
In the town center I frequently saw bears (sign on top reads "restaurant").
Regarding architecture, I must say that it's on a rather low level.
In general, I departed Russia with heavy impressions.

terms; he took a more measured stance, showing that the Soviet Union had both friends and foes at mainstream American newspapers. The play gave a relatively nuanced portrayal of the enemy, making a clear distinction between the "America of Hearst" and the "America of Lincoln and Roosevelt." Simonov suggested that while the former sought to besmirch the Soviet Union and promote the Cold War, the latter was a potential partner in the Soviet struggle for peace. Even the most villainous antagonists, such as McPherson, displayed a certain humorous charm and appeared animated by complex (albeit wrong) ideological motives. True to the principles of socialist realism, which called on writers to look into the bright future, Simonov ended the drama on a hopeful note: American enemies of the Soviet Union stood no chance thanks to people like Harry Smith, who remained committed to the joint fight against fascism and the bonds of friendship forged during the war.

*The Russian Question* demonstrates how Soviet commentators' perception of US media was shaped by Soviet ideology and practices. Simonov's play focused on the politically conscious individual reporter, whose search for truth confronted the machinery of false consciousness propelled by the bourgeois press. In so doing the play illustrated a distinctly Soviet belief in the dialectics of individual and collective, subjective and objective forces in history. On a practical level, the Soviet tradition of rewarding outstanding writers with the best material conditions informed the idea that American journalists received institutional support and hefty payoffs for defaming the USSR. Like other publications targeting the American press, *The Russian Question* emphasized both the persuasive power of individual journalists and the institutional patronage of their work, tapping into Soviet fears that endless resources were being poured into anti-Soviet propaganda and its worldwide circulation. Read against the backdrop of Soviet concerns with the American press and anti-Soviet propaganda, the play helps to explain both the origins and the extent of these fears.

The timing of the play—precisely when Soviet leadership was preoccupied with American anti-Soviet propaganda—enhanced the educational potential of *The Russian Question* and made it a perfect instrument for teaching audiences about the differences between socialist and bourgeois news media. A review in *Pravda* by Mikhail Galaktionov, Simonov's co-delegate to the US, stressed the play's instructive potential. Audiences, Galaktionov wrote, would learn how the machine of American media produced its slanderous anti-Soviet reports: "Correct information about Soviet Russia is printed to preserve an appearance of 'objectivity.' But this item will be relegated to page 16, whereas the slanderous announcements will appear on the front page under a clamorous headline."[45] Audiences could also learn about "the dirty tricks of warmongers, those who strive to undermine the cause of peace and create an atmosphere of anger and suspicion around the Soviet Union." Simonov's realistic portrayal of the American press would teach viewers and readers "that lies and slander are the most important weapons of the agents of imperialism and militarism."[46] Soviet readers and viewers were expected to approach the play from a comparative perspective, to draw links and parallels between Soviet and American journalists, writers, and newspapers, and to deduce the moral superiority of the socialist press.

*The Russian Question* reflected Soviet views of American news media and shaped them at the same time. Simonov's play, as well as the public responses it garnered, amplified the prominence of the American press in the Soviet imagination. American media owners appeared omnipotent; the links between capitalists and press proprietors, unbreakable. Foreign journalists became dangerous enemies sabotaging the Soviet Union's credibility and purposefully ignoring Soviet communism's advantages over western capitalism. As the next chapter will show, with the fictional Harry Smith and McPherson nearly ubiquitous on stage and screen and in print, Soviet officials and ordinary citizens turned their eyes to real-life American correspondents in Moscow, sizing them up in new ways.

## "Unmasking the American Way of Life"

Convinced that American journalists were part of an organized propaganda campaign against the USSR, Soviet officials launched a similar campaign of their own.[47] That they were motivated by concerns about American media is suggested in the wording of the 1949 Agitprop "Plan of Activities for Increasing Anti-American Propaganda," which instructed Soviet publishers, newspapers, and broadcasters "to publish systematically materials, articles, and pamphlets unmasking the aggressive plans of American imperialism and the inhuman character of the social and state order in the USA; to debunk American propaganda fables about the 'flourishing' of America, and to show the deep contradictions within the US economy, the falsity of bourgeois democracy, the decay of bourgeois culture, and the customs of contemporary America."[48] The anti-American campaign united the dispersed efforts of various Soviet propaganda initiatives under one official umbrella. These earlier campaigns had typically shared a fundamental goal: to excise "alien" influences from Soviet culture by attacking "kowtowing before the West" and focusing substantially, but not exclusively, on Jews (euphemistically referred to as "root-less cosmopolitans").[49]

"Unmasking the myth of the so-called American way of life" was at the heart of Agitprop's plan for the new anti-American campaign. It inspired the twenty-nine topics that formed the thematic foundation of the campaign and figured prominently in Agitprop's prescriptions to Soviet radio broadcasters and publishing houses, the Union of Soviet Writers, and the Ministry of Cinematography.[50] The entire strategy rested on the idea that the campaign would show the superiority of Soviet socialism by "unmasking America" and "debunking myths" associated with the United States. This propaganda strategy targeted both domestic and international audiences, especially the new people's republics and communist parties in Europe and the US. Also implicit in the campaign was Agitprop's belief that at least some of the Soviet statements would be reported in the "bourgeois press" and thus would reach fellow-traveling readers, pundits, and policy makers in capitalist countries.

The campaign's focus on unfavorable comparisons between capitalism and socialism was not new. From the very origins of the Soviet state, the meaning of socialism was based on a "rejection of capitalism." While a precise definition of socialism often remained elusive, it was nonetheless clear that it was *not* capitalism.[51] Still, the anti-American campaign was not just a reproduction of old propaganda tactics. This time, the campaign unequivocally positioned the United States as Soviet socialism's ideological "other." Before the Cold War, "capitalism" had no geographical center and could be anywhere: in Britain or France, in Fascist Italy or Nazi Germany. Popular and official perceptions of the United States were more complex: it was at once condemned for its cultural shallowness and admired for its speed, technology, and efficiency.[52] Ilya Il'f and Evgeny Petrov's seminal travelogue, *Little Golden America,* combined both trends as late as 1937. America was both criticized and admired: one could denounce the slums of Chicago and New York and at the same time dream about American efficiency and technological sophistication.[53] The anti-American campaign of 1949 eliminated any virtuous aspects that had characterized Soviet perceptions of the United States before 1945. Now, America's only redeeming features were its dormant proletariat and its oppressed racial minorities.

Soviet writers responded to Agitprop's call. In his capacity as the deputy chairman of the Union of Soviet Writers, Simonov pledged new plays, scripts, short stories, essay collections, and novels that would "expose the American way of life" and "strengthen anti-American propaganda."[54] New anti-American books, plays, and films, elaborating on Agitprop's major themes, spread like wildfire. Soviet strategists believed that literary accounts based on first-hand experience in the US would be the most effective educational tools in the anti-American campaign. Agitprop instructed Soviet publishers to pre-pare attractive new editions of American travelogues written by the giants of Soviet literature Maxim Gorky and Vladimir Mayakovsky. Even *Without a Tongue*, written in 1895 by Vladimir Korolenko, a rather controversial figure for the Bolsheviks, was reprinted.[55] Consistent with the Soviet view of litera-ture as a leader in propaganda efforts, works by "progressive" (read: commu-nist) American writers in Russian translation also saw increased publication.[56] By contrast, ambivalent accounts, such as the ones written by Il'f and Petrov or Sergei Esenin, were not included in massive reprints of anti-American literature.

To be most effective, Simonov stressed, the anti-American campaign re-quired fresh narratives based on contemporary observations and events. To that end, anyone with firsthand experience in the United States had to be mo-bilized. Simonov expanded the list of anti-American literature reprints to include the accounts of every Soviet writer who had spent time in the United States in the preceding five years. He asked Agitprop to commission new se-ries of documentary books, which would be written by Soviet officials and cul-tural figures who had recently returned from the United States and would "expose the so-called 'American way of life' and the disastrous situation of US workers." Finally, Simonov proposed creating a special committee that would conduct interviews with Soviet citizens who had recently visited the United States so that the Union of Soviet Writers could use these materials to prepare new anti-American accounts.[57] Through Simonov's proposals, the Writers' Union reoriented the campaign and put eyewitness accounts at the center of anti-American propaganda. Simonov and his colleagues viewed this type of literature as the core of the Soviet offensive in that it most effectively commu-nicated the crucial differences between capitalism and socialism.

The time was ripe for expanding the Soviet press corps in foreign coun-tries. At the end of 1949, Agitprop confirmed *Pravda*'s list of its first *sobkory* ("own correspondents") around the world. The fact that the highest priority was given to reporting on the US is evident from the candidates for the bu-reaus in Washington, DC, and New York: they were the renowned writer and *Pravda* war correspondent Boris Polevoi and Agitprop instructor I. A. Filippov.[58]

## TASS and the Problem of International Information

*Pravda* correspondents were a welcome addition to the anti-American campaign, but in 1949 TASS was still in the best position to create the firsthand descriptions that Simonov longed for. TASS had two bureaus in the United States: the Washington bureau covered Congress, the State Department, and the White House, while the New York bureau covered the United Nations and other more general topics. In total, TASS American offices employed about thirty people. More than twenty of these employees were US citizens with communist sympathies, and as native English speakers, they could easily supply TASS and Soviet writers with fiery up-to-date essays unmasking the American way of life.

In reality however, writing articles for the Soviet newspapers was never the first priority. TASS's main task in the United States was to prepare "special information bulletins" ("information," for short)—voluminous compendia of American publications on a diverse array of subjects such as agriculture, the US budget, or nuclear energy. The "information" consisted of materials gathered from publicly available sources: newspapers, magazines, trade press, and reports published by the US government. These bulletins were dispatched to Moscow and distributed among Politburo members and senior officials on a regular basis. Another special compendium, known as "White TASS," collected every publication, broadcast, speech, and observation of TASS correspondents on subjects requested by Soviet leaders. "White TASS" also gathered every reference to the Soviet Union that appeared in print, in the news media, or in statements of politicians and government officials. Every TASS bureau in the world prepared these compendia and dispatched them to Moscow weekly or, in some cases, daily. In the early Cold War years, these compendia were designated only for the eyes of the twenty-four senior members of the Politburo.[59] The compilation of these reports occupied the lion's share of TASS employees, both English and Russian speaking.

In addition, the agency's international reporting lacked poetic imagination and fell short of the writers' expectations about wide-ranging and expertly crafted educational narratives on capitalism and socialism. TASS functioned as the official voice of the Soviet Union, and its international announcements were often written by Foreign Minister Andrei Vyshinsky or his predecessor, Vyacheslav Molotov, neither of whom was famous for sparkling prose. To underscore the agency's standing as the authoritative voice of the state, no TASS item was published with authorial credit. In short, this most depersonalized source of news had no room for individual literary skills or broad analysis, such as Simonov had envisioned.

The shortcomings of TASS style became especially evident after it lost its monopoly on foreign news. Soviet writers and war correspondents, who frequently traveled abroad as members of various delegations, began to deliver international features based on their impressions.[60] The difference in the quality of information provided by TASS and that provided by traveling journalists did not go unnoticed. The editorial boards of Soviet newspapers began to consider the benefits of having their own on-site correspondents around the world. During a discussion of an *Izvestiia* issue featuring an article by Ehrenburg, a member of the editorial board observed, "This year we have finally realized our aspiration to show everything, the people and the faces, to show our country, juxtaposing it to the capitalist world. One man, Ehrenburg, went and saw what happens there and here. The form we used was convincing and accessible."[61] As this comment suggests, Soviet editors believed that firsthand experience in a capitalist country facilitated deeper and more personalized ideological insights, which were more effective in explaining the differences between capitalism and socialism. Ehrenburg's literary skills were no small matter, but the editors of *Izvestiia* equally appreciated the depth of analysis that he provided.

TASS directors were eager to expand the agency's contribution to the campaign and to make more relevant materials available to the Soviet press and to the agency's clients in socialist countries.[62] Shortly after the launch of the campaign, TASS director Nikolai Pal'gunov asked his correspondents to begin composing lengthy articles on various anti-American themes with a special emphasis on "manners and morals" (*byt i nravy*) in the US and the "ideological hollowness" (*bezydeinost*) of American culture.[63] Pal'gunov's request included a master list of required article topics, which roughly corresponded to Agitprop's thematic plan for the campaign. Pal'gunov provided the journalists with a portrait of the United States, as conceived through the prism of Marxism-Leninism in Agitprop's offices in Moscow, and then urged his people to report how this portrait manifested itself in American reality. For example, an article on American literature and the arts "must show how the fascist circles in the USA de facto control the entire ideological front in the country, regulating literature and the arts and taking revenge on progressive elements."[64] Pal'gunov did not ask his journalists to bend the facts or lie. On the contrary, he stressed that the articles should illustrate the required themes with "concrete facts" and "real life examples."[65] It simply did not occur to Pal'gunov that

*Figure 1.3.* Boris Efimov, "Freedom American Version." State publishing house "Isskustvo," 1950. (Image courtesy of the Keston Center for Religion, Politics, and Society, Baylor University, Waco, Texas.)

Agitprop's view of America might be at odds with his correspondents' experience. The premise of his instructions, and indeed of the anti-American campaign as a whole, was that Agitprop's ideological portrayal represented the United States as it truly was.

The reports that Pal'gunov received from the US, however, fell far short of what he had envisioned. Time and again, he lamented that the TASS correspondents were "indulging in verbose commentaries" and "redundant epithets" such as "warmongering" and "Wall Street crony."[66] For one thing, explained Pal'gunov, this writing style resulted in unnecessarily lengthy pieces that were expensive to transmit. More important, stylized yet inaccurate language could make TASS the subject of formal American reprimand and thus endanger the agency's entire operation in the United States.[67] The anti-American campaign, stressed Pal'gunov, must rely on facts and real-life stories that would illustrate the socialist critique of capitalism.

Pal'gunov had legitimate reasons to worry about the preservation of his agency's operations in the United States. TASS had been on thin ice since September 1945, when it became entangled in the Gouzenko Affair—the first

Cold War spy scandal that rocked North America. Igor Gouzenko, a cipher clerk in the Soviet Embassy in Ottawa, defected to the Canadian authorities and revealed that the Soviet Embassy ran an extensive spy ring that penetrated the highest levels of the Canadian establishment and civil service.[68] Two months later, Elizabeth Bentley, an American Communist who spied for the Soviets, exposed the existence of a vast Soviet espionage network in the United States, which included agents within the federal government.[69] In July 1946, the press reported that a Royal Commission of Inquiry, which investigated Gouzenko's allegations in Canada, found that the head of TASS in Ottawa played a central role in the spy ring.[70] The North American spy scandals fed the escalating fear of communist infiltration. Canadian developments in particular attracted attention to TASS representatives in the United States, who had until then enjoyed fairly comprehensive access to information and government institutions.[71]

In 1946, President Harry Truman revoked a wartime directive that exempted news media of the Allied countries from registering as agents of foreign governments under the Foreign Agents Registration Act (FARA). The act had been introduced in 1938 and required individuals and organizations "acting as agents of foreign principals in a political or quasi-political capacity" to disclose the nature of their relationship with foreign governments and to account for their activities on behalf of foreign powers.[72] While the lawmakers' original concern was Nazi propaganda, the postwar anxiety about communist subversion led to renewed use of the act.[73]

TASS officially registered as an agent of a foreign government with the Justice Department in 1947.[74] FARA provisions required that the agency keep copies of all its announcements, accounts, and correspondence. The Justice Department had the right to examine these records at any time, and the FBI routinely conducted inspections of TASS offices.[75] The agency's American and Soviet employees had to report their salaries, other incomes, and addresses to the Justice Department. Soviet correspondents in Washington, DC, could not live more than forty miles from the site of their professional activities, in this case the White House. Correspondents in New York enjoyed a slightly wider radius because of their work at the UN. To travel anywhere beyond their permitted residence boundaries, Soviet correspondents were required to submit their proposed itineraries in advance to the Justice Department for approval.[76]

Despite these regulations, the ties between TASS and the Soviet government continued to generate American antagonism toward the agency. Several pundits remained unconvinced that FARA provided an adequate degree of control over

TASS's activities. American news media often questioned the nature of TASS's ties to the Soviet government and the demeanor of TASS correspondents.[77] For example, in May 1948, an editorial in the *New York Times* charged that TASS was a convenient cover for Russian spies in the US and therefore should be monitored more closely.[78] Individual officials also began to take matters into their own hands. In 1948, Aleksandr Aleksandrov, TASS bureau chief in New York, informed Moscow that several government departments refused to supply TASS with standard reports that previously had been made publicly accessible and available to the press. In each case, Aleksandrov appealed to the press secretary of the department in question, but to no avail. After querying colleagues from other foreign news services, Aleksandrov learned that TASS was the only agency that could no longer receive the reports.[79]

The antagonism and mistrust toward TASS correspondents contributed to their already solitary existence. This isolation also made it difficult to produce the eyewitness accounts that were considered so essential for the anti-American campaign. Pal'gunov wanted his correspondents to be well versed in American theater, literature, and philosophy; to demonstrate deep understanding of American manners and morals; and to be familiar with the daily lives of oppressed workers and impoverished farmers. Most Soviet correspondents, however, were not fluent in English, which compromised their ability to gain insights into American philosophy or the local arts scene. The meager living allowance they received from TASS was not enough to allow them to buy furniture or proper winter clothing, let alone travel to meet "real" Americans or host them at home. Soviet correspondents usually eschewed contacts with foreign colleagues and socialized exclusively with other Soviet representatives. Aleksandrov noticed that some of his employees, especially those who had no families, spent the little free time they had alone in their empty apartments, getting drunk.[80] Soviet anti-American propaganda made the journalists even warier of contacts with anyone but fellow expatriates. The suspicion of all things foreign, especially American, slipped into TASS offices and undermined the relationship between the agency's Soviet and American employees. The latter became spectral presences in the bureau, and their considerable expertise in American politics and everyday life remained unused precisely when it was so needed.

Things had begun to go awry at the end of 1948 when Aleksandrov asked Pal'gunov to recall TASS correspondent Iliashchenko. Aleksandrov lamented that Iliashchenko had failed to maintain the honorable demeanor required of a Soviet representative overseas and appeared unable to resist the temptations of the American way of life that he was supposed to unmask. According to

Aleksandrov, Iliashchenko and his wife had accumulated $600 in debt, bought items on credit in American shops, and routinely borrowed money from American cooks who worked in the Soviet embassy. The couple was overheard grumbling to American employees about the piffling salaries and difficult lives of Soviet citizens in the United States. Professionally, Aleksandrov complained, Iliashchenko was "a kind of 'dead soul,' who decreases the productivity of the bureau" and whose employment was a "waste of foreign currency."[81]

Iliashchenko was promptly recalled. Upon his return to the Soviet Union, he wrote a long letter denouncing Aleksandrov and warning Pal'gunov of the New York bureau's ideological degeneration. While Iliashchenko's denunciation was clearly written in self-defense, it is significant that his accusations were steeped in the rhetoric of the anti-American propaganda campaign. Iliashchenko's account pitted the hard-working, *Russian* collective against malignant American saboteurs and spies. American journalists, he explained, took over the bureau's operations, intentionally produced "ideologically sterile" materials based on publications in the bourgeois press, and actively prevented "the Russians" from doing their work.[82] What allowed the situation in the first place, according to Iliashchenko, was Aleksandrov's "kowtowing to American employees." Iliashchenko accused Aleksandrov of stifling the initiative of Soviet correspondents and of delaying, or even destroying, their dispatches to Moscow to eliminate competition. Iliashchenko complained that Aleksandrov preferred his "American cronies" over "Russian journalists" and "would rather spend his family vacations [. . .] among Americans in American mansions."[83] The letter concluded with a warning against trusting American employees, "most of whom are doubtlessly working for the American intelligence," and their champion Aleksandrov, whose "reliance on Americans more than on Russians, is bordering on helping our enemies."[84]

Iliashchenko's letter shows how the anti-American campaign transformed the agency's work and undermined it at the same time. The Soviet propaganda narrative that warned against foreign enemies and their domestic fifth column appeared fitting and plausible in the unique circumstances of TASS offices in the United States. Iliashchenko blamed the bureau's poor contribution to the ideological front on American saboteurs and Aleksandrov's subservience to Americans, and repeatedly drew the boundaries between Russian (as opposed to Soviet) and American journalists. The thwarted literary ambitions of Soviet journalists figured prominently in Iliashchenko's story and in the stream of denunciations that subsequently flowed from TASS's New York offices to Moscow.[85]

Soviet writers emphasized the importance of anti-American literature and in so doing, inflamed the aspirations of TASS journalists, who dreamed of becoming writers and publicists and of seeing their literary efforts appear in print. These ambitious journalists believed their talents were hindered by the agency's stylistic conventions and preoccupation with "information."[86] However, a literary approach, and especially personalized reports (as evidenced by Aleksandrov's refusal to allow his journalists to sign their articles), was completely at odds with TASS practices. Elsewhere, Pal'gunov lamented to his superiors that "journalistic egos" were becoming an ever-bigger problem.[87] TASS correspondents, he explained, neglected their duties for the agency and spent too much time writing feature-length articles for Soviet newspapers and journals that were published under the journalists' own byline.[88] These side jobs contributed to the chaotic atmosphere in TASS offices and undermined its work. Pal'gunov's handling of the conflict further weakened the agency's ability to contribute to the campaign.

In the tense anti-American atmosphere, a failure to act upon Iliashchenko's denunciations could have had serious repercussions. Thus, although TASS suffered from a real shortage of experienced journalists fluent in foreign languages, Aleksandrov, a veteran correspondent who had headed the New York bureau since 1944, was instructed to ask for his own recall from the US.[89] His skills and experience likely saved him, however, for Aleksandrov continued working for TASS as Pal'gunov's aide in Moscow. Senior correspondent Vladislav Morev was appointed acting bureau chief after Aleksandrov's departure. Morev was convinced that the bureau fell short of Pal'gunov's high standards because American employees, who dominated the bureau's work, failed to see the United States through a critical ideological perspective.[90] Morev's plans for improvement revolved around a "Sovietization campaign," which he carried out with Pal'gunov's blessing. A new chief, Mikhail Fedorov, was appointed to the Washington bureau, where he replaced the American Laurence Todd. Another Soviet journalist was dispatched to the capital to increase Soviet representation. More and more responsibilities, such as the preparation of "information" and anti-American articles, were transferred from senior American correspondents to their inexperienced Soviet colleagues, many of whom had only recently arrived from the USSR.[91]

These measures backfired, and the bureau plunged into chaos. On paper, Soviet journalists carried more duties, but in reality, these duties were neglected. While Soviet correspondents struggled to keep up with their tasks, American employees remained unutilized. Morev proved to be a poor leader:

he failed to win the respect of his Soviet colleagues, and he alienated the American journalists with constant threats and crude hints at their ideological incompetence. Tensions in the bureau grew high, and by the end of 1949 Soviet and American employees were barely on speaking terms. The latter were especially aggrieved by the new treatment and complained that their expertise and years of hard work for TASS were unappreciated. The situation in the bureau became so dire and its shortcomings so glaring that during his trip to the meeting of the United Nations General Assembly, Soviet foreign minister Vyshinsky gathered all US-based TASS journalists and reprimanded them personally.[92]

Rather than using the full potential of TASS's location, talent, and expertise, the anti-American campaign impaired the agency's work. The general suspicion of all things Western undermined Soviet journalists' trust in their American colleagues, contributed to cross-cultural tensions, and prevented Soviet reporters from exploring their surroundings and reaching out to Americans. The anti-American campaign also shaped the language of the journalists' reports, which Pal'gunov found so frustrating. In an absence of real knowledge about their host country, Soviet correspondents fell back on the familiar slogans of anti-American propaganda, failing to produce the beautiful comparisons between socialism and capitalism that Soviet writers envisioned.

## The Campaign against TASS

A veteran of the Russian Civil War from a working-class background, Ivan Beglov graduated from the Higher Party School in Moscow in 1939 and began to write and lecture on international themes in Vladivostok. Beglov spoke no foreign languages, had no ties in the Soviet diplomatic world, and was a complete outsider in TASS. His 1949 appointment as TASS New York bureau chief therefore was a bit of a surprise. At the time, Beglov was studying at the newly established Central Committee's Academy of Social Sciences, where he pursued an advanced degree and completed his high school diploma at the same time.[93] Presumably the appointment of this unlikely candidate represented Pal'gunov's last-ditch effort to impose order on the New York bureau by bringing in a complete outsider, someone previously untainted by the bureau's intrigues or accusations of "kowtowing to the West."

Mending the sour relations between Soviet and American employees was one of Beglov's first priorities as bureau chief. He defended the American correspondents and recommended using their intimate knowledge of US politics. Beglov also lobbied Pal'gunov to increase American correspondents' salaries to make their earnings more commensurate with those of other news agencies.[94] After thoroughly reviewing the bureau's work, Beglov reported to his directors in Moscow that TASS in the United States suffered first and foremost from the inexperience of Soviet journalists: "The problem is the insufficient preparedness of our correspondents for independent work and their ignorance of the socio-political and economic life in the US; they lack a sufficient command of the English language and literary skills. The traditions of the New York bureau, which too often relegated its foreign correspondents to proofreader positions, did not cultivate the expertise necessary for independent work."[95] Beglov promised to help develop his journalists' professional skills: he proposed convening meetings that would examine the strengths and weaknesses of his staff's reporting and holding discussions that would help Soviet correspondents gain better knowledge of current affairs, American politics, and foreign relations. Beglov agreed that Soviet journalists should perform the most important duties in the bureau but suggested that a gradual transition would make them better prepared for reporting on American life.[96] However, Beglov's attention and energies were soon consumed by yet another international scandal involving foreign correspondents and TASS.

In April 1951, William N. Oatis, the Associated Press bureau chief in Prague, was arrested on charges of espionage and later confessed under duress. Despite US objections, the Czechoslovak government held a show trial of Oatis and two local AP employees. In July 1951, Oatis was convicted of espionage and sentenced to ten years in prison. Shortly after the announcement of the verdict, Alexander F. Jones, the president of the American Society of Newspaper Editors (ASNE), publicly demanded a government investigation of Mikhail Fedorov, TASS bureau chief in Washington, DC.[97] It was well known among the capital's journalists and among those who kept abreast of political news that during the war and before becoming a correspondent for TASS, Fedorov had served as an aeronautic engineer in the Soviet military.[98] Citing this aspect of Fedorov's biography, Jones charged that Fedorov was not a newsman but a Politburo trainee and, as such, should not be allowed to access government press briefings.[99]

While the government did not act on Jones's proposal, the House Foreign Affairs Committee did. Representative Christian A. Herter sent Beglov a letter containing a series of "frank questions" that aimed to establish the "factual truth" about "the status of TASS as a world news gathering agency."[100] Herter inquired about TASS's ties to the Soviet government and the Soviet Embassy, queried whether the agency had any official relationship with the Communist

Party USA, and asked whether the communist newspaper *Daily Worker* was a branch of TASS.[101] Eager to forestall another attack on TASS, Ivan Beglov dispatched a cordial letter, which replied to Herter in "the spirit of the questionnaires that TASS submitted to the Department of Justice."[102]

In September 1951, the ASNE president resumed his attack on TASS. Jones charged that TASS and Fedorov daily applied themselves to the task of destroying the US and "installing Communist world domination."[103] He demanded that TASS correspondents be barred from Congressional news galleries. Shortly after, the ASNE chapter in Washington, DC, presented a similar request to the Standing Committee of Correspondents—an elected body of five journalists that regulated admission to the Congressional press galleries. The Standing Committee decided that no new correspondents from the Soviet Union would be admitted to the galleries until TASS could prove definitively that it was not an agent of Soviet intelligence and propaganda. Letters requesting the relevant information were submitted to the State and Justice Departments. While the Standing Committee was awaiting the government's assessment, ASNE put the entire weight of its influence and publicity against TASS. *Editor and Publisher*, an influential trade magazine closely associated with ASNE, supported the measures against TASS on its editorial pages. Other newspapers followed, and the campaign against TASS was in full motion.[104]

Ivan Beglov pleaded with Pal'gunov to "rebuff" the attacks in the Soviet press and expose the "slanderous statements against TASS."[105] Upon consulting Molotov and the new foreign minister Vyshinsky, Pal'gunov decided that the best measure against the campaign would be self-restraint.[106] He explained to Beglov that the campaign was the logical outcome of American capitalists' fear of Soviet journalists and urged his people to remain calm and to preserve the ideological rigor of their reporting:

> Explain to the comrades that we could expect similar, and perhaps even more venomous and vicious, attacks of American reactionary circles on TASS workers. Impress upon the Soviet comrades that they must retain complete self-control, must keep working as if nothing is happening, not to be afraid, and continue to attend press conferences, the Congress, and other places where they usually go. At the same time, particularly impress upon them that they must not allow others to provoke them to irresponsible words and actions and must not provide [the American press with] excuses for attacks and provocations.[107]

Pal'gunov made sense of the attacks on TASS through the prism of Soviet ideology. He was convinced that the campaign against TASS was another instance of carefully orchestrated anti-Soviet propaganda and that American "reactionaries" attacked TASS because they were ordered to do so by the capitalist overlords who controlled the press. He inquired about the well-being of his people and urged them to carry on with their duties and unmask the capitalist world order.[108]

The State and Justice Departments conducted themselves with extreme caution and did not rush to weigh in on the matter of TASS. The US attorney general explained that, for reasons of confidentiality, the Justice Department could not reveal any information beyond the fact that TASS was registered as an agent of a foreign government. Assistant Secretary of State Jack K. McFall said that representatives of the press should be the ones to decide on TASS's access to the Congressional galleries. Behind the scenes, State Department officials shared the popular conviction that "TASS as a whole was not a news agency" and said as much to the agency's American employees.[109] However, the same officials thought that banning TASS would jeopardize American correspondents and other US interests across the Iron Curtain and would fail to help Oatis.[110] On September 21, 1951, the Standing Committee of Congressional Correspondents announced that it had decided against barring Fedorov or other TASS journalists from Congressional galleries. Although the accusations against TASS continued to appear in US press, the campaign subsided by the end of October.

The attacks on the agency took a heavy toll on its American employees. Beglov reported that Soviet correspondents remained more or less unperturbed and "did not show any tendency to panic," but the American staff members were clearly affected by the campaign: "The bourgeoisie press's witch hunt of TASS and the FBI's open invasion of our New York and Washington offices led many of them to depression and even—in unique cases—panic."[111] For example, Jean Montgomery, a Washington bureau correspondent, told Beglov that since the public accusations had begun, hooligans had twice smashed the windows of her apartment. Montgomery agreed to continue working for TASS only on the condition that she be transferred to New York.[112] Another Washington correspondent, Laurence Todd, notified Beglov that "his health demands a lengthy, and maybe even permanent break from his work for TASS."[113] Beglov reported that the campaign against the agency reached former employees as well. For example, Travis Hedrick, who no longer worked for TASS, was called to testify before the McCarran Committee (US Senate Subcommittee on Internal Security). Beglov worried that other Americans on his staff would also be summoned.[114]

These reports confirmed the impression that the American press was waging a propaganda campaign against the Soviet Union. They also reinforced TASS's concerns about the reliability of their American employees and the need to train more Soviet cadres for journalistic work overseas.[115] Pal'gunov urged Beglov to transfer the agency's core activities to "Soviet comrades" and promised to dispatch additional correspondents from the Soviet Union in the near future.[116] Rather than being deterred by the attacks on their journalists in the US, Soviet officials continued to increase the scope of their anti-American propaganda and expand their network of international correspondents.

## Cadres Decide Everything

Soviet officials agreed that the press and the government urgently needed reliable, well-rounded, and timely information about foreign countries. The proposed solutions invariably stressed the importance of capable and adequately trained professionals and lamented the shortage of such staff. The problem of information, therefore, became the problem of cadres. In 1950 the Central Committee put forward a series of measures that aimed to improve the quality of TASS's coverage of foreign countries and help the agency attract and retain talent. Material rewards were introduced for "publishable" information that exhibited "political significance, originality, timely transmission" and "brevity," as well as for information of "exceptional value."[117] From now on, part of foreign correspondents' salaries was to be paid in foreign currency. Salary bonuses were introduced to reward uninterrupted work within TASS and employees' salary scales and nomenklatura privileges were brought into line with those of central government ministries. In a major shift from previous policy, "significant" TASS dispatches could be published with the author's byline.[118]

The efforts to improve the quality of international information proceeded in two parallel directions: the expansion of the Soviet press corps abroad and the introduction of "international commentators" at home.[119] While the former were to provide original information from overseas, the latter were to offer an analysis of international affairs and to situate foreign news in the appropriate ideological context. The importance attributed to international commentators was manifest in their entitlement to various nomenklatura privileges, such as special health clinics and dining rooms.[120]

As Soviet officials orchestrated the expansion of international coverage, they stipulated that the training for foreign correspondents and international commentators must include two years of study at the party's High School of

Journalism and that only people with undergraduate degrees, work experience in the press, and exceptional professional achievements should be considered for training.[121] These requirements were rather difficult to meet. Adequate staffing of the international departments and bureaus abroad also required area specialists with language proficiency, who were in constant shortage after the war. Often newspapers preferred candidates with area and language expertise and chose to compromise on journalistic credentials. For example, in 1951, Vsevolod Ovchinnikov, a third-year student in the Chinese Department at the Military Institute of Foreign Languages, was assigned as a translator for a visiting delegation from China. During the delegation's tour of *Pravda*'s offices, the editor was so impressed with the young translator's command of foreign languages that he immediately offered Ovchinnikov a job in the international department. With no journalistic experience whatsoever, Ovchinnikov started working for the most powerful Soviet newspaper.[122]

One of the most sought-after sources of new professionals for the news media's expanding international departments was MGIMO—the Moscow State Institute of International Relations. MGIMO was established in 1944 as an outgrowth of the Moscow State University's (MGU) School of International Relations. MGIMO was entrusted with the academic preparation of Soviet cadres for work abroad and was central to the postwar efforts to cultivate Soviet professionals in international relations.[123] While the institute did not have a department of journalism in its early days, aspiring students who wanted to try their luck with the pen could do so by joining *Mezhdunarodnik*, the institute's highly popular wall newspaper, which was later converted into a printed newspaper.[124] Many of the most famous Cold War era correspondents graduated from MGIMO in these early years: Valentin Zorin (1948); Melor Sturua (1950); Evgenii Blinov, Leonid Kamynin, Nikolai Kurdiumov, Stanislav Kondrashov, and Gennadii Shishkin (all 1951); and Genrikh Borovik and Vitalii Kobysh (1952).

It did not matter whether one wanted to become a journalist after graduation. In fact, many of the people just mentioned did not dream of career in journalism at all. Like other university graduates in the Soviet Union, MGIMO students were unable to choose their place of employment. Even at this prestigious institution, work placements were the prerogative not of the students themselves, but of the Personnel Department at the Ministry of Foreign Affairs.[125] Most MGIMO graduates were destined for careers in the Soviet Foreign Service or in intelligence. An assignment to TASS or one of the newspapers was usually reserved for graduates who lacked establishment connections or whose backgrounds were considered problematic.

Just before his graduation in 1952, Genrikh Borovik was invited for an interview with a "recruiter" from intelligence. These interviews were common at the institute, though reserved only for its top students. The interview seemed to go well, and the recruiter complimented Borovik on his grades and command of foreign languages. Just before the end of the interview, the recruiter took another look at the front page of Borovik's file and queried him about his unusual patronymic: Aviezerovich. Borovik, whose father was Jewish, replied that it was a biblical name meaning "with God's help." The interview concluded within a few minutes with a promise that Borovik would receive a phone call, which he never did. After graduation, Borovik was assigned to the international department of *Komsomol'skaia Pravda*. He was soon told, however, that he could not work there after all because the Central Committee did not approve the newspaper's expansion of staff. The anti-cosmopolitan campaign was in full swing, and despite his top grades and multiple talents, Borovik could not find a place either in intelligence or at an important newspaper because his father was Jewish. Desperate and anxious, Borovik was at a loss about what to do next. Eventually he received an invitation to work at the international department of *Ogonek*, an illustrated weekly specializing in sociopolitical and literary features. Even this placement was arranged thanks to Boris Strel'nikov, Borovik's friend from *Komsomol'skaia Pravda*, who had put in a good word for him at *Ogonek*.[126]

Melor Sturua's father, Georgii, was a professional revolutionary and had been a close associate of Stalin since 1901. During the Civil War, Georgii Sturua was the special commissar for the South Caucasus and subsequently held the highest political and administrative offices in Georgia and Azerbaijan. Doubtless this prominent standing within the party helped his son Melor (whose name was an acronym of the words Marx, Engels, Lenin, October Revolution) to enter MGIMO in 1944 without an exam and to receive a Stalin Stipend. As the son of one of Georgia's top officials, Melor Sturua would have expected a brilliant career in the Soviet Foreign Service. However, not long before Melor's final exams, his father was accused of "nostalgia for Trotskyism" and relieved of all his duties in the party and the regional administration. Sturua's career prospects were suddenly closed off, and he feared that he would not be able to find any placement at all. An unexpected rescue came from Anastas Mikoyan, senior Politburo member and Stalin's close associate, who personally called the editor of the government newspaper *Izvestiia* to request a place for Sturua.[127]

Unlike the Foreign and the Intelligence Services, TASS and the Soviet newspapers could not be picky. Their international departments were expanding and urgently needed people who spoke foreign languages and had some knowledge of foreign countries. As a result, a new cohort of young graduates from prestigious universities joined the ranks of Soviet journalists in the early 1950s. Borovik's first assignments at *Ogonek* consisted of writing captions for illustrations and photographs.[128] Others had to become familiar with every step in the process of newspaper production, from organizing the international news section to writing general commentary articles on international themes.[129] Melor Sturua remembers the pressing sense of responsibility in these early days:

> At this time [in 1950], there were only three of us in the [international] department. Therefore, although I was still very young and inexperienced, I immediately joined the main activities. And then, *Izvestiia* was the official newspaper of the Soviet Union. [. . .] Therefore, it didn't matter that someone as young as I was wrote the material. It was examined through a magnifying glass, and diplomats and employees of intelligence services were scouting *Izvestiia* and looking for clues to the intentions of the Soviet government. It placed a lot of responsibility on our shoulders.[130]

Sturua's comments reveal the objectives of Soviet international reporting and the important duties bestowed on individual correspondents. He and his colleagues served as the official voice of the Soviet state, communicating its positions to foreign governments.

The great significance attributed to international items explains the elaborate structure of checks and balances that governed Soviet news reporting on international themes. In the major newspapers, *Pravda* and *Izvestiia*, international departments were divided into four sections that reflected the developing bipolar world: a general information section, a section devoted to socialist countries, one on Asia and Africa, and one on capitalist countries; the latter was considered most important. Each section was headed by its own editor, and together the editors worked under the direction of the international department's general editor and the newspaper's deputy editor in charge of international coverage.[131] International departments were supervised directly by the Ministry of Foreign Affairs. Thus, an average international news item traveled from the journalist to the section editor, to the international department editor, and finally to two ministry officials: one with expertise on the item's particular subject and one who scanned the item for its more general political meaning.[132]

Items on foreign affairs usually came from one of three sources: the newspapers' correspondents abroad, TASS, or Moscow-based political commentators. Although the number of regular international correspondents increased, their articles did not differ much from those written by their colleagues in Moscow. All the sources were connected through an intricate scheme of verification: if a correspondent's article lacked something that TASS had already reported, the appropriate passage was inserted into the item. Each article, often a political commentator's analysis of the international situation or a particular event, was sent to the Ministry of Foreign Affairs for comment or correction.[133] Finally, every Soviet newspaper had a resident censor who read the item in the context of the entire edition before allowing it to go into print.[134] This byzantine supervisory structure shows the importance the Soviet leadership attributed to international news. Each publication was subject to meticulous strategizing and refinement, and journalists often worked directly with the highest official source: the Ministry of Foreign Affairs. As Melor Sturua recalled,

> Usually they invited three of us: *Pravda, Izvestiia,* and TASS. We sat in Molotov's cabinet, later Gromyko's, sometimes in Vyshinsky's office, and he [the minister] would talk to us, as if he was thinking out loud—"this is how I think this issue should be covered," or "this is how I think that question could be resolved." And we, naturally, wrote everything down. Thus, we knew from the most important source what the state needed. It made it easy for us to navigate. The most important thing was to have two or three such theses; the rest was up to us. [ . . .] Since *Pravda* was the Party newspaper it could discuss international affairs in a sharper tone than *Izvestiia,* because *Izvestiia* was the government's official newspaper. Sometimes a *Pravda* journalist and I would write an article on a similar topic, but mine would come out harsher, and his would be softer. So my article was sent to *Pravda* and published under his name, and his article came to *Izvestiia* and was published under my name.[135]

As evident from these recollections, news reporting was a collaborative project, with the party articulating the content and journalists contributing the form. Writing was depersonalized, and individual authorship was not valued. Sturua saw the essence of his work as the articulation of the theses given to him. The journalists' most important function was to be the official voice of the state and to communicate the state's positions. Even the editorial articles on international relations usually appeared without any single byline. The anonymous signatures "observer" (in *Izvestiia*) and "commentator" (in *Pravda*) signified near perfect alignment with party or government talking points.[136]

While both young and experienced journalists wrote the newspapers' international commentaries, their most senior colleagues covered the foreign countries on site. Still, the newspapers were not the ideal media for exploring in depth the differences between capitalism and socialism as envisioned by Simonov and other advocates of anti-American literature. Space constraints inevitably limited narrative breadth and depth. TASS items, news from "brotherly countries," foreign communist parties, and reports from UN sessions took precedence, leaving little room for anything else.

The most crucial limitation, however, was the newspapers' general style of writing on international themes, which made it difficult to fit in more personalized narratives and individual impressions. Many editors and senior correspondents began their professional careers in TASS and carried the agency's terse writing style to the editorial rooms of Soviet newspapers. Stanislav Kondrashov, MGIMO class of 1951, worked in *Izvestiia* for a whole year before he was allowed to write his first item, which dealt with the situation in Cuba. When he finished the item, Kondrashov took it to deputy editor (and former TASS correspondent) Boris Vronskii. Kondrashov watched nervously as Vronskii deleted or rewrote nearly every sentence in the article. Finally satisfied, Vronskii crossed out Kondrashov's title and wrote "Reactionary Orgy in Cuba" instead. Although Kondrashov's name appeared in the byline, he could not recognize the item, which now resembled a TASS announcement, as his own.[137] These recollections make clear that the collaborative depersonalized writing style held sway, irrespective of publication or medium. Eventually, individual correspondents followed the ideological imperative to infuse their personal voices with the authoritative voice of the Soviet state.

Soviet international reporting was by and large a product of the Cold War. It began to develop during the early postwar years in direct response to Soviet officials' anxieties about the might of American propaganda. Thanks to the involvement of the Union of Soviet Writers in the anti-American propaganda campaign, international reporting was first envisioned as an educational literary form that would provide beautifully written and thoughtful discussion of Soviet socialism's superiority over American capitalism. As the project of making Soviet Restons began to take shape, however, conflicting forces pulled it in many different directions. Individual journalists' styles and literary aspirations, the institutional culture of the Soviet information establishment, and the priorities of Soviet foreign policy were often at odds with each other. Even though the journalists and the state often appeared to speak with one voice, Soviet international reporting, and anti-American propaganda more broadly, remained a far cry from the well-oiled, highly coordinated, efficient machine imagined by worried observers in the United States.

# CHAPTER TWO

# The Heralds of Truth

On June 24, 1945, the Soviet government held an illustrious Victory Parade in Red Square. Among the hundreds of dignitaries from all over the world who watched the Soviet troops marching by Lenin's mausoleum were more than twenty American journalists. Six years later, at the May Day Parade of 1951, only five American correspondents were present. Even though American interest in Soviet affairs was stronger than it had ever been before, these five journalists constituted the entire US press corps in Moscow.

As the superpowers' relations deteriorated in the postwar years, US correspondents found themselves caught in the crossfire of Soviet anti-Americanism and American anti-communism. Convinced that American correspondents served as the agents of hostile propaganda, Soviet officials introduced restrictions that severely circumscribed the journalists' work. These included censorship, restrictions on access and movement, and surveillance. The anti-American propaganda campaign, which explicitly targeted US correspondents, made the assignment in Moscow even more distressing. Some correspondents returned home or withdrew into insular expatriate communities. Others devised creative strategies to outsmart the censors and continued to seek out new avenues for reporting. At home in the United States, publishers, editors, and government officials agreed that as long as American correspondents in the Soviet Union were censored, their reports could not be trusted; some proposed getting rid of correspondents in socialist countries altogether. The anti-communist campaign exacerbated the situation because it prompted the establishment to scrutinize the personal allegiances of individual Moscow correspondents and to question their loyalty to the United States. To make the news from Moscow trustworthy again, US news media embraced a range of strategies that eventually altered the principles and practices of American reporting on Soviet affairs. News making became a collective enterprise and at times a contested terrain, which involved journalists in Moscow as well as "Russia experts," editors, readers, and government officials in the US.

Embittered by Soviet mistreatment and domestic mistrust, American correspondents in Moscow emphasized their unique ability to refute Soviet propaganda with objective facts and highlighted their contribution to America's battle against international communism. In so doing, these journalists, and the US news media more broadly, were drawn into the US government's information programs at home and abroad. Foreign correspondents did not see themselves as participating in government propaganda. Rather, they were convinced that they were helping to fight Soviet lies and censorship with the weapon of truth.

## "Living under Siege behind the Enemy's Lines"

On November 7, 1945, the twenty-seventh anniversary of the October Revolution, the Soviet minister of foreign affairs, Vyacheslav Molotov, hosted a banquet for the diplomatic corps in Moscow. As the festivities progressed, Molotov began to make the rounds in the great ballroom accompanied by Andrei Vyshinsky and a wine bearer. Each time Molotov came to another favored foreign ambassador of the moment, he stopped and proposed a public toast. In one such round, Molotov halted in front of Eddy Gilmore, the Moscow correspondent for the Associated Press, and proposed a toast to the American journalist. This unexpected attention made Gilmore feel as if he had been "knocked over with the Kremlin."[1] After a brief exchange through a loud and drunk translator, who slightly forgot his English during the celebration, Molotov made an unexpected move. The minister asked Gilmore what he would say if Soviet censorship of foreign correspondents in Moscow were to be abolished. Staggering and wondering if he had heard correctly, Gilmore answered that the removal of censorship would be a fine thing. Molotov then proposed a toast "for better understanding of one another," and Gilmore insisted on drinking the toast in vodka to show his respect for the Soviet minister. The following days showed that Molotov's promise was sincere. "Not a word has been taken out of any story of mine and they've been passing political commentary without [. . .] referring us upstairs to Vyshinsky and Molotov," wrote Gilmore to his editors at the AP several days after the banquet.[2]

The idyll was short lived. One month later, in December 1945, foreign journalists became a source of a small scandal in the Politburo. While vacationing in Sochi, Stalin opened the most recent dossier on foreign press coverage of the Soviet Union and came upon "slanderous fabrications" in the reports of Moscow correspondents for the *Daily Herald* and the *New York Times*.[3] The first item suggested that the members of the Politburo disagreed in their assessment of the London Conference of Foreign Ministers. The second item reported rumors that Stalin was planning to resign his post as the chairman of the Council of People's Commissars. Stalin blamed the publication of these "repugnant inventions" on the loosened censorship of foreign correspondents.[4] He charged that Molotov's eagerness to appease Great Britain and the US had sapped his ideological vigilance. The "villainous fabrications" of foreign correspondents proved that Molotov had blundered when he thought that relaxation of censorship would promote better understanding between the USSR and its former allies. Molotov's "liberal attitude" undermined Soviet foreign policy and presented the bourgeois press with an opportunity to besmirch the USSR and depict it as weak and prone to concessions.[5] Stalin urged his comrades to understand that the uncompromising treatment of foreign correspondents must be part and parcel of a Soviet "policy of fortitude" toward the United States and Great Britain.[6]

The new "policy of fortitude" toward foreign correspondents went into effect in February 1946. It manifested itself first and foremost in the tightening of Soviet censorship. During and after the war, censorship of the international press corps had been under the jurisdiction of the Press Department of the Ministry of Foreign Affairs. The censors met the journalists face to face, often explained why certain parts of a dispatch were forbidden for transmission, and occasionally surrendered to the journalists' arguments, allowing the copy to go unaltered.[7] Now, the domestic censoring body—the Main Directorate for the Protection of State Secrets in the Press (Glavlit)—became responsible for censoring foreign correspondents.[8] Under Glavlit the censorship of foreign correspondents was tightened and revamped. Correspondents were instructed to take their copy to the Central Telegraph building in Moscow. There, the censors worked in a special closed room and remained invisible to the journalists and deaf to their questions or pleas.[9] It appeared that censorship was blind—the dispatches were blackened out, sometimes almost entirely, and immediately transmitted abroad. Correspondents had no way of knowing what had been erased, nor could they revise or recall the dispatches. Frustrated and confused, journalists rushed to the US Embassy and via unmonitored channels alerted their editors that no dispatch from Moscow should be published without verification.[10]

After a few weeks, this blind censorship was lifted. The journalists could consult the censored versions of their dispatches and decide whether to transmit them in an altered form. Still, they were given no explanation for why certain aspects of their reports were "killed."[11] After several weeks of following

their censored copy and seeing what was erased or left untouched, the correspondents were able to deduce at least some of the rules governing the censors' work. Occasionally, when a particular dispatch took a long time to
clear, it became apparent that the censors had consulted their higher-ups and
that the fate of an item could be decided in the topmost echelons of Soviet establishment. Filing personalized analyses or assessments—especially concerning Soviet politics, the economy, or foreign relations—was impossible.
Glavlit censors essentially reduced the journalists' dispatches to contextualized
quotes from TASS or the Soviet press. Yet these too were sometimes erased
without explanation, and correspondents could not be confident that even a
direct quote from *Pravda* would be cleared.[12] The journalists' personal mail
and professional correspondence with editors moved through the diplomatic
pouch, but they were not allowed to use it to transmit copy.[13] Any correspondent caught doing so would face immediate deportation from the Soviet
Union, so few journalists took the risk.[14]

Censorship was not the only obstacle to news reporting from the Soviet
Union. Foreigners were prohibited from traveling by car any farther than fifty
kilometers from Moscow. Even these trips were confined to ten specific roads.
Any trip outside of the city required advance approval from the Soviet authorities. When the journalists submitted requests to visit sites or to travel outside
of Moscow, they were most often denied, sometimes after several weeks' delay. Thus it was all but impossible to report from anywhere other than the Soviet capital.[15] Interacting with locals also became difficult after the enactment
of the 1947 law on "the revelation of state secrets," which effectively criminal-
ized all contacts between Soviet citizens and foreigners.[16]

The new rules brought foreign journalists under the jurisdiction of institutions and practices that the Soviets had developed during the 1930s in response to anxieties about foreign threats. The Bolsheviks abolished censorship when they came to power, but they reintroduced it in 1922 as a temporary
measure to prevent enemies of the revolution from using the press against the
new socialist regime.[17] Glavlit began as a modest organization charged with
scanning the press for signs of anti-Soviet propaganda and state secrets.[18] During the 1930s, as each wave of purges escalated the fear of foreign enemies
and their domestic henchmen, Glavlit acquired new functions and expanded
its staff. The Central Committee urged Glavlit to emphasize vigilance, broadened the definition of a state secret, and installed a censor in every newspaper.[19] During the Second World War, Glavlit gained a powerful military arm
and new functions. By 1945, it was a vast empire that employed thousands of

censors throughout the Soviet Union. Glavlit decided what constituted a state secret and provided pre- and post-publication censorship of all printed matter. It monitored every Soviet broadcast for domestic and foreign audiences and screened literature departing and arriving through the Soviet borders. Glavlit employees also oversaw the removal of "politically harmful" literature from libraries and publishing houses.[20]

The deteriorating Soviet-American relations reintroduced anxieties about existential threats to the Soviet regime, and these anxieties came to shape Soviet policies toward foreign journalists. The official approach to "bourgeois correspondents" was influenced by an ideological postulate that mass media could not operate independently from its motivating class interests. As shown in the previous chapter, Soviet officials saw "bourgeois journalists" as the agents of hostile governments, inevitably linked to the ruling elites of their countries and seeking to undermine the Soviet Union on behalf of their capitalist masters. The restrictions on foreign journalists, especially censorship, sought to minimize the damage that these "enemy agents" could cause and to regulate the production of the Soviet image overseas.

The journalists began to devise creative strategies to outsmart the censors. Many correspondents relied on euphemisms, rare idioms, or complicated sentence structures, hoping that critiques so disguised would pass unnoticed by the censors. Drew Middleton of the *New York Times* often repeated sensitive information several times in the same dispatch, hoping that in one of these instances the censor would fail to spot the problematic fragment.[21] Members of the AP bureau discovered that if they buried the most critical part of the story in the third or fourth paragraph, rather than put it in the lead, it tended to escape the censors' attention.[22]

Soviet limitations on news gathering also changed the nature of traditional competition between the journalists and led to the development of collaborative practices that were unique to American correspondents in the USSR. The rivalry between two American wire services—Associated Press and United Press—and their respective heads, Eddy Gilmore and Henry Shapiro, dominated the Moscow press corps. In the 1940s, each agency established a consortium of sorts, where representatives of different foreign news media grouped together and shared information, tips, and resources, such as drivers, subscriptions to Soviet newspapers, and TASS teletypes. On several occasions, the consortium's members made "gentlemen's agreements" not to scoop one another, deciding that all correspondents would file certain items at the same time.[23]

Soviet propaganda warnings about "kowtowing before the West," attacks on all things American, and repeated calls for vigilance made some American journalists convenient targets for the Soviet spy mania. Robert Magidoff, a Russian-born American, had worked in Moscow since 1935 for NBC, the British Exchange Telegraph Agency, and the publishing house McGraw-Hill.[24] During the war, Magidoff's wife, Nila, campaigned extensively on behalf of Russian War Relief—the largest foreign war relief organization in the US. On April 16, 1948, Magidoff opened the morning's edition of the Soviet daily *Izvestiia* to learn that he was an American spy. In a "letter to the editor" on page 4, Magidoff's secretary, Cecilia Nelson (American-born, now Soviet citizen), accused her boss of espionage and of sending his intelligence reports via the embassy's diplomatic pouch.[25] Although US ambassador Walter Bedell Smith and Magidoff denied the accusations, he was instructed to leave the Soviet Union within forty-eight hours.[26]

Soviet anxieties about malevolent spies in the American press corps also figured prominently in another publicized episode in 1948—the defection of Annabelle Bucar, an information officer in the US Embassy. In her 1949 book, *The Truth about American Diplomats*, Bucar denounced the embassy's involvement in anti-Soviet slander and propaganda and accused its employees of espionage and intelligence gathering. A series of *Pravda* articles entitled "American Diplomats Unmasked" accompanied the publication of Bucar's book, making her exposé available to larger audiences.[27] In January 1949, shortly before the publication of Bucar's book, the Soviet authorities arrested Anna Louise Strong, a member of Communist Party USA and a staunch supporter of the Soviet regime, who spent several years in Moscow working for Soviet foreign-language publications. Strong was charged with espionage and deported. These events convinced American journalists that the Soviet regime singled them out as potential targets and that nobody, even famous "fellow travelers" such as Strong, was immune to the secret police.[28]

The ranks of American correspondents in Moscow dwindled. In November 1946, direct broadcasting from Moscow was banned, which led to the departure of CBS correspondent Richard Hottelet.[29] The *New York Times* closed its bureau in 1947 when its correspondent, Drew Middleton, was refused a reentry visa after a vacation abroad. In 1949, the *New York Herald Tribune* closed its Moscow bureau after the Soviet authorities refused a return visa to bureau chief Joseph Newman. A few months later, the *Christian Science Monitor* recalled Edmund Stevens, who had lived in Moscow since 1934 and worked for various American and British newspapers. The *Monitor* closed its

*Figure 2.1.* Harrison E. Salisbury. (Photo: Carl Mydans/The LIFE Picture Collection via Getty Images.)

Moscow bureau because it was unsatisfied with the reduced amount and quality of coverage after the tightening of censorship. Reuters also closed its bureau in 1949, but its American correspondent, Andrew Steiger, remained in Moscow as a freelance journalist.[30]

The only new member of the American press corps in these turbulent years was Harrison Salisbury, who arrived to reopen the *New York Times* Moscow bureau in March 1949. With Salisbury's arrival, the entire American press corps in Moscow consisted of five people.[31] In addition to the *New York Times*, only the wire services, United Press and the Associated Press, retained their bureaus.[32] The remaining journalists—Thomas Whitney and Eddy Gilmore of the AP, Henry Shapiro of the UP, and Steiger—were prisoners of sorts. Their wives were Soviet citizens denied exit visas by the Soviet authorities. These

journalists believed that they could protect their wives from arrest or deportation only by staying in the Soviet Union.[33] Even though Salisbury did not
have a Soviet wife, he was not free to leave as he pleased. After the bitter experience of 1947, the editors of the *New York Times* were concerned that if
Salisbury left for a vacation, his visa would not be renewed and the *Times*
would lose its Moscow bureau again.[34]

Salisbury arrived in Moscow shortly after the launch of the anti-American
campaign, and his first impressions from the Soviet capital were understand-
ably grim. He reported to his editors that the campaign had visibly increased
the Soviet public's antagonism toward the United States:

> The Soviet people are being not only taught to hate and fear America; they are
> being taught to despise the very word American. [. . .] I do not think it can any
> longer be said that "the people are friendly to Americans." [. . .] It is automati-
> cally assumed that a bad foreigner is an American. [. . .] If you compare the pro-
> paganda campaign against the United States with the propaganda against Hit-
> ler in Germany you will find that the Soviet press never conducted a drive of this
> magnitude against the Nazis before the outbreak of war. [. . .] The whole Amer-
> ican press corps would disappear from here in a moment, if it could.[35]

The anti-American propaganda campaign particularly alarmed Salisbury
and other journalists because of its focus on the American press. Salisbury's
letters home stressed that the general atmosphere in Moscow suggested that
the Soviet state marked American journalists as its enemies. Correspondents
encountered signs of special hostility almost on a daily basis:

> Serving as an American correspondent in Moscow in these times is very much
> like living under siege behind enemy lines. The idea is constantly hammered
> into the mind of the public that we are spies. Going to the theatre and the mov-
> ies you get the impression that Russia is swarming with American correspon-
> dents, all of them equipped with camel's hair coats, snap-brim hats and leicas,
> peering through their dark glasses at "military secrets". I don't believe there is a
> single anti-American play on the boards here—and there are more than 20
> on the repertoire—which hasn't got an American journalist spy in the cast of
> characters.[36]

Salisbury explained that in light of these venomous portrayals of American
journalists, he and the other correspondents believed they would be the like-
liest targets of the next "spy" fabrication by the Soviet secret police. "Corre-

spondents here feel quite literally as though they were living in a powder-house which may explode at any moment," he concluded.[37]

Soviet hostility prompted the journalists to reduce their social contacts to the company of other foreigners. Fears of entrapment added to the pressures of life within the narrow confines of a small community. The defections of Annabelle Bucar and another US Embassy worker, James McMillin, reverberated through the foreigner circles. Correspondents and embassy personnel believed that in both cases the Soviet secret police had exploited love affairs between Soviets and Americans and orchestrated the defections for propaganda purposes.[38] Several members of the expatriate community grew so fearful of Soviet entrapment that they eschewed locals and foreigners alike. Others worried that Americans married to Soviet women might become the next trump card of Soviet propaganda. When Salisbury first met AP correspondent Thomas Whitney, he observed that Whitney seemed "quite unstable and considerably under the influence of his Russian girl." Salisbury suspected that Whitney was likely to "go native" and become the secret police's "evidence in some concocted proceedings against the AP or other members of the press corps."[39] Later Salisbury regretted this assessment and developed a close friendship with Thomas and Julie Whitney. This initial response shows the emotional toll of the anti-American campaign and how strained and ridden with suspicion the social interactions of foreigners in Moscow could become.

The shared feeling of being trapped in Moscow brought foreign correspondents and US Embassy personnel closer together. In 1944 Eddy Gilmore founded a jazz band, the Kremlin Krows, composed of amateur musicians from among the employees of the US Embassy and other members of the diplomatic community. George F. Kennan, one of the founding members, played guitar. In its ten years of existence, the band remained popular and was often asked to perform at social gatherings of foreigners in Moscow.[40] Briefings with the ambassador became social events that journalists attended to pick up gossip and other news. Moscow correspondents could use the diplomatic pouch for private and sensitive correspondence with their families and editors in the US.

Social, professional, and pragmatic considerations created an informal network of information exchange and collaboration among correspondents and civil servants. The embassy's communications with the State Department often relied on information and observations received from foreign correspondents. For example, it was the journalists who first drew the embassy's attention to the scope and severity of the anti-cosmopolitan campaign and suggested that future purges in the Soviet intelligentsia would follow.[41] Reports from Moscow correspondents often figured in the State Department's dossiers of information that could help battle Soviet propaganda.[42] Before their departure from Moscow, Robert Magidoff and Edmund Stevens advised the US Embassy how to improve the newly launched Russian-language broadcasts of the Voice of America.[43] Subsequently, both journalists used their professional authority to support the Voice of America and other government information programs.[44]

The journalists' contacts in the embassy and the diplomatic community often went a long way to help with tips, information, and analysis. The AP's Eddy Gilmore had a special talent for turning friendly personal relationships to his professional advantage. In August 1949, for example, he was "tipped off" (most likely by someone at the embassy) about Stalin's forthcoming meeting with the newly appointed US ambassador, Alan Kirk.[45] Half a year later, in January 1950, Gilmore secured another scoop, this time on the demilitarization of Austria. This was thanks to a tip from Ambassador Kirk and additional help from the US counselor Walworth Barbour, who even lent Gilmore his car, allowing him to make it to the Central Telegraph building and file his story ahead of others.[46] There was nothing official about these social interactions.[47] The interests of American journalists and civil servants often coincided, blurring the boundaries between the US government and the fourth estate.

The special relationship that developed between diplomats and journalists in Moscow was emblematic of an important challenge that confronted American news media in the postwar world. On the one hand, the press was eager to assert its independence from the government, which many felt had been compromised during the Second World War. On the other hand, most American publishers shared the government's anti-communist agenda and wanted to support its standoff with the Soviet Union.[48] These two aims were difficult to reconcile not only in the closed environment of the expatriate community in Moscow. Back in the United States, a shared interest in circumventing Soviet restrictions drew American publishers and State Department officials closer together: both viewed censorship as a dangerous instrument of Soviet propaganda; both agreed that Moscow correspondents could no longer be considered a truthful source of information about the rival superpower.

As a result, reporting on Soviet affairs began to change. New actors became involved in producing and interpreting news from the USSR. Reports dispatched by correspondents in the USSR were subjected to substantial editorial involvement back home, much more extensive than what was typically applied to overseas news. Foreign desks often modified the dispatches to accommodate what the editors *thought* their correspondents meant to say. In other cases, editors incorporated additional information that they believed was missing because of the intervention of Soviet censors and thus changed dispatches altogether. More and more news outlets began to rely on the services of experts or consultants on Soviet affairs. The consultant was usually a journalist, an academic, or a former foreign correspondent who had a working knowledge of the Russian language and a certain degree of familiarity with Soviet affairs. The expert wrote articles on Soviet developments based on the Soviet press, academic sources, and information from the State Department.[49] At the AP, the UP, and the *New York Times,* the in-house expert often used information provided by the resident correspondent in a diplomatic pouch. The item would appear under the expert's name and with an American byline without mentioning the correspondent in Moscow as the source. Newspapers and agencies that did not have a resident correspondent came to rely on the experts almost exclusively. Media professionals and civil servants alike believed that such measures helped to safeguard American readers against the dangers of communist propaganda and assured the integrity of the coverage of Soviet affairs.

Paradoxically, Soviet restrictions on American correspondents forced US news media to adopt informational practices resembling the Soviet model, which combined reports from resident correspondents with analyses by international commentators and editorial intervention. Although the US government's intervention in actual news reports was minor compared with that of the USSR, American coverage of Soviet affairs became a collective enterprise that included foreign correspondents, consultants on Soviet affairs, and editors.

## "Playing, Even Innocently, the Russian Game"?

Despite the precautions that were taken with news from the USSR, many in the United States continued to worry about the Moscow press corps and its coverage of Soviet affairs. American fears of Soviet subversion escalated in the late 1940s, and anxious anti-communists cast their worried gaze on the State Department, the film industry, and the nation's newsrooms.[50] In this context, Moscow correspondents became the center of two different scenarios for potential communist infiltration. The first pointed out that by publishing censored reports or quoting Soviet leaders and newspapers, American media helped enemy propaganda infiltrate the United States. The second scenario suggested that prolonged presence in the Soviet Union and marriage to local women compromised American correspondents' immunity to enemy ideology.[51]

Mistrust often arose in the editorial offices where the dispatches from Moscow first landed. For example, at the end of 1948, Tom Whitney submitted a report describing a moderate rise in the Soviet standard of living. The AP's foreign desk cut about two-thirds of the original story, eliminated several examples and details, and delivered the shortened report to the agency's subscribers nationwide.[52] Will Lissner, the *New York Times*'s expert on Soviet affairs read the shortened report and concluded that it was "largely false" because Whitney had essentially echoed *Pravda*'s exuberant assessments of Soviet economy.[53] Confronted with Lissner's virulent critique, Whitney rushed to defend his professional integrity and anti-communist credentials, insisting that he had always given full attention to the shortcomings of the Soviet system.[54] Although it was later determined that many nuances of the original dispatch had been lost in the editing by the foreign desk, critics at the *Times* and the AP continued to pay special attention to Whitney's reporting and the language he used.[55]

The critics of Moscow correspondents expected the wire services and the *Times* to disclaim every item from Moscow with a reminder that their correspondents were complying with Soviet censorship. Otherwise, critics pointed out, the press was deceiving its audiences by presenting Soviet propaganda under the guise of factual reporting.[56] The State Department, the US Embassy in Moscow, and the journalists themselves heartily supported these proposals.[57] Despite the journalists' appeals and the growing critiques of reporting from Moscow, the wire services and the *New York Times* refused to attach the censorship caveat to the Moscow bylines.[58] The AP directors and the *Times* publisher Arthur Hays Sulzberger believed that since "censorship exists in so many other places in the world [. . .] it would be scarcely fair to single out Russia."[59] It is also conceivable that Sulzberger and others refused precisely because in the anti-Communist atmosphere of the time, a daily reminder of Soviet censorship would have made their decision to maintain their Moscow bureaus more difficult to defend.

In 1950, a large dispute broke out over Salisbury's series on the Soviet reaction to the Korean War. The series and the dispute shattered the editors' conviction that the Moscow bureau was providing them with useful facts and tested their decision not to call attention to censorship of their Moscow copy. The series came out at a crucial time. The war had begun only a few months earlier, and US foreign policy makers feared that the Soviet Union might join the fight on the side of China and North Korea. The principal message of Salisbury's series was that the Soviet Union was not going to participate in the war. Salisbury gave as evidence the massive projects for civilian reconstruction all over the country, the increase in the availability of food and produce in the Soviet stores, and the general absence of war rumors on the Soviet street. All of these, wrote Salisbury, pointed to the Soviets' decision to concentrate on domestic improvement and abstain from military conflicts abroad.[60] The last article in the series focused on Soviet public opinion and argued that Soviet citizens "took the view that the United States was the aggressor in the Far East."[61] In matters of foreign policy, explained Salisbury, "there is little difference between the views of expressed by ordinary Soviet citizens and those placed on record by such leading organs as *Pravda* and *Izvestiia*."[62] Salisbury cautioned against American hopes for a developing rift between the Soviet people and the government, warning that "any supposition abroad that such a cleavage does in fact exist or is likely to develop, is wishful thinking at best and may be extremely dangerous."[63] Even if they occasionally listened to the broadcasts of the Voice of America, the Soviet people still had "no sympathy for the American viewpoint," Salisbury concluded.[64]

Salisbury's discussion of Soviet public opinion and his assertion of the basic harmony between the regime and the people challenged the conventional wisdom of the time. State Department officials and Kremlin watchers close to the Truman administration believed that there was a large gap between the suffering Soviet people and their ruthless oppressive leaders. American officials hoped it would be possible to exploit this gap and bring down the Soviet regime by promoting popular discontent and pro-American sentiments in the USSR through, for example, the Russian-language broadcasts of the Voice of America.[65] The Voice's supporters in the State Department and the US Embassy in Moscow believed that listeners behind the Iron Curtain welcomed the station as the only truthful alternative to the Soviet government's lies.[66] Salisbury's assertion that the Soviet people associated the Voice of America with American propaganda came across as dangerously subversive.

When Salisbury's articles arrived at the *New York Times,* the editors debated whether the series was fit for publication.[67] The detractors argued that the articles' close resemblance to communist propaganda proved that Salisbury's allegiance was compromised and demanded his recall from Moscow.[68] Government officials joined the chorus of Salisbury's critics and helped undermine the editors' faith in their correspondent. The US Embassy in Moscow made it known that it felt strongly that the series should not be published.[69] The US military attaché in Moscow warned that the series could "lull the American people into a false sense of security."[70] At home, State Department officials told Arthur Hays Sulzberger that Salisbury should be recalled from Moscow because he was unable to manipulate the censors with clever language and had thus become a vehicle of Soviet propaganda.[71] These angry responses demonstrate that US civil servants had come to expect that media coverage of, and reporting from, the Soviet Union would corroborate and popularize the government's assessments of the Soviet menace.

The strong opposition to the series presented the editors with a genuine dilemma. Should they trust Salisbury and publish the series? Or should they preserve their rapport with the government, shelve the series, and protect the public from Soviet propaganda? After considerable delay, the series was published with some alterations. One installment was scrapped altogether, although at the time Salisbury thought it contained the best evidence of the Soviets' lack of intention to join the war.[72] A careful introduction, crafted by the managing editor Edwin James and personally approved by Sulzberger, prefaced each installment: "As is the case with all dispatches from Moscow, these articles were subject to Soviet censorship and were written with that fact in mind. The correspondent reported unusual cooperation in transmitting these particular dispatches; however, the Times did not receive certain requested material to make them more complete, such, for instance, as specific prices and wages and other items for American comparison."[73]

On the face of it, this introduction used censorship to explain the unorthodox views expressed in the dispatches. However, the reference to "unusual cooperation in transmitting" them suggested that the Soviets could have been pleased with Salisbury's reports. The wording also obscured whether the lack of "certain requested materials" derived from difficulties posed by the censors or from purposeful omission by the correspondent. Although the *Times* printed Salisbury's series, the editors remained undecided about whether he was "playing, even innocently, the Russian game."[74]

The *Times's* cautious approach to the Korea series demonstrates how difficult it was for news media to reconcile their ethos of independence from government intervention with their commitment to support the US fight against Soviet communism.[75] Sulzberger believed that Salisbury's appointment as the Moscow correspondent expressed the editors' trust in his reporting. There was no point in having Salisbury in Moscow if they were going to second-guess his dispatches at every stage, Sulzberger told his editors.[76] On the other hand, neither Sulzberger nor his more conservative colleagues were willing to ignore the officials' concerns or to expose the *Times* to accusations of spreading Soviet propaganda. The compromise, whereby the *Times* published Salisbury's series but distanced itself from his conclusions, failed to resolve the tension and left everyone unhappy.

The publication of the series outraged readers and critics on all sides of the political spectrum. The Communist Party newspaper, the *Daily Worker,* accused the *Times* of misleading the public and stirring anti-Soviet sentiments by relegating the description of the USSR's unwillingness to join the war to its back pages.[77] By contrast, *Time* magazine criticized Salisbury's "naïve conclusions" and labeled the dispatches a "useful piece of Communist propaganda."[78] The lion's share of critics sided with *Time.* For example, Eugene Lyons, a well-known journalist and commentator who worked in Moscow between 1928 and 1934, argued that Salisbury's assessment of Soviet public opinion was outrageous because people living under a communist dictatorship were too scared to speak their minds.[79] Another reader suggested that Salisbury's sources must have been "officials of the regime posing as ordinary citizens" and that he had been duped by Soviet propaganda. "Even *Pravda* would not hesitate to carry those dispatches," the reader concluded.[80] Notions of truth and trust informed the negative responses to the Korea series. Many readers and commentators found it difficult to qualify or reconsider their existing notions of the Soviet communist world. Salisbury's arguments ran against the grain of the anti-communist campaign, which explained that in contrast to Americans, Soviets were not free to express their true opinions. Whether they thought that Salisbury had gone soft on communism or fallen victim to cunning Soviet censors, readers and fellow journalists decided that his reports could not be true.

The outcry over the Korea series registered with the editors of the *New York Times* and prompted them to doubt Salisbury's subsequent dispatches. About a month after the series' publication, Salisbury suspected that in handling the materials from Moscow, the editors preferred to use AP copy.[81] When he asked the newspaper why his material was bypassed, the foreign editor Emanuel Freedman replied that the "lack of qualification in some of your copy as it reaches us sometimes troubles us. We shall continue to go on the assumption that the omissions represent the work of the censor, and hence will feel free to qualify whenever we feel that we are able to do it accurately. In other cases we shall simply continue to eliminate questionable material."[82]

From a professional point of view, Freedman's response was perfectly logical: the *Times* did not publish Salisbury's dispatches because the author failed to provide important additional information that would help contextualize his reports. Still, despite the traces of censorship in *all* materials dispatched from Moscow, the *Times* did not give up on these items altogether but rather selected those that seemed "less questionable." By giving preference to the agency copy, Freedman signaled to Salisbury that, Soviet censorship notwithstanding, positive items from the USSR should have some "qualifications." Moreover, while the editors assumed "that the omissions represent the work of the censor," they surely hoped that the omissions did not stem from the correspondent's declining immunity to Soviet ideology. Eager to protect their readers from Soviet manipulation, the editors applied their own censorship by means of "qualification," "elimination," or selection of what they thought least questionable.

Freedman's comments reveal how anti-communism and Cold War anxieties about Soviet propaganda changed American reporting on Soviet affairs. As they scrutinized the dispatches of foreign correspondents, the editors not only had to guess what the correspondent had meant to say and where the censors had intervened. They also tried to anticipate the reactions of readers and critics, making sure that the printed item did not stray too far from conventional wisdom and squaring the reports from Moscow with the assessments of experts and government officials. While Soviet censorship certainly restricted the scope of American reporting, editorial tampering in the form of framing and contextualizing further limited the already narrow coverage of the Soviet Union. Although the United States did not have a centralized censoring institution comparable to the Soviet Glavlit, editorial and journalistic practices performed the function of censorship and made sure that international reporting toed the anti-Soviet line.

## "News from Russia"

Anxieties about the compromised loyalties of Moscow correspondents and fears of Soviet propaganda infiltrating the United States permeated the reception of Salisbury's Korea series. After the 1951 arrest and imprisonment of the AP's William Oatis in Czechoslovakia, these anxieties developed into a fullfledged professional debate about American international reporting from the communist world. In 1951, the trade journal of the American Newspaper Guild published an open letter from *New York Times* expert on Soviet affairs Harry Schwartz to the editor of the *Moscow News*. Schwartz argued that Soviet treatment of journalists undermined Americans' trust in news reports from Moscow and called on the Soviet government to abolish censorship. Schwartz blamed the situation squarely on the Soviets' censorship and "inhumane attitude" toward the journalists' family members. At the same time, his article questioned the ability of Moscow correspondents to report truthfully on Soviet affairs: "How can we believe that what our correspondents send from Moscow is even that limited portion of the whole truth which they are able to learn?" he concluded.[83]

A few weeks later, a liberal anti-communist magazine, the *New Leader*, carried Schwartz's letter with a preface by Arnold Beichman, a columnist well known for his anti-communist writing. Whereas Schwartz's letter focused on censorship and journalists' working conditions, Beichman's commentary concentrated on the problem of the journalists' Soviet wives. Beichman stressed that the American people remained "privy to blackmail reporting" as long as their information was coming from "newspapermen whose personal happiness depends entirely upon the Kremlin barbarians."[84] A picture of Edmund Stevens accompanied Beichman's article. Its caption, "Ed Stevens sent pro-Soviet dispatches until his Russian wife could leave the country," stressed that reporting from Moscow was deeply subjective and not trustworthy.[85] Both Schwartz and Beichman expressed concern that instead of factual reporting, Americans were getting Soviet propaganda. While both blamed Soviet policies for this situation, they nevertheless expressed a general mistrust of Moscow correspondents and their work. Both Schwartz and Beichman positioned a journalist's ability to criticize the USSR at the heart of what it meant to report objectively from Moscow. Although each writer seemingly avoided personal attacks, the Moscow press corps emerged as part of the problem with reporting from the Soviet Union rather than a solution. The boundary between questioning the professional capacities of foreign correspondents and doubting their personal loyalty to the United States was thin in both articles.

The debate on Moscow correspondents tapped into a broader discussion about American international reporting in the postwar world. A few days after Schwartz's and Beichman's pieces appeared in the *New Leader*, the *Saturday Review of Literature* published another polemic article on the subject. The piece, by Russell F. Anderson, McGraw-Hill's influential foreign editorial director, was entitled "News from Nowhere: Our Disappearing Foreign Correspondents." Anderson argued that the scope and the quality of US international reporting were declining precisely when the national interest depended on knowledge about the outside world. He charged that American foreign correspondents were ill prepared for their jobs and lacked the necessary language skills and in-depth understanding of foreign countries. According to

Anderson, coverage of the Communist Bloc was particularly afflicted.[86] The news media and the State Department were not doing enough to fight the restrictions on American reporters and instead opted for a lazy solution: relying on the services of "would-be experts and second guessers outside of Russia."[87]

The debate about the Moscow press corps positioned international reporting as key to the US national interest and engagement in world affairs. Everyone agreed that the United States needed reliable information about socialist countries, now more than ever. It was also agreed that the working conditions in these countries were incompatible with the principles and practices of American journalism and that the coverage of the Eastern Bloc was unreliable as a result. The proposed solutions depended on the politics of the participants and their role in the production of news from abroad.

In 1952 the question of Western coverage of the USSR was raised in *The News from Russia*—one of the first and most talked about surveys conducted by the International Press Institute (IPI). The IPI was founded in 1951 in Zurich under the leadership of Lester Markel, an influential editor at the *New York Times* and an outspoken advocate for the freedom of the press. Funded by the Rockefeller and Ford Foundations, the IPI aimed to improve the flow of information across borders. The institute's activity focused on conducting surveys of international press on select issues, and its reports usually drew on research and interviews with journalists and editors from different countries.[88] *The News from Russia* was IPI's second survey, which suggests that it considered news coverage of Soviet affairs an important challenge confronting the profession worldwide. That American anxieties heavily influenced IPI's framing of the problem was evident in the survey's aim of helping an "objective editor" prevent his or her news service from becoming a "propaganda outlet for the Soviet Union."[89]

The report's opening sections explained that the combination of Soviet censorship and Moscow correspondents' eagerness to protect their Soviet wives made the news from the USSR "defective in almost every respect." Rather than delivering factual information, the reporting of Moscow correspondents subjected the public to the dangerous influence of Soviet propaganda.[90] IPI proposed to solve the problem by increasing the role of experts in coverage of Soviet affairs and strengthening the interpretive side of the news. The ideal expert, the survey maintained, combined the qualities of an academic researcher and an intelligence officer. All experts should have spent some time living in the Soviet Union and should demonstrate in-depth knowledge of the Russian language, culture, and history. The experts' daily work would consist

of careful reading of Soviet sources and other information (including information from the US government). The experts would draw on these sources
to write broader interpretations of Soviet developments.[91] In contrast to the
reporting of Moscow correspondents, "interpretive reporting by specialists"
would furnish the editors and the public with factual and objective information on Soviet affairs.[92]

IPI urged shifting the coverage of Soviet affairs from news to interpretive
analysis and thus appeared to propose radical changes in the principles and
practices of international reporting from the USSR.[93] In fact, however, the survey was endorsing developments that had already been in motion, especially
in the United States. Leading voices in the profession had advocated for interpretive analysis of international news as early as the 1930s. After the Second
World War, growing US involvement in world affairs and the perceived threat
of Soviet propaganda convinced many editors that it was the duty of the press
not only to report the news but also to interpret it.[94] In a keynote address to
the Association for Education in Journalism convention at Columbia University, Arthur Hays Sulzberger stressed that such interpretive analysis of foreign news must be the essence of the newspapers' leading role in the international battle for "men's minds."[95]

Still, IPI's highly publicized endorsement of experts suggested that Moscow
correspondents had little to contribute to the task of keeping the public
informed. Incensed by the IPI report and its subsequent discussion in the
mainstream press, Gilmore and Salisbury dispatched angry letters to their editors pointing out that the survey relied on outdated information, contained
many factual errors, and misrepresented the working conditions in Moscow.
Both journalists, especially Gilmore, were angered at the suggestion that marriage to Soviet women compromised the trustworthiness of Moscow correspondents. Neither Gilmore nor Salisbury was against interpretive reporting
as such, and neither argued that reporting from the USSR was unaffected by
Soviet censorship. Nonetheless, they stressed that Moscow correspondents
"lean over backwards" to provide well-rounded coverage of Soviet realities and
that the IPI report was unfair in its judgment and its personal attacks on the
journalists' wives.[96] Gilmore was convinced that the "very articulate people
who are building themselves up as Russian experts in the USA" had tried to
enhance their own prestige by purposefully undermining the credibility of the
Moscow press corps.[97]

The core question of who was best positioned to write truthfully about the
Soviet Union was at the center of the debate. The conflict, as the journalists

*Figure 2.2.* The Associated Press correspondent in Moscow, Eddy Gilmore, reads an account of his interview with Joseph Stalin, in *Pravda,* Moscow, March 23, 1946. (Photo: Associated Press Photo/AP Images.)

saw it, was between professional reporters, who sought to show how things really were, and philistines with various axes to grind. Many of the experts were former émigrés or "fellow travelers" who had converted to an almost evangelical anti-communism.[98] The journalists supposed that given these political leanings, the experts refused to accept anything but disparaging reports from the USSR and cast doubt on the loyalty of the Moscow correspondents when they reported otherwise. Gilmore warned that it was the experts' anti-Soviet bias, rather than foreign correspondents' reporting, that endangered America's interests and undermined the truth: "I realize that editors and a larger number of people probably want to hear nothing good from here, but that, of course, should have nothing to do with the way the AP covers the news. [. . .] I know that a lot of that crap about Russia in the report came from that group of Trotskyites [. . .] who've finally gotten their feet in the editorial door and are not only criticizing legitimate newspapermen, but are being listened to."[99] Gilmore turned the accusations against him back onto the accusers. While "legitimate newspapermen" struggled to deliver informed and nuanced descriptions of Soviet life, the experts bent news analysis to serve their political agenda and personal interests. While Moscow correspondents took a bashing for saying what the US *needed* to hear, the experts scored popularity points by saying what everyone *wanted* to hear. The choice of the word "Trotskyites" in Gilmore's letter could not have been coincidental. In response to repeated attacks on his and his colleagues' loyalty, he reminded his editors of the political backgrounds of those who accused him. The most vehement anti-communists in the present, Gilmore charged, were the most die-hard communists in the past.

The Moscow press corps as a whole agreed that the attacks against them derived from the unwillingness of editors, experts, and readers to reconcile their expectations of Soviet life with the realities that the journalists reported. "The fact is, that conditions in places which I have visited are by no means as black as seems to be generally supposed among the public at large," wrote Salisbury to his editors. "Thus, when I write about, for example, the really quite pleasant conditions of life in Georgia it seems to the casual reader that I am gilding the lily or singing paeans of praise for the Soviet system instead of merely offering a factual report."[100] While the journalists raised these concerns in private correspondence with friends and colleagues, they had limited options for defending themselves from afar. Moreover, insisting that life in the USSR was not as bad as commonly believed was a dangerous strategy at a time when the US news media were preoccupied with the threat of Soviet propaganda and communist subversion.

The debate on foreign correspondents shows how professional journalists thought about international reporting in the context of America's changing role in the world. All agreed that it was the duty of the press to explain the foreign world to the American public. The AP, UP, and the *Times* all believed that their Moscow bureaus played an essential role in their efforts to keep their readers informed. Other editors and publishers remained convinced that censored reporting was dangerous to the national interest and that the American public would be better served by relying exclusively on the interpretive analyses of experts. Whether one believed that Moscow correspondents were "going native" or toning down their reports in self-preservation, all agreed that

Soviet censorship was at the heart of the problem. It was the twin evils of censorship and lack of freedom of information in the USSR that prevented Americans from learning what the Soviet Union was really like and from developing a realistic assessment of the adversary. It was also censorship that brought the American press dangerously close to aiding Soviet propaganda. As far as US journalists, publishers, editors, experts, commentators, and readers were concerned, Soviet censorship was a major weapon in the Cold War.

## "Russia Uncensored"

Only after correspondents left Moscow could they confront Soviet censorship and answer the challenges of domestic critics. Upon returning to the US, most correspondents wrote lengthy analyses—books or article series that summarized their assignments and their views of the Soviet Union. The journalists used these accounts to stress their opposition to the Soviet regime and assert their loyalty to the United States. The post-assignment accounts were introduced as the ultimate reports on Russia, unhindered by censorship.[101] The critical stance of these reports conformed with readers' expectations from descriptions of life under a communist dictatorship and reinforced the idea that censorship severely curtailed the Moscow copy. In time, pundits and readers would attach greater importance to what the journalists wrote *after*, rather than *during*, their assignments. Whereas the latter was perceived as part of the Soviet plan to beam propaganda to the United States, the former became equated with the objective truth about communist dictatorship. The post-assignment account was central to how foreign correspondents shaped their careers after leaving Moscow. Given the newspapers' increasing turn to the services of Soviet experts and the limited availability of commentators with recent experience in the USSR, former Moscow correspondents were in great demand. Post-assignment publications created opportunities for editorial columns, lecture tours, talks, public recognition, and further professional commitments. The post-assignment account thus became a perfect stepping-stone to a new professional career as an expert on Soviet affairs.

In 1949, after their departure from the Soviet Union, both Edmund Stevens and Joseph Newman summarized their views on the USSR in two separate series of articles. Stevens's series comprised forty installments and ran in the *Christian Science Monitor* between October 1949 and January 1950. The series won the Pulitzer Prize and was released as a book in 1950. General Walter Bedell Smith, US ambassador to the Soviet Union from 1946 to 1948, wrote a warm foreword to the book—a clear sign of the establishment's endorsement.[102] Newman's series comprised thirteen installments published in the *New York Herald Tribune* and in the *Washington Post*.[103] The series also came out in a book format, where Newman expanded the original articles and added two previously unpublished installments.[104] Both Newman's and Stevens's series carried the title "Russia Uncensored" and emphasized the primacy of censorship in the work of Moscow correspondents. Robert Magidoff also wrote a post-assignment book. Entitled *In Anger and Pity*, it offered a retrospective analysis of Magidoff's time in Moscow and recounted in detail the events that led to his expulsion.[105] Both Newman's and Stevens's series addressed the same topics and often overlapped with the ones covered in Magidoff's book. All three journalists described how the Soviet regime deprived its people of the most basic rights and freedoms. In so doing, journalists echoed US diplomats and information officials, who believed that publicizing the dire conditions of Soviet life and the oppressive nature of the communist regime would be the most effective way to counteract Soviet anti-American propaganda.[106]

American correspondents emphasized the contradictions between the Soviet ideology and the daily lives of the Soviet people. They attacked the Soviet Union's self-representation as a workers' democracy and pointed out that Soviet elections were rigged and that citizens had no leverage against their leaders. Articles dedicated to living standards criticized the Soviet state for prizing the military and heavy industry above the welfare of the people and thus depriving its hardworking citizens of the most basic daily needs. The average Soviet citizen's diet consisted of cabbage, potatoes, and black bread. The majority of Russians, wrote the journalists, could not afford suits or decent clothing and walked around in shabby dresses and worn-out coats. At the same time, all the correspondents agreed that, compared with wartime and the immediate postwar years, Soviets' daily lives were gradually improving. They noted a greater availability of consumer goods, a larger variety of foods, and the abolition of food rationing.[107]

Edmund Stevens and Joseph Newman emphasized that, contrary to Soviet statements, a planned economy was not an adequate alternative to capitalism—that in fact the communist system of economics led to food shortages, industrial theft, and low-quality products.[108] Newman pointed out that persistent reports on the inefficiency of Soviet production "suggest that the waste in the planned Soviet system may be greater than in the unplanned capitalist country."[109] Stevens argued that waste and inefficiency were inherent attributes of a managed communist economy and derived directly from the lack of a "commercial competitive element, which operates as a powerful corrective to incompetence under a free economy."[110] Such statements affirmed both the might and right of American capitalism, industry, and living standards. Surveys of the Soviet economy and consumption also sent an encouraging message to American readers and commentators, who viewed the economy as the primary indicator of Soviet readiness to launch a war against the United States.

Stories about the plights of religious worshipers in the USSR also highlighted the inconsistencies between Soviet words and deeds.[111] Newman argued that the Russian Orthodox Church was nothing but a mouthpiece for Soviet propaganda, which "summoned all the faithful into the Soviet camp."[112] Edmund Stevens explored the plight of Roman Catholic clergy in the newly annexed Baltic states and described how show trials, based on false evidence, convicted Lithuanian monks and clerics for "indoctrination of youth and anti-Soviet activities."[113] Distraught by the "anti-cosmopolitan campaign," American correspondents discussed in great detail Jewish acquaintances who lost their jobs or were attacked in the press.[114] Stories about the disappearance of famous Soviet Jews, such as the wife of Foreign Minister Molotov, or the mysterious murder of Solomon Mikhoels, a renowned theater director and the chairman of the Jewish Anti-Fascist Committee, supported the journalists' assertions that the repressive machine of the Soviet state could turn against anyone.

Although the journalists set out to demonstrate how the Soviet state was oppressing its citizens, the accounts contained few descriptions of actual Soviet people. Most of the time, the journalists' insights about Soviet life were illustrated through the experiences of fellow foreigners. Discussions of state oppression focused on the refusal to grant exit visas to the Soviet wives of British and American citizens.[115] Stories about the secret police focused on surveillance of foreigners in Moscow. Surveys of consumerism explained that in the Soviet stores it was impossible to find items that most Americans considered essential. Stevens used a story of "Aunt Dasha," a peasant woman who sold him fresh milk, as a segue into an article on peasant markets. But the article told little about "Aunt Dasha" herself, except that owing to the Soviet planned economy she and her fellow peasants on collective farms struggled to make ends meet.[116] Most of the time the Soviet people appeared in journalists' accounts as faceless masses of downtrodden shoppers, workers, or peasants.

The journalists' descriptions of rights that the Soviet regime denied to its citizens corresponded to the notion of the four freedoms: freedom of speech, freedom of worship, freedom from want, and freedom from fear. President Franklin D. Roosevelt articulated the idea of the four freedoms in 1941 and defined them as the most basic human rights, which the US promised to defend from the "new order of tyranny."[117] Subsequently, Roosevelt's view of the world as divided between tyranny and freedom became one of the central metaphors of the Cold War.[118] Since 1946, the notion of the four freedoms had informed American political rhetoric, especially in the realm of foreign affairs.[119] The journalists' implicit use of this concept positioned the United States as the defender of the cause of freedom and contrasted it with the tyranny of international communism.

Foreign correspondents agreed that the decisive battle in America's war against communism would be fought "in the realm of ideas—and for the possession [. . .] of men's minds."[120] The journalists argued that America's victory in this battle depended on its ability to appeal to the people of the Soviet Union and around the world. Foreign correspondents explained that although the Soviet Union was a menacing police state, the Soviet people were "basically humble, fraternal and good."[121] For example, Edmund Stevens concluded his account on a hopeful note, predicting that it would not be long before the Russians would come to disdain the communist dictatorship and rise against it:

> There are in Russia today legions of thinking, intelligent people who chafe under the omnipotent police state and long with their whole being for freedom. The Russians are a race neither domineering not aggressive nor xenophobe. They are warmly human, gregarious, and endowed with an avid and friendly curiosity about other peoples. All these qualities tend to instinctively alienate them, if not from the Soviet system, at least from its present policies at home and abroad. [. . .] It is essential that the West learn to distinguish between the police state and the Soviet people, for if the former are implacable foes, the latter, unless stupidly antagonized, are potential friends and allies.[122]

This view of the Soviet people offered a radical alternative to the image of the communist enemy, which permeated American Cold War culture. Popular representations of communists alternated between subversive evil geniuses and emotionless inhuman robots.[123] In contrast, the journalists portrayed the Soviets as likeable, reasonable, and humane; as regular people who feared the secret police and wanted to protect their loved ones. The journalists emphasized that although the Soviet police state duped its people with propaganda, it was still possible to talk sense to the good, freedom-loving Russians. If only the Russians could learn the truth—that America was committed to freedom and that life in the USSR was so much worse than elsewhere in the world—they would reject the Soviet regime and pull away from their oppressors. Foreign correspondents thus reaffirmed the idea that censorship was the cardinal problem of the Cold War. It was censorship and the lack of freedom of information that accounted for the absence of rebellion in the communist world, the Soviet people's allegiance to their leaders, and their animosity toward the United States. Censorship, in short, is what kept the Soviet monolith standing.

If censorship was the primary cause of the Cold War, then truth, which the journalists defined as a free flow of reliable information, was the best weapon. Former Moscow correspondents stressed that their professional ethos and intimate knowledge of Russia made them uniquely equipped to battle Soviet censorship and propaganda. For example, in the conclusion to his series, Joseph Newman pointed out that people with first-hand experience in the USSR were the ultimate antidote to Soviet lies and manipulation:

> He who can distinguish between fact and fiction soon learns that the debate raging abroad is over two different countries, related to each other only in name. One is the Russia of Marxism, the other is the Russia of Russia. The former is the Russia of which many discontented workers and intellectuals dream as the land where order, justice and prosperity have been brought to all men. This is the Russia in which Moscow encourages the troubled people of other countries to believe and to which they are invited to lend their support. The other [. . .] is Russia of [. . .] hatred of the foreigner; wide-spread poverty in a progressively industrial economy; exploitation of the worker by the state to further its ambitions in foreign policy, injustice, fear and oppression. This is the Russia the Kremlin would conceal from the outside world.[124]

"He who can distinguish between facts and fiction" was of course an American journalist who had the opportunity to witness the Soviet Union first-hand. According to Newman, it was the duty of the journalists to open the eyes of misguided Soviet supporters and to illuminate the gaps between truth and propaganda. Other correspondents concurred. Robert Magidoff emphasized that "the traditional freedom of our profession to report events fully and objectively" empowered journalists to bear witness to the truth about the Soviet regime.[125] While domestic critics questioned the value of the Moscow press corps, its former members stressed that they, much more than anyone else, were uniquely positioned to stand up to censors and tear the mask off the oppressive Soviet dictatorship. Foreign correspondents aligned themselves with the American battle against Soviet propaganda and insisted that their work was indispensable to their country and the free world.

The idea that "truthful information" was the best weapon against Soviet propaganda enjoyed great popularity among US media professionals and political establishment. Like their Soviet counterparts, US policymakers recognized the importance of the competition for hearts and minds at home and abroad, and made information integral to their Cold War strategy. The Truman and the Eisenhower administrations actively courted US publishers and journalists and recruited them to support the government's information programs.[126] It is not a coincidence that President Truman first unveiled his "Campaign for Truth"—a broad initiative to combat Soviet propaganda around the world—at the annual convention of the American Society of Newspaper Editors. In his speech, the president stressed that "deceit, distortion, and lies" were "one of the most powerful weapons the communists have" and that it was the duty of the United States to reach out to people around the world and make sure that "the truth about communism is known everywhere."[127] Throughout the speech the president equated "plain, simple, unvarnished truth" with information emanating from the American news media, such as "the newspapers, radio, newsreels and other sources that the people trust."[128] US journalists and government officials alike described their own efforts as "information"—a neutral term associated with facts and objectivity—and labeled the enemy's practices "propaganda"—a negative term associated with brainwashing and deceit.[129]

The story of Moscow correspondents offers new insights into the dynamics of the press-government relationship in the early Cold War. It shows how individual journalists became active participants in the US government's battle against Soviet communism.[130] American journalists believed that it was their professional duty to take a stance against Soviet propaganda and saw their own writing as honest reporting that publicized the "truth" about the Soviet dictatorship. In this way, their objectives aligned with those of US foreign policy and information officials. In 1947, for example, Ambassador Smith urged the State Department to launch an American information program that would "debunk Soviet propaganda and clarify our own policies."[131] Smith attached a list of topics that could be useful in such campaign, including the inefficiency of the Soviet economy, the exploitation of working people by the Soviet state, the mistreatment of foreigners in the USSR and the plight of their Soviet spouses, and the overall totalitarian nature of the Soviet regime.[132] The topical similarity between Smith's proposed information program and the accounts that Moscow correspondents published after coming home is striking, if not surprising. For one, journalists occasionally advised the US Embassy on information initiatives, especially the Voice of America's Russian-language broadcasts.[133] More profoundly, American journalists and government officials viewed the world through a shared ideological perspective, held similar ideas about the USSR's true nature, and agreed that "truthful" information was the best weapon against Soviet propaganda. The articles and books that the journalists wrote for domestic consumption after concluding their assignments brought the major tenets of the US government's Cold War propaganda into millions of households around the country. While the Smith-Mundt Act prohibited the US government from disseminating its international propaganda materials to the American public, no such restriction applied to journalists' work in the nation's newspapers and beyond.[134] In publishing their reports, foreign correspondents shaped popular understanding of the Cold War as a conflict between truth and lies and between a police state and the republic of freedom. Fellow journalists, editors, readers and pundits embraced this distinction.

The superpowers' concerns with internal and external enemies had a formative impact on the work of American correspondents during and after their assignments in Moscow. Soviet anti-American campaigns embittered the journalists, increased their negative attitude toward the Soviet regime, and reduced the scope of reporting from the Soviet Union. Domestic anticommunism and persistent scrutiny of the correspondents' ideological allegiances necessitated vigilant reaffirmations of their loyalty and professional credibility. In response to attacks at home and abroad, foreign correspondents stressed their anti-Soviet opinions, emphasized their ability to contribute to American efforts to refute Soviet propaganda, and highlighted their personal inalienable connection to American values.

Several important precedents were established during this period. Foreign correspondents' clear stance against the Soviet regime became a staple of good reporting and facilitated public acceptance of the journalists as authoritative voices in the national discussion about the Soviet Union. The post-assignment accounts became a popular and respected format for articulating the journalists' insights on the Soviet adversary. These trends manifested themselves in American coverage of the Soviet Union throughout the Cold War, even after the conditions of reporting had improved and domestic concerns about the journalists' loyalties had long since subsided.

# PART TWO

# PENS INSTEAD OF PROJECTILES, 1953–1965

During the early days of March 1953, Melor Sturua, Stanislav Kondrashov, and many of their colleagues stood on a balcony of the *Izvestiia* building and watched the masses moving silently toward Red Square to pay their last respects to Joseph Stalin. Several blocks away, on Red Square itself, Harrison Salisbury, Eddy Gilmore, Henry Shapiro, and Thomas Whitney stood in the crowd, frantically scribbling in their notebooks, gathering their impressions of the sights and sounds of Stalin's funeral. Soviet and American journalists alike understood that they were facing the dawn of a new era but could not yet imagine how dramatically their lives were about to change.

Stalin's successors in the Kremlin transformed Soviet domestic politics and international relations. Nikita Khrushchev and Soviet foreign policy officials recognized the importance of "peaceful coexistence" between the socialist and the capitalist world, emphasized energetic outreach to foreign countries, and made international dialogue the center of superpower relations. While the Eisenhower and the Kennedy administrations differed in their response to Soviet initiatives, US policymakers abandoned their hopes of the USSR's imminent collapse and came to accept the inevitability of superpower coexistence. These developments transformed the style and the substance of Soviet-American relations. Government officials, politicians, dancers, singers, writers, artists, musicians, scientists, students, doctors, and farmers now crossed the Iron Curtain in an effort to promote mutual understanding between the superpowers. At the same time, anxieties about the rival's military and ideological superiority persisted. Events—such as the downing of the U-2 spy plane and the Cuban missile crisis—reminded Soviets and Americans that the rival superpower was a tangible threat. As a result, American-Soviet interactions in this period swung from vibrant dialogue to intense conflict.

Changes in Soviet-American relations introduced new opportunities and new challenges into foreign correspondents' work. The ranks of American correspondents in the Soviet Union and of Soviet correspondents in the US rapidly expanded, and so did the number of American and Soviet news organizations that now had representatives on the other side. Inspired by liberalization in domestic journalism and the demise of the anti-American campaign, a new generation of enthusiastic Soviet correspondents promoted new styles of reporting from the United States. Concise transmission of official policy statements and hyperbolic language were replaced with engaging human-interest stories and well-written analytical commentary. American correspondents in the Soviet Union, animated by the opening of Soviet society, began to take advantage of the newly available access to Soviet institutions, officials, and citizens. With the thaw in international relations, anxieties about the enemy overseas gave way to curiosity on both sides. Foreign correspondents were eager to satisfy readers' demand for new and different information. International reporting began to feature a broader cast of Soviet and American characters and introduced readers to daily life in the socialist East or the capitalist West.

The binary of "truth" and "lies" still shaped American and Soviet understanding of international reporting. Cutting through the "lies" of enemy propaganda and revealing the "truth" about the rival superpower remained the ultimate professional goal of Soviet and American correspondents alike. However, the "truths" that foreign correspondents now brought to their readers were much changed. In tune with the broader shift in Cold War rhetoric, international reporting now foregrounded topics such as science, education, space, domestic appliances, consumer goods, housing, lifestyles, and the welfare of regular citizens. As they explored these new topics, Soviet and American journalists confronted a challenging question: How could they write about positive developments on the other side without alienating their readers or the establishment and without losing the essential "truth" of the ultimate superiority of their own ideologies and political systems? Thus, even as they told new stories about the rival superpower, foreign correspondents continued to emphasize the comparative advantages of socialism or liberal democracy and capitalism.

Information specialists on both sides realized that foreign correspondents played a key role in shaping popular perceptions of the adversary and sought to harness the potential influence of international reporting. Although contemporaries did not use the terms "public diplomacy" or "cultural diplomacy," foreign correspondents became both the *objects* and the *subjects* of the two camps' cultural diplomacy initiatives. Organized tours, exhibitions, and people-to-people cultural events sought to attract the rival's foreign correspondents, inviting them to appreciate the institutions and achievements of the host country. The Soviet Union actively promoted such initiatives and made an effort to engage American correspondents. Eisenhower administration officials, who regarded communist journalists as irredeemable hardliners, invested little effort in reaching out to the Soviet press corps in the United States. By contrast, the Kennedy administration tried to draw Soviet correspondents into the orbit of cultural diplomacy and established working relationships with a number of senior Soviet journalists and editors. At the same time, diplomatic talks and cultural exchanges negotiations often focused on the working conditions of the press corps and their access to travel and information. More and more correspondents were drawn into the diplomatic process as journalists' exchanges of opinion with colleagues and officials in the host country became an important channel of dialogue between the USSR and the US.

Changing international relations and domestic developments in the Soviet Union and the United States also altered the dynamics of journalists' interactions with their own governments. Stalin's death prompted Soviet officials, information specialists, and journalists to reconsider the role of the press in Soviet society. New ideas and professional practices were put forward to support the state's emphasis on mobilization without violence. Soviet correspondents continued to see themselves as the voice of Soviet foreign policy. Now, however, they had to reconcile this duty with the professional imperative to produce genuinely engaging reporting that would stimulate readers' interest in and thoughtful interaction with international news. In the United States, news media and the government disagreed whether national security considerations justified withholding government information from the press. As discontent and turmoil began to engulf the US in the late 1950s and the early 1960s, the press and the government increasingly found each other in opposing camps. American correspondents in Moscow, whose work depended on having a good rapport with the State Department and the US Embassy, had to navigate a shifting landscape of press-government relations at home and abroad. American and Soviet publishers, editors, and journalists relied a great deal on their own governments' assistance. It was government officials and diplomats who could secure visas and permissions for opening new bureaus, help with access to coveted sources, or resolve disputes with the host country's officials. In Moscow and Washington, Leningrad and New York, journalists balanced the need to work closely with their own government officials and uphold their country's foreign policy in their reporting with their desire to tell new captivating stories about the lives of regular people on the other side.

# CHAPTER THREE

# Overtake America

In 1967 one-half of the Grand Prix at the Fifth Moscow International Film Festival went to *The Journalist*, a film by Soviet director Sergei Gerasimov.[1] At the heart of the film is a love story between a talented Moscow journalist and a young factory worker from a provincial town. The second part of the film finds the protagonist assigned as a foreign correspondent to Paris, where he partakes in a bohemian lifestyle, meets the actress Annie Girardot, and attends a rehearsal of the singer Mireille Mathieu. On his Paris adventures, the journalist is accompanied by a new friend—an American correspondent. The two spend much time in friendly debates over the international situation. In these discussions, the Soviet journalist comes across as a confident, friendly, and worldly youth who carries himself with dignity and passionately advocates the superiority of socialism.

Gerasimov's protagonist demonstrated how professional journalism, particularly international reporting, had changed in the period between Stalin's death in 1953 and the film's arrival on Soviet screens. A huge gap separated Gerasimov's journalist from the ideal foreign correspondent of the first postwar decade. Gone were the reticence, suspicion, and besieged mentality. The trademarks of postwar international reporting—dry, laconic, institutional language—had been left behind. The new ideal for international correspondents envisioned journalists who would actively explore the host country, reach out to foreign surroundings, and promote the Soviet viewpoint abroad. They would become their readers' eyes and ears in foreign lands and capture their imaginations with engaging and well-written reports.

Under the leadership of Nikita Khrushchev, the Soviet Union adopted a new course in international relations, one that emphasized a wide-ranging outreach to the world. International reporting played an important role in this process. Soviet foreign correspondents were tasked with explaining the USSR's involvement in world affairs to Soviet readers and expanding their knowledge about foreign countries. While abroad, they were also expected to carry the Soviet viewpoint to foreign interlocutors and audiences. Between 1953 and 1964, a new generation of journalists took over the bureaus of Soviet newspapers and news agencies in New York and Washington. As they brought along the professional innovations that excited journalists and editors across the USSR, these foreign correspondents transformed Soviet coverage of the United States. Domestic and international reporting alike now stressed the importance of good writing and liveliness, paid greater attention to human-interest stories, and highlighted the contributions of individual journalists to the collective enterprise that was the Soviet press. At the same time, Soviet international reporting remained the principal voice of Soviet foreign policy. As such, it came to reflect the overall state of international relations under Nikita Khrushchev: multifaceted, subject to the influence of different actors, often inconsistent, and polyphonic.

## The Polevoi Delegation Rocks the Establishment

In 1955, a delegation of seven Soviet journalists left the French port of Le Havre on board a New York–bound ship. All of them felt a mixture of excitement and anxiety, as theirs was the first delegation of journalists to be hosted by the US State Department since 1946. Boris Polevoi, a renowned writer and *Pravda* war correspondent, led the delegation. Other members consisted of senior figures in the journalistic establishment and one newcomer, Alexei Adzhubei—one of the first graduates of Moscow State University's new Department of Journalism, recently appointed editor of *Komsomol'skaia Pravda,* and Nikita Khrushchev's son-in-law.

The very existence of the delegation, an outcome of the 1955 Geneva Summit, pointed to the changing tides of the Cold War. During the summit the leaders of the USSR, the US, Great Britain, and France came together for the first time in ten years and discussed how to reduce international tensions in the nuclear age. This was the first meeting of the "Big Four" since 1945. Among the proposals considered was the strengthening of ties between East and West through exchanges of visitors and cultural products.[2] One of the first exchanges—of delegations of American and Soviet journalists—followed shortly after the summit.

The Polevoi delegation traveled across the United States and met with American colleagues, sympathizers, and people who were simply curious to see real Soviets. The guests visited newspaper offices, toured cultural and historic sites, and even attended a Hollywood party, where they rubbed elbows with Marilyn Monroe, Grace Kelly, and a young politician previously unknown to them—John F. Kennedy. Each journalist filed accounts of the trip with his newspaper, and for the first time in many years the Soviet public was able to read about a different America. No longer an abstract citadel of

*Figure 3.1.* Polevoi delegation at the *Los Angeles Examiner*, November 5, 1955. *Seated:* Eddie Adler (reporter); *standing (from left to right):* Alexei Adzhubei, Anatolii Sofronov, Viktor Poltoratskii, Valentin Berezhkov, Nikolai Gribachev, Boris Izakov, and Boris Polevoi (leader of group). (Photo: Mack, Los Angeles Examiner Photographs Collection, 1920–1961, University of Southern California Libraries.)

capitalism and monopolies, but a place of sights, sounds, and people. The hitherto faceless "average American" was replaced with the names, voices, professions, and home interiors of the people whom the Soviet journalists had met during their trip. After their return home, the journalists promoted another theme—the growing convergence between Soviet and American people—in lectures and public appearances and in three books published by different members of the delegation.[3]

Upon returning home, the delegation members submitted a report summarizing their experiences and insights from their visit.[4] They also shared their impressions in presentations to the staff of their newspapers and to fellow members of the Union of Soviet Writers. American people, they believed, were generally well disposed toward the Soviet Union and were sincerely interested in a dialogue with the Soviet people. Interestingly, the delegation members often used the American press as an indicator of their hosts' sincerity.

Favorable news reports were seen as evidence that the American counterparts meant business and were committed to "the spirit of Geneva."[5]

Stressing the growing importance of cultural exchanges and international dialogue, the delegation recommended that Soviet international propaganda learn from American know-how and get better at "promoting the Soviet image abroad."[6] Changing the official treatment of foreign journalists in the USSR could be an important step in the right direction, argued Polevoi. Foreign correspondents should have better access to Soviet officials, cultural figures, and public institutions; they should be allowed to travel around the Soviet Union, and censorship of their dispatches should be abolished. Overall, the delegation members urged Soviet authorities to build a system of cooperation with foreign news media, including media from the US.[7] Officials dealing with foreigners should be professional, efficient, articulate, and polite. The quality of every outward-facing aspect, such as the service on Aeroflot flights or the quality of the paper used in books and photo albums for export, should be comparable to that in the capitalist world. Soviet representatives overseas in particular should not fall behind their foreign counterparts. Polevoi and others stressed that the competition with the West had to be on the West's own terms and that nobody would take the Soviet representatives seriously unless they looked, sounded, dressed, and traveled like their hosts.[8]

The delegation members pointed out that the trip made them acutely aware that Soviet coverage of the United States had been so inadequate that it had become one of the main impediments to improving Soviet-American relations: "We realized how harmed we are by inadequate understanding of American life, by superficial and vulgar coverage of the developments in that country [. . .] and how disruptive for establishing good relations is our incessant emphasis on the dark sides of American life."[9]

A special report dedicated to TASS bureaus in the US lamented that its correspondents labored in "hard and outright humiliating" conditions unworthy of the official Soviet wire service, and that in so doing the agency had inadvertently undermined Soviet international outreach.[10] Hinting at the long shadow that the anti-American campaign had cast over TASS operations in the US, Polevoi reported that correspondents appeared "imprisoned by outdated rules and restrictions, eschew interactions [. . .] with their American colleagues, and [were] afraid to participate in any discussion or debate."[11] Unlike the representatives of American and European wire services, TASS correspondents steered clear of the journalistic opportunities in Washington such as press conferences, press clubs, or congressional sessions.[12] TASS correspondents were perpetually underpaid and "could not risk entertaining a colleague in a restaurant or at home."[13] The New York bureau's car was such a clunker (*drandulet*) that it became the laughingstock of the entire press corps.[14] Inadequate material conditions "brought shame on" the Soviet press and compromised the journalists' professional reputations.[15] Rather than sounding the Soviet viewpoint and challenging US officials with pointed critiques, Soviet correspondents remained silent and invisible. When one TASS reporter summoned the courage to ask a question during President Dwight Eisenhower's press conference, it was front-page news, wrote Polevoi.[16] Most important, the structure of Soviet communications made TASS reporting wasteful and inefficient. All too often, Soviet officials insisted on personally vetting TASS's reports from the UN General Assembly, often multiple times, and then "improving" the reports by inserting citations from their own speeches. The agency's editorial process, in which every statement was checked by a succession of editors in New York and then Moscow, further impeded timely reporting and took a toll on correspondents' time.[17] In short, charged Polevoi and his colleagues, Soviet journalists in America were missing valuable opportunities to explore the United States, to cover interesting stories, and to advance the Soviet viewpoint abroad.[18]

Delegation members not only described existing problems but also laid out a vision for the future of Soviet reporting from the United States: "We think that the time is ripe to reconsider [our] system of propaganda on American topics, to forego the bravado of our publicistic writing, and to move to principled, yet deep and calm coverage of American life and its problems."[19] Their criticism of TASS operations likewise put forward a new ideal of a foreign correspondent: no longer a trumpet of the party, who coordinated everything with the authorities "above," but a journalist-activist, who would be intimately familiar with local culture and local language, exhibit a keen interest in foreign affairs, take initiative, and sound his or her own voice. The new foreign correspondent was envisioned as an assertive propagandist, who would actively reach out to international audiences and miss no opportunity to promote the Soviet viewpoint.

## "The Spirit of Geneva"

The very existence of the Polevoi delegation, as well as the scope of its remit and recommendations, demonstrates how writer-journalists continued to shape Soviet engagement with the outside world. The delegation's report was especially striking given that all participants were senior members of the Soviet establishment and hardly prone to reformist attitudes of any kind. Veteran Pravdist Boris Polevoi was a decorated writer and war correspondent and the recipient of two Stalin Prizes. Polevoi's writing celebrated the New Soviet Man and sacrifices for the socialist cause. Another delegation member, Nikolai Gribachev, was also a decorated war correspondent, also a laureate of two Stalin Prizes in literature, and the editor in chief of *Sovetskii Soyuz*, the principal organ of Soviet international propaganda. Valentin Berezhkov, representing the journal the *New Times (Novoe vremia)* on the tour, was a Soviet diplomat and journalist, as well as Stalin's and Molotov's personal translator during the Second World War. Anatolii Sofronov was the former secretary of the Union of Soviet Writers and the editor in chief of the Soviet Union's only—and massively popular—glossy magazine, *Ogonek*.[20] The high profile of the delegation's members made the report impossible to ignore, and the Central Committee endorsed most of their suggestions. In the following months TASS, the Soviet Embassy in Washington, and various ministries were instructed to introduce plans for improvement in the spirit of the delegates' recommendations.[21] Soviet leadership's support of these changes reflected the far-reaching transformation in the Soviet approach to foreign relations following Stalin's death.

The rethinking of the Soviet Union's relationship with the world began as early as 1953. New ideas—about the importance of international outreach and peaceful coexistence between the socialist and the capitalist world—gained more and more support among Soviet elites. Ostensible Soviet interest in establishing an international dialogue on disarmament, positive responses to certain American proposals, and the Geneva Summit marked the new course in international relations.[22] In 1956 Khrushchev delivered his "Secret Speech" at the Twentieth Congress of the Communist Party. The speech denounced Stalin's "cult of personality" and mismanagement of the Great Patriotic War and held Stalin personally responsible for the violence inflicted on innocent citizens and party members.[23] Party members across the Soviet Union welcomed Khrushchev's revelations and critical appraisal of the Stalinist past.[24]

The reforms in domestic and foreign affairs that swept the USSR after Stalin's death, and especially after the Twentieth Congress, propelled a new generation to the center stage of Soviet cultural and political life. Collectively known as *shestidesiatniki* (the people of the 1960s), this generation came of age amid the hardships and deprivations of the war and was touched by it, either as young adults or as young soldiers. They enthusiastically joined in the postwar reconstruction of their country and sought to contribute to its remaking. The *shestidesiatniki* believed in the superiority of socialist ideas and saw the

Twentieth Party Congress as the dawn of a new era, marked by a return to true socialism and the Leninist values that had shaped the Soviet state before their corruption at the hands of Stalin.[25] The activist spirit also extended into the Soviet establishment. Under Khrushchev, younger cadres, characterized by critical thinking and reformist intentions, rose in the state and party bureaucracies. The regime's promise to achieve communism by 1980 further spurred the reformist enthusiasm of the young generation.[26] Explaining his reforms as a return to true Leninist principles, Khrushchev revamped the means and practices used to build socialism during Stalin's time. Mobilization, reasoning, and engagement with the public became the favored modes of action.[27]

Khrushchev's reforms also brought dramatic changes to the Soviet understanding of the press and its role in society. To begin with, the press was to become a platform for coming to terms with the Stalinist past and for thinking about the future. Second, the press was expected to furnish readers with information they needed to educate themselves and develop as socialist citizens. Finally, the press was to play a central role in the state's efforts to mobilize citizens' enthusiasm for building socialism, without the use of violence.[28] New journalistic practices were put forth to achieve these vaunted goals. Newspapers expanded their engagement and interaction with their readers. Publications ran opinion surveys and staged "debates" by inviting and publishing readers' letters on a certain topic. Editors geared material more and more toward readers' interests and sought to be responsive to their experiences and concerns. Departments dealing with readers' letters were significantly expanded. *Izvestiia* editors rewarded their journalists for "sensing a letter"— identifying correspondence that could lead to an interesting story. In many cases, the newspaper took it upon itself to "protect the small person" from injustice and would run journalistic investigations or follow-ups to a reader's letter. The newspapers strove to become the public's interlocutors and to *inspire* readers to think rather than instruct them to do so. Journalists agreed that to inspire, articles had to be compelling reading first and foremost, and thus a great deal of emphasis was put on engaging writing styles and interesting stories.[29]

At the heart of the innovation was the idea of "journalism of the person"— whereby stories about particular situations or individual persons would be used to illustrate larger phenomena.[30] "Journalism of the person" facilitated an activist approach to reporting and emphasized the importance of the individual journalist in the collective endeavor of the Soviet press. Personal insights and interests informed a journalist's selection of a random episode as a vantage

*Figure 3.2.* Readers' Correspondence Department of *Izvestiia* newspaper, February 1, 1962. (Photo: Yuri Skuratov/Sputnik Images.)

point from which to look at larger universal issues that socialist subjects were expected to explore. Literary skill and individual writing style also determined whether an item would resonate with the audience. There was a growing realization that each journalist's unique style and interests were assets that made newspapers more interesting to readers. The press began to shift its source of educational and moral authority from the party to the journalist's personality.[31]

Alexei Adzhubei, who was closely associated with journalistic reforms, underlined the importance of the journalist's educating role:

> Reporting a fact is not enough. Journalists must offer commentaries [on the fact], supply it with additional details, in order to generalize more. [. . .] For example, a small article relates that in one of our cities someone underwent a

complicated heart surgery. And that's it. But if we add that the five months of treatment, the surgery, the medical supplies cost 700 rubles, all funded by the government, and that the removal of an appendix in the United States costs 500 dollars, to be paid by the patient himself—and that not everyone has this kind of money!—a small fact will shine thanks to a sharp publicistic commentary.[32]

It was revealing that Adzhubei chose the difference between socialism and capitalism as an example of the universally important truths that journalists should convey. International news in general, and reporting about the US in particular, occupied a significant place in the cultural and ideological transformations of the period, for several reasons.

First, a significant marker of the Khrushchev era was an increasing openness in foreign policy: a reaching out to other countries and a gradual decline in the Soviet Union's isolation. Diplomatic relations were restored with Yugoslavia; cultural and scientific exchanges were initiated with the capitalist West. Willing to showcase socialism's achievements, the USSR began to welcome visitors from all over the world. Soviet leaders expressed confidence that the people's faith in the socialist project would not weaken, but strengthen, if they knew more about foreign countries. The beacons of the new agenda were the 1957 Moscow Youth Festival, which welcomed thousands of young people from all over the world to the Soviet Union, and Khrushchev's highly publicized 1959 visit to the United States. This internationalist spirit culminated with Yuri Gagarin's 1961 flight into space, which inspired the Soviet people to imagine the world as a unified civilization. The rest of the world was no longer perceived as an unavoidable, even undesirable, addition to the Soviet world, but as an inseparable and necessary part of domestic culture.[33] In this context, foreign correspondents were expected to promote Soviet international outreach both by personally engaging with their host country and by providing information about the outside world. Foreign correspondents embodied the idea of peaceful coexistence in their personal experiences as well as in the stories they told.

Second, international reporting was essential for publicizing the advent of socialism in the world. The party considered the construction of communism in the Soviet Union to be a project of universal human significance—"a great international task, reflecting the interests of all humankind."[34] It was therefore important to chronicle the unfolding of this universal task in the international arena, especially in the new European socialist countries and the decolonizing countries in Africa and Asia. By highlighting the achievements of the socialist countries and presenting the gains that socialist ideas were making around the world, the Soviet press stressed the significance of the socialist project, its universal appeal, and its moral superiority.[35]

Third, international news grounded Khrushchev's emphasis on peaceful competition with the West in real-life examples. As the famous "kitchen debate" between Nikita Khrushchev and Vice President Richard Nixon demonstrated, the Soviet leader readily acknowledged that his country had much to learn from the United States. Yet he also expressed unwavering confidence that the Soviet Union would be able to "reach and surpass" America in just a few years.[36] Soviet international reporting took it upon itself to highlight the areas where Soviet socialism had already gained superiority over American capitalism. Adzhubei's statement, quoted above, emphasized how such a comparison represented the core of the universal and educational value of international news. At the same time, reports about life overseas showcased the material and technological achievements that awaited the Soviet people in the communist future.

International reporting and high-profile events such as the 1959 American National Exhibition in Moscow or Khrushchev's trip to the United States encouraged the Soviet people to engage with information about life abroad, especially in the US, from a comparative perspective. Comparative reading taught audiences that the Soviet Union, as the superior social system, had already overcome America in the areas of welfare and communality. At the same time, the comparative approach encouraged Soviet readers to look ahead to the horizons of communism and to remember that American technological and material progress would soon be available in Soviet Union. Behind the encouragement to compare socialism and capitalism stood the Soviet conception of its citizens as conscious Marxists who understood that socialism offered a viable and compelling alternative to the capitalist system.[37]

Soviet journalists realized that coverage of international affairs, and Soviet-American relations in particular, had to uphold the "spirit of Geneva" and the politics of peaceful coexistence. "Everyone must recognize that we can't report on international affairs as we did a month ago," stressed one member of *Izvestiia*'s editorial board shortly after the conference. "It is impossible, because we don't want to make any mistakes that might harm the improving relations."[38] Yet "strengthening the spirit of Geneva" did not mean that criticism of the United States was abandoned altogether. Improving Soviet-American relations also involved "unmasking all those who oppose reducing international tensions and who strive to ignite new fires of military confrontation."[39] Whether in celebrating the "spirit of Geneva" or criticizing its foes, foreign correspondents and their editors saw it as their personal responsibility to support Soviet international outreach and contribute to its success.

## The New Voices of Soviet International Reporting

As newspapers grappled with their new tasks in Soviet society, many professional discussions focused on what constituted good reporting on foreign affairs. Journalists agreed that international material should be well written, interesting, and accessible; that it should put forward a coherent and compelling analysis, capture readers' imaginations, and respect their interests and intelligence.[40] However, the exact meaning of these categories, and whether an item met these requirements, became subject of much debate. What was more important—ideological clarity, style, or readability? Should international reporting be straightforward and unambiguous, or should it use ornate diplomatic language?

Journalistic reform emboldened the newspapers to openly challenge TASS's dominance in Soviet international reporting.[41] In *Izvestiia's* editorial meetings, for example, "TASS" became synonymous with boring journalism, to be avoided at all costs. Viktor Poltoratskii, a senior editor in the newspaper's International Department, believed that abandoning TASS's writing conventions was the essential first step for cultivating good international reporting: "It so happens that many of the comrades who are now writing on international themes, for two, three, or four years have learned [about foreign countries] not as much from real-life experience, but from TASS materials. And there is nothing more horrible than TASS materials. If you want to ruin someone, let them read TASS for a year. It may sound harsh, but stylistically speaking, it's true."[42]

There was a growing consensus that the dry, unimaginative style of TASS reports was inadequate for the new tasks facing international reporting. The three major newspapers, *Pravda*, *Izvestiia*, and *Trud,* began to develop their own network of correspondents overseas. Initially these efforts focused on the coverage of large international events such as the Geneva Summit or Khrushchev's 1955 trip to India. Editorial boards took pride in the fact that both the analytical capacity and the literary style of the reports produced by their special correspondents far surpassed those of TASS.[43] These successes were used to justify dispatching newspapers' own correspondents (*sobstvennyi korrespondent* or *sobkor*) to permanent posts overseas. In 1954 Victor Maevskii opened *Izvestiia's* first London bureau. In 1956 Nikolai Karev departed to establish *Izvestiia's* operations in the United States. A year later, *Trud* was allowed to open its US bureau as well. The number of TASS announcements in foreign news sections gradually decreased, while articles from the newspapers' own international correspondents and commentators grew more prominent.[44]

The changing status of international news manifested itself in the physical layout of the newspapers. In 1955 *Izvestiia*'s entire international section fit into half of page four—the last page of each issue. In 1958 international news moved to pages two and three and occupied between one-and-a-half and two pages. *Pravda* also moved its international news from pages five and six forward to pages three and four. While front pages had previously been dedicated strictly to domestic news or party statements, from the late 1950s onward they featured international items from correspondents around the world.

The search for new ways to engage readers introduced an element of competition between Soviet news outlets. Initially, the competition focused on the material's readability and accessibility. *Pravda* and *Izvestiia* compared themselves with TASS and at the same time carefully followed each other's reporting, taking notes and evaluating whether the other paper's materials were more accessible or better written.[45] Gradually the competition shifted to content as well—editorial meetings compared the conceptual approaches of international reports and the quality of the international analyses they provided.[46] Alexei Adzhubei, who became *Izvestiia*'s editor in chief in 1959, intensified the competition between *Izvestiia* and *Pravda* and even introduced the idea of beating the rival newspaper to a scoop. One *Izvestiia* legend is telling: "A cosmonaut landed. The *Pravda* correspondent beat us—he picked up the cosmonaut and drove him to Moscow in his car. Adzhubei was livid: 'Take over!' And a journalist raced to the cosmonaut's house. He put his wife and daughter in an *Izvestiia* car and set out to meet the procession. Somewhere on Lenin Boulevard the cars were parallel to each other and the cosmonaut's daughter waved to her father. He got out and went into the *Izvestiia* car. We won."[47] Adzhubei himself readily acknowledged that his trip to the United States with the Polevoi delegation had been an invaluable learning experience that had shaped his professional approach and management style. The lessons learned on that visit continued to reverberate throughout the world of Soviet newspapers over the course of the entire Khrushchev period.[48]

The relationship between international reporting and the establishment also began to change, and the latter's involvement in the coverage of foreign affairs decreased. In 1955 Polevoi criticized Soviet diplomats who insisted on personally vetting TASS's reports and recommended liberating journalists from the duty to triple-check their dispatches. TASS representatives in New York begged their directors to heed this advice.[49] The newspapers likewise lamented that state officials often hampered good reporting and reduced its efficiency.[50] Journalists recognized that, since newspapers and news agencies functioned as the official voice of Soviet foreign policy, international reporting often had to follow diplomatic conventions and use vague and obscure language. At the same time, they insisted that the Soviet reader would be better served by well-written, clear, and compelling stories and that good writing and interesting reporting should be as important as the policy angle. As one *Pravda* correspondent observed, "We cannot use dry official language when talking about great international developments. The readers are tired of it."[51]

Routine meetings such as the ones described by Melor Sturua, where Ministry of Foreign Affairs officials instructed journalists on how to cover international themes, gradually disappeared, and official input became subtler. Now the choice of topics was dictated by activities in the international arena. Delegations, summits, and cultural exchanges provided ample material. Another source of potential news stories was life overseas. Foreign correspondents were expected to identify important and interesting events in the lives of their host countries and report them to their readers. This gave foreign correspondents room to exercise their own judgment and personal initiative. The journalists concurred that what made good reporting was interesting analysis from the correspondent on site and the ability to convey the atmosphere of foreign events.[52]

The extent of independence enjoyed by journalists and editors should not, however, be overstated. Newspapers still served as the voice of Soviet foreign policy and were subject to Glavlit's intervention. Phones rang on editors' desks with party or Ministry of Foreign Affairs officials on the other end explaining how to present or analyze certain aspects of the international situation.[53] And there was no room for independent assessments of some of the more sensitive international events, such as the 1956 Suez Crisis or the Hungarian uprising.[54]

Soviet journalists saw no contradiction between personalized reporting and the need to write within the boundaries of official ideology, foreign policy interests, and censorship. Ideological integrity, unity with the party-state, and the educational mission remained the pillars of Soviet journalism even after Stalin's death. Yet in crafting their educational messages, journalists were now encouraged to take the initiative and rely on their personal style and interests. Individual correspondents had more room to maneuver and greater influence over their own work. The growing number of people engaged in writing about foreign affairs created new opportunities for negotiations with editors, officials, and censors.

Some journalists, though, found the innovations difficult to cope with. Ambivalence about the new measures, and even harsh criticisms of them, cast long shadows over many editorial meetings and party gatherings, where some wondered if the press was turning its back on its duties to the state and the people.[55] Many of these doubts were rooted in the notion that it was the duty of the press to serve as the voice of Soviet foreign policy. Some journalists found the occasional differences between *Pravda* and *Izvestiia* unwelcome and worried that such differences created the impression that the Soviet Union's international positions were weak. While many reporters believed that by presenting different analytical approaches, the newspapers would arouse readers' interest and help them become better-informed citizens, others claimed that the divergence between the major newspapers robbed readers of a clear explanation of Soviet foreign policy. Whereas many journalists argued that beautifully written reports made Soviet propaganda creative and more appealing, others insisted that it weakened the polemic tone of the press and undermined its ideological rigor.[56]

Were the Soviet people ready to deal with multiple perspectives and different opinions? Had the public attained the appropriate level of Marxist consciousness? These questions preoccupied the entire Soviet establishment in the wake of Khrushchev's reforms and became the subject of much discussion in government offices and party meetings across the country.[57] Journalists, editors, and information officials likewise debated whether the public would be able to sift through different interpretations and focus on the essence of the press's message.[58]

Debates about new professional practices frequently became a platform for expressing uneasiness about the rapidly changing attitude toward the West and the impact of foreign practices on the profession. For example, in 1956 *Izvestiia* arts correspondent Anna Begicheva urged her colleagues to remain vigilant of the dangers of foreign influences: "[What] we have [is] an ecstatic, obsequious worship of western culture. [...] Even our biggest essayists lean over backwards to write about anything foreign and say how great life is overseas— the nature, the landscapes, and the people. There is no critical attitude towards what's going on abroad; somehow it is considered impolite to write about it. [...] These are no political mistakes, but something is absent, still. There are things that we cannot tell our people and kolkhozniks yet."[59]

Depictions of life overseas, according to Begicheva, were particularly dangerous, because unless carefully controlled, they could subvert years of educational propaganda: "I went to an average cinema and saw a seemingly pleasant picture titled *A Policeman and a Thief*. Regular people come out of the cinema saying 'our propaganda always says that things in America are horrible, but look how well the policeman treats the thief in that movie.'"[60] As a long-term crusader against "cosmopolitan enemies," Anna Begicheva was especially attuned to "potentially harmful influences from the West."[61] Yet many shared her concerns about the influence of bourgeois culture and about Soviet audiences' ability to maintain a critical attitude toward all things foreign.[62] Journalists who opposed the innovations found it difficult to part from the old categories of analysis and believed that, in sounding the alarm against bourgeois culture and propaganda, they were serving the interest of their readers.

Tensions in international relations magnified and exacerbated these concerns, and some journalists wondered whether the new style of international reporting was to blame. For example, in the wake of the 1956 Hungarian Revolution, *Pravda*'s party cell held a long, soul-searching meeting on the role of the press in Soviet society. One after another, remorseful Pravdists stood up, accused the intelligentsia of taking comradely critique too far, and stressed the importance of vigilance against bourgeois propaganda.[63]

International reporting appeared as both cause of and solution to the problem of foreign influences. In a report on the challenges to the Soviet press posed by bourgeois propaganda, veteran foreign correspondent Victor Maevskii criticized *Pravda* for what he called its "impartial" reporting from the West. "Today, for example, there was a publication about a detonation of another radioactive atom bomb in the USA. Is it good or bad? I could not find [in the newspaper] what was our attitude towards this explosion."[64] Maevskii's comments reveal that the gap between the Soviet socialist and the American liberal press remained deep. American colleagues would have marveled both at Maevskii's assertions of *Pravda*'s impartiality and at the fact that he saw this as a liability. American journalists considered impartiality a vaunted goal, to be attained by adhering closely to a set of reporting practices, and saw it as their professional duty to remain as impartial as possible. Maevskii, on the other hand, held that any news item lacking a clearly pronounced value judgment was dangerous and that the role of the press was to explain international developments as unequivocally as possible. The ideological ethos of the Soviet press posed no problem for Maevskii and his colleagues. On the contrary, ideological clarity was the ideal. Even as some Soviet journalists and editors began to turn to American know-how, the Soviet press remained committed to the ideas and values of socialist reporting.

## Remaking TASS

TASS—the bastion of conventional international reporting—was forced to catch up with the times. Communicating Soviet positions to international audiences was deemed crucial for the success of the new foreign policy. Getting TASS materials into the international press would help promote the Soviet viewpoint abroad.[65] Nikolai Pal'gunov believed that to achieve these goals, TASS had to become a news agency of international caliber, "fully competitive with major international agencies from the capitalist world" in the global news market.[66] These new goals—"popularizing Soviet foreign policy" and making TASS competitive with foreign news services—were a radical departure from the way the agency's duties had been conceived under Stalin.[67]

In 1955 TASS began to sign agreements for information exchange with all major international wire services and foreign newspapers. Yet these agreements in themselves were not enough to ensure that TASS materials would reach audiences beyond Soviet borders. TASS articles, steeped in "propagandistic sharpness," struck foreign editors as too long and boring. Even the photographs, which were in great demand outside the USSR given that foreign news services were seldom allowed to take pictures of Soviet sites, were often rejected because of their poor quality. How to ensure that the foreign press would actually print TASS items? The agency's offices in the US figured prominently in Pal'gunov's plan: "You are working in close proximity to American news agencies," he told Beglov, "and there's nothing to stop you from adopting positive experience."[68] TASS bureaus in the US—best positioned to learn from American and international news services—would lead the way in making TASS materials meet Western standards.[69]

Pal'gunov went so far as to instruct Ivan Beglov to abandon long-standing TASS practices and transform the New York bureau in the American image. Dispatches from the US were expected to become efficient, accurate, and ready for print without much editing.[70] In a complete reversal of previous policies, Beglov was instructed to make greater use of TASS's American employees because they knew much more about the US than their Soviet colleagues.[71] Pal'gunov even envisioned a Soviet equivalent of an American columnist and told Beglov that a journalist with his knowledge and experience should not waste time writing "information" but rather concentrate on reports that provided "explanation and commentaries on current affairs."[72] Pal'gunov wanted

*Figure 3.3.* TASS chief Nikolai Pal'gunov at Nikita Khrushchev's press conference, March 1959. (Photo: Howard Sochurek/The LIFE Picture Collection via Getty Images.)

TASS correspondents to develop specializations and fields of expertise and to focus on these fields in their reporting. He urged his people to cultivate a "deep understanding" of American affairs and to develop "their own opinions" on the issues they covered.[73] TASS correspondents were expected to educate themselves, to stay on top of current affairs, to "become accustomed to making an independent appraisal of the situation, and to form their own conclusions."[74] Another novelty was Pal'gunov's emphasis on the stylistic presentation of TASS reports. Each item should not only be factually correct but also "attract readers' attention" and exhibit "literary liveliness and brilliance."[75] All the items produced by TASS in the US, Pal'gunov stressed, should be interesting not just to Soviet readers but also to foreign audiences.

Pal'gunov's objective remained unchanged: he still wanted TASS to focus on the universal truth about the differences between capitalism and socialism, and unmask "the American way of life." The means of achieving this objective, however, changed a great deal. Pal'gunov now encouraged his journalists to rely on their own experience and analysis, to apply their personal judgment, and to identify episodic events that would help illustrate broader issues and trends in the United States. Potential sources of material expanded to include the "bourgeois press and culture," and TASS journalists were invited to rely on their own ideological compass to separate the merely "sensational" from the potentially instructive.[76] The agency's ability to report on events of objective universal importance now depended on the subjective viewpoint of individual correspondents.

These reforms bore mixed results. TASS directors believed that their efforts to place Soviet materials in the foreign press could be more successful. In 1960 Dmitrii Goriunov succeeded Pal'gunov as the director of TASS. As former editor in chief of *Komsomol'skaia Pravda* and deputy editor of *Pravda*, Goriunov brought to his post a broader journalistic perspective, less beholden to TASS traditions. It is conceivable that the purpose of his appointment was to make the agency more dynamic and better equipped to keep up with the new developments in foreign policy and journalism. Shortly after taking the job, Goriunov traveled to the United States and took a tour of the Associated Press offices and operations. He also reached out to American TASS employees and asked them to share their thoughts on how to improve the bureau's work and make TASS items more appealing to the US media.

Harry Freeman, the longest-serving American TASS employee, stressed that the agency should liven the style and content of its materials and make them timelier.[77] Freeman explained that to be internationally competitive, TASS had to bring the bureau's budget up to date with financial reality. For example, journalists could not travel around the country because the correspondent's allowance of $5.77 a night was not enough to pay for lodgings anywhere in the United States. The wages of American staff were in particularly miserable shape and had fallen far behind the rest of the industry and the standards set by US trade unions.[78] Goriunov took these recommendations seriously and secured the desired increase in American journalists' salaries and Soviet correspondents' allowances.

The transformation of the New York bureau continued under Goriunov. Ivan Beglov, who for several years had been unable to leave his post owing to the absence of a suitable replacement, was finally allowed to return home. In his place, Goriunov appointed Gennadii Shishkin, a young correspondent and a graduate of the Moscow State Institute of International Relations (MGIMO). As if fulfilling the dreams of the Polevoi delegation, Shishkin and other TASS correspondents began to reach out to American colleagues and officials to pick their brains on local American developments and to discuss Soviet-American relations. TASS correspondents also began to take advantage of the privileges and institutions available to the international press corps in New York and Washington, becoming a much more prominent presence in that community.[79] Although other journalists and US officials did not shun Soviet correspondents, TASS was still not considered a bona fide news agency. In line with its reporting innovations, TASS continued to gather "information" for official Soviet use. In fact, given growing Soviet interest in learning from foreign experiences, the demand for information was constantly rising. Yet the American liberal approach to the press held that a news service should busy itself with news as current affairs and that TASS's information-gathering practices were "inappropriate for a news agency."[80] For example, in 1963 TASS was instructed to prepare a dossier on foreign trade arrangements in the American private sector. TASS distributed questionnaires to US firms that conducted business with foreign companies, querying them about their methods of pricing, licensing, and marketing. The State Department caught word of these inquiries and issued a strong reprimand to TASS and the Soviet Embassy. Soviet interest in the nuts and bolts of American foreign trade did not trouble US officials—it was the fact that a news agency was the one gathering such information that they found objectionable.[81] At home, TASS was expected to collect this kind of material in its capacity as the official information service of the USSR. In the US, it was precisely because of TASS's close association with the Soviet state that these inquiries raised suspicion. It appeared that the Soviets were using TASS to bypass reciprocal agreements for information exchange and gain vital American knowledge without giving something in return.

One of the reasons for these objections was the US State Department's growing emphasis on reciprocity in American-Soviet exchanges, particularly in the realm of the press and mass media. Parity was maintained in the size of the respective press corps and the restrictions on traveling. US visas were withheld from Soviet journalists or officials as punishment for Soviet withholding of visas from American correspondents assigned to work in the USSR. Whereas the United States did not expel foreign correspondents as often as the Soviet Union did, other restrictions, such as limitations on journalists' travel and access to officials and information, were applied to mirror the limitations imposed on American correspondents in the USSR. Nevertheless, reciprocity was never complete given the broader differences between the Soviet socialist and American liberal systems of government and information. Soviet correspondents in the US continuously enjoyed better access to public officials and institutions than their American counterparts in the Soviet Union.

## Coming to America

In 1956 Boris Strel'nikov, a junior editor in the international department of *Komsomol'skaia Pravda*, was appointed *Pravda*'s correspondent at the United Nations in New York. This was Strel'nikov's first trip to the capitalist West and the United States. Before his departure, Strel'nikov spent three months learning English from scratch, cramming vocabulary and conjugations with the help of a private tutor provided by *Pravda*. One of the first things Strel'nikov realized upon his arrival in New York was that the English he had learned was useless when it came to communicating in the US. He could not understand Americans when they spoke, and they in turn had a hard time deciphering his heavy accent. For the next two years, Strel'nikov stuck to covering the UN sessions, which were usually translated into Russian. It was some time before Boris gathered the courage to foray into a different formats and different subject matters. After *Pravda* published his feature essay "Under the Roofs of New York," Strel'nikov received a postcard from Boris Polevoi congratulating him on his achievements. Encouraged by Polevoi's support, Strel'nikov continued to perfect his work with this genre, which eventually became a trademark of his fifteen-year-long assignment as *Pravda*'s correspondent in the US.[82] The appointment of a young and rather inexperienced journalist who barely spoke English to a post of such importance reflects the sincerity of *Pravda*'s commitment to promote fresh approaches and new voices in its coverage of the US. Strel'nikov's ultimate success as an essayist came as a result of both his personal investment in the genre and the newspapers' support for his professional development.

The international departments of the Soviet newspapers sought new professional talent and a fresh spirit, and this interest facilitated the rapid promotion of young correspondents who had joined only a few years earlier to strategically important posts in New York, Washington, Paris, and London.[83] Borovik, who for several years was not allowed to do more than edit photographs for *Ogonek*, was now traveling to Cuba to meet his heroes Fidel Castro and Ernest Hemingway. Stanislav Kondrashov, a 1951 MGIMO graduate, was appointed *Izvestiia*'s first resident correspondent in Egypt, Africa, and the Middle East after his impressive coverage of the Suez Crisis. In 1961 Kondrashov became *Izvestiia*'s correspondent in New York, replacing Nikolai Karev, who, in contrast to the young Kondrashov, had thirteen years of experience working in the US for TASS and *Izvestiia*.

*Figure 3.4.* Boris Strel'nikov on board the RMS *Queen Elizabeth*, circa 1959–1960. (Photo: Vasily Strel'nikov family archive. Published by permission of Vasily Strel'nikov.)

Within a few years the Soviet press corps in the United States doubled and then tripled in size as a brand-new cohort of Soviet journalists arrived. Unlike their predecessors, they had come through elite Soviet universities and were trained for work overseas. Like other *shestidesiatniki*, these foreign correspondents shared a commitment to the socialist project and the idea of "people journalism." Hailing from the 1960s generation, these journalists defined their generation's encounter with the United States. The ideal of the new foreign correspondent first articulated by Polevoi held a lot of appeal for the new cohort. The journalists were eager to get out and understand the American world around them. They strived to develop their own unique voices, cultivate their personal writing styles, and explore topics close to their hearts. They believed that it was their duty to unveil foreign life for their readers and provide them with clear analyses of the international situation.[84]

There was a growing consensus among foreign correspondents that good journalism was about focusing on human-interest stories and using these stories as vantage points from which to observe universally significant social and cultural phenomena. For example, a feature dedicated to the hardship of one jobless person would tell more about unemployment under capitalism than a lengthy recitation of complicated facts and figures. The emphasis on observing the universal in the particular foregrounded the role of individual correspondents and broadened the thematic scope of reporting from the US. Whereas diplomatic summits, UN sessions, or international conflicts left little room for differences in interpretation, stories about everyday life allowed journalists to follow their interests and initiative and ultimately differentiated between *Pravda*, *Izvestiia*, and TASS. Dispatches from the US now included descriptions of American cities and conversations with American people, an occasional review of a movie or a book, or a journey-based essay. Although the lion's share of reporting still focused on politics and foreign relations, articles on Christmas celebrations or environmental pollution in the US began to appear in the Soviet press. Within a few years, several features central to the working of the American press had become staples of Soviet socialist reporting. Soviet newspapers now emphasized well-written and accessible stories, reader engagement, and human-interest features, and recognized that individual journalists were valuable assets who could make a distinct contribution to the paper.[85]

In 1957 six-year-old Tatiana Strel'nikova received a long-awaited postcard from the United States. The picture showed a park surrounded by towering buildings. On the other side she read: "Dear Daughter, this is New York City, where I now live and miss you very much. See how big it is? It has many funny dogs, and beautiful cats that are taken on a leash for a stroll. And in the park curious squirrels are chasing after people begging for nuts. Kisses, Daddy."[86] Hundreds of postcards featuring famous American sights and long letters densely written on foreign paper traveled between the United States and the Soviet Union, carried by diplomats, delegation members, or regular mail service. Seldom focused on presidents, general secretaries, sputniks, or nuclear missiles, they inquired after the well-being of loved ones living on both sides of the Cold War divide. In most cases, an assignment to the United States involved separation even from the most immediate family members. It was not uncommon for foreign correspondents to travel abroad without their spouses. Since the Soviet Embassy's school had only four grades, teenage children had to stay behind or be sent home when they reached the fifth grade. Given the complexities and the expenses involved in traveling between the Soviet Union and the United States, foreign correspondents were lucky if they could travel home once a year.

Moving to the United States involved a myriad of new sights, new experiences, and new skills. Everything was unfamiliar: driving, paying taxes, shopping. Melor Sturua remembers: "What the visitors from the Soviet Union were most impressed with in the US was not the science or the technology, but the American supermarket. Most of all. Why? Because we had a real shortage of products, and when you entered a supermarket and saw such an abundance of goods, it made an overwhelming impression. Especially if you saw it in Harlem or in the Bowery. [These areas] were terrifying, but their supermarkets had things that were not available even in our grandest stores."[87] Sturua's testimony is a rare reference to how difficult it was to reconcile one's first impressions with prior knowledge about the United States. Soviet visitors' first encounter with the American supermarket, and the deep impression it left, has evolved into an almost apocryphal story often used to uphold the triumphalist narratives of American superiority in the Cold War. Sturua's recollections make it clear, however, that the actual encounter was much more complicated. Sturua was surprised not only at the sight of the supermarket as such, but at the contradiction between the abundance of the supermarket and the penury of the urban ghetto surrounding it. The grandeur of the supermarket and the deprivation of the ghetto exceeded his expectations in equal measure. The resulting image of the United States was complex, nuanced, and multilayered.

## Promoting the Soviet Viewpoint Abroad

State Department officials recognized that they were dealing with a new kind of Soviet correspondent—young, urbanite, sophisticated, and more open to the world. American observers also distinguished between the young generation and their predecessors, realizing that the former were much freer and more open in their worldviews and interactions. Future ambassador Malcolm Toon, then a counselor for political affairs at the American Embassy, hosted Melor Sturua for dinner one night. Toon observed that Sturua was well traveled, "appears to have been completely outfitted in Rome," and had a good command of English. Toon reported that the Soviet journalist had demonstrated a "calculated flexibility" in his political opinions and a liberal attitude toward the arts—a topic that clearly divided Soviet elites in 1963. Toon concluded that Melor Sturua was "the prime example of the young Moscow elite, confident, sophisticated, rather flexible in conversation, friendly and poised."[88]

The observations made by American officials who came into contact with Soviet correspondents suggest that these encounters were premised on rather modest expectations. Thanks in part to the picture painted by international reporting in the first postwar decade, Americans expected that Soviet citizens encountered in official or unofficial capacity would be shabbily dressed, stern dogmatists, and strict in their adherence to the official Soviet line. Thus American officials always took notice when their Soviet interlocutor was well dressed or wore foreign clothing and expressed opinions considered unorthodox for a Soviet citizen. Even when these encounters became more frequent, American hosts continued to believe that when Soviet correspondents expressed their personal opinions they did it either because they were "authorized to" or because they were accidentally caught off guard. This, in turn, attests to the widespread assumption among Americans that a Soviet individual's private and public self were completely at odds.[89]

Official restrictions on Soviet correspondents remained in force. Journalists continued to register with the US Justice Department as "agents of a foreign government," which meant that their offices, paperwork, and financial records could be inspected by the FBI at any time. Soviet correspondents had to pay income tax, a procedure they found cumbersome, and at times humiliating, as they were subjected to meticulous inquiries about even the most routine expenses. In 1960 the US Immigration and Naturalization Service introduced a requirement that all "non-immigrant aliens" who remained in the US for more than one year have their fingerprints registered. These measures were humiliating to the Soviet correspondents, who believed that they were the only foreign journalists subjected to this procedure, which in their minds was reserved only for common criminals. While Soviet officials tried to resolve the matter with the State Department behind the scenes, Soviet journalists launched a publicity campaign against the new measures.[90] In March 1961 *Izvestiia, Pravda*, and TASS published articles on American restrictions against Soviet correspondents, each within a week of the other. The articles cited many similar grievances, including but not limited to the fingerprinting.[91] Following these objections, and considering the damage that Soviet publications on the subject could do, the State Department informed the Soviet Embassy that fingerprinting of Soviet correspondents would be temporarily suspended, thus quietly putting the lid on the whole affair.[92]

The most annoying of all restrictions was the limitation on travel, and this, too, quickly became the focus of a Soviet publicity campaign. Soviet journalists had to seek the State Department's approval each time they wished to travel outside of Washington or New York; 26 percent of the United States remained permanently off limits. These restrictions, imposed to reciprocate for the

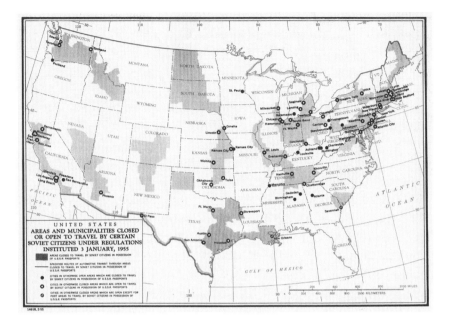

*Figure 3.5.* United States Areas and Municipalities Closed or Open to Travel by Certain Soviet Citizens under Regulations Instituted 3 January 1955. (Image courtesy of the Rockefeller Archive Center. Rockefeller Family Archives [III] Record Group: 4, Nelson A. Rockefeller—Personal, Series: Washington, DC, Files, Subseries: O.9, Special Assistant to the President Declassified Materials, 1954–1956, 1969, Box 4, Folder 94.)

travel limitations applied to US nationals within the USSR, pertained to all Soviet citizens, correspondents included.[93] There was considerable American opposition to the restrictions on Soviet journalists' travel, not least because they created the impression that it was the Americans and not the Soviets who were building an Iron Curtain of information, thus potentially damaging the US image overseas.

Bad publicity in the Soviet press prompted the State Department to undertake a review of the restrictions on travel. Eventually the system of "closed zones" was abolished, but only for Soviet tourists and visitors on the various exchange programs. Soviet officials permanently assigned to the United States, including resident correspondents, were still subject to the closed zones system and had to seek the State Department's approval before traveling. Officially, the decision to keep the restrictions on Soviet correspondents in place was designed to reciprocate for the treatment of American correspondents in the USSR. Behind the scenes, however, the State Department admitted that its position was "re-enforced by the highly distorted reporting engaged in by Soviet correspondents in this country."[94] Moreover, American officials remained convinced that "most, if not all, Soviet correspondents are primarily trained intelligence agents, and only secondarily working pressmen in our sense of the term."[95] Thus, the United States explicitly discriminated against Soviet correspondents and established a system of retaliation for their reporting from the US, although the existence of these practices was vehemently denied.

There were no rules regulating the permission to travel to non-forbidden areas, so a Soviet correspondent's ability to travel often depended on the whim of a handling official. For example, in 1964 Strel'nikov and Kondrashov asked to visit the southern states and were refused without explanation. Kondrashov wondered whether the State Department had informally decided to close the south off to Soviet correspondents since their requests to travel there had been often declined.[96] His hunch was right: a 1963 State Department memo confirmed that Soviet journalists were often barred from traveling to the Deep South because "it was feared that Soviet correspondents in the area might be subjected to violence, and it was thought wise to deny them 'eye witness' observations" of racial disturbances.[97] When the journalists called to appeal the decision, officials cited Soviet limitations on American correspondents, ignoring Kondrashov's insinuation that there was an unofficial policy in place.[98] Some years later, when Kondrashov was again barred from traveling for several months in a row, a State Department official acknowledged that it was because in Kondrashov's "rather offensive" reporting on travel restrictions, he had failed to mention that similar regulations applied to American journalists in the USSR.[99]

Soviet correspondents were often subject to FBI surveillance as they went about their daily business or traveled around the country. Journalists frequently described discovering that someone had evidently broken into their apartment (which often also served as their office) without taking anything of value.[100] While they complained about these incidents in their articles and interviews, most correspondents understood full well that American journalists in the USSR received the same treatment.[101] Soviet journalists tried to make light of the situation or even engage their "tail." When Melor Sturua got lost on one of his trips, he stopped his car and went to the surveillance team's car to ask for directions. On a few occasions, FBI surveillance could have a reassuring effect. Boris Strel'nikov's son, Vasily, remembers that once a phone rang in their apartment and the person on the other end of the line asked, in English, to talk to his mother. Vasily, who then eavesdropped on the conversation, heard the caller threaten his father. Mrs. Strel'nikova hung up on the caller and became really worried. Fifteen minutes later, uniformed policemen showed up on their doorstep, tried to calm her, and stayed with the family until her husband came home. "We didn't call them, so probably the person who was listening to our phone conversations alerted them, so that was kind of cool," Vasily concluded.[102]

Soviet correspondents believed that being recognized as a "red" journalist when traveling could be dangerous. On his trips, Boris Strel'nikov often identified himself with his UN accreditation because it did not state which newspaper he worked for.[103] In 1961 two TASS correspondents were scheduled to observe "democracy in action" as part of a trip to New Hampshire organized by the Foreign Press Association in New York. A week before the scheduled visit, New Hampshire governor Wesley Powell instructed state officials to revoke the invitation to the group because it included journalists from the Soviet Union, Poland, and Czechoslovakia.[104] Sometimes, after Soviet journalists had visited a locale in the US, concerned residents wrote to the State Department, alarmed that "reds" were allowed to roam freely around the country.[105]

The State Department itself did little to introduce Soviet journalists to "democracy in action" or to bring them into the growing orbit of cultural diplomacy initiatives aimed at foreigners in the United States. Occasionally, the participation of Soviet correspondents was declared undesirable because of the "closed zones" system. When Soviet correspondents were included in cultural diplomacy activities, US officials went to great pains to show that the programs in question were independent of the government or did not target Soviet correspondents in particular. Although there was no explicit policy to that effect, inviting journalists from elsewhere in the socialist bloc was considered potentially more productive.[106] Things changed somewhat with the arrival of the Kennedy Administration. The president's press secretary, Pierre Salinger, made an effort to reach out to Soviet journalists, cultivating personal relations with correspondents and even initiating a special program to introduce them to the United States.[107] Overall, however, while Soviet cultural diplomacy strove to win over American journalists, US officials all but gave up on Soviet journalists, writing them off as staunch communists beyond redemption.

Nevertheless, quite a few US officials and journalists did respond to the Soviet correspondents' outreach. Meetings between the representatives of both sides became routine affairs and occasions to discuss and express opinions on pressing matters in Soviet-American relations. During these meetings each side carefully assessed the other, trying to determine whether their interlocutors were sincere and really meant what they said. American hosts usually remained skeptical and unconvinced. Blind to the developments in Soviet coverage of the US, Americans believed it remained biased and failed to paint a fair picture of what the United States was like. Bitterness about Soviet treatment of US correspondents often got the better of US officials, and they wondered whether American leniency toward Soviet correspondents allowed the latter to score propaganda points off the United States.[108]

Still, the use of mass media and foreign correspondents to promote the Soviet viewpoint abroad continued apace. In 1961, the Union of Soviet Journalists, the Union of Soviet Writers, and the Union of Soviet Societies for Friendship and Cultural Relations with Foreign Countries established the Novosti Press Agency (Agentstvo Pechati Novosti or APN), which replaced the Sovinformburo as the voice of Soviet international propaganda. APN's charter stated that the agency's mission was "spreading truthful information about the USSR abroad, and introducing the Soviet public to the lives of people in foreign countries."[109] Unlike TASS, which had an extensive domestic network in addition to its foreign posts, APN focused exclusively on international news and exchanges with foreign wire services. It soon established itself as an important source of news from abroad (and a convenient cover for the foreign operations of the KGB, which was not allowed to recruit in *Pravda* and was discouraged from approaching *Izvestiia* journalists.)[110] Eager to expand Soviet outreach, APN was more creative in its strategies than the Sovinformburo or TASS. International publications could receive APN materials for free, which increased the chances that these materials would make it into circulation. On one occasion, the agency bought large ads in two American newspapers and used them to publish Khrushchev's speech on disarmament.[111] Established six years after the Polevoi delegation's visit to the US, APN embodied the spirit and practice of the mobilized, activist international reporting the delegation had envisioned. APN correspondents were not only reporting and gathering information but also actively reaching out to foreign outlets and using creative and unorthodox methods to communicate the Soviet viewpoint.

## "The Russians Are Coming"

In November 1961 Alexei Adzhubei arrived in New York on a special mission: to conduct the first interview by a Soviet journalist with the president of the United States. The interview, published in full in *Izvestiia*, was considered a

*Figure 3.6.* President John F. Kennedy interviewed by Alexei I. Adzhubei, editor in chief of *Izvestiia* and Nikita Khrushchev's son-in-law, at the president's home in Hyannis Port, MA, on November 25, 1961. *From left to right*: President Kennedy; Alexander Akalovsky, interpreter for the president; Georgii Bol'shakov, interpreter; and Adzhubei. (Photo: White House Photographs. Courtesy of John F. Kennedy Presidential Library and Museum.)

great success on both sides. Soviet officials thought that Adzhubei's questions faithfully represented the Soviet positions: he was firm but polite, friendly but not obsequious.[112] American officials believed they had scored an important victory on the propaganda front, for this was the first time that the president of the United States had addressed Soviet readers directly from the pages of their own newspaper, unedited and unmediated.[113]

As Nikita Khrushchev's son-in-law and an important figure in the Soviet leader's inner circle, Adzhubei was of course unlike any other Soviet journalist, and US officials recognized his privileged position. Yet the existence of this interview and Adzhubei's engagement in Soviet foreign policy testify to the important role that journalists came to play in Soviet foreign relations. During the Khrushchev years, the Foreign Ministry's Press Department regained the important role it had had before the war, and its officials now routinely participated in discussions with their American counterparts, taking it upon themselves to look after the interests of Soviet correspondents in the US, among other things.[114]

Senior Soviet journalists became frequent visitors to the United States. Tours, conducted in official or semi-official capacity, often involved meetings with US officials, and Soviet journalists were authorized to deliver messages directly or to discuss their government's positions on certain international issues. Alongside Adzhubei, the most prominent journalist engaged in diplomacy was the senior *Pravda* editor and veteran foreign correspondent Yuri Zhukov. Between 1958 and 1964, Zhukov undertook several trips to the United States both in his capacity as an international commentator and as chairman of the Committee for Cultural Relations with Foreign Countries. On each trip he met with senior US government officials and was authorized to discuss a range of topics including disarmament, cultural exchanges, and Germany.[115]

The Soviet practice of entrusting journalists with diplomatic missions flourished during the Kennedy administration. Pierre Salinger cultivated warm, personal relationships with Adzhubei, Zhukov, and Mikhail Kharlamov, a senior official at the Foreign Ministry's Press Department.[116] In another famous case, the Soviet intelligence officer Georgii Bol'shakov, who served as the personal go-between for Khrushchev and Kennedy before and during the Cuban Missile Crisis, made his first connections in the US media world working undercover for TASS. Senior American editors also visited the USSR during the Khrushchev years. Unlike their Soviet colleagues, however, they came first and foremost as the representatives of their own papers. The US government entrusted them with no mission, and if they shared their insights with officials at home, they did it as a good turn to the establishment. Soviet editors on the other hand, arrived as their country's envoys, delegated to raise questions or communicate positions, albeit in a semi-official capacity.[117]

Resident Soviet correspondents partook in personal diplomacy as well. Meetings with American officials, which became part and parcel of the journalists' work by the early 1960s, developed into an important channel of communication between the two sides. Whether the meeting was official, semi-official, or simply a courteous lunch, Soviet correspondents and their American interlocutors understood that they were acting as the representatives of their government and that the contents of their conversations would be reported onward. All participants were also aware that they were *perceived* as the spokesmen for their side. In these encounters the voice of the individual journalist became the voice of Soviet foreign policy.[118]

The developments in Soviet international reporting during the Khrushchev years culminated with journalists' participation in the diplomatic process. This participation reflected the growing importance of individual journalists and journalist-activism, as the success or failure of such encounters depended entirely on the correspondent. Journalists were entrusted to convey Soviet positions to American officials, to have a command of the international situation, to think on their feet, and to adequately represent the USSR in unscripted discussions. Journalists' involvement in personal diplomacy embodied the ideal foreign correspondent as imagined by the members of the Polevoi delegation in 1955. The journalist–party trumpet of the first postwar decade gave way to a professional international correspondent (*zhurnalist mezhdunarodnik*): resourceful, enthusiastic, showing initiative, knowledgeable about foreign life, and willing to reach out to the surrounding world to exchange opinions and communicate the Soviet viewpoint.

The duties of socialist foreign correspondents remained the same: their mission was to educate their readers and help them become better socialist subjects, as well as communicate Soviet positions to foreign leaders and international audiences. Yet *how* the journalists carried out their duties changed in tandem with domestic reforms and evolving international relations, and often drew inspiration from American journalism. International correspondents believed that it was their responsibility to make their stories interesting and engaging, to offer in-depth analyses of the international situation, and to attach greater value to their own voice.

# CHAPTER FOUR

# In Sputnik's Shadow

In 1954 the National Newspaper Promotion Association ran a two-page ad in newspapers all over the United States. The ad featured a photo of Eddy Gilmore, his wife, Tamara, and their daughters, holding hands, smiling, and walking away from a life-size sign of a hammer and sickle. The Gilmore family looks exuberantly happy. The youngest daughter holds a little American flag in her hand. At the bottom of the photo the caption in large bold letters reads: "Freedom is like being born again." The second page featured a text by Eddy Gilmore saying that the United States and the Soviet Union are competing for "the minds and souls of men everywhere" and that censorship of the press is a potent Soviet weapon in this struggle. The text concluded with Gilmore's tribute to newspapers in America, where nobody ever told him to write anything except the things he really wanted to write. "Thanks for the American Press, operating in Free America. Isn't it wonderful to be home!" read the final words of the ad.

The Gilmore ad captured the new tides in American-Soviet relations and foreign correspondents' place in the US media landscape. The ad celebrated the fortunes of Moscow correspondents, like Gilmore, who were now allowed to leave the USSR together with their Soviet wives and families. Gilmore's text reflected continuing American anxieties about Soviet propaganda: it positioned censorship and suppression of freedom of information as the main features distinguishing the Soviet Union from the United States. At the same time, the National Newspaper Promotion Association's decision to publish an ad that would remind Americans how important it was to preserve and cherish the freedom of the press hinted at the news organizations' growing uneasiness about the information policies of the US government.

American news media loomed large in the Soviet Union's efforts to project a new, friendlier image to the international community. As a result, the American press corps in Moscow expanded significantly, and so did its opportunities for reporting on Soviet affairs. The new cohort of American correspondents in Moscow captured the transformation of Soviet society and of American-Soviet relations under Nikita Khrushchev. Foreign correspondents

*Figure 4.1.* The National Newspaper Promotion Association Freedom Ad featuring Eddy Gilmore and his family. (Image courtesy of the Associated Press Corporate Archives. Published by permission of the Alabama Media Group.)

monitored the cooling of the superpowers' antagonism and introduced a new and different image of the Soviet Union to their American readers. Stories about regular Soviet people and their daily lives peppered American correspondents' dispatches from Moscow and foregrounded the accounts they wrote after returning home. Instead of prophesying the imminent collapse of Soviet communism, American journalists began to emphasize the stability of the Soviet Union and the pride of the Soviet people in their country's achievements. At the same time, foreign correspondents shared the anxieties felt by

US officials and the American public about Soviet advances in science and technology, as well as the gains that Soviet propaganda appeared to make around the world. In a decade that posed new challenges to press-government relations in the United States, journalists, publishers, and civil servants had one thing in common: a vehement opposition to Soviet propaganda and information policies. Thus, as they made an effort to improve their readers' understanding of the Soviet enemy, foreign correspondents also sought to reassure Americans of their country's continued superiority over the rival superpower.

## "Thawing" Relations with the US Press

On the night of March 3, 1953, Harrison Salisbury was dozing off at the Central Telegraph building in Moscow, waiting for the arrival of Soviet newspapers' morning editions. At 3 a.m., the usual distribution time, the papers did not arrive. Four o'clock came, then five o'clock, and the papers still had not arrived, at which point Salisbury surmised that something was wrong. At 8 a.m., TASS announced that Stalin was gravely ill. Commotion broke out among the international press corps as all correspondents rushed to file the news, bracing themselves for further developments. For the next twenty-four hours, Salisbury kept a "death watch" near the Kremlin, driving around and looking out for signs of unusual activity. At 3 a.m. the following night, Salisbury noticed one of the big ZIS cars, which evidently belonged to a senior government official, leaving the VIP parking lot outside the Kremlin's Spasskii Gates. Salisbury assumed that no "big shot" would leave the Kremlin if Stalin were still alive. He sped to the nearby Izvestiia building, where he was told that the morning paper would not come out until 10 a.m. Certain that this was the moment of truth, Salisbury rushed to file his dispatch. The Censor's Office and the Central Telegraph building shut down all international communications, and it was not until 7:30 a.m. that Salisbury managed to file the story that became front-page news all over the world: Joseph Stalin was dead.[1]

Within a few days, Salisbury reported, it became evident that "a <u>new</u> administration has taken over."[2] Salisbury observed that there was "an almost complete hiatus in the hate-America campaign. Not only has it been absent from the speeches of the leaders, but it has disappeared from the press."[3] In April a small delegation of editors from regional American papers toured the Soviet Union, and none of their dispatches from the visit were censored. Harrison Salisbury and Thomas Whitney organized a lavish party for the delegation at the prestigious Aragvi Restaurant in Moscow and invited several senior officials from the Foreign Ministry's Press Department to attend. To everyone's surprise, the Soviet guests showed up. The dinner turned into an amicable event, featuring many toasts to Soviet-American friendship.[4]

The new leadership's "peace offensive" moved swiftly and decisively, generating new headlines and new developments in the daily lives of US correspondents.[5] Soon, Eddy Gilmore was able to tell the readers of *Editor and Publisher* that Soviet censorship had loosened somewhat and that the Soviet authorities were actively trying to open a new page with foreign correspondents.[6] Western journalists were invited to a tour of the Kremlin. Colleagues from TASS and *Pravda*, whom they had not seen for several years, suddenly reappeared at the parties of the foreign community.[7] While American correspondents diligently recorded the minutiae of Soviet transformations, US newspapers were initially slow to catch up. Back in the United States, Joseph McCarthy began to probe the un-American activities of the American press. With the news media under attack, editors cautiously considered the dispatches from Moscow and rejected many of the reports because they sounded like "Russian propaganda."[8] Two events convinced American editors that the Soviet attitudes toward foreign correspondents were truly changing: in May 1953 Willian B. Oatis was released from a Czechoslovak prison. One month later, in June 1953, Molotov announced that the Soviet wives of American correspondents in Moscow would receive their long-awaited exit visas.[9]

The years 1954 and 1955 transformed the American press corps in Moscow. Correspondents who had covered the Soviet Union during the first postwar decade departed with their families, and new correspondents arrived to replace them. As a gesture of goodwill, and to advance the expansion of its own press corps across the Iron Curtain, the Soviet Union admitted more American journalists through its borders. In 1955, NBC dispatched its new Moscow correspondent, Irving Levine. The CBS bureau was reopened in 1955 as a sign of goodwill, following a personal appeal from Senator Estes Kefauver to Nikolai Bulganin, the chairman of the Council of Ministers.[10] By the end of 1956, the Moscow press corps had thirteen correspondents representing ten media outlets: Associated Press, United Press, International News Service, *New York Times*, *New York Herald Tribune*, *Baltimore Sun*, *Chicago Tribune*, NBC, CBS, and *Look* magazine (now represented by Edmund Stevens, who had returned to Moscow with his family).[11]

Engaging American correspondents in Moscow became an important pillar of Soviet attempts to improve relations with the United States. The Polevoi delegation had urged the Soviet government and Agitprop to become more flexible in their attitudes toward foreign journalists in the USSR. Evidently the Soviet leadership took these recommendations seriously. Soviet officials began to attend receptions and celebrations in the Moscow diplomatic community. Cultural figures and industry captains became available for interviews with foreign journalists. The Foreign Ministry's Press Department established an information service for foreign correspondents. Soviet organizations were instructed to respond when foreign journalists requested information about their activities.[12] Seeking to "influence the reporting of foreign correspondents" by means other than censorship, the Press Department began to organize special press conferences in collaboration with various ministries, cultural organizations, and creative unions. Activities for the international press corps included visits to flagship Soviet institutions such as a kolkhoz or Young Pioneer camp. Foreign correspondents were also invited to attend specially organized talks on a range of topics, including Soviet science and industry, Soviet musical production, Moscow housing construction, or the training of specialists in the USSR.[13] Following Polevoi's recommendations, regional and republican authorities began to establish committees for welcoming and hosting foreign visitors and journalists.[14] The Press Department deemed that censorship should be reduced to a minimum and kept in place only to correct "gross distortions" of Soviet official statements.[15] As a result, Soviet censors became less heavy-handed.[16] At the same time, however, Soviet information management remained clumsy and inconsistent and often undermined its own goal of publicizing Soviet achievements to the outside world. Despite the Press Department's efforts, securing access to news sources, especially Soviet officials, remained difficult, and appointments were often granted after the meeting was no longer relevant or newsworthy. When Yuri Gagarin made his first journey into space, for example, foreign correspondents could not gain access to Soviet scientists or officials.[17]

Using US media to speak directly to the American people emerged as a central strategy in the Soviet "peace offensive." Soviet information initiatives thus bore a resemblance to the American tactic of "reaching out to people above the head of their government," advocated by US embassy and journalists in the postwar years. Soviet leaders demonstrated how far they were willing to go in their attempts to court the American press in the spring of 1955, when they welcomed to the Soviet Union the unlikeliest guest: William Randolph Hearst Jr., the owner of a conglomerate of conservative publications and editor in chief of the *New York Journal-American*. The harsh anti-communist tone of the Hearst publications had made him and his media empire the central villains of Soviet anti-American propaganda in the late 1940s and the early 1950s. Now, to the consternation of resident Moscow correspondents, Hearst and his entourage (consisting of J. Kingsbury-Smith and Frank Conniff) were received by Khrushchev, granted access to the highest Soviet officials, and allowed to file their reports without censorship.[18] In 1956, the members of Hearst delegation received the Pulitzer Prize for international reporting—a clear sign that their interviews with the Soviet leaders were considered an important professional achievement.

The title of Hearst's reports—"Russia Uncensored"—tapped into established Cold War genre conventions, which celebrated American journalists for penetrating the closed Soviet society. The reports themselves, however, cautiously debunked old ideas, telling readers that the USSR wanted and needed peace because it recognized America's superiority in the atomic age.[19] While praising "the Western program of building armed strength," Hearst urged the US to accommodate the Soviet outreach and develop "a more flexible and imaginative strategy for 'competitive co-existence' with the Communists in every field and on every front."[20] Written, as they were, by one of the Soviet Union's staunchest opponents, Hearst's reports helped to convey the message that the Soviet peace agenda was earnest and sincere.

After Hearst's visit, senior Soviet officials' interviews with prominent American commentators became common practice. In 1957 alone, Khrushchev gave interviews to the managing editor of the *New York Times*, Turner Catledge, as well as to celebrity columnists Joseph Alsop and James Reston. In each interview, Khrushchev stressed that his interest in Soviet-American dialogue and peaceful coexistence was genuine and sincere. Since each meeting was granted on the assurance that Khrushchev's remarks would be published in full, he turned the interviews into an opportunity to present the Soviet peace program and place the blame for the slow progress in superpower dialogue on the US.[21]

Soviet efforts to engage the American public reached their apogee in 1957, when Khrushchev agreed to appear on CBS's *Face the Nation*. Khrushchev gave this—his first ever—television interview in order to speak to Americans directly and reassure them of his country's peaceful intentions. The most important aspect of the interview, according to CBS Moscow correspondent Daniel Schorr, who arranged it, was that "Khrushchev had appeared in America's living rooms—real, robust and unthreatening."[22] This degree of visibility and accessibility of Soviet leaders to the foreign press had been unseen during the Stalin era, and it helped to project the new image of a Soviet

*Figure 4.2.* Soviet Premier Nikita Khruschev (*second from left*) appears with his translator (*left*) on the television program *Face the Nation* and answers questions from the show's host Stuart Novins (*center*) and journalists B. J. Cutler (*second from right*) and Daniel Schorr, 1957. (Photo: CBS Photo Archive/Getty Images.)

Union that was open to the world. US officials recognized the propaganda value of the Soviet outreach to the American press, and they responded with reservation bordering on criticism. When asked whether he thought CBS had used good judgment in seeking the interview with Khrushchev, President Eisenhower refused to share his opinion.[23]

Soviet outreach to the American press altered the working conditions of American correspondents and introduced new challenges into their work. The expansion of the international press corps transformed the small, tight-knit foreigners' colony into a large and diverse group of people with different ambitions, aspirations, and work cultures. New correspondents arrived with their wives and, occasionally, their children and had to make arrangements for their family members. Maintaining a bureau from a hotel room was no longer possible, and correspondents spent many hours lobbying Soviet authorities for housing or figuring out how to import kitchen appliances. In the stressful atmosphere of work in Moscow, emotions ran high, making friendships, sympathies, rivalries, and enmities stronger than in other foreign posts. Many Moscow bureaus now had two or even three correspondents, introducing the challenge of teamwork and division of labor within the bureau. For example, it took the *New York Times* several shifts of personnel before it achieved a good equilibrium among its Moscow correspondents and ensured that teamwork triumphed over competition for bylines. The AP and UP continued to enjoy exclusive access to TASS wires, which drew newspaper and network correspondents into the respective agencies' orbit and perpetuated the "two camps" system. In an enlarged press corps, however, "gentlemen's agreements" on filing together or sharing exclusive news became impossible, and competition between Moscow correspondents became intense.

Moreover, the Soviet "peace offensive" deprived the Moscow foreign press corps of its status as sole eyewitness mediator between the USSR and the American public. While officials and propagandists courted and welcomed the visits of famous newsmen such as Alsop and Catledge, resident correspondents still had a hard time securing access to the topmost echelons of Soviet leadership. Whereas the visiting editors and their entourages received every possible accommodation in sending their dispatches, the reports of resident correspondents were still subject to the regular restrictions on filing from Moscow, including censorship. Moreover, hosting a visiting media dignitary added another layer of responsibility onto the shoulders of resident correspondents, who were the ones that submitted requests for trips and meetings, organized tours, or purchased Bolshoi Ballet tickets for senior colleagues that came to town. Merely filing from Moscow was no longer enough, and journalists began to seek new avenues for delivering exciting, exclusive material. Fortunately, American interest in all things Soviet boomed in the atmosphere of "peaceful coexistence." After nearly ten years of being "a riddle, wrapped inside an enigma," the USSR presented almost endless opportunities for new discoveries.

## Meet the "Average Russian"

In 1956, Harrison Salisbury went on a highly publicized tour for *American in Russia*, the new book he had written after concluding his Soviet assignment. Interactions with readers from all over the United States had taught Salisbury that Americans were ready for new information about the Soviet Union: "My overall impression is that public opinion has, generally, decided there is not to be an immediate war with Russia. In the interim there is a lively public interest in specific and realistic reports of specific segments of soviet life—schools, churches, houses, living conditions, moral problems, youth, science, technique."[24] As the sense of impending war with the USSR gradually receded, Americans were ready to learn more about what Soviets were like and how they lived. Salisbury observed another indicator of the changing attitude toward the Soviet Union—more and more readers expressed an interest in visiting it as tourists: "I received a good many personal inquiries (getting me aside after the talk) for specific information about travel to the Soviet Union. My impression is that a good many of the well-to-do and community leaders are thinking about including Russia on their travel plans for next summer. This, of course, reflects a substantial diminution in the general fear which I noted so often last year on the questions of 'going to Russia.'"[25]

Salisbury pointed out that these questions offered a valuable indication as to where the *Times* could turn its coverage and that they could be easily addressed under the new conditions of reporting from Moscow. Salisbury was not alone in noticing the change in American attitudes toward the USSR. Across the American media establishment, editors, readers, and pundits expressed a "tremendous appetite" for eyewitness reports "on Russian life."[26]

Changing policies toward foreign correspondents allowed American journalists to meet and interact with Soviet citizens and to write about their daily lives for the first time since the end of the war. In 1957, the *New York Times* featured a series of articles by its Moscow bureau chief, William J. Jorden. Titled "The People of Russia," the series described Jorden's visits with people of various occupations all over the Soviet Union. That the *New York Times* ran such headlines as "A Bus Driver in Moscow Gives His Views on Life in the Soviet Union" or "A School Teacher in Soviet Armenia Mingles Family Life and Work" on its front page shows how valued these journalistic encounters with Soviet people were as new sources of information.[27]

From the early days of the Cold War, journalists' limited access to the "average Russian" had evolved into an important trope in the narrative that constructed the Soviet Union as a closed society. The newly available descriptions of regular Soviet people and their everyday lives were particularly valued, because they allowed the readers a peek behind the facade of a totalitarian regime. As new opportunities to report on Soviet life beckoned, Moscow correspondents and their editors turned to the language of explorers and pioneers to discuss their work, stressing that it was their duty to bring the Soviet Union to their readers' doorsteps. The word "curtain" and metaphors for unveiling, lifting, and opening prevailed in discussions of reporting from Moscow. After concluding his trip to the Soviet Union, managing editor of the *New York Times* Turner Catledge urged his Moscow correspondents to seek and write on "even the smallest things that are done behind the Iron Curtain." Catledge stressed that the United States "is getting very Russian-minded, largely because of the few peep-holes they are getting through the Iron Curtain."[28] Similarly, CBS correspondent Daniel Schorr remembered that "there was an evident hunger in the United States just to see Russian faces, Russian stores, schools, subways. With the menacing Stalin gone, it was as though a curtain were parting on a hidden country."[29] Paradoxically, therefore, it was precisely with its literal and figurative "parting" that the "Iron Curtain" was reintroduced as a fixture in American reporting from the USSR.

Reporting on everyday life also helped journalists meet some of the challenges that came with the new Soviet information policies. Visiting senior editors, columnists, and press delegations enjoyed better access to Soviet officials and were usually better positioned to score "an exclusive" on American-Soviet relations. Soviet regulation of the official flow of news made scrambling for scoops all but obsolete. Under these circumstances, the competition between American correspondents shifted onto reporting on everyday life, which provided almost endless opportunities for both creativity and individual initiatives. Competition focused on getting an interview with that Soviet intellectual or a photo essay on that Young Pioneer camp.

Because regular reporting still had to contend with censorship, the journalists' post-assignment accounts remained essential sources of well-rounded information about the Soviet Union. By now it had also became an honored professional practice that brought prestige and revenue, and it was almost expected that a Moscow correspondent would round up his (or very occasionally, her) assignment with a book or lengthy article series. In the mid- and late 1950s foreign correspondents' accounts focused on daily life beyond the Iron Curtain. The 1958 book *Main Street U.S.S.R.*, by NBC's Moscow correspondent Irving R. Levine, grew out of a weekly radio program in which Levine responded to listeners' questions about the Soviet Union. The book offered answers to questions such as, How many years of schooling are compulsory in Russia? Do Russian women make their own clothes or buy them ready made? What's on Russian television? Is there a stock exchange? Do Russians keep pets?[30] Aline Mosby, who served as UPI Moscow correspondent between 1959 and 1961, provided a female angle to the Soviet story. Mosby's reporting for the UPI included such triumphs as interviews with Gary Powers, the pilot of the US U-2 spy plane shot down by the Soviets, and with Lee Harvey Oswald. Her book, in contrast, shied away from politics and focused on her "experiences as a woman-reporter in Moscow," exploring daily life, women's fashions and hairstyles, parties, and the peculiarities of shopping and dating.[31]

The largest breakthrough in introducing a less menacing view of the Soviet Union was the 1958 publication of a Soviet-themed installment of John Gunther's famous *Inside* book series—*Inside Russia Today*. The series had been widely

*Figure 4.3.* American journalists during a weekend retreat at a Soviet dacha, February 1961. (Photo: Carl Mydans/The LIFE Picture Collection via Getty Images.)

popular in the United States since the 1936 publication of the first book, *Inside Europe*.[32] Gunther's books aimed to familiarize readers with foreign places and explain how and why those places differed from the United States. *Inside Russia Today* added the Soviet Union to a long list of places whose "otherness" needed to be explained to the American reader. At the same time, Gunther's narrative normalized the Soviet Union by treating it as just another country in the world, suggesting that it could be an interesting tourist destination and offering tips for getting around.[33]

Whereas previously readers were introduced to Soviet life mostly through stories about the experiences of foreigners in Moscow, now they learned what everyday life was like for the Soviet people. The range of characters in journalists' work expanded significantly. They now included random acquaintances, fellow passengers in the journalists' travels around the country, even people journalists approached on the street. The readers learned how Soviet citizens spent their leisure time and vacations, what they wore, and what their daily routines were. When the journalists wrote about the experiences of foreigners in the Soviet Union, stories about Soviet police surveillance and intimidation became less and less dominant. Instead, the journalists created sympathetic descriptions of Soviet attempts to accommodate tourists from overseas, particularly from the United States.[34] In another innovative move, foreign correspondents began to elucidate the rationale behind Soviet policies. Journalists in the late 1940s seldom explained the actions and motivations of Soviet leaders and institutions. On the rare occasions when such explanations were provided, they evoked Communism's expansionism and aversion to freedom. By contrast, the new accounts described the ideological origins of numerous Soviet policies such as economic planning or the national ownership of factories. The journalists emphasized that Soviet leaders sought to improve the lot of their people, even though their methods seemed wrong to the outside world.[35]

The new focus on the Soviet people helped journalists develop a more nuanced view of the relationship between the two countries. In the 1940s, a period of scarce opportunities to interact with the locals, most journalists wrote that the Russians did not differ much from the Americans. This notion of similarity facilitated the idea that there was a gap between the Soviet people and their leaders—a gap that could be exploited to bring down the Soviet regime.[36] In the 1950s, foreign correspondents began to emphasize that the gap was in fact between the Americans and the Soviets and that the latter felt an affinity for their leaders. Explanations of the Soviet political system pointed out that, contrary to the prevailing view in the US, the Soviet people did not consider themselves lacking freedom, nor did they await liberation from overseas.[37] Foreign correspondents explained that from the perspective of ordinary Soviet people, the USSR had made great progress since the revolution and their lives had significantly improved compared with their parents'. Moreover, journalists pointed out, Stalin's death introduced hopes of future improvements, and Soviet citizens supported the innovations ushered in by their leaders.[38]

At the heart of the changing descriptions of the Soviet Union was the realization that the Soviet people did not share Americans' view of the USSR as an oppressive dictatorship.[39] The new rhetoric both reflected and reinforced the US establishment's changing views of the Soviet adversary. By the late 1950s, the hopes that covert propaganda could instigate a citizen revolt against the Soviet government seemed less realistic. American policymakers and observers also began to recognize the possibility of coexistence with the Soviet Union.[40] Foreign correspondents followed the currents of political thought of their time and stressed that, despite the differences, the people on both sides had to do their best to understand each other for the sake of the world's future:

"The gulf, the chasm, the abyss, may seem too great to be bridged. But we must try to bridge it, because the world will have no rest otherwise," wrote John Gunther.[41] This prescription, which appeared in the introduction of his book, differed significantly from his predecessors' hopes to promote pro-American sentiments among the Soviet population. American journalists pointed out that the leadership's efforts to mobilize the citizens without violence had transformed the Soviet Union into a different country.[42] And this changing USSR, they argued, posed new challenges to the United States: "It is a country showing signs of emerging from absolute, centralized dictatorship [. . .] a land bursting suddenly from the age of the sickle into the era of Sputnik," explained Irving Levine.[43]

The launch of Sputnik played an important role in the changing perceptions of the Soviet Union in the United States. The Soviet head start in the space race shattered American popular belief in its scientific, technological, and military superiority and caused grave concerns across the political spectrum. The USSR no longer appeared as a country of backward peasants, but as a competitor equipped with first-rate modern technology. Sputnik also transformed the image of the Soviet education system and made Americans realize that the USSR trained world-class scientists and technological specialists.[44] In journalists' reports, Sputnik loomed large among the challenges that the Soviet Union posed to the United States. John Gunther more than any other correspondent emphasized Soviet comparative advantages in education and technology. He wrote with appreciation about his visits to Soviet schools, universities, and popular scientific exhibitions, urging Americans to treat Soviet scientific achievements with utmost seriousness: "It is always unwise to underestimate adversaries. For a generation, it has been part of the American folklore to think that Russians are hardly capable of operating a tractor. Not since Pearl Harbor has the United States suffered such a jolt. [. . .] The United States can no longer claim with reason to be the world's first scientific power, in an era when science, as well as prestige, counts for so much."[45] Gunther enjoined his compatriots to reevaluate the Soviet adversary and not to take American superiority for granted. The Soviet head start in the space race demonstrated that the USSR could eventually surpass the US.[46]

The writings of other journalists spoke to similar concerns. In 1959, *New York Times* correspondent Max Frankel wrote a series of articles about Siberia, which focused on Soviet campaigns to revive the region. Like other correspondents, Frankel pointed out the changes that were sweeping the Soviet Union and described young Soviets' optimism about the future of their country. Two articles in the series emphasized that the developments in Siberia had the potential to tip the scales of superpower competition in favor of the USSR: "Thousands [of people] toil there in summer heat and winter cold to overtake the United States some day in industrial output and standard of life. The American learning about the Soviet Union can no longer look only to Moscow, unfamiliar enough as are its ways. [. . .] Throughout Siberia there are pride and hope. Soviet plans for Siberia are grandiloquent, and many Russians seem willing to work and wait for the new world of communism."[47] Frankel suggested that the US beware of Soviet plans for Siberia and popular mobilization in the area. His editors in New York agreed and supplemented the series with headlines and subheadings that emphasized the Soviet promises to "reach and surpass" the United States. The subheading on the first article, on the reconstruction of Siberia, stated: "Vast, Rich Area Is a Basis of Hope of Excelling U.S."[48] The headline on the second item, describing life in major cities of the region, proclaimed, "Four Siberian Centers Typify Soviet Efforts to Overtake U.S." While Frankel pointed out that "reaching and surpassing" America was still far away, neither he nor the *Times* would dismiss these goals as impossible.

References to Sputniks, schools, and the transformation of Siberia presented a new image of the Soviet Union, but they did not dispel the old notions of the Soviet menace. On the contrary, by pointing out the areas of potential disadvantage to the US, journalists' accounts exacerbated domestic concerns about the Communist enemy. The implicit proposition that American superiority might not last forever angered several readers. One such response to Frankel's Siberian series reprimanded the *New York Times* for giving a false impression of Soviet progress: "Frankel's recent visit to Siberia and the Soviet Far East [. . .] would lead people to believe that Russia is just around the corner from the high standard of living the United States now enjoys. Nothing can be farther from the truth. It will probably take quite a while longer than the articles imply for the Russians to even come close to the standard of living of the average U.S. citizen today."[49] Although the American attitude toward the Soviet Union was transitioning from fear to curiosity, readers still found it difficult to think about the USSR outside of familiar patterns and worried about the specter of Soviet propaganda. In an atmosphere of concern about the Soviets' overtaking the US, the reader evoked the high American standard of living as indisputable evidence of American superiority.[50]

Many foreign correspondents used similar tactics. References to Soviet scientific accomplishments often reiterated that Soviet living standards remained far behind those of the United States or that the Soviet dictatorship was no match for American freedom. Irving Levine reminded readers that "there were sputniks in the sky, but for Russians on the ground there were no cars to be bought, shortages of everyday goods, and cramped housing."[51] Such implicit and explicit references to American material culture reaffirmed the continuing superiority of the United States over the Soviet Union. To a large extent, this writing style derived from habits inculcated by domestic anti-Communism, whereby readers and correspondents alike identified descriptions of Soviet advantages over the US with the attitudes of "fellow travelers." Forty years after the conclusion of his Moscow assignment, Max Frankel explained in his memoir that his reporting on Soviet everyday life sought to reassure audiences of American superiority and at the same time to protect himself from being labeled an enemy sympathizer: "Stalin had made *Soviet* a synonym for *aggressive*, and in the overheated atmosphere of the 1950s, my minority view that Khrushchev had a primarily domestic agenda could have marked me as the Communists' dupe. Americans were simply not ready to be reassured. I nonetheless tried to reassure them by contrasting the spectacular success of Soviet rocketry with the pathetic poverty and inefficiency of daily life."[52]

International reporting in the wake of Sputnik exposed the tension between American fascination with all things Soviet and American anxiety about communist propaganda. On the one hand, correspondents welcomed the opportunity to report about regular Soviet people and their daily lives. On the other hand, journalists worried that if they wrote about the Soviet Union as if it were a "normal" country, just like any other, they would give their readers the wrong impression or, worse, help Soviet socialism present itself as a viable alternative to American capitalism. These concerns were informed by anticipation of readers' criticisms as much as by the journalists' own reflections on Soviet international outreach. Thus Max Frankel's memoir may have been not entirely accurate when he wrote that his tone of reporting was shaped first and foremost by readers' expectations. Several months after he was criticized for his Siberian series, Frankel wrote a soul-searching letter to his editors and urged them to exercise greater caution toward reports about Soviet daily life: "I fervently believe that we are getting careless and are being exploited, for in its basic objectives, I am convinced Soviet propaganda seeks only to have the Soviet Union projected and talked about like any other western country. This right it has not earned and its standard of living will not be comparable for many years to come."[53] The fear of being exploited for Soviet propaganda had accompanied Moscow correspondents since the inception of the Cold War. Frankel's concern that Soviet openness had actually increased the danger posed by propaganda was widely shared by fellow correspondents and American officials. As a result, many journalists were moved to qualify their reports on Soviet achievements with references to the comparative advantages of the American way of life. In so doing Frankel and other correspondents reinforced American self-representations at home and abroad, which focused on material culture and high standards of living in the US.[54] Reporting on everyday life in the Soviet Union thus became an extension of the journalists' American ideology.

## Of Truths and Censors

Despite Soviet outreach to foreign correspondents, the working conditions of western journalists in the USSR were still difficult compared with those in other European or even socialist bloc countries. Soviet information policies centered on controlling the production of the Soviet image overseas, an objective that became even more urgent in the context of the "peace offensive." Until 1961 censorship remained the primary means of regulating the flow of news and information from the Soviet Union. Soviet censors and officials viewed censorship as necessary for protecting truth and peace and insisted, in public and in private, that information control was an indispensable intervention against the anti-Soviet bias of American media.[55] In his interview with Turner Catledge, Khrushchev explained that the Soviet Union had no choice but to "take measures" against "correspondents who distort conditions and the real life of our country." According to Khrushchev, he was actually doing American media a favor, helping them "not to waste means such as ink, paper and paint on information that only creates harm."[56] Aware of the accusations against it leveled by foreign journalists, Glavlit insisted that censors did not make cuts when they disagreed with correspondents' analyses on ideological grounds but rather intervened only in cases where journalists' dispatches were "clearly tendentious" and factually inaccurate.[57] However, comparing the reports of American journalists with the comments of Soviet censors reveals that even their respective understandings of "facts" and "interpretations" were colored by their different ideologies and remained incompatible.

Glavlit prepared regular roundups summarizing foreign correspondents' dispatches and its own interventions in the filed texts. Censors routinely accused "bourgeois correspondents" of "purposefully misrepresenting the true nature" of Soviet foreign policy, inaccurately reporting the statements of Soviet leaders, and thus harming the USSR's relations with other states. Gravest concerns revolved around "distorted depictions" of Soviet domestic reality and "slanderous attacks against the Soviet people."[58] Censors' special scorn was reserved for items in which foreign correspondents used negative stereotypes of the "Russian national character." These included references to Soviet people's passivity, lack of political agency, life in perpetual fear of totalitarian oppression, and obsession with the material advantages of the United States.[59] In one roundup of reports filed by foreign journalists after the elections to the Supreme Soviet, a censor commented that "bourgeois correspondents strive to depict the Soviet electoral system as undemocratic, attributing the high turnout of voters to Soviet people' fear of repression."[60] Another roundup, compiled in conjunction with the 1959 American National Exhibition in Moscow, criticized correspondents for trying "to play down the living standards of the Soviet people, and to depict them as apolitical, ignorant, and concerned only with their daily bread."[61]

Was the Soviet electoral system undemocratic? Did Soviet people enjoy high standards of living? The answers obviously depended on the respective ideologies, lived experiences, and comparative reference points of the beholders. Journalists' reports on Soviet life were shaped by implicit and explicit comparisons with the United States. Censors' engagement with these reports was informed by their understanding of the bourgeois press as purposefully misrepresenting the Soviet Union to please its capitalist masters. Such views were reaffirmed on a daily basis, as censors peered over dozens of reports that contradicted either their own experiences of Soviet life or the ways it was reflected to them through Soviet media. According to Glavlit, by exercising "information control" over the dispatches of foreign correspondents, censors were not trying to *hide* the truth but to *protect* it.

Still, compared with the Stalin era, censorship became much more lenient. After 1953 foreign correspondents could file dispatches consisting of analyses or commentary. Reports in which journalists relayed official Soviet materials such as TASS announcements or press conference proceedings were no longer subject to Glavlit inspection.[62] In practice, information control was never uniform and depended on the watchfulness or the negligence of individual Glavlit employees, who often found it difficult to navigate the changes introduced by de-Stalinization.[63] In the absence of clear and precise guidelines on how to regulate the dispatches transmitted abroad, blame for any problems often came to rest on the individuals involved. For example, in 1958 AP correspondent Roy Essoyan was expelled because he "rudely violated censorship"—in this case a report assessing Khrushchev's approach to the crisis in the Middle East as a "diplomatic and public setback." Essoyan's dispatch was

*Figure 4.4.* Associated Press reporter Roy Essoyan leaving the USSR after being declared persona non grata by the Soviet Ministry of Foreign Affairs, October 1958. (Photo: Howard Sochurek/The LIFE Picture Collection via Getty Images.)

cleared by a censor. When he dictated it over the phone to the AP, Essoyan inserted additional comments and remarks that had not been cleared, and he had to shoulder the responsibility for doing so.[64] Senior censors likewise occasionally faced reprimands for showing lack of "political sharpness" and allowing problematic reports to slip through.[65]

Occasionally, Soviet attempts to police "crude slander" extended beyond individual correspondents in Moscow to their parent organization in the United States. At different times, CBS, NBC, ABC, *Time,* and the *Washington Post* temporarily lost their Moscow bureaus in retaliation for "anti-Soviet materials" that had been broadcast or published at home.[66] The first, and one of the most famous, cases was of CBS, which lost its Moscow bureau in 1958 after broadcasting *The Plot to Kill Stalin*—a TV play suggesting that Stalin had been killed by his closest associates. The broadcasting of the play, particularly one scene showing Nikita Khrushchev convincing his comrades that they had better not call the doctors and let Stalin expire, was cited specifically as the reason for the sanction against CBS.[67]

US correspondents, officials, and editors were convinced that these Soviet actions constituted heavy-handed attempts to manipulate the American media and their coverage of Soviet affairs.[68] This, however, was only part of the story. Understanding Soviet policies of information control also requires an appreciation of how unprecedented the interactions between Soviet leaders and foreign correspondents were under Khrushchev, and the emotional dimension of Soviet attitudes toward the American press. The Soviet "peace offensive" and the leadership's efforts to cultivate relations with the American press brought Soviet leaders and American correspondents into a proximity that was unmatched even during the Second World War. Now officials and journalists rubbed elbows at parties, receptions, and events at the foreign embassies. They interacted at summits and press conferences that were part of the Soviet "peace offensive." American journalists joined the press corps that followed Soviet leaders on their trips around the world, which offered numerous opportunities for informal, more personal interactions. Having a press car, such as the one that accompanied Khrushchev on his visit to the US and to France, or being followed by a press corps, such as the one that trailed Anastas Mikoyan during his trip to the US, were wholly new experiences for Soviet officials.

Khrushchev's memories of his foreign voyages are suffused with descriptions of the press following his every step and scrutinizing his every action or gesture. During Khrushchev's visit to the UN General Assembly, one correspondent, whose name the Soviet premier did not remember, sent a note warning him against spending too much time on the balcony of his residency as someone might assassinate him. Years later, Khrushchev remembered this episode as "emotionally touching."[69] On a flight from Los Angeles to New York, Mikoyan, prompted by Salisbury, agreed to sit down with American journalists for an "informal, completely off-the-record chat." Mikoyan was at ease, gesturing with his hands, and frequently "put his arm around the correspondents sitting at each side of him." The conversation soon moved from Soviet domestic affairs and superpower relations to personal matters, and Mikoyan told the journalists about his sons, his ninety-two-year-old mother, and his ailing wife. He also shared some stories from his life as a young revolutionary in Baku.[70]

Occasions such as these may have caused Soviet leaders to interpret their interactions with American correspondents as highly personal, almost intimate, encounters and to expect intimacy in return. This is especially likely

*Figure 4.5.* Members of the US press interview Soviet premier Nikita Khrushchev during his state visit to a farm in Iowa. (Photo: Jerry Cooke. © Jerry Cooke Archives. Published by permission of Mary Delaney Cooke.)

given that the only available model for relationships with journalists available to them was the comradely fraternization between Soviet officials and senior editors of the Soviet press. Although Soviet leaders would seldom go so far as to call American journalists their friends, they were arguably under the impression that the personal rapport they developed with foreign correspondents entitled them to expect a friendly, or a more considerate, attitude in return. It is not surprising that Khrushchev hailed Schorr as his "friend" during a reception, given the latter's investment in organizing the Soviet leader's appearance on *Face the Nation.* The episode featuring Khrushchev was considered highly controversial at the time and made Schorr and the network the subject of public criticism and even official scorn.[71] While Schorr was doing what he thought was his job—securing an important exclusive for his network— Khrushchev had likely assumed that Schorr was sticking his neck out for him. In this context, it is easier to understand why the Soviet leader was so outraged with CBS for broadcasting *The Plot to Kill Stalin* that he resorted to the strongest punitive measure and ordered the bureau closed. The broadcasting of a program that made such a grave personal allegation against Khrushchev must have come across as particularly treacherous, and as a betrayal of the special relationship Khrushchev thought he had with the network.

Soviet explanations for sanctions against American correspondents often used the language of emotions. In his defense of the closing of the CBS bureau, Soviet ambassador Mikhail Men'shikov accused the station of "inciting . . . mistrust and hostility toward the Soviet Union." Likewise, Men'shikov explained that the USSR was jamming the Voice of America because its broadcasts were "insulting" to the Soviet people: "They are very hospitable, very friendly, and as a matter of fact, they are very friendly toward the American people. When there are some of those insulting things said about our people, our country, our people don't like that sort of thing."[72] Men'shikov repeatedly juxtaposed the "hospitality" of the Soviet people to the "insulting" broadcasts of the Voice of America, suggesting that these broadcasts were an ungrateful response to Soviet hospitality and friendly attitudes toward Americans. Similarly, in 1960, the Press Department's chief Mikhail Kharlamov told journalists that International News Service (INS) correspondent Priscilla Johnson had lost her accreditation because she had written an "incorrect and insulting" report alleging Mikoyan's political downgrading. Kharlamov said that Johnson's reporting was particularly insulting because it was Mikoyan who had helped her get accredited in the first place, suggesting that her ingratitude made Johnson's case especially grave.[73]

Reports from Glavlit, Press Department officials, and the personal experiences of Soviet leaders showed that American journalists refused to share in the enthusiasm for Soviet domestic developments and international peace proposals. US correspondents continued to produce reports that the Soviet leaders considered hostile, biased, and at times personally offensive.[74] At one official function, UPI's Henry Shapiro overheard Mikoyan tell Malenkov that he was "fed up with Western press."[75] As they struggled to strike the right note in their relationship with the American press, Soviet leaders' engagement with the Moscow press corps could swing from friendly fraternization to threats of expulsion. At both ends of the spectrum, however, the relationship with the foreign press was often understood in highly emotional and intimate terms.

This emotional engagement with American journalists was consistent with the overall Soviet understanding of the "bourgeois press." Soviet culture considered the written word a powerful weapon and attributed great significance to American reporting. Soviet outreach to US journalists was based on this view and on the assumption that journalists held the key to American hearts and minds and could tip the scales of public opinion toward war or peace.

Thus another explanation invariably evoked to justify Soviet sanctions against American correspondents was that information control helped to protect "mutual understanding" between the Soviet and American people. In this worldview, journalists' personalities mattered a great deal. Soviet officials closely followed the reporting of each American journalist, trying to assess whether or not he or she promoted the cause of peace.[76] Foreign Ministry officials also scrutinized each candidate for permanent accreditation, often rejecting journalists whose previous writing they deemed to be particularly biased against the USSR.[77] While they were under no illusion that they could make the "bourgeois press" nominate correspondents with a healthy socialist consciousness, Soviet officials nevertheless tried to limit the damage to public opinion in the US. Thus, while there were regulations applicable to the foreign press corps as a whole, in many cases particular restrictions or special access to information were administered on a personal basis to punish or reward individual correspondents.[78] This personalized attitude was also consistent with Soviet understanding of access to information as a privilege that could be awarded, portioned, or revoked as needed.

In 1961, Soviet censorship of foreign correspondents was abolished, and journalists were allowed to file their stories without supervision or intervention. Nevertheless, many other restrictions—especially on travel and access to officials—remained in place. Between 1956 and 1965, twelve American correspondents were expelled from the USSR; numerous others received official warnings from the Press Department. The tactic of expelling correspondents proliferated after censorship was abolished, when the USSR could no longer control the dispatches of individual journalists. Two correspondents—*Newsweek*'s Whitman Bassow and *Time*'s Donald Connery—were expelled in 1962 alone, for writing "crudely slanderous dispatches."[79]

## US Press and Government versus Soviet Information Management

American journalists, editors, and government officials viewed Soviet sanctions against foreign correspondents as a brazen attempt to control US media and deprive American citizens of truthful information about the USSR. In a 1958 address to the annual convention of Civitan International after the launch of Sputnik the previous year, Assistant Secretary of State for Public Affairs Andrew H. Berding equated Soviet censorship to psychological warfare. Like his Soviet counterparts, Berding described propaganda as a military campaign and stressed that the war of information "needs to be conducted with the same tenacity, vigor, and skill that we would use in countering any military offensive."[80] Using information policies as the superpowers' defining features, Berding emphasized that censorship and suppression of truth were what distinguished the Soviet Union from the United States. According to Berding, censorship also accounted for the apparent success of Soviet propaganda around the world. Soviet restrictions on the free flow of information and limitations on American news reporters, Berding concluded, had to be fought at all costs.[81] It was not a coincidence that Berding's reaction to Sputnik focused on denouncing Soviet censorship and propaganda. Psychological warfare and the threat of mind control preoccupied US pundits and officials in the Eisenhower administration in the 1950s, especially after the launch of the first Soviet satellite into space.[82] Censorship and psychological warfare appeared to be weapons from the same arsenal.

At the time when Berding was preoccupied with Soviet propaganda, his own government's information management faced heavy domestic criticism. The Truman and the Eisenhower administrations increased their use of executive orders that classified government information and kept many aspects of government activities from the prying eyes of the press.[83] While Berding dwelled on Soviet censorship and suppression of truth, journalists and editors around the country wondered whether the US government's own information policies were fit for democracy.[84] In this context, attacking Soviet restrictions on American correspondents both diverted attention from the government's increased reliance on secrecy and provided a cause for policy makers and the press to unite around.

Even though news media and government officials agreed that Soviet restrictions posed a serious problem, they had a hard time coordinating a strategy to combat them. The State Department urged news organizations to work together and develop pathways for adequate retaliation against Soviet sanctions. Over the years, senior US government officials made several attempts to lead the news media toward a coordinated response to Soviet restrictions.[85] In 1959 Berding himself initiated one such meeting and invited State Department officials and senior representatives of news organizations to discuss the problem of maintaining correspondents in the Soviet Union.[86] These efforts, however, bore little fruit. For one, the extreme competitiveness among the news services made them disinclined to take any action that could jeopardize the future of their operations in Moscow. Ambassador Llewellyn Thompson lamented that when facing expulsions and warnings targeting their journalists, news organizations usually tended to "roll with the punch," fearing they might upset the Soviets and lose their bureaus. Thompson regretfully commented that the news media were unable to agree on even the bare minimum, such as publicizing the cases of Soviet sanctions against American journalists, which, he believed, would have helped a great deal to resist the Soviets.[87] The news services, in contrast, believed that if they were to publicize Soviet restrictions, it would signal that these tactics were working. Others worried that publicity would give the erroneous impression that American news organizations "bowed" to Soviet "pressures" and wanted to avoid another debate about the desirability of having correspondents in Moscow.[88]

Furthermore, government officials, news organizations, and even Moscow correspondents themselves could not agree on an adequate retaliation for Soviet restrictions. Some proposed harsh, tit-for-tat measures such as expulsions of Soviet correspondents, withholding of their visas, and denunciations of their anti-American dispatches. Others argued that such measures would be counterproductive, hurt American correspondents in Moscow, and further limit their access to news.[89] Although the demands for reciprocal retaliation for Soviet sanctions became more frequent by the mid-1960s, officials and news organizations still could not find common ground. In the absence of a joint strategy, the State Department responded to Soviet sanctions on an individual basis and in close consultation with the news agency affected.[90]

News organizations' unwillingness to publicize Soviet restrictions and the State Department's acquiescence with these policies were put to the test a few months after Soviet censorship of foreign journalists was abolished. UPI correspondent Aline Mosby was relatively new to the Soviet scene and was the only female member of the US press corps. As a newly arrived writer of features, she was eager to establish local contacts. So when a local man whose acquaintance she had recently made invited her to dinner, Mosby accepted the invitation. They met in a local restaurant and shortly after toasting to "peace and friendship" with her companion, Mosby began to feel unwell. She made her way out and collapsed outside the restaurant. A policeman reprimanded Mosby for being intoxicated in public and orchestrated her transition to a "sobering-up station," while a photographer, who conveniently "happened to be on the scene," took photos. A few hours later the US consul was summoned to retrieve Mosby from the station and took her to the American Embassy. The embassy doctor who examined Mosby determined that she was not intoxicated but heavily drugged.[91]

A week later, *Izvestiia* printed an article titled "Miss Mosby in a Sobering-Up Station." It featured two photos of Aline Mosby—one of her being carried to an ambulance and another of her scarcely clad, barely covered by a sheet, on a clinic bed. The five-column article (a relatively long piece by Soviet standards) portrayed Mosby as an example of corrupt American morals. According to *Izvestiia*, Mosby's passion for abstract and religious art had brought her to the restaurant for an evening of decadence, excessive drinking, and shady dealings: "It is unknown where Mosby picked up the black-haired dandy with an icon concealed in his jacket. But we do know that they spent the evening together in 'Ararat.' The dandy showed his 'damsel' an edge of the icon, touting his goods and pushing up the price. Mosby poured the brandy, knocking down the price of the icon and pushing up her own."[92] The article proceeded to discredit Mosby, stressing that her "dirty doings and orgies" in Moscow were a logical outcome of her previous beat as a reporter in Hollywood, where she "penned 'juicy' stories about the intimate life of film stars" for a "gutter sheet."[93]

The American Embassy in Moscow took the incident very seriously and urged UPI to file an official complaint with the Soviet authorities and publicize the affair. The State Department concurred. However, Mosby herself and her boss in Moscow, Henry Shapiro, implored the State Department to do nothing of the sort, stressing that any publicity would further tarnish Mosby's reputation and result in her losing her accreditation.[94] American correspondents in Moscow united behind UPI, and no journalist filed a report on the incident. UPI's competitor, AP bureau chief Preston Grover, explained to his bosses that "the consensus is that our only self-protection is to show the authorities here that they are not going to get the hoped-for smear publicity abroad when they attack correspondents here."[95] Ultimately, US officials in Moscow also came to support Mosby's decision. "Any reporter who filed the story would henceforth be virtually boycotted by his fellow newsmen and the diplomatic corps," explained Grover.[96]

The exact purpose of Aline Mosby's frame-up remains unclear. It is plausible that her position as the sole female correspondent made her a target. *Izvestiia*'s insinuation that Mosby was trying to seduce her companion and the rather revealing—by Soviet standards—photograph showing Mosby's bare shoulders and upper chest support that conclusion. Interviewed thirty years later, Mosby thought it was not only her gender, but also the fact that she was an "adventurous" correspondent who "wasn't timid about doing any stories in Moscow" that had made her the target of a frame-up.[97] There may be truth to that supposition as well. One of the charges *Izvestiia* leveled against Mosby was that she did not use her knowledge of the Russian language "to learn more about the Soviet Union and report objectively about it, but for dirty dealings, drunken parties, and debauchery."[98] Such a formulation hinted at Mosby's efforts to establish unofficial contacts in Moscow and to report on routine aspects of daily life.

Mosby's colleagues in the Moscow press corps believed that she was singled out because of her ability to cut through Soviet barriers and report as she liked.[99] The incident fed into a larger narrative that began to develop in the 1960s, which held that sanctions targeted those American correspondents who got to know the Soviet scene well and were in a position to report things that the Soviets wished to keep hidden. "The government is having its trouble on many fronts and of course we are all writing about it," explained Preston Grover. "The reaction is to attack members of the press publicly, to scare away our news contacts."[100] Similarly, after the expulsion of Whitman Bassow in 1962, a confidential memo from the American Embassy to the State Department explained: "Newsweek has warned Bassow six or seven months ago that he should be more active if he wished to continue in their employment. Apparently his increased interest in the Soviet scene from that time satisfied his employer's requirements, but not the security preoccupation of the Soviets."[101] Crucially, American journalists and officials held that the information the Soviets wanted to keep hidden did not consist of political secrets, but descriptions of everyday life under socialism and how it compared with the capitalist world.[102]

The idea that fighting Soviet suppression of truth required Moscow correspondents to join forces with diplomats further strengthened the relationship between news organizations and the US government. Even though the press corps expanded a great deal after Stalin's death, a sense that US journalists and civil servants formed a small community united against the Soviets remained one of the defining features of reporting from Moscow. In fact, collaboration between the government and the press expanded through the 1950s and the 1960s, posing new challenges to the ideal of an independent fourth estate. American correspondents were allowed to purchase imported goods at discounted rates from the embassy's commissary. Because regular mail was routinely screened by the Soviet authorities, journalists continued to use the diplomatic pouch for private communications with their families and offices at home. On Fridays, Moscow correspondents took part in closed, off-the-record meetings with the ambassador, where they discussed important developments and exchanged opinions in an informal atmosphere. The fact that American journalists representing Communist publications were not included in these meetings and were not allowed access to the diplomatic pouch suggests that these privileges were allocated on the basis of a shared ideological approach rather than being automatically granted to all US citizens working in Moscow.[103]

News organizations routinely reached out to the State Department and the American Embassy for help with visas, access to Soviet officials and institutions, housing, and accreditation for their correspondents. Government officials increasingly took it upon themselves to mediate between the news services and the Soviet authorities over questions of working conditions, bureau openings, or expulsions. Unlike their predecessors in the early postwar years, American correspondents showed much less uneasiness about sharing information with government officials. Unofficial exchanges of intelligence became routine, and many journalists either willingly offered information to embassy officers or easily acquiesced when asked to do so.[104] In the last week of March 1958, for example, the State Department recorded twelve official contacts between its officers and American journalists.[105]

This is not to suggest that all correspondents had an equally close relationship with government officials. The dynamics of journalists' interactions with civil servants varied depending on the personality of individual correspondents and their organization's general approach to such a relationship. On his visit home in 1958, CBS's Daniel Schorr reached out to the State Department, offering to share his impressions from the Soviet Union and discuss "a number of useful ideas concerning the Soviets."[106] Undersecretary Berding met Schorr for lunch and also arranged for him to meet with Secretary of State Dulles. Although other journalists were rarely so forthcoming, it is likely that foreign correspondents found nothing controversial in their relationship with US officials. A 1959 letter from Max Frankel to Clifton Daniel at the *New York Times* reflected on working in close proximity with the government: "We feel the State Department should know more about the discrimination against western reporters here and believe the embassy may not strongly report the situation to Washington. [. . .] It isn't pleasant to hind behind State's skirts but around here we'll never get anywhere unless we have official cooperation."[107] In Frankel's view, desperate times called for desperate measures, and the circumstances of work in Moscow required—indeed demanded—that journalists develop a close relationship with the State Department. In fact, writing in 1959, Frankel thought that the government was neither helping nor getting involved *enough*.

In the following years the relationship evolved into a direction that Frankel probably would have considered favorable. The Kennedy and the Johnson administrations took an openly activist approach to the question of the press in Soviet-American relations. Secretary of State Dean Rusk urged American correspondents to come forward and seek the government's help in dealing with the Soviets.[108] The State Department and the US Embassy in Moscow actively promoted further expansion of the American press corps in the Soviet Union. The *Washington Post* was allowed to reopen its Moscow bureau after Ambassadors Llewellyn Thompson and Foy D. Kohler raised the matter repeatedly with the Soviet ambassador to the US, Anatoly Dobrynin.[109] While collaboration between American correspondents, news organizations, and diplomats remained unofficial, unstructured, and largely dependent on individual personalities, it came to share certain features with the Soviet model.

Although news organizations were still reluctant to publicize Soviet maltreatment of American correspondents, they raised much fewer objections to US government's move toward "strong retaliation" against Soviet journalists in the United States. By 1966, the State Department insisted on parity in the numbers of journalists on both sides and withheld visas to Soviet journalists until Moscow-bound American reporters received theirs.[110] "Reciprocity" became an unofficial—yet widely applied—policy of retaliation for "Soviet blackmail tactics," and more and more officials began to push for tit-for-tat expulsions of Soviet correspondents from the United States.[111] However, "reciprocity" failed to deliver the silver bullet against Soviet information management. One reason was that the number of correspondents that Soviet news services wanted to dispatch to the US usually exceeded the number of candidates for work in Moscow put forward by American news services. The State Department occasionally reached out to American news organizations and actively invited them to open new bureaus in Moscow, only to maintain parity with the Soviet press corps in the US.[112] More fundamentally, the insistence on reciprocity often set off a chain reaction in which visas were withheld from several Soviet and US journalists at a time. The protracted "visa wars" undermined the normal functioning of the foreign press corps in both countries, making it difficult to open new bureaus and to maintain smooth transitions of personnel in the existing ones.[113] In the late 1960s and throughout the 1970s, Soviet officials would use "censorship by expulsion" time and again to prevent American correspondents from building close relationships with the Soviet dissident movement.

After Stalin's death in 1953, Soviet leaders had embarked on a new path in foreign policy that led to a gradual opening of the Soviet Union to American foreign correspondents. American journalists recorded the changes that took place after Stalin's death and the Soviet people's optimism about the future. Journalists also pointed out how the transformation of the rival superpower, and especially its advances in science and technology, introduced new challenges to the United States. Having greater access to Soviet society allowed foreign correspondents to focus their accounts on Soviet everyday life. An important feature of these accounts was the comparison between Soviet and American standards of living. Through these comparisons, foreign correspondents both satisfied readers' curiosity about life across the Iron Curtain and demonstrated the comparative advantages of American political and material culture. International reporting thus offered American readers a safe framework for exploring the Soviet Union while also reassuring themselves of the superiority of their own country. In the years to follow, the topic of the contrast between Soviet and American standards of living would take on a life of its own, becoming the most important theme in American writings about the Soviet Union.

Cultivating better relations with the international press corps in Moscow played a central role in the Soviets' international outreach policy. Yet many traditional information management tactics remained in place and ultimately undermined Soviet efforts to engage American journalists. In 1961, *New York Times* bureau chief Seymour Topping observed that certain Moscow correspondents had "become so enraged and frustrated at the censorship, delays in communications, police surveillance, and denial of information and some amenities that they began to concentrate on needling the Soviet Union rather than covering it."[114] American correspondents and editors were once again convinced, as they had been in the first postwar decade, that Soviet efforts were directed first and foremost at preventing foreign audiences from learning the "objective truth" about the USSR. By the mid-1960s, journalists began to distrust the official programs that introduced them to life in the Soviet Union. There was a growing sense that the *real* experience of the "ordinary Russian" was hidden from view and that it was the foreign correspondents' duty to bring it to light. By the early 1970s this narrative would become a dominant trope that shaped Moscow correspondents' understanding of their profession as well as their approach to reporting on Soviet everyday life.

# PART THREE

# YOUR FIGHT IS OUR FIGHT, 1965–1985

On June 12, 1977, NBC News aired a special feature entitled *Human Rights: A Soviet-American Debate*. Three Soviet and three American citizens faced the cameras and the audience at Georgetown University's Gaston Hall, ready to discuss a subject matter that could not have been timelier. It appeared that the Soviet-American détente had hit a dead end and that the future of superpower relations and nuclear arms control now hinged on the issue of human rights. Edwin Newman moderated the discussion between the two teams, each comprising a renowned legal scholar, a human rights expert, and a foreign correspondent. The journalist on "Team USSR" was Genrikh Borovik—the bureau chief of the Novosti Press Agency and of *Literaturnaia Gazeta* in New York City. "Team USA" featured Robert G. Kaiser, recently returned from Moscow, where he had worked for four years as the bureau chief of the *Washington Post*.

The journalists joined the panel as experts whose intimate knowledge of the other side could buttress their team's critique of the opponents. Within a few minutes, however, they were dominating the discussion, bitterly debating the reasons for mutual mistrust that undermined the détente. Robert Kaiser argued that the Soviet people would never trust the United States as long as their only source of information about it consisted of loyal communist journalists like Borovik. Genrikh Borovik swiftly retaliated, charging that Americans distrusted the Soviet Union because all they knew about it came from reports that Kaiser and his colleagues wrote, based on the experience of a handful of dissidents. Although Kaiser and Borovik blamed the rival's press for the stalemate in Soviet-American relations, they appeared to agree that the first duty of foreign correspondents was to make the two nuclear superpowers more intelligible to each other.[1]

The years between 1965 and 1985 were marked by intense fluctuations in superpower relations. Hostility rose as each side regarded with fear and distrust the other's growing involvement in Southeast Asia and the Middle East. The Soviet-American détente saw a relaxation of international tensions, increased superpower dialogue, and made important strides toward reduction of nuclear weapons. The détente collapsed in the late 1970s under the weight of mutual accusations of human rights violation and involvement in armed conflicts in the decolonizing world. Hostile rhetoric and diplomatic standstill further escalated after President Ronald Reagan and General Secretary Yuri Andropov assumed their leadership posts.[2] At times of incredible optimism as well as at times when it seemed that two countries were on the brink of a new world war, foreign correspondents offered ongoing commentary on superpower relations, told stories about regular people on the other side, and guided readers on how to understand themselves in relation to the Cold War adversary. To do so, more and more correspondents on both sides turned to long-form journalism: lengthy article series or books written after the conclusion of their assignment abroad.

The commitment to exposing the adversary's "lies" and revealing "the truth" about what the other side was really like remained central to foreign correspondents' personal and professional self-understanding. On both sides, "truth" in international reporting was shaped by the experiences of individual journalists, their ideological allegiances, and their publications' editorial policies. On both sides, "truth" in international reporting was also closely attuned to the host country's domestic political agenda and to developments there. Soviet correspondents were drawn to the civil rights and antiwar movements in the United States, and the critical insights articulated by these movements informed much of Soviet reporting on the Vietnam War and on American political and social structure. American journalists were deeply moved by the courage of Soviet dissidents and their principled stance against the oppressive state apparatus. As a result, American coverage not only paid a great deal of attention to the dissident cause but also often drew on the dissidents' insights, experiences, and criticism of Soviet society.

American and Soviet correspondents alike argued that the most important "truth" about the adversary's society was that it was experiencing a deep ideological crisis, with the majority of the population no longer invested in the revolutionary principles of socialism or, conversely, disappointed in the false promises of the American way of life. American journalists pointed out that Soviet Union's failure to provide its citizens with standards of living comparable to those of the West resulted in rampant cynicism and mass disillusionment in socialist ideology. Unable to claim that the Soviet standards of living were superior to the United States, Soviet journalists highlighted the experiences of those who were excluded from the American Dream and explored the disastrous results of the war in Vietnam.

Foreign correspondents on both sides engaged in a form of comparative writing and reading that glossed over domestic shortcomings and contrasted the rival superpower with an ideal image of the home country that delivered the socialist utopia or the American Dream. In this way, international reporting reaffirmed readers' faith in their own country's creed and helped to popularize the respective Cold War ideologies. When examined side by side, it becomes evident that both Soviet and American correspondents engaged in subjective writing and both actively promoted the ideas and values of the Cold War.

What was different was how the respective ideologies operated in the journalists' accounts. Soviet correspondents explicitly applied Marxist ideology to daily life in the United States, using the concepts of alienation and capitalist imperialism to frame their insights. Soviet correspondents explored the moral erosion triggered by liberal ideology, capitalism, and market economics, fully expecting their readers to engage with these ideas and decode them as antithetical to the Soviet system. By the early 1980s, however, the reports of Soviet correspondents were met with indifference or incredulity; the journalists' educational message was ignored or discarded in favor of information about what life in America was really like. American correspondents, on the other hand, presented their reports as unmitigated reflections of Soviet reality. Although their coverage of the Soviet Union was steeped in the liberal understanding of rights and freedoms, American journalists used these concepts implicitly, as if they were synonymous with human nature. Unlike the reports of Soviet correspondents, American coverage of the Soviet Union proved popular with readers, who turned to it for insights about the enemy as much as for confirmation of America's continued superiority. The divergent patterns in audiences' reactions illustrate the difference in the mobilizing power of the respective ideologies in what were to become the final decades of the superpower conflict.

# CHAPTER FIVE

# Notes from the Rotten West

On January 31, 1968, Stanislav Kondrashov was glued to the television set in his New York office. On the screen, CBS news anchor Walter Cronkite was telling viewers about the Tet Offensive in the Vietnam War and of the Viet Cong's takeover of the US Embassy in Saigon. Right after delivering these dramatic headlines, Cronkite disappeared from the screen to make time for a commercial break, featuring an advertisement for a new brand of dog food. A modest man of working class origins, Kondrashov found it hard to get used to the commercials punctuating all programming on American television, even after seven years spent in the United States. He turned to his diary to record his dismay and disgust:

> You know that Walter will be back on the screen momentarily, and that he will tell you more about those 19 heroes-martyrs [who died defending the embassy], but during this commercial break, dedicated to ALPO's dog food, you have once again been insulted and once again splattered in money-grabbing filth. And you are offered yet another opportunity to loathe this country and to feel the impotence of your loathing and of your pen, which will be never able to describe THAT [. . .] in a way that will make readers understand and share your revulsion.[1]

The sharp contrast between the unfolding drama in Vietnam and the cheerful dog food advertisement, the television program's unwillingness to forgo a commercial break even while reporting on the most dramatic events of national significance—these struck Kondrashov as offensive testimony to the triumph of American consumer culture over human tragedy. Though he was a veteran observer of the United States, Kondrashov still could not reconcile himself with what he saw as its crass materialism and consumerism.

Kondrashov had begun keeping a diary only a few weeks earlier. Struck by the magnitude of the changes in American politics and culture unfolding all around him, he had decided to chronicle his commentaries of 1968—the last year of his first assignment in the United States. Begun as a collection of short observations about his life, his family, and his profession, the diary soon evolved into an extraordinary record of a Soviet man's perspective on one of the most turbulent periods in American history.

The Soviet press corps in the United States shared Kondrashov's sense of bearing witness to a watershed moment in US politics and culture. In 1968, there were twenty-six accredited Soviet journalists in the United States, representing nine different news media. Most of them were experienced foreign correspondents and seasoned political commentators who began their careers in early and mid-1950s and knew a great deal about the US. As 1968 unfolded, each new event—the dead end of the war in Vietnam, the assassinations of Martin Luther King Jr. and Robert F. Kennedy, the violent suppressions of antiwar demonstrations—made it seem as if the America that Soviet journalists knew was unraveling all around them. Many of them realized that, as lifelong professional observers of the United States, it was their duty to chronicle these developments and explain them to readers at home. The events of 1968 led to an explosion of written impressions, vignettes, and analyses that the two pages usually reserved for international news in Soviet newspapers simply could not contain. As a result, Soviet foreign correspondents in the US began to explore different formats, increasingly turning to long-form journalism: lengthy analytical essays, article series, and books. The events of 1968 alone were the subject of Kondrashov's books *American Crossroads* (1969) and *The Life and Death of Martin Luther King* (1970), Melor Sturua's *Ferment* (1971) and Genrikh Borovik's *One Year of a Restless Sun* (1971).[2] Thus came a sea change in Soviet reportage on the United States. As more and more journalists committed their impressions to the long-form format, producing a universe of books, novels, and article series dedicated to describing the vicissitudes of the Cold War adversary, the following two decades became a golden age of Soviet writing about the United States.

Soviet writers' American travelogues from the Cold War era remain relatively unexplored.[3] In the past, contemporary observers and scholars alike argued that Soviet Cold War accounts of life in America were officially manufactured, similarly sounding propaganda pieces dictated "from above" by party ideologists. Another piece of conventional wisdom held that if Soviet journalists had been free to express their true opinions, they certainly would have told their audiences that life in the United States was better than in the Soviet Union.[4] More nuanced and insightful analysis of Soviet travelogues from the Cold War has emerged recently, thanks to scholars' growing attention to socialist internationalism and the USSR's relations with the world.[5] Still, the reports of foreign correspondents are usually regarded as lacking sincerity and toeing the Soviet establishment's line and as a result are rarely analyzed on their own terms.[6] Such criticism is seldom leveled against reports by American correspondents who worked in the Soviet Union during the same period.

In reality, Soviet journalists' accounts reflected the different personalities and interests of their authors, focused on different facets of American life, and exhibited as much variety as the accounts produced by US correspondents in the Soviet Union. Genrikh Borovik, who grew up in the theater where his parents worked, was drawn to the world of American progressive intelligentsia. He wrote about experimental music concerts, fringe theater productions, and conceptual art exhibitions and cultivated friendly relationships with Norman Mailer and Jane Fonda, among others.[7] The dashing and cosmopolitan Melor Sturua was attracted to high politics and diplomacy and felt comfortable in elite circles both at home and abroad. Sturua's dry, biting sense of humor established him as one of *Izvestiia's* leading writers of political features.[8] By contrast, Stanislav Kondrashov's thoughtful nature and modest background made him uncomfortable in the world of high politics and big cities. Hailing from a remote town in the Soviet heartland, he believed that to truly understand America, one had to see its small towns and rural areas, which he did whenever the opportunity allowed.[9] Boris Strel'nikov, one of the few war veterans in the press corps, was shaped by his wartime experiences and his deep, personal commitment to antifascism. Strel'nikov wrote extensively and thoughtfully on racial violence, the struggle for civil rights, and US involvement in Vietnam, often to the consternation of the officials at the State Department. As *Pravda's* most veteran US correspondent, Strel'nikov was also tasked with hosting the visiting Pravdists and chaperoning them on their tours around the country. An avid traveler, Strel'nikov embraced these opportunities to get away from New York or Washington and thus revived the genre of Soviet American travelogue.[10]

Despite the different interests and personalities reflected in Soviet reporting about the United States, the long-form accounts of Soviet correspondents shared many features. In that too, Soviet journalists resembled their American colleagues, whose writing explored many similar experiences, ideas, and themes. First, it was the journalists' professional imperative to chronicle the political, social, and cultural events around them and to explain these developments to their readers. The assassination of Martin Luther King, the rise of American counterculture, and the election of Ronald Reagan were important events in the United States and could not be ignored by professional Soviet "Americanists." Second, many journalists in the Cold War era were shaped by the accounts of prewar Soviet travelers to the United States, especially their moral stance toward capitalist society and their imaginary geography of America. Following in the footsteps of writers such as Maxim Gorky and Vladimir Mayakovsky, Cold War correspondents reflected critically on the contrasts between wealth and poverty in megalopolises such as New York or Chicago. In homage to the best-known Soviet American travelogue—Il'f and Petrov's *Little Golden America*—they undertook automobile road trips through rural United States, often to the same destinations visited by the famous duo in 1935.[11] Finally, Soviet journalists brought a shared ethos, which distinguished their particular generation and profession, into their work. They viewed themselves as the custodians of universal truths whose duty was to instruct their readers about the fundamental differences between capitalism and socialism and to explain the advantages of the latter.

The influence of Soviet information policies, censorship, and potential sanctions, such as the loss of travel privileges or of one's job, must not be ignored.[12] These were *not*, however, the most important factors shaping Soviet coverage of the United States. Much more influential were the personal interests of individual journalists and their professional self-understanding as socialist writers and educators. Ideology was important in journalists' accounts about the US, but it did not take the form of depersonalized party dogma or a shield hiding ulterior motives or insecurities. Rather, a socialist critique of capitalist modernity was deeply ingrained in virtually all Soviet journalists' interpretation of American society. The socialist structure of thought was their prism for understanding both the United States and themselves, and it was through this prism that their experiences and observations became meaningful. Seen in this perspective, journalists' accounts of the United States were as much products of socialist ideology as its creators.

What neither the journalists nor their editors could anticipate or control was Soviet audiences' engagement with long-form writing about the US, at a time of steadily rising fascination with all things Western, and especially American.[13] For many readers, the reports of foreign correspondents reinforced their sense of good fortune to live in a morally superior country that looked after all its citizens. Others, however, ignored the educational lessons that journalists sought to impart and scouted their writings for information about what American life was really like. Yet others discarded the literal meaning of the texts altogether, read between the lines, and found additional fodder for their critical views of the socialist system. As the Soviet public gradually lost faith in the ultimate triumph of Soviet socialism over American capitalism, the reporting of foreign correspondents, much like the socialist project itself, became the subject of alternative readings and subversive interpretations.

## The Soviet Press after Khrushchev

Nikita Khrushchev was ousted from his post in an intraparty coup and sent to early retirement in 1964. The new leader, Leonid Brezhnev, and his colleagues began to implement increasingly conservative policies, seeking to reinstate ideological rigor and calm what they saw as the cultural turmoil of the Khrushchev Thaw. Soviet leadership abandoned the revolutionary outlook of the Khrushchev era: the inspirational slogans of the Twentieth and Twenty-Second Party Congresses and of the 1961 Third Program of the Communist Party of the Soviet Union (CPSU) disappeared from their statements. The 1971 declaration that the Soviet Union had reached the era of "developed socialism" signaled that the Party no longer posited itself as the leader of the revolutionary movement toward communism and would now focus on attempts to deliver a modest welfare state for all citizens instead.[14]

A tightening of the screws in all areas of Soviet culture followed Khrushchev's departure. Controversial themes were purged from literature, the press, and the arts scene. Reformist newspaper editors and commentators were replaced with more conservative figures. In 1965, new editors in chief were appointed to the three major newspapers—*Pravda*, *Izvestiia*, and *Komsomolskaya Pravda*. Dmitrii Goriunov was relieved from his post as TASS director in 1967. Aleksandr Tvardovskii, the editor of the flagship literary journal of the Thaw *Novyi Mir*, was removed from his post in 1970. Many of the brightest thinkers of the Thaw were demoted to diplomatic posts abroad, often in faraway countries.[15] The newspapers' language became more and more formulaic; the human-interest stories gradually lost their edge. The press, which since the Thaw had seen itself as an active agent in the education of socialist persons, now had to repeat orthodoxies and transmit "the myths that constructed the leadership's own version of itself."[16]

In 1968, the Communist Party of Czechoslovakia initiated a series of reforms aiming to liberalize the country's political system and introduce "socialism with a human face." Czechoslovak writers and journalists played a leading role in the reform movement, and after censorship of the press was abolished, even formerly conservative communist publications readily supported liberalization and criticized the Soviet Union. Czechoslovak liberalism appeared contagious. The younger generation of reform-minded Soviet *apparatchiks*, establishment consultants, and foreign correspondents in Prague applauded their Czechoslovak colleagues for their efforts to address the problems of the system head on. The Soviet intelligentsia rooted for the reforms and eagerly anticipated the arrival of a "Moscow Spring."[17] Fearful of a domino effect in the rest of the socialist world, the Soviet leadership decided to move against the Prague Spring. The arrival of Soviet tanks in Czechoslovakia in August 1968 made the Soviet position on reforms very clear.

The demise of the Prague Spring was a crushing disappointment for the younger members of the Soviet establishment.[18] *Izvestiia* correspondents in Prague Vladlen Krivosheev and Boris Orlov refused to toe the official line, which portrayed Soviet intervention as an indispensable measure against counterrevolution in Czechoslovakia. Both correspondents were recalled home and summarily fired from the newspaper.[19] In the aftermath of the Prague Spring, many young *apparatchiks* remained in their posts, trying to influence the aging, conservative leadership; others became disillusioned and moved into policy think tanks and study centers. The limited-circulation studies produced at these think tanks discussed the country's problems in honest terms and proposed dramatic remedies, most of which would not be adopted.[20] Brezhnev's political advisers, such as Georgy Arbatov, Anatoly Chernyaev, and Alexander Bovin, tried to change the opinion of the general secretary and described the subsequent years as a "struggle for Brezhnev's soul."[21] The events in Prague reminded Soviet leaders, yet again, how important it was to control the press and the intelligentsia. Official scrutiny of mass media increased and further dulled its critical edge. However, as Simon Huxtable observed, it was precisely at the time criticism was suppressed that it came to play an even more important role in the journalists' professional identity—"one of the few things that made their work worthwhile."[22]

Soviet journalists' responses to the new developments varied. With years of experience in the system, journalists had a good sense of what would and would not pass the censors, and they made sure that excessively controversial themes did not even make it into their drafts.[23] Still, censors' reactions remained hard to anticipate. In 1975, Stanislav Kondrashov's article on the Soyuz-Apollo Test Project (the first joint Soviet-American space flight) was censored, shortened, and reedited to emphasize Soviet superiority in space exploration. Kondrashov complained that he could barely recognize the end product as his own piece and felt ashamed that the article even bore his name. Kondrashov protested against the changes to his editors, but to no avail.[24] At times, and often with the backing of their editors, journalists chose to submit controversial materials for publication, hoping to avoid the wrath of censors or officials.[25] In one such case Genrikh Borovik conducted an interview in New York with Alexander Kerensky, the exiled leader of Russia's Provisional Government in 1917. The editor of *Literaturnaia Gazeta* cleared the interview for publication, but Glavlit pulled it off the printing press at the last minute.[26] Unwilling to compromise on their professional standards, some journalists continued to try and sneak controversial ideas into their articles and broadcasts.[27]

The weakening of the newspapers' edge became especially evident when they faced strong competition from another player that had emerged on the Soviet media scene: foreign radio broadcasting. Public access to foreign radio grew with the advancement of shortwave technology in the 1960s. By mid-decade a majority of Soviet households sported a radio set that could beam "enemy voices"—the Russian-language services of Voice of America, Radio Liberty, and the BBC—into every household.[28] Immensely popular because of its cultural and musical programming, foreign radio also posed an important challenge to Soviet news services. To begin with, foreign radio stations broadcast information about domestic events, such as accidents or dissident activities, that was unavailable elsewhere. Unlike their Soviet counterparts, foreign radio stations did not have to wait for the censors' clearance or an official announcement from TASS and could report on events as they unfolded. Moreover, foreign radio stories about life abroad were much more diverse than the ones presented in Soviet newspapers and thus undermined the latter's position as the primary source of information about the world.[29]

Interestingly, Soviet experts in media and international affairs—foreign editors and correspondents—felt the problem most acutely, and they cautioned their colleagues and superiors against the explosive potential of information from overseas. As early as 1963 *Pravda*'s foreign editor Victor Maevskii urged fellow party members to develop creative responses to foreign broadcasting and to improve *Pravda*'s analysis of life overseas.[30] Another senior Pravdist with ample experience in foreign affairs, Yuri Zhukov, pointed out that the Soviet press failed to report about international developments in a timely fashion and warned that Soviet readers could fall prey to "bourgeois propaganda" as a result.[31] Concerned international news specialists pointed out that the problem was not just foreign broadcasting itself, but the Soviet approach to this challenge.[32] In 1970, *Izvestiia* correspondent in France Sergei Zykov warned Agitprop that the conservatism of the Soviet media establishment, and its unwillingness to learn from bourgeois press how to adapt to a changing media landscape, allowed the enemy to score propaganda points off the Soviet

Union.[33] That same year, the editor of *Literaturnaia Gazeta,* Aleksandr Cha-kovskii, warned Brezhnev that the "boring and formal" tone of Soviet media pushed audiences to explore other—foreign—sources of information, which caused irrevocable damage to listeners' "spiritual health."[34]

Despite these warnings, the conservative media landscape of the late 1960s and the early 1970s made it impossible to implement creative solutions to the problem of "enemy voices." The question of timeliness became a particularly important issue, as the tightening control on the press further encumbered the already complicated process of vetting materials for publication and broad-casting. In one case it took twenty-three days to clear a Soviet response to a program broadcasted on Voice of America.[35] Over the years, the problem of timely reporting on international affairs became so severe that Brezhnev him-self was forced to address it during his speech at the 1978 Central Committee Plenum. Brezhnev urged officials to provide the Soviet people with timely re-porting on and well-rounded analysis of the most recent developments in foreign affairs.[36] Nonetheless, the problem of timeliness continued to plague Soviet newspapers and news agencies, and the popularity of "enemy voices" did not diminish.

## The Turn to Long-Form Journalism

Soviet foreign correspondents developed their own unique path for coping with the challenging media landscape. They turned to long-form journalism—lengthy accounts, usually in the form of books or article series, that offered all-encompassing descriptions of life and culture overseas. In part, social analysis and generalization dovetailed with a broader turn in Soviet journal-ism, whereby journalists increasingly saw themselves as "social researchers" with a duty to offer meaningful commentary on the world around them.[37] At the same time, this shift drew inspiration from the professional practices of American colleagues: the printed press's emphasis on analysis to compensate for its inability to compete for timeliness with broadcast media, as well as the long-standing popularity of post-assignment accounts authored by US foreign correspondents. Similarly, the long form freed Soviet correspondents from the newspaper's constraints of space and pertinence to current affairs. The focus on in-depth analysis of the American national character, as opposed to the most recent news, liberated journalists from the competition with foreign ra-dio. The turn to long form meant that Soviet journalists could reach out to readers outside their own newspapers and address their audiences directly in their capacity as writers and experts on international affairs.

Although Soviet leaders gradually de-emphasized the promise to "reach and surpass" America, the demand for reliable information about the US did not diminish. The United States remained the USSR's most important geo-political and ideological rival, one that defined the meaning of Soviet social-ism.[38] Moreover, the internationalist ethos underlying the socialist ideology encouraged Soviet citizens to cultivate their curiosity about the foreign world as long as such curiosity did not amount to "kowtowing."[39] Journalists' work, especially their publications beyond newspapers, offered a perfect medium to advance the public's general knowledge about the United States while main-taining a healthy socialist criticism of all things American. Paradoxically there-fore, the personalization of international reporting that had begun during the Khrushchev Thaw culminated precisely in the period of an increasingly conservative media environment in the late 1960s and the 1970s.

This professional evolution was made possible by the fact that Soviet for-eign correspondents straddled the worlds of news media and foreign policy and thus enjoyed more freedoms and privileges than their colleagues in other branches of journalism. A complex network of generational, social, and pro-fessional ties bound international correspondents to the Soviet foreign policy establishment. The majority of Soviet journalists working in the US during the Brezhnev era came from the same cohort of the first postwar graduates of elite institutions such as the Moscow State Institute of International Relations (MGIMO) or Moscow State University. Their classmates, who had followed a different professional path, now formed the core of the foreign policy estab-lishment, serving as Leonid Brezhnev's speechwriters and advisers and se-nior staff members in the Central Committee's international departments, the Ministry of Foreign Affairs, and foreign policy think tanks.[40] These men (and all of them were men) were shaped by the ethos of the 1960s generation, es-pecially the Thaw in arts and culture, de-Stalinization, and the international outreach of the Khrushchev decade. The "enlightened *apparatchiks*" consid-ered themselves true socialists and Soviet patriots, and they tended to priori-tize pragmatic politics and state interests over ideology.[41]

Journalists and foreign policy officials were also bound together by a par-ticular culture of male friendship that developed in elite academic institutions and was further strengthened by years of circulating in the same social and professional milieus. As they came together at official functions, during over-seas assignments, in their day-to-day work in think tanks and foreign policy apparatuses, during long stints at government dachas as part of Brezhnev's speechwriting teams, and within social circles involving their wives and children, these men had ample opportunity to interact, exchange opinions, and share their knowledge and experience.[42] It was through participation in these networks that journalists and *apparatchiks* came to shape each other's worldviews and gained indirect access to Soviet leaders and the Soviet reading public, respectively. Foreign correspondents' affiliation with these networks endowed them with a privileged status that marked their separation from other journalists and was rivaled only by senior editors and international commentators. That privileged status allowed foreign correspondents to explore alternative formats and to transcend the confines imposed by the newspaper and by the conservative media environment.

Explaining their turn to long form, journalists themselves pointed out that one of its advantages was the scope. Unlike newspaper articles, which were constrained by the need for relevance to current affairs, essays and books allowed for more detailed discussion of life abroad and provided an opportunity to engage in a deeper analysis of foreign culture and national character. While a newspaper story offered a mere glance at a foreign country, a book allowed for the presentation of a more complete picture and as such was better suited for conveying the universal differences between capitalism and socialism. For example, in the introduction to his book *Americans in America*, published in 1970, Stanislav Kondrashov wrote that while reporting from the United States during the "the explosive 1960s," he had "accumulated many impressions as well as the desire to relate them in greater detail." The dense newspaper pages, explained Kondrashov, could not fit all his impressions, and therefore he had chosen to write a book that would convey the bigger picture, by setting Americans "against the backdrop of their country, their society, and their problems."[43]

Kondrashov wrote about Americans in America by knitting together a series of short stories about the people and situations he had encountered during his years abroad. Most of his colleagues covering the US exercised a similar tactic. Rather than presenting their readers with an impersonal analysis of the country as a whole, long-form accounts were composed of small stories about the people journalists had met or their encounters with a particular phenomenon in American society. In this manner, Soviet journalists upheld one of the key principles of Thaw journalism—the focus on individuals. At the same time, the bigger picture came through in the narrators' commentaries and explanations of how a small episode fit into wider social and cultural tendencies. Moreover, they deliberately devoted their books and articles to social and cultural themes to counterpoise the newspapers and their near exclusive emphasis on politics and diplomatic relations. Melor Sturua made this connection clear:

First of all, it was important for me to distance myself from [writing on] foreign policy, which was dry and didn't interest me. I was more interested in life. Second, it showed the people here that there were people there, too. Human beings are human beings, no matter where they live. And this is the most important thing that we have in common. And more. Here [in the book] one could really philosophize on the development of the West. Where it was going. [...] I distanced myself from politics and was able to touch on the questions that equally preoccupied us and [the people in] the West. Where are we going? Who are we?[44]

Sturua's recollection demonstrates how committed he remained to the educational ethos of socialist journalism. He maintained his interest in the lives of regular people and his aspiration to talk about universal ideas and values; he continued to educate his readers by simultaneously showing shared human interests as well as the differences between the Soviet Union and the West. It is significant that Sturua used "the United States" interchangeably with "the West" and that, according to him, an examination of the West was inevitably a comparative endeavor. Thinking about the West advanced his understanding of "us"—Soviet society and culture.

In writing books about "Americans in America," Kondrashov, Sturua, and other Soviet foreign correspondents thus acted on a set of important commitments that in part stemmed from the traditions of the Thaw and in part had a longer prehistory. These commitments included the expert's desire to share knowledge and offer deep analysis, the writer's mission to educate and convey universal truths, and the proclivity to think comparatively about competing worldviews and Russia's place in the world. Many of these commitments harked back to the ethos of critical realism imparted by the Russian intelligentsia in the nineteenth century and rephrased by subsequent Russian and Soviet generations.[45] They could be summed up as a shared responsibility by any critical thinker, whether a writer or a journalist, to enlighten his or her readers, to engineer their souls.

## "The Rotten West"

A socialist critique of American capitalism permeated the reporting of Soviet correspondents from the United States. All correspondents understood capitalism as an ideology (rather than merely an economic or political system) and believed that, as such, it informed the attitudes, patterns of thought, and everyday experiences of Americans from all walks of life. The journalists interpreted the United States through a prism that mixed Marxism-Leninism with the basic pillars of anti-American propaganda and conceived of American society as a matrix of conflicts between classes, races, and rival capitalist interests. Correspondingly, "Americans" were also categorized according to their class and race. Soviet accounts thus described the hardship of "a typical farmer," the plight of "a typical worker," or the "typical examples" of racial discrimination. Soviet correspondents portrayed the United States as plagued with the kinds of troubles the Soviet Union had left behind long ago: class and racial rifts, child poverty, and illiteracy. In doing so, journalists' narratives indicted the American system and implicitly challenged US assertions of superiority over the Soviet Union. The emphasis on injustice and inequality, and the correlated criticisms of American modernity, remained a constant theme in Soviet reporting on the United States from the mid-1960s to the mid-1980s.

Soviet journalists seldom ventured into overreaching abstract declarations about all Americans. Committed to Thaw principles of "journalism of the person," correspondents demonstrated how class struggle manifested itself in the lives of regular Americans by telling the stories of the people they met. These narratives were usually accompanied by the journalist's commentary, which explained how the specific story related to a broader American phenomenon or how it represented the capitalist social order. While journalists avoided lumping the American people into broad universal categories, they did universalize the socioeconomic system of American capitalism. The advantages of socialism were seldom mentioned. It was up to the Soviet readers, who were expected to read such narratives comparatively, to deduce the merits of the socialist system from the tale of a worker who had lost his job, of a disenfranchised person of color, or of a hungry immigrant child. Both Marxist analysis of American society and Thaw humanism thus shaped the accounts of Soviet correspondents and their choice of the universal themes and values that they sought to impart to their readers.

In a sketch entitled *A Dead Town*, Boris Strel'nikov used the story of one man and a small mining community to explore the plight of workers in capitalist America. In his story Strel'nikov recalled how, during a trip to West Virginia, he had visited the abandoned coal-mining town of Stotesbury, where he had met Russell, the town's last remaining resident. Strel'nikov told his readers that Russell had been born into a family of Stotesbury coal miners, had attended the local school, and married his high-school sweetheart. For forty years he had been happily married, worked in the mine, and enjoyed living side by side with his fellow miners. All this had been swept away when a new technology—"an electric miner"—was introduced into the neighboring mine to increase productivity. The workers, driven to desperation by the prospect of hunger and unemployment, had turned their wrath on the machines that were about to replace them. It didn't help, and the Stotesbury mine eventually had to shut down, unable to sustain the competition.[46] "Three hundred miners were fired. The town received a death sentence," wrote Strel'nikov. "People fled from the dying town one by one, driven away by the sound of the crying children and the howling of abandoned dogs. . . . Where did they go? Where were they led by the endless roads?"[47] In a last, desperate effort to save the town, its remaining residents turned Russell's house into a museum, hoping that it would attract drivers from the nearby highway and turn Stotesbury into a picnic area. These hopes were futile, Strel'nikov explained, for "who would want to have a picnic in a graveyard?"[48] Two years passed, and Russell remained the town's only resident, guarding the long-abandoned mine and preserving the memories of those "who lived, worked, loved, and prayed under these beautiful Appalachian skies."[49] The American journalist who accompanied Strel'nikov on his trip told him that the establishment of the museum was an example of a "private enterprise," and Strel'nikov could not figure out whether she was joking or not. Strel'nikov's parting description of Russell paraphrased the museum's promotional materials and hinted that this story was indicative of the changes that swept over America: "a man-ghost, the keeper of the past—and of the inevitably evaporating present."[50]

Stories about the plight of honest American workers (often miners) were a recurring feature in the accounts of Soviet correspondents. In his Stotesbury story, Strel'nikov used one individual to demonstrate how Marxist theory played itself out in the reality of one particular town. Most Soviet readers would have recognized the Marxist analysis in this story about greedy capitalist owners trying to maximize their profits (in this case by introducing labor saving machines), driving the workers into poverty and desperation, and thus turning a bustling community into a ghost town. The vignette about Stotesbury's failed attempt to save itself by establishing a museum illustrated that "private enterprise" (or in other words, capitalism) was no remedy for fundamental social ills such as unemployment, poverty, or failing social institutions. Strel'nikov's readers were invited to compare their own lives with the lives of the Stotesbury miners and to deduce that the socialist system would never abandon its workers to unemployment and destitution.

*Figure 5.1.* Boris Strel'nikov on one of his trips around the US, circa 1968–1969. (Vasily Strel'nikov family archive. Published by permission of Vasily Strel'nikov.)

Soviet journalists stressed that the contrast between classes and races in the United States derived from the very nature of the capitalist system. The importance that American society attributed to financial gain rather than to solidarity, Stanislav Kondrashov explained, accounted for the misfortunes of the American poor: "The state spending on the social needs is trifling. [. . .] The authorities are more willing to spend money on all kinds of services for the 'middle class,' than on helping the poor's vital needs to have work, food, and home. Strangely, this approach is justified by considerations of fairness: 'the middle' class is larger, pays more taxes than the poor and therefore deserves to see its 'tax dollars' spent on satisfaction of its needs."[51]

Kondrashov's account did not merely label the American social system as wrong; he also explained how and why it made sense to the people who lived in it. Kondrashov stressed that American attitudes toward welfare had their own internal logic. The educational mission of Kondrashov and the other Soviet journalists made it important to communicate this logic to Soviet audiences and to explain how capitalist thinking worked. The conscious socialist reader would see that capitalist society did not operate upon the whims of mindless actors. Instead, readers would identify the ideological foundations of this policy and condemn it, based on a comparison with their own country, which had a universally accessible welfare state. As shown in the previous chapter, comparative readings of these accounts were facilitated by Soviet traditions of contrasting socialism and capitalism, by Soviet culture's emphasis on competition with the United States, and at times by the journalist's own commentary. Soviet foreign correspondents challenged the staples of US international propaganda such as "American progress" or "the American Dream" and put forward an alternative, socialist vision of modernity. Journalists' stories demonstrated that social welfare and support for the weak and the vulnerable were the true markers of modernity that trumped technology and high standards of living. In their view, a society had no right to call itself advanced if it failed to rid itself of unemployment, child poverty, and racial prejudice.

Soviet correspondents stressed that these problems were perpetuated by the American political system, which was tantamount to the subjugation of the lower classes by the propertied classes.[52] American politics were depicted as being driven by class interests only: property owners appeared as ideologically conscious actors, concentrated on protecting their profits and disenfranchising the poor. Therefore, Soviet correspondents pointed out, American democracy was an empty vessel that masked the uneven distribution of political power in the US and allowed the rich plenty of means to influence and manipulate the votes of the poor. Boris Strel'nikov illustrated this point with a story about his visit to another small town—Lamont, Wyoming: "Sometimes you are driving on the main road, read the billboards and are surprised to see: 'Miller's Bank,' 'Miller's Restaurant,' 'Miller's Department Store,' almost everything belongs to some Miller. Out of curiosity you ask who is the town's mayor and you discover that it is the same Miller. These towns must be a good introduction to the basics of the political economy of capitalism. Many of the things described by Karl Marx in 'Das Kapital' appear in vivid and real form."[53] The Miller example demonstrates how Strel'nikov projected Marxist categories into his analysis of American society, which he then imparted to his readers. Strel'nikov's colleagues likewise positioned class conflict at the heart of American life, as the force affecting not just election results but also the minutest details of one's daily activities. In their discussions of politics in the US, journalists represented the American people as the victims of capitalism: the "small man" could be crushed by capitalist interests without expecting any protection. This political system, journalists explained, could not be improved by any means, for control by the rich precluded any change from within. The biggest tragedy, Soviet correspondents suggested, was that "average Americans" suffered from a false consciousness: they believed that they lived in freedom and democracy and remained unaware of their exploitation by the proper-tied class.

Moreover, Soviet correspondents argued, capitalist self-interest infiltrated the whole of American society; it fueled racial conflict and precluded cross-racial solidarity among the poor. Genrikh Borovik was particularly interested in racial conflict and racial politics, in part perhaps because of his own expe-riences during the anti-cosmopolitan campaign in the 1940s. Borovik greatly admired the civil rights movement and dedicated much of his writing to ana-lyzing and denouncing racism as a social, cultural, and political phenomenon. Several essays and stories in Borovik's book about 1968, *One Year of a Restless Sun,* introduced readers to the sorrows of racism and to the struggle for civil rights. A whole chapter focused on the presidential campaign of Alabama gov-ernor George Wallace, whose political platform enshrined racial segregation. Borovik traveled to Alabama, visited the Wallace campaign headquarters, and met with the governor's supporters. Having carefully analyzed the Wallace phenomenon, Borovik concluded that it was the capitalist instinct that bred racism in the United States:

> They say that Wallace is a racist who skillfully appeals to the element of irratio-nality present in every person. But, first of all, racism is carefully nourished by the entire system of life in a capitalist country. Second, the racism to which Wal-lace appeals is not a zoological, unconscious racism. It is based on the rather concrete economic foundations created by capitalist America. [. . .] When Wal-lace promises that Negroes won't have same entitlement for jobs as the whites will, he does not appeal to the irrational. He means a very concrete threat of unemployment, which he promises to eliminate at the expense of the Negroes if he becomes the president. The most important thing that Wallace plays on is not racism. The most important is the sensibility of a petty proprietor. And this is also a dangerous feeling. Quite often, racism derives from it.[54]

Borovik projected patterns of class struggle on racial divisions and pre-sented racism as a logical outcome of capitalism. In fact, he excluded the possibility of non-ideological racism and showed his readers that racism was endemic to capitalist society.[55] Although Borovik clearly denounced Wallace and his supporters, he still paused to offer a rational explanation of their po-litical thought. Borovik's chapter on Wallace featured a detailed presentation of the governor's views and political platform as well as lengthy quotations of his supporters. In this way, Borovik actually gave the stage to one of the

staunchest critics of socialism and of the Soviet Union and exposed his readers to an ideological position radically different from their own. While Borovik gently guided his socialist readers toward a repudiation of Wallace's ideas,
he did not label these positions as irrational, illogical, or untenable. Therefore,
the textual presentation of Wallace's opinions did not exclude a potential iden-
tification of the reader, not with Borovik, but with Wallace.[56] The choice of a
morally appropriate position depended on the readers' own level of political
consciousness.

Looking at the US through the prism of Marxist theory, Soviet analyses
stressed that the capitalist instinct was the main source of estrangement between classes and races and even between individuals of the same class or race.
The capitalist system, they insisted, robbed people of their ability to care for
one another, resulting in widespread social alienation.[57] Stories about lonely
Americans, lacking any network of social and financial support, often driven
to poverty by old age or large medical bills, featured prominently in the writings of Soviet correspondents.[58] Arguably, these stories preoccupied Soviet
journalists because in their view, the absence of even the most basic welfare
provision for the sick and the destitute represented the most frightful aspect
of American society. In his interview, Melor Sturua recalled that the contrast
between American loneliness and Russian communality struck him as one of
the most important differences between the two countries that needed exploring.[59] It is also possible that stories about loneliness had a special resonance
with the specific experience of Soviet correspondents in the United States. Although the journalists brought their families along and participated in the
social world of Soviet diplomatic community, they spent many days traveling
alone and feeling like strangers in a strange land.

Many journalists repeatedly turned to the word "soul" or the term "searching for a soul" to describe Americans' yearning for empathy and compassion,
and their difficulty in establishing meaningful emotional connections with
other human beings.[60] Several correspondents stressed that soullessness far
outweighed even those perks of American life that were available to the select
few members of the propertied classes. For example, Stanislav Kondrashov
contrasted the bounty of consumer goods with the paucity of interpersonal
relations:

> The main street of the town spreads out in front of me. A symbol of abundance.
> [. . .] The teasing triumph of shiny store windows showing off the might, the
> flexibility and, unimaginable for us, sophistication of American industry; its

multitude of brands and international economic relations. [. . .] It had everything! And the symbol of spiritual emptiness. Everything available, but what's
next? The street is empty and silent. [. . .] The silent, longing people, blocking
their hearts and souls and longing to pour them out in front of an open human
soul. But where could you find that open human soul?[61]

Kondrashov, whose modest proletarian origins made him the staunchest critic
of American consumerism in the Soviet press corps, discussed material abundance in conjunction with spiritual emptiness and thus established a link of
cause and effect between the two. He created the impression that atomization
was the natural outcome of consumerism and suggested that interest in commodities was alien to the human spirit.

It was the journalists' treatment of American consumer culture that most
vividly demonstrated their self-understanding as socialist educators. For many
Soviet citizens in the period of late socialism, foreign consumer goods were
an object of desire and aspiration.[62] As early as the Khrushchev period, even
Soviet authorities and publications tacitly acknowledged the superiority of
American consumer products.[63] The Soviet public's enthusiasm for foreign
goods was the biggest challenge to Soviet arguments for socialist superiority.
While Soviet newspapers regularly criticized popular interest in foreign goods,
official rhetoric did not reject consumption in and of itself; nor did it represent interest in foreign commodities as entirely negative. Instead, Soviet criticism focused on excessive shopping for its own sake and on the unequal distribution of goods under capitalism.[64] Descriptions of American consumers
emphasized their irrationality and excess and thus reinforced the ideal of a responsible and "rational" Soviet consumer, which had begun to appear in the
Soviet press starting in the late 1950s.[65] Official attacks on "unhealthy" and "extreme" fascination with Western consumerism coincided with an acceptance
of "modest" popular interest in Western commodities, which was attributed
to internationalist engagement with the foreign world.[66] However, Soviet ideological proclamations rarely spelled out the boundaries between "extreme"
and "acceptable" interest in Western commodities, and they did not elaborate
on the dangers of Western bourgeois influences. The result was paradoxical:
the official ideology simultaneously encouraged interest in foreign goods and
labeled it as dangerous.

Soviet correspondents in the US took it upon themselves to explain the potential dangers of consumerism. No journalist denied that American stores
surpassed Soviet ones in abundance or variety. Yet journalists stressed that the

glowing fronts of American stores were an empty veneer, a façade concealing the dark side of American everyday life. Journalists linked consumption to atomization, selfishness, and social injustice; they pointed out that consumer culture fed on and encouraged lust, violence, and greed.[67] In another tirade against consumer culture, this time prompted by an excursion to a strip club, Kondrashov demonstrated how American consumerism commodified the most intimate sides of human life:

> Topless girls were trying to justify the high prices charged for the beer. On a small stage, a small black girl clumsily danced and waved her unattractive breasts. She was working—and this word is the most appropriate here—without inspiration, accompanied by music from a record machine. At another small stage, right at the entrance, dutifully and unwillingly, a very young blonde jumped from leg to leg. The whole bar is organized in the most rational and economically efficient way: a music machine (instead of a jazz band), the dancers are constantly changing to allow the clients a wider choice of products and the opportunity to examine them from all directions. [. . .] Topless dancing became just another commodity for mass consumption. The mechanized, rationally organized sale of sex, accessible to all, just like the cheap Woolworth stores.[68]

Kondrashov's description of the strip club was a warning to his compatriots: attractive and shiny on the outside, American consumer culture was in reality dull, desperate, and dehumanizing. Kondrashov's use of topless dancing as the metaphor shows how, in their attempts to illustrate the pernicious effects of American consumerism, Soviet journalists turned to gendered language and imagery.[69] Soviet journalists described American consumers as superficial, irrational, and beguiled by changing fashions. Shoppers often appeared in the journalists' accounts as conspicuously consuming American women or emasculated American men.[70] The capitalist system, journalists explained, duped the American people into believing that material possessions could cure their loneliness and alienation. Another emasculating effect of capitalism, then, was that it lured Americans away from society-changing action.

The relationship between Soviet correspondents and American consumer goods remains controversial. Recollections of people who lived through the Brezhnev era point out that in the Soviet context, where international travel was available to only a select few and Western goods were notoriously hard to come by, foreign correspondents' condemnation of American consumer culture and way of life often rang hollow.[71] US observers likewise accused Soviet foreign correspondents of hypocrisy because they warned against the dangers of Western consumerism while wearing Western suits, riding in Western cars, and enjoying a Western lifestyle. "His words were pure party line, but his clothes were Oxford Street in London, where he spent four years as *Pravda* correspondent," wrote David K. Willis about Vsevolod Ovchinnikov in 1985.[72] It is likely that Soviet foreign correspondents were aware of such disapproval, yet did not see their own purchase of foreign products as inconsistent with their critique of American capitalism. The main focus of their criticism was not the possession of Western goods per se, but rather the consumer culture that glorified commodities and turned consumption into the pinnacle of human existence—an approach consistent with the Soviet ideal of a responsible consumer.[73] Moreover, for Soviet foreign correspondents, wearing Western clothing was as much a professional imperative as a choice. Like all Soviet representatives abroad, journalists were required to maintain the same level of wardrobe and well-groomed appearance as their foreign counterparts. However, as Soviet popular interest in Western goods and the frustration with their unavailability grew in the late 1960s and the 1970s, these particular guidelines and journalists' access to foreign products could come across as markers of duplicity.

The long-form accounts authored by Soviet journalists introduced readers to a range of American protagonists from all walks of life. Sympathetic characters, such as Russell, the unemployed miner, were featured in journalists' books alongside deplorable figures, such as George Wallace, accompanied by detailed explanations of their worldviews and commitment to the American system. Perhaps ironically, the Soviet long-form accounts, usually perceived as tightly controlled and unfree, exposed their readers to a variety of political doctrines different from the one advanced by the dominant Soviet ideology. A "correct understanding" of these accounts demanded active intellectual work. As the Brezhnev era progressed, the hope to "reach and overtake" American standards of living became more and more distant. In telling stories about the hardship experienced by many ordinary Americans and their hopes for better lives, foreign correspondents invited readers to appreciate the superiority of Soviet socialist ideals and values.

## Caught in the American Ferment

In the 1960s, Soviet journalists found their critiques of American society and consumer culture reinforced by the myriad social and youth movements that characterized this turbulent period. Soviet correspondents contended that young Americans' rejection of the norms and values of capitalism revealed a crisis in the American social structure. The mass conversion of young bourgeois Americans into hippies, journalists explained, reflected the youngsters' desperate yearning to escape consumerism and commoditization and find a supportive community. However, Genrikh Borovik, who explored the hippy movement at great length, discovered that it was impossible to escape the soul-wrecking effects of capitalism. In "Journey to the Hippie-land," an account of his trip to San Francisco, Borovik described how capitalist America had turned the naïf symbols of the hippie movement—flowers, beards, and colorful garments—into marketable (and expensive) commodities. "Racketeers are already fighting each other to the death over the ownership of the market of flowers, love, and kindness," he observed.[74]

The only viable alternative to soul-wrecking American capitalism was the dedication of many young Americans to what the Soviet journalists saw as the essentially socialist causes of justice and social equality—the civil rights and antiwar movements. In the mid-1960s, select journalists such as Boris Strel'nikov began to cover the struggle for civil rights and to express their admiration for the activists in the southern states. Soviet correspondents' initial response to the antiwar movement was cautious though—probably because journalists initially conflated it with the hippie movement. The events of 1968—the assassination of Martin Luther King Jr. and the violent antiwar demonstrations throughout the country—profoundly shocked Soviet correspondents. More and more journalists began to explore the movements at great length, celebrating the courage and commitment of their participants. After witnessing the violent suppression of an antiwar rally outside the 1968 Democratic National Convention in Chicago, Melor Sturua, whose writing on the 1960s focused heavily on youth protests, declared the demonstrators the only remnants of social consciousness in America: "Oh, Yankees-Puritans, who look with disgust on mini-skirts and jeans! Bend your heads before them! They are covered with blood and torn into pieces by the Gestapo from Chicago! They are your conscience, wide awake in Lincoln Park, while you sleep in your warm, habitable, bought-on-credit nests!"[75] Like Sturua, many Soviet journalists described American youth protesters as the only alternative for those who wanted to rescue their souls from the corrupting effects of capitalist culture. Projecting patterns of class analysis on American domestic turmoil, Soviet journalists presented the war in Vietnam and racial segregation as the ultimate outcomes of America's colonialist policies and capitalist greed.

Depictions of racial conflict in the United States had played a central role in Soviet anti-American propaganda even before the Cold War, as well as in

*Figure 5.2.* Melor Sturua in August 1970. (Photo: Nino Meliya/RIA Novosti via Sputnik Images.)

the early years of superpower confrontation.[76] Denunciations of racism and segregation became even more prominent in the 1950s, when the USSR began to reach out to the decolonizing nations in Africa, Southeast Asia, and the Middle East and to compete with the United States for the hearts and minds of people emerging from under the colonial yoke.[77] The war in Vietnam was likewise fitted into the overall narrative of US racism and colonialism. The oppression of African-Americans in the US and the brutal military campaign in Vietnam were presented as two sides of the same coin, and both dominated Soviet representations of the US from the mid-1960s to the early 1970s. The struggle for civil rights, the condemnation of the Vietnam War, and the suppression of peaceful demonstrations against the US government became important themes in Soviet anti-American propaganda.[78] It was the writing of Soviet correspondents in the US that brought alive both the civil rights and the antiwar movements and turned their leaders, such as Martin Luther King Jr. and Dr. Benjamin Spock, into household names in the USSR. Moved by the commitment of the protesters and shaken by the violence of reprisals against them, Soviet journalists became personally committed to carrying these stories to their readers.

The fascination with Dr. Spock in Soviet society illustrates the broad impact of narratives about American protest. Spock's political activism and his persecution by the authorities became a focal point of many reports on the opposition to the Vietnam War. Soviet journalists depicted Dr. Spock as an icon of consciousness and morality and stressed the high personal costs he incurred for opposing the war. Genrikh Borovik's lengthy essay on Dr. Spock explained that, as a pediatrician whose advice shaped the upbringing of millions of American young adults, Dr. Spock could not simply look away while "his children" were sent to butcher and be butchered in Vietnam. Others linked Dr. Spock's child-rearing philosophy directly to the youth's opposition to the war. Children reared on Dr. Spock's principles, journalists explained, had grown into conscious adults with high moral standards that made it impossible to avoid taking a decisive public stance against the war.[79] In 1970, Dr. Spock's book *Baby and Child Care* was published in the Soviet Union. When censors approved its publication, they justified their decision with the argument that it was not only Spock himself who opposed the war in Vietnam, but also children brought up on his principles.[80]

Possibly because they were aware of the Soviet regime's uneasy attitude toward accounts of civil disobedience and public protest, especially after Prague, Soviet journalists celebrated the courage and engagement of their American protagonists and tried to portray them as essentially socialist heroes fighting for freedom and equality. As a quote from Melor Sturua's book *Ferment* illustrates, participants in American counterculture often appeared as ideological subjects, sometimes even groping toward the Marxist light: "Of course, among the protesting students one could find a large diversity of ideologies, perspectives, and temperaments. And although everyone considered themselves Marxists, only a minority were Marxists in reality. [. . .] But here I would like to point out one thing: the unique renaissance in Marx's popularity among the new generation of the New World. Marx is attracting and fascinating [people]. Marx is read over and over. For some it's a necessity, for others it's a fashion. But fashion is very telling, isn't it?"[81] American counterculture held an enormous appeal for many young women and men in the Soviet Union.[82] Descriptions such as Sturua's stressed that those aspects of American culture that so fascinated Soviet youth actually derived from socialist values and that many heroes of American protest movements criticized the US in terms similar to those used by the Soviet state. Journalists' descriptions of young American bourgeois converting to Marxism and protesting against the evils of capitalism demonstrated how socialism was conquering hearts and minds around the world. The coverage of countercultural movements also reinforced the idea that socialist ideology provided the only feasible ground for effective moral action.

Soviet reporting stressed that there were two sides to American counterculture. The civil rights and antiwar activists were celebrated for their courage and commitment to high ideals. By contrast, hippies and avant-garde artists were presented as a decadent, escapist, and misguided bunch who inadvertently played into the hands of oppressive capitalists. In applauding the ideological engagement of the protest movements and criticizing the escapism of the hippies, the journalists tried to channel Soviet youth's admiration of American radicals in a proper, socialist direction.

In the late 1970s, the stories about American counterculture saw a sad new postscript. Several foreign correspondents reported that upon revisiting the hotbeds of the 1960s rebellion, they discovered that the flame of protest had been extinguished, suppressed, or domesticated by the establishment. Stanislav Kondrashov's 1975 book, *Rendezvous with California*, illustrated the changing fortunes of American counterculture. Divided into two parts, the book chronicled Kondrashov's impressions from two reporting trips to California: in 1968 and in 1975. In the first part (previously published as a separate book) Kondrashov criticized the hippies' naiveté; admired the political awakening of students at the University of California, Berkeley; and offered a sympathetic account of his visit to the Black Panthers' headquarters. In his 1975 account, Kondrashov revisited the same sights: the home of the hippie movement in the Haight-Ashbury district, the UC Berkeley campus, and the urban ghettos where the Black Panthers had launched their assault on the American establishment.

Kondrashov found these sites much changed, betraying few of the traces of past turmoil. Haight-Ashbury was now a regular middle-class neighborhood. "The symbols of American standardization" that the hippies had rebelled against—chain stores and banks—now stood triumphantly where "psychedelic shops" had been.[83] On the fourth anniversary of "Bloody Thursday"—the

*Figure 5.3.* Stanislav Kondrashov in January 1981. (Photo: Prihodko/Sputnik Images.)

most violent day of clashes between students and police in May 1969—Berkeley was silent. Students had left for the summer break; the streets that had witnessed their outraged marches now boasted colorful new shops and multiethnic food trucks. Reflecting on the changes that had taken place, Kondrashov pondered the "metamorphosis of conformism (and non-conformism) in America," where challenges to common tastes and practices were easily absorbed and commercialized, and soon became a new standard everyone was compelled to follow.[84] Kondrashov's impressions reiterated his and his colleagues' original assessment of the hippies as unprincipled and easily swayed by any current common craze. The hippies' easy transition into mainstream consumer culture demonstrated that their renunciation of the American system had been hollow from the start. Reiterating these criticisms in 1975 was important. Back in the USSR, Soviet Union's own hippie movement had been growing and attracting young people from elite families, including foreign correspondents' own children. One of the earliest and the most sympathetic articles about the hippies had been written by Boris Strel'nikov, whose eldest daughter, Tatiana, was a Moscow hippie (and a friend of Kondrashov's eldest daughter, Natalia).[85] Addressing not only the nation's youth but also perhaps their own children, journalists sought yet again to impress on their readers that the hippie rebellion in the US had been naïve and misguided and was not to be taken seriously.

And what of those whose opposition to the American system stemmed from true commitment to universally important ideas? Where were the civil rights and the antiwar activists? What had happened to the Black Panthers, who, according to Kondrashov at the time, had the potential to become "that persistent force that would finally unite the radical elements of the Negro movement"?[86] Kondrashov discovered that, although they had abandoned their former iconoclastic strategies and as a result no longer dominated the national headlines, many of the former members of these movements continued to engage in political activism. Now their political work focused on the local municipal level and on improving lives in the black urban ghettos. Bobby Seale, the cofounder of the Black Panther Party, was running for mayor of Oakland. Kondrashov emerged from these meetings with admiration for the activists' continued commitment to civil rights and their tireless efforts to improve the lives of their communities. Yet he remained skeptical about their chances of bringing about any fundamental change in the American system itself.[87]

In revisiting the sites and the heroes of the turbulent 1960s, Soviet correspondents reiterated their criticism of capitalist America. The "American system" emerged from their accounts as an all-encompassing ideological, political, social, and cultural structure, strong and stable enough to contain, absorb, or suppress any challenge from within. The fate of American counterculture illustrated both the power of "the American way of life" and its endurance. Delivered in the mid-1970s, this lesson in the stability of the American system spoke directly to, and supported, the Soviet Union's ongoing efforts to find ways of coexisting with the United States. Back in the USSR, however, the appeal of American counterculture and its symbols, such as the hippie lifestyle, garments, and music, only grew stronger. Young Soviet readers' imagined version of American culture was increasingly at odds with the educational message of the foreign correspondents.

## Soviet Reports, Soviet Readers

Did readers indeed embrace the journalists' critiques of the United States and become more appreciative of their own system? While there is little documented evidence that would allow us to analyze how contemporaries engaged with specific accounts, close attention to the cultural context of late socialism, oral history interviews, and memoir literature help to discern several patterns of readers' engagement with writings about America in the Brezhnev era and beyond.[88]

For readers, one potential response to the long-form accounts was to read comparatively and share the journalist's assessment of the superiority of Soviet socialism over American capitalism. Soviet correspondents implicitly and explicitly encouraged their readers to compare and contrast the two systems.[89] As already shown, this kind of comparison was one of the founding blocks of Soviet culture, especially in the wake of Khrushchev's Thaw and international outreach. The Soviet Union continued to emerge favorably from such comparisons well into the Brezhnev era. In a 1976 survey of the Soviet population, respondents graded the quality of their life at 4 on a scale of 0 to 5, while awarding the United States a grade of 2 or 3.[90] Respondents in documentaries and oral history interviews often mention how they were struck by the stories of unemployment, greed, and lack of welfare provision in the United States and describe how fortunate they felt to live in the socialist "here" and escape the problems in the capitalist "there."[91]

Other readers consciously chose to ignore the educational message of stories about life in the US. "I watch Zorin's documentaries about America with the sound off" was a popular Soviet saying.[92] It referred to Valentin Zorin, a prominent international commentator on Gosteleradio whose famous series of documentary films about the US were broadcast on Soviet television in the 1970s. For travel-starved Soviet viewers, the lens of Zorin's camera offered a rare opportunity to see America. Watching "with the sound off" meant that audiences enjoyed the footage from the US while tuning out Zorin's narration, which situated the footage in the appropriate ideological context. Similarly, many readers turned to the journalists' published long-form accounts to satisfy their curiosity about American cities, culture, and everyday life. As they read, audiences brushed off the journalists' ideological commentary and instead scoured the texts for raw information about life in the United States.

An interesting example of such reading appeared in the 2001 memoir of Andrey Makarevich, the front man of the band Mashina Vremeni and one of the founding fathers of the Soviet rock and roll scene. A key moment in this retrospective account of his transformation from a regular Soviet boy to na-tional rock legend was Makarevich's growing awareness of Western youth cul-ture: "By the 1970s the hippies became the center of our world. It was an ar-ticle in a journal *Vokrug Sveta* [Around the World] that opened our eyes to reality. The essay was called 'A Journey to the Hippie-land.' We [. . .] copied quotes from the article of hippies declaring their program (I, for instance, remembered everything by heart). The hippie platform was adopted in its entirety."[93]

The essay "A Journey to the Hippie-land" was Genrikh Borovik's aforemen-tioned account of his trip to San Francisco. Originally published in *Vokrug Sveta,* the article was later included in Borovik's collection of essays about America in 1968, *One Year of a Restless Sun.* Borovik's article treated the hippie culture in a rather humorous manner, describing the hippies and their aspi-rations as naïve and at times ridiculous. The part of the story Makarevich re-fers to—where Borovik asked a hippie about his program—actually sought to demonstrate that the hippies had no program at all; it provided another layer in Borovik's gentle mockery of the hippies' lack of any ideology whatsoever.

Oblivious to Borovik's sarcastic tone, or perhaps dismissing it as the offi-cial voice, Makarevich's interpretation of the article was completely the oppo-site: he embraced the hippie "platform" as his own. Apparently he was not alone. As Juliane Fürst has shown, many young Soviet hippies adopted Boro-vik's article as their guide to the hippie lifestyle.[94] It is impossible to say whether Borovik intentionally wrote this article to satisfy his readers' interest in the hippie movement or whether his critique of their lack of ideology was only a veil that would ensure that the article cleared the censors. Regardless of Boro-vik's intentions, Makarevich and his contemporaries mined this account for "raw" information about America while ignoring its didactic message.

In post-1991 interviews, former foreign correspondents took pride in their coverage of American youth and counterculture, stressing that these reports were specifically attuned to the interests of their younger readers.[95] Arguably, these recollections could have been influenced by the journalists' retrospec-tive knowledge about readers' engagement with their reports. It is clear, how-ever, that Soviet correspondents broadened the scope of the discussion about American culture and introduced such phenomena as rock music and hippies into the Soviet picture of the foreign world. As they expanded readers' per-spectives, the journalists were not trying to deliver a subversive message. Neither Soviet correspondents nor their readers saw any contradiction in a simultaneous appreciation of both socialism and Western culture.[96] Moreover, while journalists such as Genrikh Borovik and Melor Sturua discussed various facets of American youth culture, their respective analyses signaled that each phenomenon should be treated differently. While Borovik's stories about the hippies stressed their naïveté and presented the whole movement in a rather comical light, Sturua's reports of the antiwar movement emphasized the ideological rigor of the protesters and described them as brave and worthy of admiration. What the journalists, and those who approved their accounts for publication, perhaps did not foresee was that the commentary would be ignored altogether, that their descriptions would be de-contextualized and read in isolation from their analysis, "with the sound off."

Sometimes, this form of reading involved a dismissal of any criticism of the US simply because it was relayed by official Soviet media. Upon immigrating to the US in the late 1970s, the writer Vassily Aksyonov commented that Soviet readers tended to ignore Soviet discussions of American shortcomings and problems only to learn, after immigrating to the United States, that much of the critique was accurate:

> Soviet propaganda has piled up so many lies in its lifetime that it now gives reverse results: a certain brand of "critically thinking" Soviet citizen—and most of the new émigrés fall into the pattern—no longer believes a word of it; the critically thinking Soviet rejects both the lies of Soviet propaganda and the scraps of truth the propaganda machine needs to make the lies to appear true. [. . .] As a direct result of anti-American propaganda the CTS [Critically Thinking Soviet] forms a picture of America as an ideal society, prosperous and romantic. [. . .] Thousands of Soviet émigrés were cruelly disappointed with what they found instead.[97]

In this case, ignoring the text's didactic message promoted an explicitly subversive reading. Ironically, this mode of engagement was similar to the one intended by the journalists, for they too imagined America as an inverted mirror of socialist society and asked readers to form their perceptions of the US in comparison with the Soviet Union. What differed in the case of subversive engagement was the readers' inherently negative attitude toward the Soviet state, which led them to cast the United States in an ideal light.

Another potentially subversive form of engagement was Aesopian reading, which was widely practiced in educated circles. The term refers to the Greek storyteller Aesop, whose fables often used animals, endowed with human traits, to criticize human nature. Lev Losev, a scholar of Russian literature and former Soviet journalist, defined Aesopian language as "a special literary system, one whose structure allows interaction between author and reader at the same time that it conceals inadmissible content from the censor."[98] Intimately familiar with the inner workings of the Soviet press, Losev argued that the use of Aesopian language emerges under conditions of state censorship in literature. In the Russian context it was part and parcel of a literary tradition dating back to the nineteenth century.[99] The use of Aesopian language rested on the assumption that the actual meaning of a text was different from the literal one. Like socialist-realist writing, Aesopian writing presupposed an audience of conscious, thinking readers. While the former envisioned the reader engaging with the *literal* meaning of the text, the latter invited critical, and at times cynical, reading between the lines. As the writer Kornei Chukovskii pointed out, the attribution of Aesopian meaning to a text could occur independently of the intentions of its author.[100] In the context of Russia's longstanding tradition of censorship and critical reading, audiences could find a hidden message in almost any given text.

Soviet writing on the United States was especially susceptible to Aesopian reading. First, the official language of Soviet newspapers was often an Aesopian text in and of itself. Since the information published in the Soviet press was tightly controlled, the newspapers developed a wide range of euphemisms and figures of speech to discuss topics that otherwise would have been ideological taboos.[101] The constant use of euphemisms in official newspapers endowed every journalistic text with a potential hidden message and fostered a tradition of reading newspapers with an eye for sub-textual meanings.[102] Soviet editors and censors were acutely aware of this potential and paid close attention to every detail in newspapers, seeking and finding subversive meaning in many apparently innocent formulations and expressing constant concern with texts' ability to evoke "uncontrollable associations."[103]

At the core of all Aesopian devices, according to Losev, is the principle of metonymicity—the substitution of one concept for another. In the context of Russian political writing, one of the manifestations of this principle was discussing foreign countries as a way to comment on domestic phenomena or events.[104] Fedor Burlatskii, Khrushchev's speechwriter and later a *Pravda* commentator, identified this as a prominent tactic among political and international commentators. Burlatskii recalled that when he wanted to criticize Brezhnev and his colleagues' fascination with "the cult of personality," he decided to use Aesopian language and wrote a brochure about the cult of personality in Communist China. Burlatskii hoped that a text criticizing China would raise no objections and that when it was published, readers would infer that his criticism was in fact aimed at the Soviet leadership. The party's chief ideologue, Mikhail Suslov, personally intervened to prevent publication of Burlatskii's brochure, underscoring that the Soviet establishment was well aware that texts dealing with foreign countries invited reading between the lines.[105]

The Aesopian potential of reports from the US was further enhanced in the context of Khrushchev's call "to reach and surpass America" and the Soviet journalistic culture of the Thaw, which encouraged the public to read information about the West from a comparative perspective. However, the conclusion that socialism was better than capitalism was not the only available outcome of a comparative reading; it was also possible to read the journalists' accounts as a critical commentary on the USSR. For example, Mikhail Barshchevskii, a Russian legal expert, journalist, and former politician, remembered how his criticism of the Soviet penal system was reinforced by press reports on life overseas:

> I remember reading in one of our Soviet newspapers, *Pravda* or *Izvestiia*, an item that left me literally in a state of shock. The article discussed a strike in one of the Danish prisons. Naturally, everything was presented as an example of rotten, collapsing capitalism, "their" customs, and so on. Danish prisoners started a strike, or perhaps even a hunger strike, demanding to replace black-and-white TV sets in their cells with color ones. And when this was announced in the Soviet press (and we knew what went on in our own [penal] system), it sounded like mockery.[106]

Barshchevskii realized that the article in question was meant to encourage him to criticize the penal system of capitalist countries. Yet upon reading it, and conducting an almost inevitable comparison with the Soviet Union, he took an entirely different lesson from the article and saw it as evidence of the backwardness of the Soviet penal system and of the contradictions between the socialist state's proclamation of its humane principles and the reality he was familiar with. Even if Barshchevskii "invented" this particular memory, the invention nevertheless indicates a pattern of engagement with information about life abroad.

The Aesopian potential of Soviet coverage of the United States was especially strong in reporting on the civil rights and the antiwar movements. Read against the grain, journalists' descriptions of civil disobedience and public protests could have been interpreted as indictments of the Soviet Union's harsh treatment of dissent within its own borders and across the socialist bloc. In the context of the Prague Spring and the subsequent unrest among the intelligentsia, stories about rank-and-file Americans challenging the authority of their government and the older generation, and sticking to their principles even in the face of reprisals, could have been interpreted as a call to arms and a celebration of domestic dissent.

On August 28, 1968, Soviet correspondents in the US witnessed Chicago police forces violently suppressing a large antiwar rally held to coincide with the Democratic National Convention. Only a few days earlier, on August 21, 1968, Warsaw Pact forces had invaded Czechoslovakia to trample the reforms of the Prague Spring. On August 29, 1968, the front page of *Izvestiia*'s evening edition featured, side by side, an article praising "Soviet brotherly help to Czechoslovakia" and an account of the "brutal reprisal against demonstrators who spoke up against the Vietnam venture."[107] The proximity of the two events in terms of both time and content—that is, two violent suppressions of demonstrations opposing foreign interventions by superpowers and calling for reform and change—made it possible to read the descriptions of Chicago as an allegory for Prague. The highly emotional language of the second article, its detailed descriptions of Chicago police brutality, and the ultimate sympathy it expressed toward the young activists could be read as an indictment of the Soviet intervention in Prague and a call to support the Czechoslovak people. The imperative to tell a story about the moral degradation of capitalism, combined with the desire to provide an appropriate ideological explanation for Soviet repressive policies in the socialist bloc, created the potential for subversive reading.

Even outside the immediate context of Prague, journalists' descriptions of the antiwar movement could have been misconstrued as an implicit criticism of the domestic political order. The following excerpt from Borovik's description of an antiwar rally in New York's Central Park showed "the American masses" branding their country's policy in Vietnam as shameful and unjust:

> Thousands and thousands of people are standing, closely pressed to each other on the enormous field of Central Park in New York. [...] They are demonstrating against the war in Vietnam. [...] In 1966 people also met in Central Park for a demonstration against the war. What has changed in the last two years? First of all, there are more people now. Two years ago the police counted 22,000 participants. This year, *New York Times* correspondents equipped with special "counters"

concluded that 87,000 men and women showed up. The organizers themselves argue that between 100,000 and 150,000 people came to protest. [. . .] Back then [in 1966] the predominant feeling among the protesters was victimization. Now they are feeling their own power. It is not that speaking out against the war is less dangerous today. [. . .] The sense of power did not come because the authorities have "softened." It came because the most amazing thing happened: the American conscience has awoken and became manifest. [. . .] Apparently, those lonely individuals who stood silently on Times Square two years ago with posters, "Stop the shameful war!" have achieved surprisingly large results.[108]

Borovik turned to the well-rehearsed tactic of using American voices to condemn American policies, thus rendering Soviet criticism of the US more effective. It would not have escaped his audience, however, that they were reading about an *officially sanctioned* hundred-thousand-strong demonstration protesting a major US policy in a major US city. Even if one did not consciously pause to ponder the meaning of this information, every Soviet reader knew that nothing of the kind could happen in his or her own country. Even the modest anti–Vietnam War demonstration organized by the Soviet hippies, on the model of the American rallies such as the one described by Borovik, had been unacceptable to the local authorities and the KGB.[109] A simple comparison between Borovik's paragraph and the commonly known practices of political repression could undermine official declarations that pitted Soviet freedom against American oppression.[110]

The different paths of engagement with the reporting of foreign correspondents outlined here were not necessarily incompatible. It was possible to recognize the critical potential of stories about antiwar demonstrations in the United States and identify with the journalists' critiques of American capitalism at the same time. In fact, the official sanctioning of the journalists' accounts itself relied on expectations of an Aesopian reading of sorts, whereby conscious Marxists audiences were to extrapolate the advantages of socialism from the descriptions of the evils of American capitalism. While the journalists applied the prism of socialist ideas to present a critical appraisal of the American system, the structure of their accounts did not forestall other conclusions, including ones that could undermine the official proclamations of the Soviet state or the literal meaning of the texts. In opening the prism and allowing their readers to form their own conclusions, Soviet correspondents may have unintentionally opened the gates for subversive interpretation.

*Figure 5.4.* Genrikh Borovik's photo from a demonstration against the Vietnam War, New York City, June 30, 1966. (Photo: Genrikh Borovik/Sputnik Images.)

## Soviet Reports, American Readers

Shortly after publication, the long-form reports of Soviet correspondents would find their way to the desks of American officials. Carefully translated, the reports were disseminated to the relevant offices in the US Embassy in Moscow, the State Department, or the US Information Agency (USIA), occasionally accompanied by a commentary on their content. These American readers evaluated the Soviet reports through the prism of the norms and practices of US liberal media and charged that Soviet coverage of the US was decisively shaped by the ideological rigidity and anti-American bias of the Soviet press.[111] State Department officials were convinced that Soviet correspondents criticized the American way of life either because they were induced to do so by their state-controlled publications or because they were irredeemable hard-liners, unable to transcend their own ideological lenses. For example, the embassy translator of Boris Strel'nikov and Il'ia Shatunovskii's 1969 American series in *Pravda* marveled that, after visiting Hollywood and Oklahoma City, "the two managed to find enough negative aspects to fill up a dozen columns"—suggesting that the journalists were explicitly seeking ways to misrepresent the United States to their readers.[112] The question of whether the reports of Soviet correspondents were raising potentially valid points seldom came up. Convinced that it was mandatory for all Soviet writing about the US to tick certain boxes, American officials paid little attention to what the journalists actually had to say. Although US civil servants believed that there was nothing unusual about critical Soviet reporting, they often found the harsh tones difficult to ignore, especially in light of the Soviet treatment of American correspondents and the escalating tit-for-tat of expulsions and visa denials, which became known as "visa wars." One embassy official who reviewed Zorin's visa application suggested that the US could take a page out of the Soviets' book and reject visas for "all Soviet tv commentators" in retaliation for "distorted critical reporting" about the United States on Soviet television.[113]

Soviet reporting on Vietnam was one area where US civil servants paid close attention. Soviet journalists' treatment of the Vietnam War, and the overall emphasis on Vietnam in Soviet propaganda, exasperated US officials, for they understood that such coverage had a strong potential to turn public opinion, within and outside the USSR, against the United States. Ambassador Foy D. Kohler, particularly attuned to matters of propaganda following his tour as director of the Voice of America, took Soviet press coverage of Vietnam seriously and frequently brought it up with his superiors in the State Department and his Soviet counterparts.[114] Controlling the public relations damage over Vietnam was a challenge for American diplomats and propagandists alike. In response to an essay by Strel'nikov describing one day of violent race riots and antiwar demonstrations across America, the embassy asked the USIA to produce a special Russian-language program for Voice of America highlighting all the positive things that had happened on the same day and that Strel'nikov had failed to mention.[115]

Efforts to control the publicity damage often descended to the level of individual articles. A few months after Strel'nikov's riot essay, another of his pieces, entitled "Arsonists," caused a furor among American officials. It opened with the story of Smokey—a little bear cub miraculously rescued from a wildfire in a New Mexico forest. Strel'nikov went on to tell his readers how successful

American efforts to prevent wildfires in many forests across the United States had been. Strel'nikov then cited a *New York Times* item about a new tactic used by the US military in Vietnam: starting wildfires in order to "smoke out" Vietnamese rebels from their hiding places in the jungle. The experts who fought against wildfires in the United States were brought in by the military as consultants on how to use fire to ravage forests in Vietnam. The concluding paragraph contrasted American children visiting Smokey the bear cub in the zoo with Vietnamese children being smoked out of their forests and villages by the same people who saved Smokey. A copy of Strel'nikov's article circulated among State Department officials as an example of the uses of Vietnam in Soviet propaganda. A small typed note pinned to the article said that Strel'nikov's piece was "seemingly very effective" and hardly innocuous. "Although sadly not unjustified," replied an unsigned handwritten comment added below.[116]

Because they understood all Soviet reporting to be directed by the state, US officials scouted it for insights into the positions of the Soviet government. For example, in November 1968, *Izvestiia* published an article by its international commentator Vikentii Matveev, who argued that the American public had drawn important lessons from the Vietnam War and that, soon enough, domestic opposition to the war would usher in a real change in US foreign policy. The piece appeared in the wake of a turbulent summer of fighting in Vietnam and shortly after Richard Nixon's victory in the presidential election. Matveev's opinions were so unorthodox that *Izvestiia* prefaced his piece with a disclaimer that the editorial board "may not entirely agree with the opinion expressed by the author"—a rare occasion in the newspaper's handling of international themes.[117] US Embassy officials hastened to make a "courtesy call" on senior international commentators from *Pravda* and *Izvestiia* to discuss US-Soviet relations, taking particular interest in *Izvestiia* journalists' take on Matveev's piece. While embassy officials found their Soviet interlocutors "guarded in their remarks," their overall impression was that "the question of whether the USSR can 'do business' with the US is a subject of continuing and deep discussion not only among journalists, but more particularly within the Soviet leadership."[118] In the next few years, as superpower relations moved into détente, US officials frequently turned to the Soviet press and international commentators when they wanted to ascertain the sincerity of the Soviet leadership's overtures to the United States.[119]

Personal diplomacy was at the heart of Soviet-American détente, and it was during this period that foreign correspondents' involvement in person-to-person diplomacy attained unprecedented levels.[120] Even before the establishment of a back channel between Secretary Brezhnev and President Nixon in 1969, Soviet journalists in the US expanded their interactions with American colleagues and State Department officials, invariably stressing how important these interactions were for maintaining a dialogue between the two sides.[121] Back in Moscow, US officials also scaled up their outreach to Soviet journalists and editors specializing in foreign affairs, visiting the editorial offices of major Soviet newspapers to discuss international developments and US-Soviet relations.[122]

Even though these encounters became more frequent, American officials were invariably surprised to discover that their Soviet contacts were a far cry from what one might expect from a communist dogmatic. The Americans continued to be struck by the Soviet journalists' apparent sincerity. A State Department official who had met *Ekonomicheskaia Gazeta*'s correspondent Vasilii Gromeka in the US described the meeting as "pleasant and factual."[123] When Soviet interlocutors made comments deemed inconsistent with Soviet political orthodoxy, these statements were attributed to a journalist's falling off guard or to the positive influence of American culture.[124] American embassy officers who met Gromeka after his return from the US took special notice of Gromeka's "relative frankness and 'liberal' attitudes," suggesting that it "probably reflects his recent exposure to the United States."[125] Still, despite the growing contact between them, national character stereotypes continued to shape American civil servants' perceptions of Soviet journalists.

By the late 1970s, deteriorating superpower relations took a toll on journalists' participation in personal diplomacy. Interactions between Soviet journalists and US officials were reduced to practical matters such as visa applications or travel permits. Back in the USSR, authorities adopted an increasingly harsh attitude toward American journalists' reporting on the dissident movement, which in turn eroded any remnants of goodwill toward Soviet correspondents in the United States. Although Soviet journalists no longer engaged in personal diplomacy, they continued to tour the US, make new acquaintances, and persist in their efforts to present a broad range of American characters to their readers.

In October 1982, after several years' absence, Stanislav Kondrashov went on a short assignment to the United States. A few months earlier, Melor Sturua had not been allowed to resume his post as *Izvestiia*'s Washington correspondent, in retaliation for the Soviet expulsion of *Newsweek* correspondent Andrew Nagorski. Kondrashov was accredited as a temporary replacement while

*Izvestiia* made the arrangements for a new permanent correspondent. Few of Kondrashov's colleagues from the old days still worked in the United States. In 1980, Boris Strel'nikov had died from a heart attack on a train en route to his new assignment in London. Genrikh Borovik no longer worked as special foreign correspondent for *Literaturnaia Gazeta* and Novosti Press Agency; he now dedicated himself to theater, film, and a new TV program on foreign affairs called *The Camera Is Looking into the World*. Kondrashov himself was now *Izvestiia*'s senior political commentator and a frequent presenter on *The International Panorama*—a popular weekly TV magazine on foreign affairs. Kondrashov's 1982 assignment to the US came at a time when Soviet-American relations were at one of their lowest points in years. Commentators on both sides, including Kondrashov, worried that the world might be on the brink of nuclear war.[126] Not since the late 1940s had the international sections of the Soviet newspapers been so entirely dominated by articles on the military threat posed by the United States.[127] Arriving in New York in October 1982, Kondrashov found few reasons to remain optimistic. Seeing the rift in Soviet-American relations, Kondrashov also wondered whether the twenty-odd years he had dedicated to reporting on the US had really mattered and whether he had ever managed to bring about a better understanding between the two sides.[128]

The cohort of Cold War correspondents who had ushered a new style into Soviet international reporting in the wake of Stalin's death and spent more than twenty years reporting on the United States were now mostly Moscow-based. Nevertheless, they remained highly influential in the Soviet media landscape as international editors and senior political commentators. They also continued to reach out to readers by writing books and exploring new formats such as television, documentaries, theater, and fiction. International correspondents remained active in their country's foreign policy circles and participated in their contemporaries' efforts to influence the aging leadership. Several generations of Soviet readers had encountered and understood America through the eyes of journalists who belonged to the *shestidesiatniki* generation. Their analyses of the United States had been decisively shaped by this generation's shared ethos: a combination of Marxist universalism, Thaw humanism, and faith in the power of the written word to enlighten and educate the public. Journalists first reached out to readers from the pages of the newspapers and, when those were not enough to contain the breadth and depth of their knowledge and impressions, through alternative formats such as long essays and books. It was in these alternative formats that Soviet correspondents finally came to realize the ideal coverage of America as imagined in the early Cold War years by writers such as Konstantin Simonov and Boris Polevoi. Foreign correspondents spent many years living in the US, spoke good English, were well traveled, and were attuned to local social, political, and cultural currents. Their criticism of the "American way of life" was no longer based on slogans, proclamations, or ideological postulates designed in Moscow by Agitprop or the Ministry of Foreign Affairs. Rather, it was composed of local vignettes and individual human interest stories, of detailed episodic observations of America that were then translated into larger universalized tales about the essence of socialism and capitalism. Soviet reporting about the United States flourished even when Soviet-American relations did not. Writing about America was central to the journalists' efforts to engage their public and to their self-understanding as socialist writers and engineers of the human souls.

As the time went by, the journalists and their readers had fewer and fewer things in common. Years spent overseas and the privileged access to international travel, information, and commodities that foreign correspondents enjoyed as members of the Soviet elite had set them apart from many of their compatriots, especially the younger ones. As the mobilizing power of socialist ideology began to wane and the state's promises to match Western standards of living rang increasingly hollow, many readers began to turn to alternative sources of information about the world and developed their own ways of interacting with the journalists' work.

Overwhelmed by thoughts and impressions, Kondrashov transformed the diary entries he wrote during and immediately after his 1982 American assignment into a book-length essay reflecting on his professional career and on Soviet-American relations in the nuclear age. Although he completed the book in 1984, more than two years passed before he published it. It appeared in 1986 under the title *The Americanist's Journey* and featured a hopeful postscript that marked the arrival of a new era.

# CHAPTER SIX

# Reports from the Backward East

In 1976, more than twenty years after the publication of his *American in Russia*, Harrison Salisbury reviewed two recent books by correspondents fresh out of Moscow and proclaimed, "The simultaneous appearance of two such excellent reports on Russia is a double blessing and, incidentally, a remarkable demonstration of the ability of American reporters to crack the famous enigma wrapped in a riddle—as Winston Churchill liked to characterize Russia."[1] The "excellent reports" were *The Russians,* by the former *New York Times* Moscow bureau chief Hedrick Smith, and *Russia: The People and the Power,* by his counterpart at the *Washington Post,* Robert Kaiser. Both worked in the Soviet Union from 1971 to 1974. Both took advantage of the Soviet-American détente, and both managed to complete their tours even though their reporting often displeased the Soviets.

Tall, handsome, and boisterous, Smith was recruited to the *Times* in 1962 by James (Scotty) Reston, the influential head of the Washington bureau. Since joining the *Times,* Smith reported on the civil rights movement in the South, did two stints as a foreign correspondent in Vietnam and in Cairo, and held the prestigious post of diplomatic correspondent in the Washington bureau. After Smith received a job offer from CBS in 1969, Reston asked him what sort of assignment would keep him at the *Times.* Smith replied that he wanted to go to Moscow—"Everest" for journalists. Reston picked up the phone, called Harvard University, and asked them to consider a late submission for a Nieman Fellowship. Within a few months, Hedrick Smith was in Cambridge, where he studied Russian language, history, economics, foreign policy, and literature with leading specialists in the field. In the spring of 1971, Smith was called to New York to work on the Pentagon Papers. Throughout, he continued with his language training.[2] The Smiths—Hedrick, his wife, Ann, and their children—arrived in Moscow in the summer of 1971. Within a few days, Smith realized that "the one investment that clearly was worth every expensive penny that the *Times* put into it was language training."[3] The *Times*'s senior management must have shared Smith's viewpoint, especially in 1974, after he won the Pulitzer Prize for International Reporting for his coverage of the Soviet Union and the socialist bloc.

Robert Kaiser, a dashing, ambitious, and brilliant youth, joined the *Washington Post* as a summer intern while still attending college. He was only twenty-one when he began working as the *Post*'s correspondent in London, a job he held while pursuing his master's degree at the London School of Economics. The legendary editor Ben Bradlee, who joined the *Post* while Kaiser was in London, was impressed with Kaiser's work without even knowing how young his "London byline" really was. In 1970, when Kaiser returned to the US from a year-and-a-half-long assignment in Vietnam, he was asked where he wanted to go next. Kaiser said that he wanted to go to Moscow, on the condition that the *Post* would let him take language training before his departure. The *Post*'s foreign editor, Philip Foisie, used his connections at Columbia University to secure a fellowship, which allowed Kaiser and his wife, Hannah, to take a special course that crammed two years of college-level Russian into one.[4] The Kaisers arrived in Moscow to reopen a bureau that had been vacant for several months and that had a troubled record with the Soviets. In 1969, the *Post*'s bureau chief, Anatole Shub, had been expelled for his coverage of the Soviet dissident movement, while Kaiser's immediate predecessor, Anthony Astrachan, had left in spring 1971 following a series of warnings for his reporting on dissidents. Kaiser therefore faced the challenging task of keeping the bureau intact while upholding its tradition of covering the opposition to the Soviet regime. In 1974 Kaiser won the Overseas Press Club award for best reporting from abroad.

The two journalists had much in common. Before coming to Moscow, both spent time reporting from Vietnam—the unfortunate new forge of American foreign correspondents. Both insisted on undergoing extensive training in the Russian language before their departure—a relatively uncommon practice for American journalists until then.[5] Their books were often reviewed in tandem, were featured together on the nonfiction bestseller lists, and won important awards.[6] The books reflected the characters of their writers: while Smith's account was sharp and animated, Kaiser's was thoughtful and level-headed. The Moscow assignment, and the celebrated books that emerged as a result, established both Smith and Kaiser as important commentators on Soviet affairs and paved the way for distinguished journalistic careers after Moscow.

Smith and Kaiser became the most recognizable representatives of a cohort of American journalists who reported from Moscow starting from

Khrushchev's ouster, through the Soviet-American détente, to the advent of Gorbachev's reforms. By the mid-1960s the press corps was restored to its prewar capacity, boasting between twenty-two and twenty-five permanent members. The importance of the Soviet Union as a maker of international news, the challenging conditions of the assignment, and the American public's enormous interest in all things Soviet made the Moscow posting attractive to the best reporters of the generation. Almost every year saw publication of a new book by an American correspondent just out of Moscow. For many journalists, the Soviet assignment (and the long-form accounts they produced after returning home) became a springboard for distinguished careers in the world of media or foreign policy. All these factors made the period between 1965 and 1985 a golden era of American reporting from the Soviet Union.

In contrast to the early Cold War days, journalists now arrived with their families. The presence of spouses (most correspondents were men) and children gave journalists new insights into Soviet society and offered new opportunities to interact with the Soviet people. Playground conversations with local parents or grandparents, visits to the doctor, teacher-parent conferences, and shopping in local shops helped journalists gain a different perspective on Soviet life. Reporting from the Soviet Union often became a family adventure whereby parents and children exchanged experiences, observations, and daily insights that made up the fabric of journalists' stories.[7] Soviet authorities opened new areas for journalists to travel to, and the Press Department expanded the range of press conferences, organized trips, and events for international correspondents. Novosti Press Agency, now in charge of accommodating foreign journalists, helped with travel plans and facilities. Further concessions were made in travel and access during the détente and following the 1975 Helsinki Accords.[8] Finally, the proliferation of Soviet dissident groups gave the journalists unprecedented critical "inside" access to Soviet society.

This is not to say that Moscow correspondents enjoyed working conditions similar to those of their colleagues in Western Europe or even elsewhere in the socialist bloc. Journalists and their families still lived in foreigners' compounds—specially designated buildings usually located in prestigious quarters of central Moscow. Local policemen were posted at the entrances of every such building—ostensibly to ensure safety, but in reality to screen the comings and goings of the residents and their visitors. Forming local friendships remained difficult, and journalists' social interactions were usually confined to the expatriate and diplomatic communities. Outside the foreigner colony, the only meaningful social relationships correspondents were able to

*Figure 6.1.* The Moscow staff of the Associated Press pose for a group portrait in Red Square on March 11, 1965. *From left to right*: Photographer Brian Calvert from the London bureau, translator Boris Zagoruiko, driver Nikolai Samoilov, translator Tamara Devyatkina, newsman George Syversten, translator Emilia Taubkina, Chief of Bureau Henry S. Bradsher, teleprinter operator Vladimir Firsov, newsman Fred Coleman, photographer Vasily Gritsan. (Photo: AP Photo/Associated Press Corporate Archives.)

develop were with Soviet dissidents and nonconformists, who were willing to take greater risks and face the consequences of their interactions with American journalists. Securing access to Soviet officials, gaining permission to cover certain stories, and writing features about "average people" remained notoriously difficult and were often subject to official whim. For example, Hedrick Smith's application to travel to Kazakhstan to cover the harvest was denied for two years in a row.⁹ Journalists whose connections with dissidents displeased the Soviet authorities faced surveillance, harassment, and, at times, expulsion.

Inspired in part by these peculiarities of the Soviet scene and in part by the rise of investigative and socially mobilized reporting in the United States, American correspondents saw it as their professional duty to uncover the truth about Soviet life, which they believed the Soviet regime was desperately trying to hide. Between 1965 and 1985, American reporting from the USSR emphasized the oppressive apparatus of the Soviet state, described the failures of Soviet institutions, and focused on the faults in Soviet standards of living. A new narrative stressing the erosion of Soviet citizens' commitment to the socialist ideology highlighted the competitive advantages of American liberal capitalism over Soviet-style socialism. In this context, the long-form accounts journalists wrote after their return home enjoyed a renaissance and assumed new political significance. Only after returning to the United States, the journalists explained, were they truly free to express their opinions of the Soviet state and to shed light on what life there was really like.

## Investigative Reporters in the Land of the Soviets

The rebellious spirit of the 1960s transformed journalism's role in American society and journalists' relationship with the US government. Journalists played a pivotal role in the turmoil of the 1960s and the 1970s. Coverage of the civil rights movement and the war in Vietnam, as well as the exposure of the Pentagon Papers and the Watergate scandal, brought these contested issues into every household and increasingly put the press in opposition to the governing elites. The triumphs of investigative journalism also elevated the prestige of the profession and reinforced the idea of a "fourth branch of government"—it appeared that journalism had the power to transform politics and society. The atmosphere of the early Cold War, when the press mobilized to support the US government and its interests, was no longer tenable. More and more voices in the profession claimed that the journalists' duty was to protect the public, to act as the government's watchdog, and to help rectify social injustice with their reporting.¹⁰

In fact, many of the triumphs of investigative reporting in the 1960s occurred on the Cold War front. In 1960, the Moscow bureau of the Associated Press broke the story of the Soviet shooting down of the U-2 spy plane, which the Eisenhower administration attempted to cover up.¹¹ The most radical clash between journalists and the national security state occurred in Vietnam, where the government and the news media's senior editors initially attempted to squelch reports about American troops' violence against civilians. Incidentally, Harrison Salisbury was one of the first journalists who clashed with editors and civil servants over his reporting from Vietnam.[12] The government's attempts to silence news from Southeast Asia worked to amplify the importance of eyewitness reporting from all around the world.[13]

The rotation of foreign correspondents from one international hot spot to the next brought investigative reporting into American coverage of the Soviet Union. Interviewed in 2010, Robert Kaiser made an explicit connection between investigative journalism at home and abroad:

> In Washington, as we know from the history of this newspaper, we can find out important things that could bring down the government. I didn't have any such ambition in the Soviet Union. But because of the fog created by Churchill and that whole view of the Soviet Union, that it was a mystery and we could never figure it out, my challenge was to resolve the mystery. It was to say, "No, this can be figured out." Not in the sense of knowing the names of all the Soviet Union's spies or all the secrets of the Politburo, but more in the sense of how this system really works, what matters, what doesn't, and why things happen the way they do.[14]

In Kaiser's case, the object of his investigative gaze was the Soviet system as a whole, which made him interested in everything—from the structure of the Soviet government to what the average person had for lunch. What ignited Kaiser's curiosity, first and foremost, was Russia's perpetual status as an unknown, a mystery: "We were in America, as they were in the Soviet Union, the victims of stereotypes and misleading notions about what the other guy was really like. So I had a lot of fun, always, writing about unexpected things and trying to explain to Americans that this was just a different kind of human organization and enterprise. But it was recognizably human, and the people in it were, too."[15]

Both Kaiser and Smith, whose work in Moscow coincided with the détente in superpower relations, related their quest for a more nuanced understanding of Soviet society to the reduction of tensions between the US and the Soviet Union.[16] However, their goal—to understand what Russia was really like—was shared by each new generation of American correspondents in Moscow, including those who would succeed them in the press corps. In part, this continuity derived from the journalist's professional imperative to remain in tune with the times and to report on the most recent developments. At the same time, the idea of Russia as an impenetrable mystery and a closed society

had become so ingrained in the American collective consciousness that it superseded the reports produced by individual journalists. Moreover, from the
mid-1960s onward, it was often foreign correspondents themselves who
contributed to this impression by presenting their reporting as unveiling
the perpetually hidden "real Russia." The ethos of investigative reporting fit
well with the journalists' growing conviction that the Soviet authorities were
trying to prevent them from learning the truth about life in the USSR. More
and more correspondents became convinced that uncovering those hidden
truths was their professional duty, and they began to direct their investigative
efforts at what, in their view, were the most fundamental aspects of everyday
life.

　　The ethos of liberal watchdog journalism, which seeks to uncover hidden
realities, scrutinize the government, and rectify wrongdoing, was bound to
clash with Soviet information policies and, at times, the Soviet culture of hospitality. Foreign correspondents were invariably frustrated by the requirement to seek official permission to travel, by Soviet officials' reluctance to respond to questions about the problems facing the Soviet system, and by their
inability "to communicate with intelligent non-dissidents."[17] Soviet officials
treated American journalists' requests to travel or meet with various post hold-
ers with suspicion. Applications for individual travel were often denied without explanation, and correspondents were told instead to apply for group trips
organized by Novosti Press Agency. The number of participants in such tours
was often limited, and journalists with a history of criticizing the Soviet establishment were often barred from participation.[18] When on tour, reporters
found that they seldom could roam free and talk to whomever they wanted.
Journalists complained that the tours were heavily orchestrated and that they
were conducted from site to site, from one official meeting to the next, from
one lavish meal to another. The Soviet hosts—for many of whom this was
their first encounter with foreigners—were also keen to put up the best show
for their guests, showcasing local achievements and concealing shortcomings.
The visiting correspondents assumed that these arrangements had sinister
motives, and they could not shake off the impression that their hosts were trying to hide something.[19] For example, in their eagerness to impress their foreign guests and give them the best possible welcome, the Soviet hosts often laid
out lavish receptions, as per the Russian tradition of treating guests with the
best things one had to offer. Foreign correspondents, noticing that these receptions offered foods seldom available to the average Soviet shopper, interpreted their hosts' efforts as an attempt to create a false impression of what life

in the Soviet Union was really like or even saw these as manifestations of a Russian sense of inferiority vis-à-vis foreigners.

The myth of the Potemkin village framed journalists' expectations of official trips, as well as their efforts to make sense of their interactions in the Soviet Union. The myth takes its name from Count Grigorii Potemkin, who allegedly constructed cardboard villages in advance of Catherine the Great's naval tour of Crimea in 1787, to bedazzle Catherine and impress on the accompanying foreign dignitaries how well developed Russia's new domains were.[20] Over time, the idea of the Potemkin village became an idiom for presenting a false picture, a glossy veneer to hide something's true state. The idiom is especially associated with perceptive foreigners who were able to discern the shabby Russian reality behind the official attempts to impress them with fake displays. As Michael David-Fox observed, the Potemkin village became such an enduring myth precisely because it reflected oft-recurring political practices and engaged the notions of superiority and inferiority that underlined the relationship between Russia and the West for more than three hundred years.[21] Indeed, foreign correspondents often turned to the story of the Potemkin village to demonstrate that their experiences had historical precedent, thereby giving a better grounding to their frustrations. Whether or not they questioned the veracity of the Potemkin story itself, foreign correspondents treated it as an important indicator of the Russian national character. "Potemkinism seems to be a Russian trait that predates by centuries the birth of Prince Grigory Potemkin," wrote *Newsweek*'s John Dornberg.[22] The myth offered journalists a framework that tapped into both their reporting experiences and their position as investigative reporters, who endeavored to lift the official façade and discover the true state of life in the USSR.

The Soviet hosts, though, never abandoned their hopes, dating back to the dawn of the Soviet era, of winning over visiting correspondents with their ideas and their plans for a better future.[23] They asked journalists to take a leap of faith, associated with socialist realist art, and to appreciate the achievements that had already been made as well as the Soviet designs for a bright future. Refusing to be impressed, American journalists criticized the Soviet state for failing to live up to its promise to deliver a lifestyle comparable to that of the West. "We don't give them a great deal of credit. And they want credit that they don't deserve. As a result, the gap is enormous between what they want and what we give them," reflected Peter Osnos of the *Washington Post*.[24]

Several correspondents recognized the differences in the two superpowers' approach to journalism and did their best to report about Soviet life despite

*Figure 6.2.* A press conference organized by the Press Department of the Soviet Ministry of Foreign Affairs for Soviet and foreign journalists, October 1, 1969. (Photo: Tishenko/Sputnik Images.)

the challenging circumstances. Many journalists believed that Soviet information policies were explicitly targeting their freedom to report truthfully, a belief that dovetailed with their expectations of a closed society that sought to shield itself from international scrutiny.[25] Popular books and article series produced by foreign correspondents after they returned home highlighted the difficulties of reporting from Moscow and the obstacles Soviet officials erected before journalists whose only desire was to do their job. Foreign correspondents stressed that it was impossible to interact with "regular Soviet people" without official supervision, and they described in detail Soviet attempts to discredit enterprising journalists and obstruct their access to Soviet life.[26] Stories about the difficult working conditions experienced by Moscow correspondents contributed to the impression that the journalists were doing important investigative work and unveiling the hidden Soviet reality.

Many journalists were well aware of how Soviet information policies influenced their reporting on Soviet society. "There is a tendency among westerners to take a kind of ideological position when they write about the Soviet Union. We tend to reflect our own personal distaste for this kind of a system, and think it comes through," explained Osnos.[27] Although Osnos was not alone in observing the potential biases of American journalists against the Soviet system, this kind of self-reflection was rare, and it seldom featured in the journalists' written reports. What the public read came across as the objective results of a journalist's dogged efforts to shed light on what the Soviets wanted to keep hidden, the fruits of a reporter's relentless investigation of how Soviet everyday life really worked.

Despite the investigative ethos, in many ways the long-form accounts produced by American correspondents in those years resembled in principle their Soviet colleagues' writing about the United States. Both Soviet and American journalists criticized the rival's political system for betraying its own people; the Soviets exposed the empty promises of the "American way of life," and the Americans revealed the false vision of the socialist utopia. Soviet and American correspondents alike seldom dealt with abstract generalizations; they explored daily life in the host country through the stories of people they met or read about in the local press. In so doing, both Soviet and American journalists frequently drew on the experiences of the most unhappy or disenfranchised. Both sets of correspondents invited audiences to contrast reports about life on the other side with daily experiences in their own country. The major difference was that in Soviet accounts the invitation to read comparatively was usually implicit and embedded in the overall fabric of postwar culture, while American journalists often drew explicit parallels between daily lives in the USSR and the United States.

The question of whether Americans and Soviets could find common ground preoccupied American correspondents as much as it did their Soviet colleagues. However, in American reporting this question often developed into an implicit inquiry that had animated US observers of Russia since the nineteenth century: Could the Russians become more like us?[28] While presuming a potential similarity between the Americans and the Russians, this question also rested on the premise that the United States was the superior civilization and that the Russians were an altogether different breed of people to be examined and analyzed. By returning to this question and drawing parallels between the Soviet Union and the United States, each successive generation of US correspondents reflected on their own society and on America's place in a fast-changing world.

## The Unimaginable Plight of Soviet Everyday Life

In 1972, on the eve of President Richard Nixon's visit to the Soviet Union, the *Christian Science Monitor* published a series of five articles by its Moscow correspondent Charlotte Saikowski. Addressing each piece "Dear Mr. President,"

Saikowski's series offered "an American's" perspective on "some of the basics about Soviet life [. . .] how Russians work, how they view their government, how they spend their leisure, what they see on television."[29] In the first installment, titled "Russians Rarely Worry about Losing Their Jobs," Saikowski told her readers that although Soviet everyday life "is still generally drab and often lacking in simple necessities," most Russians were convinced that socialism was "morally superior," and they took pride in the progress their country had made since the revolution.[30] Saikowski had arrived in Moscow in 1969. Born in Chicago, she was fluent in Polish and Russian. Having spent time teaching English and studying violin in postwar Warsaw, she spent ten years working at the *Current Digest of the Soviet Press*. Respected for her generous, level-headed attitude and her expertise in Soviet affairs, Saikowski got along with her Soviet hosts and the American press corps alike. Her series "How Russians Live" was published by the *Monitor* and then reprinted in many newspapers across the nation.[31]

Ten years later, shortly after President Ronald Reagan had won the election—in part by campaigning against détente—*Washington Post* correspondent Kevin Klose visited Donetsk, a major mining city in the Ukrainian SSR, to interview local workers and residents. Traveling with a dissident friend, mining engineer Alexei Nikitin, Klose visited a housing complex for retired miners. Klose was dismayed to discover that none of the apartments had running water or functioning lavatories and that elderly residents had to rely on a "community well in a weed-choked field" and "foul-smelling, rough-hewn outhouses."[32] The visit left Klose appalled with the living conditions experienced by regular Soviet people. His article series on Donetsk exposed the glaring gaps between the proclamations of Soviet propaganda and the daily lives of Soviet workers and described how Nikitin's efforts to improve the lot of the local miners were brutally repressed by the state. Klose's series were so damning that the *Washington Post* published an editorial condemning the Soviet regime for its treatment of Nikitin and his fellow workers.[33]

Almost ten years—and radically different political climates—separated Saikowski's and Klose's accounts. What persisted was the two journalists' interest in the most mundane aspects of Soviet everyday life, an interest shared by their contemporaries and predecessors alike. Saikowski's and Klose's approaches to Soviet society and their overall conclusions represented two opposite ends of the spectrum. As the years progressed, the tone of reports about Soviet daily life, especially in long-form accounts, grew harsher, and journalists' assessments became more critical. This shift derived from the logic of Soviet commitments on the one hand and the investigative ethos of American reporting on the other. For years, Soviet Cold War propaganda had promised that the USSR would "reach and surpass" the United States. By the late 1960s, the Soviet failure to realize these promises became apparent, especially in view of the public's growing demands for better consumer goods and higher standards of living.[34] Foreign correspondents captured these frustrations with the system's inability to fulfill the public's needs. At the same time, the professional imperative to examine the Soviet regime carefully and expose its wrongdoings often pushed journalists to adopt a harsher, more scrutinizing position.

While reports about the hardships of Soviet daily life featured prominently in American coverage throughout the postwar years, new elements entered these stories in the late 1960s. Previously, journalists had compared their observations of Soviet living standards with those of prerevolutionary Russia or the immediate postwar years. They had emerged from these comparisons convinced that life in the Soviet Union had greatly improved over the years. Many journalists in the late 1950s had also pointed out that the Soviet people themselves were for the most part content with the material state of their lives and believed that it would improve in the future.[35] In the late 1960s, correspondents began to contrast everyday life in the Soviet Union and in the United States. When journalists encountered statements expressing satisfaction with Soviet standards of living, they often interpreted them as examples of Russian lack of knowledge about the world or fear of criticizing the regime.[36] Moreover, in the late 1960s reports on Soviet everyday life became linked to an important new theme: Soviet people's loss of faith in the socialist ideology. Journalists began to point to the inferiority of the Soviet standards of living and consumer culture as the source of mass disillusionment with socialist ideas. The state's failure to fulfill its promise and deliver a lifestyle comparable to that of capitalist countries was presented as eroding popular support in the Soviet project itself.[37]

American correspondents explored at great length the purchasing power of salaries; the conditions of housing, schools, and hospitals; and the availability of consumer goods in Soviet stores. In describing the everyday lives of average Soviets, journalists stressed the gaps between official propaganda and their own eyewitness observations. While recognizing the appeal of benefits such as free housing, health care, and universal education, foreign correspondents explained that in reality the Soviet welfare state was plagued by serious problems. Universal housing, they showed, usually meant a total lack of privacy:

a room in a communal apartment might host three generations living together. They pointed out that the health care system was under such strain
that it failed to provide decent treatment. The idea of free universal education, journalists reported, also collapsed under closer scrutiny, given that
greasing the palm of someone on the admissions committee increased one's
chances of entering a prestigious university. Moreover, foreign correspondents
explained, the socialist system's inability to meet the basic needs of its people
had set in motion a whole economy of corruption, which contributed to the
erosion of confidence in state institutions.[38]

The Soviet store figured as the major symbol of the challenges faced by regular Soviet people on a daily basis. Although Soviet consumer culture had
attracted correspondents' attention since the dawn of the Cold War, in the late
1960s journalists' scrutiny of Soviet stores became more intense and comparison with American stores more frequent. Journalists often pointed out that
American readers could not even begin to imagine the plight of Soviet consumers. The following fragment, from an account by *Christian Science Monitor* correspondent David K. Willis, explained that the daily task of food shopping in the Soviet Union could be a gruesome experience: "I went down two
steps into a dark room. Shelves were almost empty. The floor was filthy. The
white coats on the sales assistants had not been laundered for some time, if
ever. Large bottles containing various pickled parts of unnamed animals stood
here and there. A single twenty-watt bulb without a shade provided the only
light."[39] Willis concluded his description by observing, "By Western standards,
much of what the Soviet Union sells as meat to ordinary citizens is almost in-
edible."[40] Willis's emphasis on his dismay upon encountering such squalor
was not unique. Vivid language was often used to describe, down to the smallest detail, the limited variety of produce in Soviet shops and its inferior quality, the shortages of goods or foods, and the complicated queuing system. Most
correspondents ascribed the dire state of Soviet stores to the inefficiency of the
state, the absence of free market competition, and the malfunctioning of the
planned economy.[41] Some, like Hedrick Smith, invited their readers to appreciate the advantages of their own lives by comparing their experiences
with those of Soviet consumers: "the figures do not begin to convey the tex-
ture of Soviet consumer life, and the enormous gulf between the daily ordeal
of the Russian shopper and the easy life-style of Americans. My Russian
friends were amused to hear about the American suburban housewives getting into the station wagon and dashing off to the supermarket or shopping
center for groceries a couple of times a week."[42] Writing in 1976, Hedrick

Smith surely knew that the "suburban housewife" was by no means represen-tative of American society. Yet his and others' use of the middle class to refer to the American experience as a whole was consistent with the way the United States projected its own image at home and abroad.[43] Throughout the twentieth century, but especially during the Cold War, consumer plenty be-came a central pillar in the construction of "American exceptionalism."[44] Detailed descriptions of the long lines and empty stores in the Soviet Union invited American audiences to imagine themselves as a nation unified by a high standard of living. Beyond the traditional importance of consumerism in Cold War rhetoric, these accounts had a special significance in the mid-1970s, when the United States was going through its first recession since the Second World War.[45] The vivid picture of Soviet shoppers' plight reinforced readers' faith in the strength of the US economy and its ultimate advantages.

American correspondents' critiques of Soviet consumption suggested that material abundance and consumer plenty were universally important. The So-viet people's apparent readiness to do with much less was portrayed as a dis-tinctive mark of the Russian national character. As Hedrick Smith explained: "The regime has failed to make good on all kinds of promises, yet Russian consumers are appeased if there is a steady supply of bread, cabbage, potatoes, and vodka, an occasional shipment of oranges, and a chance once in a while to go to a Western movie. They will settle for less than consumers in any other industrialized nation—and that is an important element of the regime's stabil-ity."[46] Soviet people's unwillingness to challenge the regime's policies, even if it meant having a limited variety of inferior goods, ostensibly set them apart from consumers and citizens in the West. The observations of the Soviet people's willingness to put up with scarcity went hand in hand with descriptions of their insatiable desire for, and fascination with, Western consumer goods.[47] Like the descriptions of Soviet stores, stories of Soviets' passion for blue jeans and foreign records showcased the ultimate advantages of the American eco-nomic model and the political system that enabled it.

On a deeper level, reporting about Soviet everyday life challenged decades-old American ideas about the Soviet threat. Foreign correspondents often stressed that the dire Soviet reality undermined the official propaganda state-ments about Soviet triumph over the West. David K. Willis explained: "Above the clouds circled Soviet space capsules and killer satellites. In their remote bun-kers sat ICBM missiles. Down on earth, in the capital city of Communism itself, which is allocated the best food and consumer goods in the country, soldiers and mothers stood in the slush for thirty minutes or more to buy candy available

*Figure 6.3.* Pilot-cosmonaut Vladimir Shatalov (*second from left*) shows Soviet space technology to US journalists, 1973. (Photo: Alexander Mokletsov/Sputnik Images.)

in even the most ordinary shops in most of the rest of the world."[48] The gap between the advanced military-industrial complex and the backward standard of living vividly illustrated socialism's failure to deliver the good life it promised. That failure, in journalists' view, was the Soviet regime's biggest secret, which it found increasingly hard to keep "behind the Potemkin-village front of its propaganda."[49] To be sure, the contrast between Soviet military technologies and standards of living had been a fixture in American reporting since the mid-1950s. In the wake of Sputnik and Khrushchev's Thaw, foreign correspondents used this contrast to illustrate America's continuous superiority in the superpower confrontation and thus to alleviate readers' fears of the Soviet Union. However, the idea that the Soviet Union posed a threat to the United States was never called into question until the late 1960s, when journalists used this gap to challenge the very notion of the Soviet menace.

Robert Kaiser, for example, emphasized that the dysfunctionality of Soviet institutions and the state of the Soviet economy were reassuring signs to American audiences because they offered undeniable evidence for why the United States needed *not* fear the Soviet Union.[50] A close look at Soviet realities, he argued, revealed that the USSR was encumbered by internal shortcomings to such an extent that it was incapable of posing a serious challenge to the United States:

> And this is the country which has frightened us for nearly sixty years, which convinced us to invest billions in an arms race without end, which established itself as the second super-power and a threat to peace in the minds of several generations of western statesmen. That this has been possible, given their egregious weakness, is a great tribute to the men who have ruled the Soviet Union. But this is also a tribute to our foolishness. [. . .] we have given the Russians more than due credit for military prowess, and ignored their failings in economic and technological development, social organization and the rest. We have defined strength and power in purely military terms—favorable to the Soviet Union— and then exaggerated Soviet power.[51]

Moscow correspondents were well aware that members of Congress, State Department officials, and CIA analysts were following their reports closely.[52] Journalists hoped that their experience on the ground would improve American assessments of the Soviet Union and lead to the formation of more realistic tactics. Kaiser challenged the mainstream opinion of his day and the view that the "Soviet menace" justified continued expenditures on the armament race. Kaiser urged his compatriots, including policy makers, to see that America had the ultimate lead in the superpower contest and implied that national attention and funds should be diverted elsewhere.

This advice, however, was ignored. In 1976, the Committee on the Present Danger (CPD), a foreign policy pressure group, commissioned a select team of conservative public figures to assess the Soviet threat. The resulting document, known as the Team B report, criticized the CIA for underestimating the Soviet threat, stated that the Soviet Union had a strategic superiority over the United States, and offered a bleak view of the US capability to contain the USSR in the future. The report was based on limited evidence, yet its analysis, and the resulting calls to increase investments in countering the Soviet threat, dominated the national headlines in the winter of 1976–1977, not long after Kaiser's book was published.[53] The emphasis on the Soviet threat and the public traction of the Team B report eventually worked to undermine the Strategic Arms

Limitation Talks (SALT) II agreement. In 1980, Ronald Reagan, who was closely associated with several CPD and Team B members and had campaigned on the promise to restore American military greatness and step up containment of the Soviet threat, was elected president of the United States.[54]

On the face of it, the American journalists' descriptions of Soviet everyday life were devoid of ideological bias. Foreign correspondents emphasized that theirs were eyewitness reports of Soviet realities and of Soviet people's actual experiences. Yet written and read, as they were, in the context of the superpowers' ideological confrontation, these reports had broader political meaning. Stories about Soviet citizens scrambling for commodities, craving Western products, and ceasing to care about socialist principles highlighted the strength of US economy and suggested that material culture and consumer plenty were the true measures of a good life. Appraising Soviet everyday life against the living standards of the American middle class glossed over a reality where high-quality education, healthcare, and housing, remained out of reach for many Americans. Inevitably, journalists' conclusions about the backwardness of the Soviet standards of living and the popular loss of faith in the socialist ideology illustrated the superiority of the American political and economic system—precisely when its own foundational principles were being contested at home.

## "Eternal Russia"

Foreign correspondents agreed that the Soviet system was stable and unlikely to collapse anytime soon despite its many shortcomings and the declining faith in socialist ideas. To explain this puzzle, journalists usually turned to the past. The features of the Soviet state and the behavior of Soviet citizens, they argued, were rooted in the specifics of Russian history. While the contents of such explanations varied, journalists usually relied on a set of pseudo-historical notions that might collectively be referred to as the idea of Eternal Russia.

Journalists explained that Russia's historical development differed significantly from that of the West, resulting in authoritarian political culture, submissive national character, and a widespread aversion to change. The Communists, foreign correspondents argued, had not changed Russia in any fundamental way.[55] John Dornberg, who imprinted this idea into the very title of his book—*The New Tsars*—explained that contemporary Soviet customs were shaped not as much by socialism as by the "legacy of a millennium."[56] To understand the Soviet Union, journalists stressed, one should not look at Marxism or socialist ideology but turn to the Russian past. An important notion embedded in this description was that of Russia's eternal, unchanging nature.[57]

The concluding remarks of Hedrick Smith's best-selling book *The Russians* offer an excellent example of how the concept of Eternal Russia was used as a broad explanation for Soviet realities and are worth quoting at length. According to Smith, the most influential factors in the Soviet political system, and the most powerful impediments for change, were "the deep-seated influence of history on Russian character and institutions—the centralized concentration of power, the fetish of rank, the xenophobia of simple people, the futile carping of alienated intelligentsia, the passionate attachment of the Russians to Mother Russia, the habitual submission of the masses to the Supreme Leader and their unquestioned acceptance of the yawning gulf between the Ruler and the Ruled. The longer I lived in Soviet Russia, the more Russian it seemed to me and hence the less likely to undergo fundamental change."[58]

The particular traits of the Russian national character were forged, enshrined, and perpetuated by history itself. In contrast to people elsewhere, stressed Smith, the Russians were content with being ruled by an oppressive dictatorship and well suited to it. It was the Russians' aversion to change that set them apart from the West and explained why they did not make an effort to improve their lives and political culture:

> Gradually it came through to me that Russians—unlike Westerners—do not take it for granted that Russian dictatorship must inevitably evolve into democracy for they know its power and its permanence; they recognize its ability to adapt without surrendering the essence; they find comfort in the stability and order that it provides. Fearing what seems to them the chaotic turbulence of Western liberal democracies, most of them do not want democracy for Russia.[59]

Writing during the Soviet-American détente, Hedrick Smith cautioned against excessive optimism and exaggerated hopes for convergence between Russia and the West. Foreign trade or improved diplomatic relations, he stressed, were highly unlikely to generate "grassroots pressure" for more freedom. Smith urged readers to remember that, despite the lack of obvious exotic features, they should not make the mistake of assuming that Russians were "like us":

> here is alien culture, one which did not pass through the Renaissance, Reformation, and the era of constitutional liberalism which shaped the West. But

here is a culture that absorbed Eastern Orthodox Christianity from Byzantium, endured Mongol conquest and rule, and then developed through centuries of czarist absolutism with intermittent periods of opening towards the West followed by withdrawal into continental isolation. [. . .] The forays into the West brought some changes but did not fundamentally dilute the strong authoritarian strain in the Russian body politic in any lasting way. If anything, Western innovations were simply used to reinforce Russian methods.[60]

Whereas every important milestone in the history of the West brought it one step closer to liberal democracy, Russian history had led to the development of an authoritarian state. Russia's embrace of Orthodox Christianity (a religion that, according to Western observers, elevated the sovereign), followed by several hundred years of the Mongol yoke, and a long succession of autocratic monarchs, had had a detrimental effect on the Russian people. The Russian national character, journalists contended, had developed in these historical and political circumstances, rendering the Russian people accustomed to authoritarian rule and fearful of change. In Robert Kaiser's words, "thinking about what Russians are like can be made easier by considering what they are not like—us."[61]

There was considerable novelty in this analysis of Russian history, which challenged the conventional wisdom of the time. As David Foglesong has shown, from the late nineteenth century onward US relations with Russia had been permeated by hopes and aspirations to remake Russia in America's image, and by the assumption that Russia would inevitably follow in America's footsteps and adopt the same economic and political system. Idealistic hopes for Russian "liberation" from Communism often focused on consumer goods, supposing that images of American abundance and living standards would impress on the Soviet people the advantages of capitalism and liberal democracy.[62] Thus, for example, in a 1977 radio interview, Ronald Reagan evoked the gap between the "Soviet military machine" and the scarcity of consumer goods and famously suggested: "We could have an unexpected ally if citizen Ivan is becoming discontented enough to start talking back. Maybe we should drop a few million typical mail-order catalogues on Minsk & Pinsk & Moscow to whet their appetites."[63] Foreign correspondents, in contrast, asked their contemporaries to acknowledge that Russia had a unique historical path and that its transformation in America's image, through consumerism or otherwise, was highly unlikely. The Russians were not craving liberation from the communist yoke, nor were they eagerly awaiting the coming of democracy. Somewhat ironically, this conception of Russian history and the emphasis on its importance were pseudo-historical. In the journalists' rendition, history was an impediment to change rather than a vehicle for it. Russian history appeared in these accounts as a pickle jar preserving the Russian "national character." This was a frozen history, a constant that originated in a distant past, replicated itself in the present, and would likely last in the future.

To reinforce their claims, journalists turned to historical precedents. They stressed the parallels between their own observations and the experiences of Western visitors to the tsarist empire, noting how little Russia had changed over the years.[64] John Dornberg, who dedicated the concluding chapter of his book to such parallels, told his readers that Russia "has remained remarkably unchanged from the sixteenth century to the twentieth."[65] Like the travelers to tsarist Russia, American journalists in the Soviet Union found a country where "for centuries secrecy, police surveillance, rewriting of history, the omnipotence and arrogance of rulers, adherence to a doctrinaire ideology, idleness, poverty and Potemkinism have been institutionalized."[66] The gaze of the historical traveler merged with that of the contemporary observer, creating a picture of seamless continuity and impressing upon the readers the notion that Russia, unlike the West, remained impervious to time and to change.

The most important and most frequently cited account to demonstrate such continuities was the 1839 travel narrative *Empire of the Czar*, written by a French observer, Astolphe-Louis-Léonor, Marquis de Custine. De Custine had traveled to Russia after the French Revolution in search of examples to bolster his objection to representative government. However, the account he produced criticized the practices of the Russian autocracy and the apparent collaboration of the people in their own oppression. De Custine's most caustic remarks were reserved for the Russian court and the nobility, whom he mocked for hiding their barbarous Asiatic nature under the veneer of European civilization. De Custine used the very same historical arguments listed above to explain his observations, contending that Russia's shortcomings were the result of the backwardness of the Orthodox Church, the years spent under the Mongol rule, and the repressive policies of Peter the Great.[67]

References to de Custine were ubiquitous in the long-form accounts written by American correspondents between 1965 and 1985.[68] John Dornberg, whose book quoted de Custine in the epigraph to the first chapter, stated that no text was "more revealing of the twentieth-century Soviet Union than this nineteenth-century classic."[69] David K. Willis even arranged his entire book as a modern-day parallel to de Custine's report: most chapters opened with a quote from the Marquis's text and then proceeded to demonstrate to readers how Willis's own experience and observations in the 1980s matched de Custine's from a century and a half earlier.

De Custine's *Empire of the Czar* was much beloved in Cold War America.[70] Over the years, it captured the attention of diplomats, journalists, and intellectuals. A new US edition was published in 1951. Its contemporary relevance was helpfully articulated in the title—*Journey for Our Time: The Russian Journals of the Marquis de Custine*—and in the following description on the cover: "An intriguing look at the continuities in Russian politics and society."[71] De Custine's text was translated from French by Phyllis Penn Kohler, who lived in Moscow from 1947 to 1949 together with her husband, a career diplomat and "Russia-watcher," Foy D. Kohler (who would become President Kennedy's ambassador to the USSR in 1962 and a member of a Team B panel in 1976). Foy Kohler's boss, Ambassador Walter Bedell Smith, wrote an introduction to the edition, praising the marquis's account as "the single greatest contribution in helping us to unravel, in part, the mysteries that seem to envelop Russia and the Russians."[72] Stressing the continuity between the Russian past and the Soviet present implied in the title, Smith wrote: "I could have taken many pages verbatim from his journal and, after substituting present-day names and dates for those of a century ago, have sent them to the State Department as my own official reports."[73] De Custine's account, Smith told readers, demonstrated that the Russian people were nothing like their brethren in the West "because wholly different social and political conditions have retarded and perverted their development and set them apart from other civilizations."[74]

When Phyllis Penn Kohler's edition of de Custine's account was published in the United States, the idea of Eternal Russia had just begun to take hold. Among the first cohort of American Cold War correspondents in Moscow, only Harrison Salisbury argued that it was the tsarist past that had decisively shaped the Soviet present. While his colleagues wrote how millions of "freedom-loving Russians" would welcome an alternative to communist brainwashing and oppression, Salisbury told his readers about the all-enduring "Russian character," which remained impervious to "tsar or commissar."[75] Ambassador Walter Bedell Smith himself was also one of the early admirers of the idea of Eternal Russia. Most chapters in Smith's published recollections from his assignment to Moscow began with a quote from Neill S. Brown—the US envoy to Russia between 1850 and 1853. Within each chapter Smith drew explicit parallels between his own experiences and those of his predecessors, past US ambassadors to Imperial Russia and the USSR, highlighting Russia's unchanging nature.[76] By the 1970s, the idea of Eternal Russia had been well established, featuring prominently in the reports of foreign correspondents, academic studies, and the analyses of professional Russia watchers. In 1989, when Kohler's translation appeared in a new edition (this time with introductions by Daniel Boorstin and George F. Kennan), the idea of Eternal Russia was so prominent that it seeped into the very title: *Empire of the Czar: A Journey through Eternal Russia.*[77]

Beyond making Eternal Russia part of mainstream knowledge, its centrality in the reporting of American correspondents had important ramifications for readers' understanding of the Cold War adversary. The notion of Eternal Russia put forward the idea that Soviet reality inevitably derived from Russia's idiosyncratic history and national character, and emphasized the differences between the Soviet Union and the United States. The countless affirmation of Eternal Russia through references to foreigners' experiences, past and present, and the emphasis on Russia's historical separation from the West excluded alternative interpretations of Soviet life. Foreign correspondents were thus only partially successful in bringing the Soviet people closer to their American readers. While many journalistic reports endeavored to dispel the view of the Soviet Union as a dangerous and unknown foreign "other," they also made it difficult for the American public to relate to the Soviet people and understand them on their own terms.

Read comparatively, the long-form accounts of foreign correspondents invited reassuring reflections on contemporary America, particularly welcome after an extraordinarily difficult decade. The counterculture movements of the 1960s posed a serious challenge to accepted manners and morals and laid bare the gaps between generations, races, and classes. The war in Vietnam flooded the nation with feelings of guilt, shame, and doubts about the goodness of America's mission in the world. President Nixon failed to fulfil his pledge to "Bring Us Together." The Watergate scandal further undermined the standing of the nation's leaders and invited troubling ruminations on freedom and democracy in America. Finally, the oil crisis of 1973 brought about the first economic shock since the Second World War. As the cultural products of the time—especially literature and film—vividly demonstrate, many Americans no longer recognized the country they were living in.[78]

Journalists' reports about the difficulties of Soviet life invited readers to imagine the United States as the nation of "a happy middle class," where everyone reaped the fruits of the free-market economy and enjoyed access to a high standard of living and consumer goods. Stories about repression, corruption, and the unchallenged rule of the Communist Party highlighted the political advantages of liberal democracy in the post-Watergate era. The image of a stagnating Russia, unchanged by history, conjured a heartening image of America defined by progress and dynamism. It reinforced the narrative that positioned the US as incessantly striving to improve the lot of the American people and steadily moving toward the resolution of class, racial, and gender inequalities.[79]

## Your Fight Is Our Fight

Developments in the Soviet Union encouraged foreign correspondents to see their work as an important frontier for watchdog journalism. In the mid-1960s, small groups of Soviet citizens began to challenge the regime, gradually earning the label of "dissidents" from Western observers—a label which they eventually adopted. These activists first came to the attention of Western correspondents in 1965, when the writers Andrei Siniavsky and Yuli Daniel were put on trial for publishing their literary works abroad under pseudonyms. Siniavsky and Daniel were convicted of anti-Soviet agitation and propaganda and sentenced to, respectively, seven and five years in labor camps. Western correspondents who caught word of the trial hung out outside the court, mingled with the families and friends of the accused writers, and reported on the proceedings. The Siniavsky and Daniel trial was a watershed moment both in the history of the dissident movement and in its relationship with Western press corps. In the next two decades, as the dissident movement attracted more and more participants, the reporting of Western correspondents helped it capture international attention, causing much embarrassment to the Soviet authorities.[80]

The emergence of the dissident movement caught American foreign correspondents by surprise, in the same way that the American counterculture shocked Soviet journalists in the United States. For years the USSR had been perceived as a closed society, the very structure of which prevented the evolution of critical thought. The emergence of domestic criticism of the Soviet regime and the dissidents' ability to resist Soviet ideology and propaganda appeared inconceivable, and thus became incredibly exciting. Equally striking were the high profiles of the people involved—scientists, writers, and children of the Soviet elites—and the highly articulate nature of their resistance. According to Robert Kaiser, these two aspects made for an excellent news story, precisely of the kind US news media craved: "When a dog bites a man, that's a routine event, that's not news. But when a man bites a dog, that's news. And the dissidents were men biting dogs, they were challenging this authoritarian police state, and were very courageous. [. . .] American journalism loves conflict, it loves challenges to authority, and in the Soviet-American context, Soviets who seem to share American values about basic things like freedom of expression and so on, were instantly sympathetic figures."[81] Soviet dissidents both surprised and moved foreign correspondents. Their courage and commitment to the cause and their willingness to face reprisal and danger won the journalists' admiration.

The Soviet dissidents came to occupy a central place in the social lives of many American journalists in Moscow, and relationships between the two groups were quite close. Newly arrived correspondents usually "inherited" their dissident contacts from their predecessors, and they would come to Moscow bearing gifts and letters from the US. In a movement that built and thrived on networks of close relationships, the newly arrived journalists were embraced as "friends." To this day, many correspondents fondly remember their relationships with the dissidents, their warmth, and the deep intellectual conversations they had about Soviet life. It was among the dissidents that American journalists found intimacy, friendship, and kindred spirits.[82] The boundaries between "us" and "them" that underlined journalists' interactions in the Soviet Union were erased in their relationships with the dissidents. Many US correspondents came to view them as fellow crusaders who spoke truth to power, or as fellow investigative reporters who sought to expose the truth about Soviet life.[83] That sense of shared calling drew the journalists and the dissidents even closer. Reporting on the dissident movement fit well with the ethos of investigative journalism because it exposed and emphasized the gaps between the Soviet government's words and deeds on human rights.

Foreign correspondents reported on political trials that violated the Western norms of legality, on the KGB's surveillance and harassment of activists, on the brutal suppression of demonstrations and public gatherings, on activists' being forcibly committed to psychiatric hospitals, exiled to Siberia, or sent to labor camps. Told in evocative language, these stories stressed how, despite repression, Soviet activists continued in their struggle against the regime.[84] Thanks to the efforts of foreign correspondents, figures such as Andrei Sakharov, Yelena Bonner, Alexander Solzhenitsyn, Pavel Litvinov, and Natan Sharansky became household names in the United States. Journalists' descriptions of the dissidents obscured the distinctively *Soviet* nature of the dissident movement—the ways that the dissidents' actions and ideas about "right" and "good" developed in conversation with Soviet ideas and Soviet experiences and drew inspiration from the Russian and Soviet intelligentsia's preoccupation with morality and society.[85] Instead, American reporting inscribed Soviet dissidents into the global struggle for a better world, creating an imagined community of American audiences and Soviet activists who shared a commitment to freedom and democracy.

The perception of emotional and ideological bonds with the dissidents inspired many correspondents to see their struggle with the Soviet state not just as a good news story, but as an important political cause in which they themselves became personally invested. Many articles, chapters, even entire books, were dedicated to the Soviet dissidents and the harsh reprisals they faced in their struggle for human rights. Several correspondents were committed to raising awareness of dissident activities, expecting that international attention would temper Soviet reprisals against the dissidents.[86] For example, Anatole Shub's efforts to secure health treatment for the activist Larisa Bogoraz and his writing about her plight are considered crucial interventions that helped save her life. The close friendship that developed between Soviet Jewish dissident Natan (Anatoly) Sharansky and *Los Angeles Times* correspondent Robert Toth made Sharansky well known in the US and arguably helped to protect his life during the nine years he spent in a labor camp.[87]

Both Shub and Toth suffered as a consequence of these friendships. Shub's wife was detained by the KGB when she came to visit Giuzel and Andrei Amalrik, whose house was under search. Shub himself was expelled from the USSR. Robert Toth was detained immediately after meeting with a Soviet acquaintance who wanted help publishing his scientific article, ostensibly about Soviet parapsychology, in the West. According to the KGB the article contained state secrets, and Toth was accused of espionage. He was interrogated several times, but was able to depart the USSR, on schedule, a week later. The material from his interrogations was used in the KGB's case against Natan Sharansky. Dwelling on Sharansky's friendship with Toth, Soviet publicity surrounding the case accused dissidents of collaborating with US intelligence and warned activists against further association with American correspondents.[88] As these and many other examples show, in reporting the dissident story certain journalists pushed the boundaries of direct-observation reporting and became actual participants in a local political conflict.

At times, covering the dissident story as a participant was thrilling. It put the journalists at the heart of action, intrigue, and danger, all of which became

*Figure 6.4.* Andrei Sakharov (*seated in the middle*) at his house during a dissident press conference for foreign journalists held after the trials of Alexander Ginzburg, Anatoly Sharansky, and V. Piatkus, Moscow, July 15, 1978. (Photo courtesy of the Sakharov Center, Moscow.)

important tropes in the popular imagination of investigative reporting and foreign correspondents after Vietnam and Watergate.[89] Communicating with Soviet dissidents, visiting their homes, or attending their press conferences involved elaborate cloak-and-dagger techniques: calling from public pay phones, using code names for individuals and locations, and trying to elude KGB surveillance.[90] Demonstrating that stories about journalists and dissidents could be a gripping read, the following fragment from Kevin Klose's book describes American correspondents' efforts to whisk off Yuri Orlov's wife, Irina, to a safe location for an interview:

> As we rolled along the Moscow Ring Road toward it, KGB cars completely surrounded us. [. . .] Four or five beefy agents were jammed inside each car and one man in each had a small videotape camera trained on us. Then I noticed that, as if on signal, the taping had ceased in every car. *They've run out,* I thought. Immediately another thought crowded past that idea: *they're saving tape for something still to come.* This bothered me plenty. But what? [. . .] I suddenly

recognized the scenario: the car in front of me would plug the building's narrow entrance like a cork in a bottle and then the other agents would attack as
we moved on foot into the building. They were saving film for that. Even as
this realization was forming in my head, I began accelerating the Volvo. The
KGB driver ahead had to stay in front of me by reading my movements in his
rearview mirror. This man would have to be very good to stay with us. I began
weaving from lane to lane. [. . .] we led them on a high-speed chase through
winding back streets. With each turn, the KGB fell further behind. [. . .] As we
crested the last rise a block from the compound, a stumpy babushka with string
sacks groaning with groceries was square in the middle of the street. I hit the
horn. She hunkered, hesitated, then leapt aside as we flashed past. [. . .] Then I
heard the chase cars coming—horns blaring. The babushka was in the middle
of the street again! At that exact moment, I figured I was one for one and bat-
ting a thousand against the secret police.[91]

This description reads as if it was lifted entirely from a Cold War thriller, including the road-crossing babushka as an element of suspense or comic relief.
Stories such as these increased the prestige of Moscow correspondents and
endowed the profession with a certain sense of romanticism and allure, similar to what readers were familiar with from the dramatic representations of
the Cold War in popular culture. Yet, unlike characters in spy fiction or James
Bond movies, the journalists saw themselves as helping the just fight of real
individuals and as standing up to an oppressive regime.

The official Soviet response to the dissident movement and American reporting on its activities contributed to this impression. The bonds between
dissidents and correspondents greatly worried Soviet authorities. The resonance of the dissident story with overseas audiences embarrassed Soviet
leadership and caused problems in terms of international propaganda. Western reports on the dissident movement were beamed back into the USSR by
the Russian-language services of foreign radio stations such as Radio Liberty,
the Voice of America, and the BBC. Radio reports generated sympathetic responses from some listeners and emboldened others to reach out to famous
dissidents or join their activities.[92] These developments confirmed the Soviet
leadership's worst suspicions of American correspondents and meshed with
their longstanding views of the bourgeois press. Soviet propagandists believed
that American media, in their anti-Soviet bias, gave preference to the dissident
story and intentionally "created the impression that dissidents were coming

forth from every nook and cranny in the Soviet Union."[93] Purposeful misrepresentations of Soviet realities, Soviet officials argued, were both insulting and dangerous, for they undermined superpower relations and thus carried the potential threat of precipitating war.[94]

Eager to forestall the development of a "Soviet Spring" and to control the USSR's image abroad—especially after the 1968 invasion of Prague—Soviet authorities escalated their persecution of dissidents. The already heavy-handed information management techniques were mobilized to curtail foreign correspondents' reporting on the dissident movement. KGB officers and plainclothes policemen followed journalists and often tried to block their access to dissidents' apartments and press conferences. Soviet contacts were arrested while meeting American journalists in public spaces and taken away in unmarked cars. Several correspondents reported that groups of unidentified men accosted and threatened them outside dissidents' apartments and the foreigner compounds.[95]

Official Soviet reprisals were highly targeted and individualized. Journalists with extensive dissident contacts were bitterly denounced in the Soviet press and frequently summoned for reprimands at the Foreign Ministry's Press Department. At these meetings, correspondents were warned against reporting on dissident activities and threatened with expulsion if they did not comply.[96] These threats were occasionally carried through, and they could result not only in the loss of individual accreditation but in the demise of an entire Moscow bureau.[97] Five American correspondents were expelled from the USSR between 1968 and 1970 for reporting on dissident activities: Raymond Anderson from the *New York Times*, Anatole Shub from the *Washington Post*, *Newsweek* bureau chief John Dornberg, Stanley Cloud from *Time* magazine, and William Cole from CBS. Filling in a vacancy in the Moscow bureau could take a long time, leaving the organization dependent on the news agencies. Even if the editors managed to find a good candidate whose appointment raised no objections from the Soviets, their departure could be delayed by weeks or even months if their visa happened to get caught in the storm of so-called correspondents' visa wars that frequently erupted between the two sides.[98] Furthermore, Soviet officials had other ways to retaliate against journalists who covered the dissidents, such as denying access to official sources or travel.[99] For example, out of ten trip requests Henry Kamm of the *New York Times* submitted to the Press Department between August 1968 and April 1969, only one was approved, and then with a significantly reduced itinerary. By way of explanation, Kamm was explicitly berated for "circulating [the] writings of common criminals and embezzlers."[100]

At times, Soviet intimidation tactics assumed an outright sinister character. On December 25, 1967, Associated Press bureau chief Henry Bradsher, his wife, and two young sons returned from a Christmas dinner on the other end of Moscow. The Bradshers parked the family car on the street near their apartment building and went upstairs. As they were putting their children to bed, they were startled by the sound of a great explosion below. When they looked out the window they saw their family car in flames. Soviet experts who arrived on the scene determined that an explosive had been placed under the car. Although the culprit was never found, Henry Bradsher, as well as US Embassy officials, were convinced that the explosion was intended to send a warning to Bradsher for his reporting about a trial of dissident intellectuals in Leningrad.[101]

Journalists who were committed to reporting on dissidents were not deterred by Soviet intimidation. On the contrary, the official Soviet responses strengthened US journalists' conviction that there was a conspiracy to hide the truth about the USSR and that it was their duty to investigate and tell the world about Soviet violations of human rights. Some journalists assumed a daredevil attitude and became even more enterprising in their contacts with the dissidents. These correspondents reasoned that, since they were likely to be expelled anyway, they might as well give their all to the pursuit of the story. KGB surveillance, *Pravda* denunciations, and the Foreign Ministry's threats of expulsion became badges of honor that journalists wore with pride. In their opinion, Soviet reprisals showed that a correspondent was doing a good job: standing up to Soviet authorities and exposing truths they wanted to keep hidden.[102]

Reporting on Soviet dissent created a rift within the American press corps and introduced tensions in journalists' relations with their editors at home. American correspondents were by no means unanimous in their commitment to the dissident story. While some journalists were convinced that documenting the struggle for human rights was their most important professional and personal duty, others believed that there were other equally significant stories and focused their reporting elsewhere. Rumors circulating within the foreigner community and the press corps accused some correspondents of deliberately avoiding reporting on dissident events in exchange for preferential treatment from Soviet officials and exclusive access to important sources and stories. At times, journalists who committed themselves to covering the

*Figure 6.5.* General Secretary of the Communist Party of the USSR Leonid Brezhnev giving an interview to Henry Shapiro of UPI, June 1973. (Photo: Eduard Pesov/Sputnik Images.)

dissident movement and facing the consequences accused colleagues who avoided this topic of kowtowing to Soviet intimidation.[103]

Correspondents pursuing the dissident story did not receive unconditional support from their editors at home either. In January 1968, when the relatives of two dissidents—Yuri Galanskov and Alexander Ginzburg—organized a press conference, Soviet authorities warned that if foreign correspondents attended they would face "stern reprisals." Out of eighteen American reporters in Moscow, only four showed up to the press conference. The others received instructions from their editors to stay away.[104] News media differed in their attitudes toward reporting on the dissident story. At one end of the spectrum were organizations such as the *New York Times*, where the managing editor, Clifton Daniel, famously told Raymond Anderson, "You cover the news. The New York Times will take the consequences," or *Newsweek*, whose editors' assignments to Jay Axelbank struck even the US Embassy, usually supportive of reporting on the dissidents, as pushing too far.[105] On the other end of the spectrum were organizations that instructed their correspondents to stay away from dissident events in order to protect their people and their operations in Moscow. For example, in 1970, the Associated Press held back Holger Jensen's series on dissidents after an official Soviet rebuke of Jensen's reporting was followed by his arrest for hitting a pedestrian—an accident that the AP and the embassy thought had been arranged by the KGB.[106]

Reporting on the dissidents also complicated correspondents' relationships with the US Embassy and the State Department. US diplomats often took it upon themselves to look after the interests of US press corps in Moscow, including special attention to individual bureaus and correspondents.[107] Journalists often volunteered to share information with the State Department and US Embassy and solicited help in navigating Soviet restrictions.[108] US Embassy, which took great interest in developments on the dissident front, followed closely both American journalists' coverage of dissent and Soviet efforts to suppress it.[109] Soviet officials made it clear, both explicitly and implicitly, that they distinguished between correspondents who criticized Soviet leaders or reported on dissent and those who did not, and argued that they were well within their rights to retaliate against the former.[110] In their interactions with Soviet officials US diplomats refused to accept these distinctions and, citing concerns about freedom of information, made the case for the ability of *all* American journalists to report without restrictions.[111] In this context, it became more difficult to distinguish the embassy's support of journalists whose reporting on dissidents attracted Soviet reprisals from its support to the US press corps as a whole.

The State Department's retaliatory measures against Soviet correspondents in the US now received support from the American press corps in Moscow and occasionally from their editors in the US.[112] In 1969, Boris Strel'nikov and Genrikh Borovik were hit with a month-long travel ban in retaliation for Soviet travel restrictions on Henry Kamm and Anatole Shub. US officials chose Strel'nikov because his reporting on the American domestic scene had been considered "particularly scurrilous" and Borovik because he was the most frequently traveling member of the Soviet press corps. Later that year, TASS correspondent Victor Kopytin was expelled in retaliation for the expulsion of Anatole Shub. In 1970 the State Department's decision to expel *Pravda*'s Boris Orekhov for violating travel restrictions, was assumed to be linked to the expulsion of *Time*'s Stanley Cloud earlier that year.[113] Reporting on Soviet dissent facilitated a close contact, and at times, a collaboration between American correspondents, their editors, and the US foreign policy establishment—precisely at a time when professional ethos valorized journalists' opposition to the government agenda and stressed the importance of challenging the government's foreign policy.[114]

## Between Conflict and Communion

Early in 1972 Hedrick Smith and Robert Kaiser learned that they were chosen to interview Alexander Solzhenitsyn, in what would be his first interview
in nine years. Arranged at Solzhenitsyn's request by the dissident biologist
Zhores Medvedev, the interview took months to prepare. At that time the famous writer, who had just been awarded the Nobel Prize in literature, captured
Western headlines. Eager for the interview to go through without a KGB inter-
ruption, the two correspondents took numerous precautions in their prepara-
tions. Nobody except their wives knew about the forthcoming interview, and
they never discussed it indoors in case their apartments and offices were bugged.
To have privacy when they prepared their interview questions, Smith and Kaiser
went skating in the local park. On the agreed-upon day, they arrived at Solzhenitsyn's apartment and began an unusual interview experience.[115]

Solzhenitsyn told the two correspondents that he did not get the chance to
see their questions in advance but that they should not worry because he had
already prepared some material. He then handed each of them a fifteen-page
document titled "Interview with the *New York Times* and the *Washington Post*,"
and to the correspondents' amazement it contained both the questions and the
answers, all written by Solzhenitsyn himself. Puzzled, the journalists began to
read through the document. The questions struck them as artificial and
some sections of the "interview" that Solzhenitsyn prepared had no interest
for American audiences. But they were relieved to discover that Solzhenitsyn's document contained useful material that addressed some of their questions.[116] Still, Smith was surprised that, here was a major dissident writer, and
his treatment of the interview was no different from what one would expect
from Soviet leadership's handling of *Pravda*.[117]

A negotiation over the format of the publication ensued, encumbered by
language difficulties on both sides. Solzhenitsyn, who did not speak English,
communicated through his wife, who had a basic command of the language.
Solzhenitsyn insisted that the journalists guarantee that the interview would
be published in its entirety. Smith and Kaiser explained that they worked
within certain constraints and that not even President Nixon got those kinds
of guarantees. Eventually it was agreed that each correspondent would be
able to use his own questions and select roughly half of the material Solzhenitsyn had prepared.[118]

Having reached this agreement, Smith and Kaiser left Solzhenitsyn's apartment, bearing their precious material. They made it to Smith's car, and as they

were about to make a perfectly legal U-turn in the direction of Kaiser's apartment, a taxi crashed into them. Nervous and on high alert, the journalists suspected that this might be the first stage of a trap set by the KGB, which often used traffic incidents to pressure foreign correspondents. Smith urged Kaiser to leave the car immediately and take all the equipment and the interview materials while he dealt with Soviet officials. To everyone's relief, this crash was a real traffic incident, and each correspondent eventually made it safely back to his office.[119]

The interview appeared on the same day in the *New York Times* and the *Washington Post* and was hailed as a great success. A week later, Hedrick Smith received a letter from Solzhenitsyn saying that the writer thought otherwise. Solzhenitsyn charged that, rather than helping him get his point across, Smith had "hindered" his attempt to discuss "the questions that I considered most important." Solzhenitsyn did not think Smith purposely tried to undermine him. Rather, he believed that the whole encounter had been characterized by a clash of expectations and by the vast cultural differences between them:

> You appraised neither the level, nor the tone, nor the inner connections of the materials you were holding in your hands. In your indirect, descriptive statement you turned my views into vermicelli or minced cabbage, and when the radio stations wanted to grasp the significance, they picked out my information in small bits and put it together. [. . .] Even in that section where you seemingly give direct discourse, you arbitrarily reconstructed it so that *your* questions occupy the main position—maybe this is interesting to *your* public, but by *our* standards the questions are crudely direct and constantly imply the answer in their form. You interpret as "ill at ease" or "hesitation" those moments when I was simply feeling shame that you were asking me such questions, and not wanting to offend you I was, of course, answering.[120]

Hedrick Smith also thought that the situation was indicative of cultural differences. Solzhenitsyn's treatment of the interview, he wrote, "was a reflection of the myopia of Soviet dissidents who were as ignorant of the ways of the West and as unprepared for the untidiness of democracy and the awkward probing questions of the Western press as Soviet authorities themselves. Here was Solzhenitsyn, an uncompromising foe of the Soviet system, using Soviet methods because they were the only ones he knew."[121] Both Smith and Solzhenitsyn saw the interview as a reflection of their conflicting understandings of journalists' relationship to their subjects. Yet, while both parties claimed to be aggrieved, ultimately the interview proved to be mu-

*Figure 6.6.* Alexander Solzhenitsyn on *Meet the Press*, aired on July 13, 1975. *From left to right*: Panelists Peter Lisagor, Norman Cousins, Hedrick Smith, and Bill Monroe; moderator Lawrence E. Spivak; and Alexander Solzhenitsyn. (Photo: Gary Wagner/ NBC/NBCU Photo Bank via Getty Images.)

tually beneficial. Although Solzhenitsyn suggested that he would be reluctant to turn to American journalists in the future, the following year he would personally invite Smith, when he wanted to reach out to sympathetic audiences in the Soviet Union and abroad.[122]

More profoundly, the interview illustrates an oft-forgotten aspect of the relationship between American journalists and Soviet dissidents: how fraught with misunderstandings, clashing expectations, and at times frustrations the encounters between them could be. Both Andrei Sakharov and Alexander Solzhenitsyn complained that at times Western correspondents were not daring enough and neglected to report news and events the dissidents deemed important. Sakharov remembered that he often "spotted very dangerous distortions and reductions" in the materials he had given to foreign correspondents and that as a result he felt that he "came across as a fool."[123] As intellectuals deeply invested in words and ideas, dissidents saw every statement as a crucially important milestone in their struggle. In fact, the intellectual realm—thinking, writing, documenting, publishing, and speaking out—were the heart and soul of Soviet dissident activities and of the movement as a whole. In this context, careful and precise rendition of the dissidents' written and oral communications were of the utmost significance.

Foreign correspondents, however, believed that it was ultimately their prerogative to decide what to report and that in doing so, they also had to consider the
demands of their editors and the interest of their public, who did not regard
every dissident statement as newsworthy—especially as the years went by and
the novelty of Soviet dissent began to wear off.

Clashes over the interpretations of dissidents' relationship with the journalists began as early as 1971 on the pages of the *New York Review of Books*. In an
article titled "News from Moscow," a well-known dissident, Andrei Amalrik,
accused American journalists of willingly forfeiting their professional duty to
report on the crimes of a totalitarian regime in order to protect themselves
from Soviet reprisals. In particular, Amalrik criticized the *New York Times*
bureau chief Bernard Gwertzman for failing to report on important developments in the dissident movement. Amalrik also accused UPI's bureau chief,
Henry Shapiro, of shelving important dissident documents and distorting
other journalists' perception of dissident activities, in exchange for favorable
treatment from the Soviet authorities. In conclusion, Amalrik sarcastically
pointed out that the only time foreign correspondents united against the Soviet regime was when they faced a threat to their luxurious lifestyles and lost
their privileges to import food and goods from abroad.[124]

Several months later, the *New York Review of Books* published an article by
Bernard Gwertzman defending American journalists' professional integrity.
Gwertzman argued that the duty of a foreign correspondent demanded
reporting on a wide spectrum of events and opinions, which inevitably
extended beyond the coverage of dissidents. Amalrik's criticism, Gwertzman
contended, derived from a fundamental Soviet misunderstanding of what the
democratic press was all about: "It is clear that no American newspaper sends
a correspondent to Moscow to report on one aspect of Soviet life. [. . .] But
these concepts of 'balanced reporting' in which American newsmen have been
trained are alien to the Russian experience, and completely foreign to the history of the Soviet Union. The press to a Russian is something to be 'used.'
The officials want to impress the world with their achievements through the
foreign press, and the dissidents want to expose how evil is the system through
the foreign press."[125] Amalrik's misconceptions about the American press were
not unlike those of Soviet officials, charged Gwertzman: both failed to grasp the
importance of journalistic impartiality and sought to exploit American reporting to advance their own agenda. By explaining Amalrik's critiques as resulting
from the differences in Soviet and American understandings of journalism,
Gwertzman attempted to restore the distance between reporters and the sub-

jects of their reporting, which had become increasingly blurred in journalists' interactions with the dissidents. The controversy that played out in the *New York Review of Books* illuminated how difficult it was to reconcile two notions that were central to the self-understanding of Moscow correspondents at the time: the journalist as an impartial observer on the one hand, and the journalist as an investigative reporter and defender of human rights on the other.

Even though individual correspondents differed on how involved they should be in the dissidents' struggle, journalists' perspective on Soviet life was decisively shaped by their encounters with the dissidents, and with the members of the Soviet intelligentsia more broadly. After he left Moscow, Robert Kaiser went to Rome and then to Tel Aviv, where he stayed for several weeks "interviewing recent émigrés from all walks of life and from all over the Soviet Union, who could tell me how things worked and lots of very helpful material" that he then used to write his book. Without the dissidents, Kaiser admitted, it would have been impossible to understand how the Soviet Union really worked.[126] The journalists' deep inherent sympathy with the dissidents, and the dissidents' readiness to invite journalists into their lives, established a sense of friendship, intimacy, and shared commitment. These personal interactions stood in sharp contrast with the journalists' experiences on officially organized trips, which were heavily scripted and artificial, and with their general difficulty in establishing meaningful relationships with what one correspondent called "the intelligent non-dissidents."[127] At the same time, the journalists' conviction that information they garnered through official channels could not be trusted (a conviction strengthened by their interactions with the dissidents) made them turn to unofficial sources of information—people whose defiance of the regime apparently liberated them to tell what Soviet life was really like. The resulting image that journalists formed of Soviet life fit well with their ideas about the superiority of liberal democracy and capitalism.

In 1977, the *Columbia Review of Journalism* published a soul-searching piece by the *Washington Post*'s former Moscow correspondent Peter Osnos, reflecting on how the relationships between dissidents and journalists were shaping American perceptions of the Soviet Union. Osnos began by acknowledging that it was difficult "to be completely objective or critical about dissidents" when their courageous resistance to the Soviet regime and willingness to embrace foreign outsiders won the journalists' admiration and friendship.[128] Moreover, Osnos explained, the relationship was rewarding for both sides. Dissidents helped journalists get a good story and learn about the USSR;

journalists helped dissidents publicize their views and protect themselves from official reprisals. As a result, argued Osnos, there could be "a disproportionate emphasis" on dissident news in American reporting from the USSR.[129] Even when journalists turned to other topics, he went on to explain, the prominence of dissidents among their informants contributed to an inaccurate understanding of Soviet realities. By privileging the dissident movement in their reporting, Osnos warned, American correspondents ran the risk of turning into their *bête noir*: the Soviet correspondents in the United States: "Dissidents in the Soviet Union say what most Americans want—and expect—to hear about the evils of communism. Excessive dependence on them, however, creates a picture of that complex country as oversimplified in a way as Soviet reports about the United States being a land of little more than poverty, violence, corruption, and racism. The Soviet press may not be able to do a better job. But we can."[130] Osnos's reflections were outstanding both in their irreverent attitude toward American reporting on Soviet dissent and in their willingness to interrogate the very pillars of his colleagues' personal and professional self-understanding. By drawing attention to the important role dissidents played as journalists' friends and sources of information, Osnos cast doubt over foreign correspondents' claims to report impartially on Soviet affairs. In highlighting how reporters benefited professionally from their interactions with the dissidents, he called into question the prevailing views of Moscow correspondents as selfless defenders of human rights. Finally, Osnos's suggestion that there were certain parallels between American reporting from the USSR and the much-vilified practices of Soviet reporting from the US targeted a cornerstone of American journalists' professional identity in the Cold War era. Despite these controversial arguments, Osnos's reflections failed to stir a meaningful debate on the subject. In their capacity as friends, subjects of news, and sources of information, Soviet dissidents continued to shape American journalists' perceptions of the Soviet Union, which they passed on to their readers.

## American Reports, American Readers

Journalists' long-form accounts about Soviet life were usually embraced by US news media, pundits, and the reading public. Although dozens of books and article series by Moscow correspondents were published between 1965 and 1985, each new account was applauded for exposing one or another aspect of Soviet society and penetrating the grey monolith of the totalitarian state. Re-

views in major US newspapers, often written by other former Moscow correspondents or academics specializing in Soviet affairs, stressed how difficult
it was to make contact with, let alone understand, an average Soviet person
and celebrated these publications as triumphs of investigative journalism.[131]
This positive reception and the establishment's endorsement further enhanced
the professional standing of Moscow correspondents and positioned them as
custodians of the truth about the Soviet Union.

Though foreign correspondents enjoyed the support of pundits and their
professional peers, gauging the response of the general public is more difficult.
Following their initial publication in the journalist's own paper or magazine,
article series were distributed via news services to smaller regional and local
papers, reaching readers in the farthest corners of the US, sometimes months
after their initial publication. Journalists' books often made it to the national
bestseller lists and won prestigious awards, which further enhanced their appeal. Each new book attracted the attention of reviewers and editors of cultural
supplements of large and small papers alike, and the journalists secured invitations to deliver public talks or to appear on radio or television. The publishers' promotions ensured that journalists traveled far and wide to do readings,
give talks, visit book clubs, and meet readers.[132]

Hedrick Smith's papers at the Library of Congress contain scores of letters
that he received from readers across the United States in response to *The Russians*. While these letters shed light on the public reception of Smith's book
in particular, they also could be suggestive of the broader patterns in American audiences' engagement with the reporting of Moscow correspondents.

Numerous readers told Smith that his book made them appreciate their
good fortune. "I just finished reading your book *The Russians*, and I must say
it makes me feel glad that I live in the United States. Our problems may be
numerous but they are nothing compared to the can of worms society they are
faced to live in," wrote one correspondent.[133] Even those who disagreed with
Smith's conclusions articulated their critiques from a comparative perspective,
highlighting the parallels rather than the contrasts between the USSR and the
US. One reader, for example, took Smith to task for his portrayal of Soviet
elites, arguing that US politics were equally plagued by "corruption, deceit, and
diversion of wealth to those in power."[134] Although such critical responses
appeared now and again, the overwhelming majority of letter writers praised
Smith's portrayal of the Soviet Union and expressed appreciation of the comparative advantages of the United States:

*Figure 6.7.* Hedrick Smith, circa 1974. (Photo: *New York Times*. Photo courtesy of the Brooke Russell Astor Reading Room for Rare Books and Manuscripts, New York Public Library.)

Many of the things you wrote about from 1971 to 1974 were exactly the same as when [we] were in the Soviet Union in 1959. The poor construction, the poor quality of merchandise, the endless lines people had to stand in to buy, then pay for and finally retrieve what they bought. [. . .] When we came back we remarked that these people and this country, in many things, was 25 years to 50 years behind us. [. . .] I think you, in writing the book, did a great service to your country. I believe everyone in the Senate, Congress, the White House and many of the bureaucrats should read your book and they will get a clearer idea of what to expect of Russia in a showdown if that ever becomes necessary. Under their system I don't, and apparently you don't, think that they can measure up to our know-how and individual efforts. Our incentive system is much more rewarding than theirs.[135]

Having appreciated the book's discussion of Soviet everyday life, and compared it with his own experiences fifteen years earlier, the reader concluded that that United States remained the superior country. Still, this reader treated the book as a useful preparation for a potential "showdown" between the superpowers. Other readers shared this "know your enemy" approach and explained that it was their curiosity about America's largest nemesis that drew them to the book.

Many fans of the book praised it because Smith's observations resonated with their own impressions from the Soviet Union. Tourists, exchange students, scientists, and businesspeople who had visited the USSR wrote to congratulate Smith for his perceptive analysis and for showing what the Soviet Union was really like. The following excerpt from a letter written by an employee of a travel agency is representative of many letters Smith received from readers who had seen the Soviet Union firsthand:

> Quite frankly, I wasn't terribly interested in reading your book because, one, I didn't think anyone could tell me anything about the Russians that I didn't already know from my own experiences and, two, my own experiences have, for the most part, been so negative and so full of frustrations that I really didn't want to know anything else. [. . .] You have verbalized so much that I have experienced and felt and the insights that you have provided have helped me to better understand seemingly un-understandable things. [. . .] Some of the outrageous things that you describe and explain so well cannot, I think, be fully appreciated unless one has had the same experience because they are unbelievable. [. . .] From now on, I intend to tell anyone travelling to the Soviet Union that the best preparation they can make is to read your excellent book.[136]

The reader found the book valuable because Smith's *analysis* helped him to comprehend his own experiences and to make them meaningful. This response was not unique. Readers often thanked Smith for capturing in words their experiences and their sense of being different from the Russians. Many readers referred to Smith's explanation of how historical developments made Russians different from Westerners as eye-opening, and as helpful in making sense of their own impressions. For these readers, Smith's work demonstrated that theirs had been the quintessential experience of Westerners in the Soviet Union.

Emigrants from the Soviet Union—a substantial presence in the US by the time Smith's book was published in 1976—formed a distinct and formidable category of letter writers. Émigré readers usually told Smith that the most important thing about the book was that it helped to dispel the lies of Soviet propaganda and exposed Western audiences to the harsh reality of everyday life in the Soviet system and its oppressive nature. In letters from émigré readers, stories of personal hardship and experiences of oppression at the hands of the Soviet regime were intertwined with praise for the book, validating its findings:

> You are the first author who gives the real picture of, so called, free people, their life and struggles for food, clothes and living quarters. [. . .] Your book, dear Mr Smith, reawakens my memories. I saw myself again in the endless lines, in the winter poorly clad against the cold, freezing to the bones and in summer suffering from the heat. I would stand for hours for 5 kilogr. [of] frozen wet potatoes mixed with dirt. [. . .] I lost my father in conzentr. camp [in] 1937 he was 53 years old. I had 2 brothers, the oldest died in exile, Kazakhstan, in 1961 age 52. My younger brother spent 17 years in a conzentr. camp in Sibiria [sic]. He was released and then lived also in exile near his brother. [. . .] O, how I wish that the American People will read and understand your book.[137]

The reader recalled her life in the Soviet Union as a traumatic past involving state repression and struggles for daily survival—a past she was prompted to revisit by reading Smith's book. It was common for Smith's émigré readers to combine descriptions of personal experience of terror and oppression with stories about their difficulties in procuring basic foods and supplies. These readers' emphasis on stories of material hardship and shortages of consumer goods illustrates how they embraced the narrative positioning consumer bounty at the heart of US superiority vis-à-vis the Soviet Union. Reading the book and writing the letter to Smith allowed this particular reader to articulate how her new country gave her a better life.

A letter from celebrity pianist and conductor Vladimir Ashkenazi likewise praised Smith for exposing the lies of Soviet propaganda. Ashkenazi also took pains to disassociate himself from the Soviet Union and to articulate his belonging to the United States:

> It is very encouraging to see that the West is beginning to realize certain things about Russia and you show that it is and will be more and more difficult for the Soviets to fool the rest of the world about what the USSR really represents today and what we are to expect from that country in the future. I am sure you'll agree with me that to understand and evaluate the USSR correctly is of paramount and perhaps crucial importance if our concept of democracy is ever to survive.[138]

A significant portion of Ashkenazi's letter discussed Soviet émigrés in the United States and their emotional distance from their former homeland. People like himself, Ashkenazi concluded, had no other home but the United States.

The large number of émigré letters and their shared attributes—praise for exposing the truth about the USSR, stories of oppression and personal hardship, expressions of belonging to the US—demonstrate how these readers saw Smith personally, and perhaps Moscow correspondents more generally. In their eyes, American journalists were the allies of those oppressed by the Soviet regime and the voice of truth that exposed the regime's lies and evil doings. The very act of writing a "thank you" letter to the American journalist was an affirmation of one's new identity as an American and of belonging "here" and not "there." By sharing the American journalist's views of their former homeland and declaring their affinity with the journalist's positions, émigré readers inscribed themselves into their new society.

In 1988, Whitman Bassow, a veteran of the American press corps in the Soviet Union, published *The Moscow Correspondents*—a bird's-eye view of the lives and times of American journalists who covered the Soviet Union from 1917 to 1988. In his concluding remarks, Bassow wondered whether his colleagues' work had managed to change the prevailing stereotypes and to have "any significant impact on American public opinion and understanding of the Soviet Union."[139] For years, Bassow argued, negative statements of American politicians had carried more influence with the public than the dispatches of journalists in Moscow. As a result, "the Soviet Union has become such a villain in the American psyche that most of us carry a profoundly negative image of the Russians: bad, threatening, mysterious, powerful, and anti-American."[140] Many journalists whom Bassow interviewed for the book expressed concern that "despite their collective efforts over the decades, their hard work and voluminous reporting, Americans still do not, and have no desire to, understand the Soviet Union. Perceptions and stereotypes are so ingrained that most Americans will not permit the facts to undermine their tightly held opinions."[141]

American journalists who worked in the Soviet Union from the mid-1960s to the mid-1980s made genuine efforts to understand the Cold War adversary. They produced reports impressive in their scope and depth and put forward daring analyses that often challenged the conventional wisdom at home. Foreign correspondents viewed their accounts as impartial, objective descriptions of Soviet reality. Yet, their analyses and overall approach to Soviet life were shaped by the assumption that its true state was hidden behind the lies of Soviet propaganda and their faith in what one correspondent called the "self-evident" "superiority of the Western way of life."[142]

Steeped in concepts and questions central to their own culture, journalists focused on Soviet standard of living and everyday life, and discarded the Soviet claims that socialism offered a viable alternative to liberal democracy and capitalist economy. To explain the persistent longevity and the apparent stability of the socialist system, correspondents turned to exoticized discussions of the Russian national character and the historical differences between Russia and "the West." In doing so, American reporting contributed to the politicization of history, material culture, and standards of living that characterized the superpower competition. Journalists' explicit and implicit comparisons between the Soviet Union and the US, promoted the superiority of liberal democracy and capitalism, at a time when the meaning of these concepts was contested and debated at home. The reports of US foreign correspondents thus reaffirmed readers' faith in their country's superiority and helped infuse content and meaning into their understanding of what it meant to be an American.

# PART FOUR

# A MOMENT OF TRUTH?
## 1985–1991

In the early days of September 1985, Mikhail Gorbachev, recently appointed general secretary of the Communist Party of the Soviet Union, sat down with a team of editors and journalists from *Time* magazine for his first private interview with a Western news organization. The situation was unprecedented in many respects. First, the fact that it had been the Soviets to invite *Time* to do the interview was a truly outstanding occurrence in a country where gaining access to high officials had always been notoriously difficult. Second, Gorbachev had taken office only six months before—his predecessors had usually faced the Western press only once they were well established in their positions. Gorbachev struck his American guests as a new type of Soviet leader— "well informed, urbane, energetic, tough, witty, and above all in possession of a disciplined intellect."[1] After a succession of rather aged and conservative heads of state, here was a young, worldly, and spontaneous leader, willing to do away with "the familiar pedantic Soviet style."[2] Given at a particularly sensitive point in Soviet-American relations, Gorbachev's interview with *Time* urged a relaxation of international tensions and sent a message of hope.

The reciprocal interview—of Ronald Reagan with Soviet correspondents— was arranged shortly thereafter and held on October 31, 1985. A special squad of journalists, comprising Gennadii Shishkin (TASS), Stanislav Kondrashov (*Izvestiia*), Genrikh Borovik (Novosti), and Vsevolod Ovchinnikov (*Pravda*), was invited to the White House to interview Reagan in the Oval Office. It was the first interview a US president had given to Soviet journalists in twenty-four years: the last such occasion had been President John Kennedy's interview with Alexei Adzhubei in 1961. That the first presidential interview with Soviet correspondents in a quarter of a century was to be given by Ronald Reagan, a vociferous critic of the USSR, surprised even the seasoned America-watchers who were to conduct the interview. Kondrashov, recording the events in his diary, wrote that, in the highly charged atmosphere in the Oval Office, the president appeared "like a Superman-Buddha," handling even the most difficult questions in a clear and relaxed fashion.[3]

Soviet journalists interview President Ronald Reagan (*center, with back to camera*) in the White House, October 31, 1985. The journalists are (*from left to right on the left couch*) Stanislav Kondrashov (*Izvestiia*) and Vsevolod Ovchinnikov (*Pravda*) and (*from left to right on the right couch*) Genrikh Borovik (Novosti Press Agency) and Genadii Shishkin (TASS). Reagan's translator is seated to his immediate right. (Photo: White House Photograph. Courtesy of Ronald Reagan Presidential Library and Museum.)

   The full text of the Gorbachev interview was published in *Time* on September 9, 1985; the Reagan interview appeared in *Izvestiia* on November 5, 1985. Each interview was accompanied by a lengthy feature written by the journalists who had conducted it. The journalists shared their impressions from meeting the respective leaders and commented on their statements. Both American and Soviet news organizations understood the interviews as propaganda targeted directly at the citizens of the rival superpower. Therefore, both analytical pieces sought to mitigate the potential advantage that the adversary might have accrued, by pointing out whenever the rival leader's statements were seen to depart from the truth. *Time*'s piece focused on Gorbachev's personable political style and his efforts to reform domestic and foreign policy but reminded readers that, so far, the substance of Gorbachev's foreign policy was no different from that of previous Soviet leaders. Quoting Margaret Thatcher, the authors of the *Time* feature concluded with a tacit warning that Gorbachev's proposals for nuclear arms reductions might be merely a clever propaganda ruse, aimed at driving a wedge between NATO's member countries.[4] *Izvestiia*'s supplement to Reagan's interview reminded readers that it was this president's "confrontational" foreign policy and excessive military spending that had derailed the Soviet-American détente.[5] Writing in a forceful, critical tone, Soviet journalists accused the president of "direct distortion of the truth," which they set out to correct point by point.[6] Journalists' comments notwithstanding, Gorbachev's and Reagan's efforts to speak directly to the citizens of the rival superpower demonstrated that each side made an effort to engage the other, despite mutual hostility and suspicion. That an interview with the rival's journalists was chosen for such an outreach demonstrates that mass media remained an important intermediary in communications between the superpowers.

Gorbachev and Reagan's interviews became the first step in a series of exchanges, summits, and agreements on reduction of nuclear weapons—a process that took place between 1985 and 1991 and that we now associate with the end of the Cold War. Underpinning these developments was a revolution in hearts and minds that invited Soviet and American people to imagine a different world, marked not by confrontation but by dialogue and collaboration between their countries. Cold War correspondents—journalists who had been covering the other side from before 1985—actively contributed to this process. They often spearheaded and facilitated Soviet-American exchanges at both official and grassroots levels and were regular participants in the transnational conversation. They mobilized public support for superpower dialogue, communicated the changing foreign policy to audiences at home and abroad, and created more nuanced and more positive images of the rival superpower. After 1945, Soviet and American journalists specializing in foreign affairs had participated in constructing the very idea of the Cold War and had shaped its meaning over the decades. Between 1985 and 1991, these journalists would play an increasingly important role in constructing the narrative of a dissipating superpower confrontation and of the Cold War's end.

# CHAPTER SEVEN

# Cold War Correspondents Confront Old and New Thinking

When Mikhail Gorbachev took the post of general secretary of the CPSU, he was confronted with a struggling economy, a disenchanted society, and a strained international situation. Soviet-American relations had reached their lowest point in years. President Ronald Reagan's election campaign and first term in office were marked by a harsh stance against the Soviet Union. A young, energetic, and enthusiastic leader, Gorbachev introduced a series of reforms collectively known as *perestroika*, which sought to revitalize Soviet economy and political culture. In foreign policy, Gorbachev put forward the idea of "new thinking," which rejected the traditional notion of a world divided into antagonistic capitalist and socialists camps. Instead, "new thinking" emphasized shared human values and mutual coexistence, and stressed that humanity—as a whole—had to cooperate in order to prevent nuclear war and ecological catastrophe.[1] Gorbachev's proposed transformations in domestic and foreign affairs were closely linked and mutually constitutive. Even the most conservative members of the Soviet elite recognized that tackling the domestic crisis would be impossible without improving relations with the United States and its European allies.[2]

The Soviet press was assigned a crucial role in the reform of domestic and foreign affairs. A new information policy—*glasnost* (openness)—called for increased government transparency and public discussion of the nation's problems. The architects of *perestroika* hoped that by exposing systemic shortcomings and scrutinizing officials, the press would highlight targets for improvement and mobilize public support for rejuvenating the socialist project.[3] In coverage of foreign affairs, *glasnost* encouraged the press to offer new perspectives on the Soviet Union's relationship with the world and to help the public reimagine socialism "as a viable and critical alternative to capitalism."[4] Overall, *glasnost* was intended to impress upon domestic audiences and foreign observers the sincerity of Gorbachev's commitment to reform and bolster the credibility of "new thinking."[5]

Gorbachev's information policies were unprecedented in scope and nature. *Glasnost* soon superseded its original mandate, resulting in far-reaching liberalization of the Soviet press. Newspapers eventually came to reject the notion of forbidden topics, and this change gave way to a radical transformation of Soviet journalistic practices.[6] Soviet foreign correspondents, who had for years been tacitly pushing the boundaries of writing on international themes, embraced the idea of "new thinking" and expanded the breadth and scope of their analyses. Many previously published books and essays were reprinted after 1986, in revised editions, underscoring the relevance of a critical in-depth understanding of the rival nuclear superpower.[7] Gorbachev and his team expanded Soviet outreach to the foreign press, hoping to mobilize Western public opinion and pressure the US government to engage with Soviet initiatives.[8] Gorbachev's personality and polished worldliness made him better equipped to deal with foreign media than any of his predecessors. Within a short time his popularity in the West was so great that it had its own nickname: Gorbymania.[9]

Ronald Reagan, often referred to as the Great Communicator, was also well known for his skill in handling the press.[10] Foreign policy figured as an area of particular importance in the president's public relations, and the White House constantly explored new avenues of communication with audiences around the world.[11] In designing Reagan's media strategy at home and abroad, his advisers confronted a fast-changing media arena. The expanding audience of cable television and the twenty-four-hour news cycle—pioneered by CNN— prompted the White House to develop innovative approaches to communications and diversify its media outreach. It was also during the Reagan years that the influence of political commentators in elite US media reached its zenith. Cultivating a good relationship with media pundits was as important as it was difficult to enlist their support. The president's meetings with leading columnists and commentators to discuss ongoing political developments became a fixture of his two terms in office.[12]

Despite his harsh anti-Soviet rhetoric, Reagan never did, in fact, rule out the possibility of dialogue with the Soviet Union. After securing his second term in 1984, Reagan set about renewing US efforts to engage the Cold War adversary. When Gorbachev took office in 1985, Reagan hoped that this would be someone he could work with.[13] A split among the president's advisers challenged his new policy. Several key members of the administration remained convinced that "the Soviet system could not be altered in any fundamental way" and that Gorbachev's foreign policy was nothing but a publicity trick with no substance.[14] Others believed that negotiating with the Soviets was of the utmost importance. These disagreements mirrored the divisions in American society. On the one hand, public opinion polls reflected a growing support for the reduction of nuclear weapons and American-Soviet rapprochement. A vibrant and vocal anti-nuclear arms movement called for Reagan to backtrack from his confrontational foreign policy. On the other hand, Reagan's original conservative base held that the president should maintain a tough, uncompromising stance with the Soviets.[15] Convincing the American public that the Soviet Union could transform into a trustworthy partner in nuclear disarmament was particularly challenging given the dominance of the idea of "Eternal Russia" in the press, popular culture, and academia, as well as among Reagan's own advisers. The success of the president's new policy toward the USSR depended, in his words, on "US public opinion."[16]

This chapter focuses on three distinct episodes in which the press, and particularly Cold War correspondents, emerged as important subjects in the evolving superpower dialogue, and consequently also as objects of critical political assessments from overseas. Over the course of the Cold War, the press had evolved into one of the central symbols of each superpower's political system. While at the beginning of the conflict, the rival's journalism represented the perils of the enemy's ideology, between 1985 and 1991 journalism came to be seen as epitomizing the adversary's "new face." Soviet and American observers carefully examined each other's press in an attempt to establish whether the other side could truly change and become a trustworthy partner in the dialogue for nuclear disarmament. Gorbachev and his allies looked to the US media to gauge the American public's opinion of Soviet proposals and to gain a better understanding of US foreign policy goals.[17] American commentators often turned to Soviet media coverage of contentious issues such as foreign policy, domestic corruption, or human rights to assess the extent of Gorbachev's trustworthiness and commitment to change the system. As they debated and reevaluated each other's professional practices and information policies, American and Soviet actors still operated within different sets of universal categories that they projected onto the other. American coverage of the Soviet reforms suggested that the lessening of restrictions on the press was transforming Soviet people from obedient subjects into independent citizens. In the Soviet Union, journalists stressed the importance of the press in promoting joint efforts to secure a future free from nuclear weapons. While American observers focused on the global march of democracy, Soviet commentators emphasized the urgent need for world peace.

## 1986: The Daniloff Case Provokes Mutual Suspicion

On August 30, 1986, Nicholas Daniloff, a *U.S. News and World Report* Moscow bureau chief, was walking down a leafy street, having just met with Misha, a Russian acquaintance from the provinces. Daniloff held a sealed packet he had received from Misha containing what the journalist thought were clippings from regional newspapers. Suddenly a van stopped next to him. Several men rushed out, handcuffed Daniloff, shoved him inside the van, and took off at high speed. Eventually the van stopped near a heavily guarded building. A double barrier opened into a drab, secluded courtyard. Daniloff was led out of the van, through the courtyard, and along gray institutional corridors to an office, where a tall man in a well-cut suit was waiting. The man introduced himself as KGB Colonel Sergadeev and told Daniloff that he was being held on suspicion of espionage. Two people were brought in to witness as Sergadeev opened the pack Misha had given Daniloff and pulled out photographs of soldiers and tanks and two maps marked "secret." Daniloff was allowed to call his wife and in brisk English told her that he had been entrapped by the KGB. Afterward he was taken for a medical examination, issued prison clothing, and sent to a detention cell. Daniloff was in Lefortovo prison—the KGB's infamous detention center for political prisoners in the heart of Moscow.[18]

Daniloff's entrapment came as a surprise, for he was an old hand on the Moscow press corps. At the time of his arrest, Daniloff was about to round up a five-year tenure as the *U.S. News* bureau chief in Moscow—his second assignment in the USSR. Between 1961 and 1965 he had worked in UPI's Moscow bureau under the tutelage of the legendary Henry Shapiro. A descendant of a Russian noble family that had emigrated after the Revolution, Daniloff spoke fluent Russian. Thanks to this fact and his familiarity with Moscow, he had many local acquaintances and friends. During his second tour, Daniloff further expanded his networks, using his spare time to track down the history of an ancestor who had participated in the 1825 Decembrist uprising and had been exiled to Siberia. Well aware of the risks associated with work in Moscow, Daniloff was cautious of dangers and potential entrapment. Misha, who handed Daniloff the packet that led to his arrest, was an old acquaintance whom Daniloff thought he knew well.[19]

Daniloff's arrest came at a sensitive time in Soviet-American relations. Ten months earlier, Ronald Reagan and Mikhail Gorbachev had met for the first time in Geneva in an effort to reduce the tensions between their countries and to discuss nuclear disarmament. Earlier in 1986, Gorbachev had launched an international "peace offensive," calling for the cessation of the arms race and a large-scale reduction in the superpowers' nuclear arsenals. Faced with a somewhat hesitant response from the Reagan administration, Gorbachev sought the help of US allies in Western Europe, especially Britain and France.[20] Soviet foreign minister Eduard Shevardnadze and US secretary of state George Shultz were due to meet and discuss potential ways out of the stalemate, with rumors about a new summit on the horizon. On August 23, a week before Daniloff was seized on the streets of Moscow, Gennadii Zakharov, a Soviet scientific attaché at the United Nations Secretariat in New York, had been arrested in an FBI sting operation while attempting to buy classified US documents. Zakharov's arrest was the latest link in a virtual spy war between the superpowers that had been ongoing since 1985.[21] As it coincided with a vigorous media discussion of Gorbachev's disarmament proposals, Zakharov's arrest sparked new concerns about Soviet espionage in the US and undermined trust in Soviet initiatives. When the news of Daniloff's arrest reached the US, American officials immediately reasoned that he had been framed and taken as a bargaining chip to be exchanged for Zakharov.[22]

Over the next four weeks, while Nicholas Daniloff was locked in Lefortovo and later while he was in the custody of the US ambassador in Moscow, Daniloff's wife, Ruth, and *US News* editor Mortimer Zuckerman led a forceful publicity offensive. The campaign for Daniloff's release dominated the news cycle in the US, eclipsing all other agendas in Soviet-American relations and drawing in Shevardnadze and Shultz, Mikhail Gorbachev and Ronald Reagan. During that month, the Daniloff case became the focal point of anxieties about new developments in Soviet-American relations and the future of the superpowers' negotiations. Underlying the media discussion of the Daniloff case on both sides was the question of whether the other side could change its ways and become a trusted partner in nuclear disarmament.

The first reports on Daniloff's arrest in the American press drew upon themes that were central to the writing and self-representation of Moscow correspondents throughout the Cold War. Articles and editorials reminded the public that Daniloff's fate perfectly illustrated the difficulties and dangers that American journalists in the Soviet Union confronted on a daily basis: intimidation, KGB surveillance, and precarious communications with "real" Soviets. American observers explained that from the Soviet viewpoint, Daniloff was the perfect candidate for entrapment because he knew the country well and spoke fluent Russian. He thus could report on violations of human rights, the plight of Soviet dissidents, and a range of other topics that the Soviet regime

was keen to suppress.[23] In short, according to the US press, Daniloff was singled out precisely because he was an honest reporter, doggedly doing his job
exposing the truth "about conditions in the Soviet workers' paradise."[24]

The most sinister aspect of Daniloff's arrest, explained American commentators, was the painful familiarity of his story, for it illustrated that the Soviet
Union's purported new outlook was a sham. The Daniloff case clearly showed
that, despite the Soviet Union's efforts to convince the world otherwise, it remained an oppressive totalitarian system that unabashedly violated human
rights and suppressed freedom of speech.[25] A *Los Angeles Times* editorial, for
example, charged that the recent changes in Soviet rhetoric were but a "fig
leaf" covering the fact that the regime "has not changed anything except its
choice of words" and that "it continues to place the whims of the state ahead
of rights of individuals."[26]

Much of the discussion focused on the person of Mikhail Gorbachev, whose
"charm offensive" in the previous months had made dents in the armor of even
quite conservative observers. Daniloff's arrest reintroduced the question of
whether Gorbachev could be trusted. Was he strong enough to lead the change
in Soviet-US relations and make good on his offers of nuclear disarmament?
Was he sincere in his efforts to reform the Soviet system? Would he impose
his authority on the KGB, or was he really just a KGB pawn? The discussion
of Gorbachev's trustworthiness had real policy implications, as it tapped into
a broader public debate on Soviet disarmament proposals. US commentators
took different views about whether the Soviet international outreach and domestic reforms were a sham. All agreed, however, that Daniloff's arrest seriously undermined Gorbachev's credibility and that the journalist's release was
the necessary precondition for any further engagement with the USSR.[27]

US reporting on Daniloff's case reintroduced the same fears and anxieties
that had characterized press assessments of American-Soviet relations in the
first postwar years. News media used the case of Gennadii Zakharov to highlight the threat of Soviet espionage on American soil. A survey in *Newsweek,*
for example, stressed that the extent of the KGB's operations far outstripped
the CIA's, and that while the latter had a hard time recruiting American journalists, all Soviet correspondents in the US collaborated with the KGB and at
least half of them were "paid intelligence agents."[28] As they pondered the sincerity of Gorbachev's "new thinking," American commentators evoked the
specter of Soviet propaganda and wondered whether the Soviet initiatives were
yet another disinformation campaign targeting the American people and ex-
ploiting their hopes for peace.[29] While stressing the constant dangers faced by

American correspondents in Moscow, some commentators reintroduced the question of whether reporting in such conditions of personal threat could be trusted. A *Washington Post* editorial explained, "The framing of Nick Daniloff is the worst thing that could have happened to the integrity of the foreign press in the Soviet Union, and to the confidence in that press of the Western public."[30] In contrast to the early Cold War, though, the proposed solutions did not call for abolishing the Moscow press corps, but rather for pressing for Daniloff's release with the topmost Soviet officials.

Eventually this tactic brought Daniloff home. After a few days, President Reagan became personally involved in the case. He sent a letter directly to Mikhail Gorbachev and vouched that Daniloff was not a CIA agent. Gorbachev replied via the Soviet ambassador that Daniloff had engaged in unlawful activities and that his arrest should not stand in the way of Soviet-American negotiations.[31] Moving forward, however, was impossible, especially now that Reagan had become personally committed to Daniloff's release, and the publicity campaign led by Ruth Daniloff and Mortimer Zuckerman received increasing attention. US newspapers carried daily updates on the Daniloff case and urged the US government to cease all dealings with the Soviets until he was brought home.[32]

The efforts to secure Daniloff's return without surrendering Zakharov bore no fruit. On September 12, both men were released into their ambassadors' custody—effectively a house arrest in their respective embassies. On September 19, Eduard Shevardnadze arrived in the United States for a series of negotiations with George Shultz. He bore a personal message from Gorbachev to Reagan proposing a meeting in London or Iceland in preparation for the next summit. The president told Shevardnadze that Daniloff had to be returned to the US before any meeting would take place. In his diary, Reagan reported, "I gave him [Shevardnadze] a little run down of the differences between our 2 systems & told him they couldn't understand the importance we place on the individual because they don't have such a feeling. I enjoyed being angry."[33]

A few days later, Shultz and Shevardnadze concluded the final deal on Daniloff and Zakharov. Daniloff would be permitted to leave the USSR. Then Zakharov would plead a legal equivalent of guilty in a US court and would be expelled. After Zakharov's departure, Shultz would announce that the dissident Yuri Orlov would be permitted to travel to the United States. Orlov was added to the deal to allow the administration to save face and say that Zakharov was traded for the famous Soviet dissident. The president and his team were eager to create the impression that they did not surrender to Soviet black-

*Figure 7.1.* Nicholas Daniloff with President Ronald Reagan and First Lady Nancy Reagan after his return to the United States, September 1, 1986. (Photo: White House Photograph. Courtesy of Ronald Reagan Presidential Library and Museum.)

mail and did not exchange a real spy for an honest reporter taken hostage.[34] Reagan returned to this topic in his diaries and even met with the commentator George Will "to counter the impression made in his columns of US caving in on the Daniloff case."[35] On September 29, Nicholas Daniloff left for the United States. The following day, the State Department announced the Zakharov-Orlov exchange, and the White House confirmed that there would be a summit with Gorbachev in Reykjavik in mid-October.

As US commentators reflected on the Daniloff case both before and after his return home, journalism became a symbol that both defined the respective systems and illustrated the differences between them. Descriptions of the difficult working conditions of Moscow correspondents stressed that most reporting activities considered normal by Western reporters were unacceptable in the USSR. Speculation on Soviet reasons for imprisoning Daniloff reminded readers that "information control is vital for the maintenance of power by a totalitarian regime, just as the free flow of information is vital for safeguarding any democratic system."[36] As the Daniloff case drew to a close, US analyses stressed that in American democracy, freedom of the press and of the individual were inseparable. By contrast, the oppressive Soviet dictator-ship had no regard for either and was thus prone to violate both.[37] *US News* owner and editor Mortimer Zuckerman articulated this idea most forcefully in an editorial: "The Soviet Union has never known a day of democratic free-dom in its history. The United States was conceived and developed as the most open society in the free world."[38] These differences, according to Zuckerman, illustrated the broader differences in the two superpowers' conduct on the international arena: "The U.S., though passionate for the advancement of freedom in the world, is satisfied with peaceful, evolutionary change while the U.S.S.R. is a dissatisfied imperial power, revolutionary in its ideological outlook, expansionist in its historic urges."[39] Slipping the idea of "Eternal Russia" into his analysis, Zuckerman implied that it was history itself that conditioned each side's attitudes toward "freedom." For Zuckerman and other commentators, the treatment of the press came to symbolize the dif-ferences between American freedom and Soviet oppression.

Several American publications stressed that Daniloff's arrest was part of the KGB's increasing anti-American propaganda. In reality, Soviet reporting on the affair was rather muted. In contrast to the early postwar years, when media campaigns warned the Soviet public against associating with American corre-spondents, reporting on the Daniloff case discussed the individual incident in concise terms and subdued language. Soviet newspapers made a point of stick-ing to official statements and often quoted Shevardnadze saying that the Soviet government had "good relations" with American journalists overall.[40]

Daniloff's name first appeared in the Soviet press on September 7, more than a week after his arrest. A commentary in *Pravda*'s international section men-tioned Daniloff as an example of a CIA operative whose capture in the USSR sparked unjustified American outrage. All the article said about Daniloff per-sonally was: "It has been known that he was arrested by the security organs and is now the subject of an investigation."[41] The main theme of the *Pravda* piece was not the case itself, but the commotion US media and politicians raised over what the article claimed was the legitimate arrest of an American spy. *Pravda* accused the US of using the Daniloff case as an excuse for evading the Soviet disarmament proposals. The "peddlers of the exposed agent," it charged, "are keen to divert international attention from Soviet peace initiatives and from Washington's efforts to rob humanity of its nascent hope for a world without nuclear weapons and self-destructive war."[42] *Pravda* set the tone for subse-quent reporting on the affair. Daniloff himself, mentioned only briefly, was de-scribed merely as a spy caught red-handed. The lion's share of the reporting was dedicated to the scandal that the US media had conjured out of thin air in their efforts to obstruct vital negotiations that could bring about world peace.[43]

Although most Soviet reporting on the Daniloff affair kept a sober and rather restrained tone, old anxieties about the US media occasionally crept in. During the month that the Daniloff-Zakharov case stayed in the headlines, Soviet newspapers featured items on the CIA's practice of recruiting American foreign correspondents and on the collaboration between the intelligence sector and the news media.[44] While these items were few and far between, they conjured up concerns about US news media, their willingness to peddle anti-Soviet bias at someone else's bidding, and their ability to disrupt the delicate balance of Soviet-American relations. In the weeks preceding Daniloff's release, major Soviet newspapers published analytical pieces by leading international commentators, including Stanislav Kondrashov, Yuri Zhukov, and Vsevolod Ovchinnikov. These commentaries were unanimous in their take on the Daniloff case: it was an excuse to forestall meaningful discussion of the Soviet proposals, a small episode inflated out of proportion in order to undermine world peace. Warning that the Daniloff case might become a repetition of dangerous historical precedents, Soviet commentators reminded readers that small episodes (such as the U-2 spy plane incident) had derailed nuclear disarmament negotiations in the past.[45] Addressed to foreign observers as much as to domestic audiences, Soviet commentaries stressed that Daniloff case was not important enough to stand in the way of an unprecedented opportunity to do away with weapons of mass destruction.

Like their American colleagues, Soviet commentators also used the Daniloff case to reflect on the broader differences between the rival superpowers. For Soviet journalists, though, the heart of the matter was not Daniloff's arrest, but the attention it was receiving in American press and its negative impact on the superpowers' negotiations. Borrowing from Gorbachev's political rhetoric, commentators contrasted Soviet "new thinking" with American "old thinking." While the USSR was preoccupied with a peaceful future, the US was still driven by its aggressive imperialism. While the Soviet side worked tirelessly to ensure collective security, the American side was egocentric in the pursuit of its own narrow interests. These comparative reflections invariably ended on an optimistic note and expressed confidence that the Soviet people's forbearance and resilience in the face of adversity would lead to the ultimate triumph of peace.[46] Writing in this manner, Soviet journalists defined the differences between the superpowers as a binary between champions of aggression and advocates of peace.

As commentators in the American and Soviet media read the situation through different sets of binary lenses, the discussion of the Daniloff affair on the two sides effectively channeled both the hopes for a fresh start in super-power relations and the fears that these hopes were misplaced. To American observers the Daniloff affair confirmed that the USSR remained an oppressive dictatorship that trampled on the freedom of speech. Soviet commentators saw it as yet another case in which the US government and media colluded to undermine the Soviet world peace initiative. Still, things were changing: the Daniloff affair would be the last Cold War scandal that featured a journalist as a subject of espionage accusations.

## 1987: Journalists' Spacebridges Deliver a Lesson in Truth

It was a rainy day. Phil Donahue, a renowned American talk-show host, was taking in the sights on a public square in Minsk, the capital of the Belorussian SSR. Suddenly, a babushka—an old lady wearing a colorful kerchief— approached him holding a pen and paper in her hand and assertively said something in Russian. Puzzled, Donahue turned to his companion, Soviet journalist Vladimir Pozner, and learned that the babushka had seen him on television and was asking for his autograph. It was at that moment that Donahue realized he was truly famous. "Hey, I'm Elvis!" he thought.[47] What was Phil Donahue, native of Cleveland, Ohio, resident of Manhattan, and beloved American TV presenter, doing in Minsk in 1987? And how was he instantly recognized on a Soviet street?

There was nothing in Phil Donahue's personal or professional biography to suggest that one day Soviet babushkas would be asking for his autograph. Donahue was born into a middle-class Irish Catholic family and got a scholarship to attend the University of Notre Dame. After graduating in 1957, he began working in local radio and television in Cleveland. Over the next ten years, Donahue gradually built his professional career, eventually hosting his own phone-in afternoon radio show. In 1967, Donahue moved his program to television and became one of the pioneers of the talk-show format. Within three years *The Phil Donahue Show* entered national syndication. By the mid-1980s, Phil Donahue was one of the most popular television presenters in the US, with a daily show broadcast in hundreds of cities.[48]

In 1985, Donahue was approached with an unusual proposal: to cohost a "spacebridge"—a television program featuring a dialogue between regular Soviet and American people. A spacebridge (in Russian, *telemost,* or TV bridge) was a public, interactive videoconference between individuals or groups at two or more locations linked by satellite technology. The first spacebridges were organized by Soviet and American communications enthusiasts in the early 1980s. In 1983, *Moscow Calling San Diego* brought together children and filmmakers from both countries to exchange ideas and discuss cinema. Two years later, *Remembering the War* featured an emotional conversation between Soviet and American veterans of the Second World War who had participated in the Meeting on the Elbe, on its fortieth anniversary.[49] The spacebridge Donahue was asked to host in 1985 aimed to take this type of programming to the next level. A joint production of the Soviet Documentary Guild, Soviet Gosteleradio (State Committee for Television and Radio Broadcasting), and Seattle-based KING-TV, this spacebridge would involve a dialogue between roughly two hundred Soviet and American people from all walks of life. Entitled the *Citizens Summit*, the spacebridge sought to generate candid, unscripted conversation between residents of Seattle and Leningrad, moderated by an American and a Soviet host.[50]

The Soviet host, and Donahue's proposed partner in this venture, was Vladimir Pozner—a journalist of unusual talent and an equally unusual biography. Born in Paris to a Soviet Jewish father and a French Catholic mother, Pozner moved to New York City in 1934, when he was three months old. In 1938 the Pozners returned to Paris but had to go back to the United States two years later when the Nazis invaded France. Vladimir Pozner grew up in New York City, attended school in Manhattan, played baseball, and fell in love with an American girl. After the war, the family returned to Europe. The Pozners settled in the Soviet sector of divided Berlin in 1948 and moved to Moscow four years later.[51] In the early 1960s, Vladimir Pozner's talents and excellent command of foreign languages brought him into the newly formed Novosti Press Agency. He soon became a dominant figure in Soviet international broadcasting and often appeared as a guest on Western media, explaining Soviet foreign policy with an impeccable American accent.[52] In the early 1980s, when Pozner became the host of the US-Soviet spacebridges, his was a new, largely unknown face on Soviet television, for until then his formidable journalistic career had been limited primarily to foreign-language broadcasting. To some extent, Pozner's professional future in Soviet television depended on the outcome of the *Citizens Summit*. Much was at stake for Donahue as well, for working with the Soviets could be a risky endeavor, especially for someone with his fame and popularity. In preparation for the program, Pozner and Donahue reached a "gentlemen's agreement" to make the Soviet and American versions as similar to each other as possible and to ensure that mutual criticism would not be redacted.[53]

The *Citizens Summit,* broadcast early in 1986, set several new precedents for Soviet television: frank, unscripted, and often pungent comments, combined with discussions of taboo topics in the USSR, such as human rights, emigration, the shooting down of the Korean Airlines plane, and Sakharov's house arrest. Before the program came onto Soviet screens, Pozner nervously presented the final edit to his superiors at Gosteleradio. He could not believe his ears when they congratulated him for producing such a fine show. Subsequently he learned that Mikhail Gorbachev and his Agitprop (Agitation and Propaganda Department) chief, Alexander Yakovlev, had watched the recording and given it their blessing. The *Citizens Summit* was scheduled to broadcast just a few days before Gorbachev officially unveiled his policy of *glasnost.* Aired in prime time to an audience of approximately 150 million, the spacebridge sent shockwaves throughout the country and became one of the flagship programs of *glasnost* television.[54] Numerous Soviet-American spacebridges were held between 1986 and 1989, drawing in children, students, journalists, communications enthusiasts, academics, and government officials from both sides. The central principle underlying all US-Soviet spacebridge projects held that direct engagement and candid dialogue would help people on both sides of the Cold War divide to recognize their shared humanity and understand each other better and thus advance the chances of world peace.[55]

After he became an almost accidental contributor to Soviet-American dialogue, Phil Donahue continued to try to facilitate better understanding between the people on both sides. In January 1987, Donahue came to the Soviet Union and recorded five episodes of his syndicated talk show with Soviet participants. The ultimate installment of *Donahue in Russia* was a special spacebridge featuring a conversation between American correspondents in Moscow and Soviet correspondents in the United States, moderated by Donahue and Pozner. Another journalists' spacebridge—a joint production of Gosteleradio and the Center for Communication in New York—was filmed in April of the same year, in front of large studio audiences composed of professional journalists, editors, and journalism students.

The two journalists' spacebridges cast specialists in reporting on foreign affairs as indispensable to superpower dialogue. In contrast to other spacebridge programs, the journalists' spacebridges sought not only to establish a conversation between Soviet and American participants but also to create an environment where media professionals would discuss how they could help people on both sides to get to know each other better. In both programs, however, the discussion shifted from these topics and gave way instead to debates on the professional practices and values of US and Soviet reporting. American and Soviet participants thus transformed the spacebridges into didactic platforms, where they could showcase and explain the superiority of their own political systems to journalists and the viewing public on the other side. As they positioned the respective media as representative of the Soviet and the American systems, the spacebridges also examined the sincerity of the rival's commitment to change and international partnership. On both occasions, the conversation between Soviet and American participants was shaped by their respective sets of universalist values, which they projected onto the work of their foreign colleagues.

The first journalists' spacebridge, recorded and broadcast as an installment of *Donahue in Russia*, saw Soviet correspondents enjoying the advantage of both determination and numbers. Eleven Soviet journalists, representing the major Soviet newspapers, news agencies, and radio and television outlets, gathered in a New York studio. Most of them participated actively—and at times forcefully—in the discussion. By contrast, of the four American correspondents present in the Moscow studio—representing CNN, the *Los Angeles Times, U.S. News and World Report,* and the *Baltimore Sun*—only three actively contributed to the show.

Rhetorical punches began flying as soon as Phil Donahue finished the introductions and asked his guests to talk about what it was like to cover the rival superpower. At this invitation, both sets of correspondents began to air their long-standing professional grievances. Complaints about limitations on travel and access, surveillance by local security forces, and the suspicious and prejudiced reception in the host country dominated the discussion. Much of this was new to audiences on both sides: although journalists had done a great deal to publicize their own difficult working conditions over the years, they seldom acknowledged that the limitations were reciprocal and that rival correspondents operated under similar constraints. Both hosts, especially Vladimir Pozner, urged their guests to move beyond these comparative limitations and to reflect more broadly on journalists' responsibility for promoting negative stereotypes of the other. While making some effort to address these questions, correspondents kept bringing the discussion back to their working conditions and continued to air resentments harbored by several successive generations of the respective press corps.[56]

Soviet correspondents, who wanted to emphasize how absurd and disparaging American stereotypes of the Soviet people could be, charged that US schools and media failed to acquaint the public with even the most basic facts about Soviet life. Pozner asked the American correspondents whether US media were at least in part responsible for the lack of such basic knowledge. William Eaton, the *Los Angeles Times* bureau chief, replied that if Soviet citizens could travel to the US more freely, Americans might become more interested in learning new things about the Soviet Union.[57] The dialogue thus went in circles: journalists argued that negative stereotypes derived from the limitations imposed on their reporting, and the existence of these limitations was attributed to the host country's a priori negative view of the journalists and their work. Soviet correspondents tried to impress upon their colleagues that stereotypical and superficial coverage of the USSR was dangerous because it undermined world peace, poisoned Soviet-American relations, and diverted attention from Soviet proposals on nuclear disarmament. American correspondents urged Soviet journalists to understand that it was impossible to cover their country with any adequacy without having the freedom to talk to people and move around.[58]

The most animated part of the debate focused on the differences between journalism in the Soviet Union and the United States. American journalists argued that what distinguished them from their Soviet colleagues was the freedom to write objectively without attending to any ideological considerations. They stressed that a vast gap separated the work of an American journalist—a professional news reporter—from that of a Soviet journalist—a party propagandist. "*We* are not governed by ideology, we are newsmen and we want the story of the day," explained CNN correspondent Peter Arnett.[59] Upon hearing that, Iona Andronov from *Literaturnaia Gazeta* burst out: "And who [is] paying YOU? The capitalists who own your television networks. [. . .] Of course, you are not receiving orders from the White House, but [. . .] their class interests, you have to reflect. If you don't, they would throw you out."[60]

Trying to prompt his guests to consider how journalists' biases shaped the public's perceptions of the rival superpower, Vladimir Pozner pressed further and asked his American guests, "Then how come you get this general overtone that seems to be pretty common to the mass media in general? I would defy any American to turn his back to television and to say 'That's NBC on the Soviet Union, that's CBS on the Soviet Union, and that's ABC,' because they are different. But they're not. And doesn't ideology have something to do with it? Honestly speaking, can we admit that we all are influenced by ideology?"[61]

American participants acknowledged that their personal backgrounds, up-bringing, and, in one correspondent's words, "the system" they grew up in shaped their understanding of the Soviet Union and their reporting on it.[62] Yet they continued to reject the parallels between their work and the work of So-viet correspondents and insisted that ideology had no influence on their re-porting. Jeff Trimble, Daniloff's successor as the *U.S. News* correspondent in Moscow, explained,

> I don't like the suggestion that what Soviet journalists do is the same thing that we are doing here in Moscow. Unless there have been some radical changes in textbooks in the approach to teaching journalism in the Soviet Union, my un-derstanding is that Soviet journalism is a deeply ideological profession. [. . .] Lenin talked constantly about the importance of the press and the media in spreading the ideas and the ideals of communism and that's a hundred percent different than what we do as [American] journalists here. [. . .] It's a completely different business.[63]

While Trimble was willing to admit that objectivity was a desired goal, an ideal to strive for, rather than an established accomplishment of the US press, he still held that impartiality both defined US reporting and distinguished it from its Soviet counterpart. Soviet journalists, in contrast, argued that the US press was by no means devoid of ideology and did the bidding of its capitalist owners.

The exchanges on ideology crystalized the differences in the ways that for-eign correspondents on both sides understood their work. Soviet journalists openly acknowledged that communist ideas shaped their perspective on the United States as well as their reporting. Yet in their view, ideological influences were not manifest in the form of *external* pressure, but as an *internal* moral compass that came with being a communist. Andronov articulated it as fol-lows: "I am a member of the communist party, I think that the majority of the people here, they are also communists. I don't need any orders [on how to write]—I have my own orders."[64] American correspondents vehemently de-nied the presence of any external influences—ideological or editorial—and insisted that their work remained independent and impartial. Whereas Soviet correspondents saw ideology as an internal force that shaped one's worldview, American journalists equated ideology with an external pressure or a dictate, distinct from personal background or interests. Such a definition of "ideology" glossed over the bias in the US news media and helped American journalists eschew the interrogation of their own partiality.

Jeff Trimble's words, quoted above, concluded the American broadcast of the program. It appears there is no remaining recording of the Soviet version.[65] According to Ellen Mickiewicz, who viewed and compared both programs, until that point Soviet audiences saw the version that Donahue prepared for American viewers with a Russian-language voiceover. In the Soviet version, as the end credits began to roll, Pozner suddenly called "stop" and told viewers that now they would see a fragment of the discussion that was not included in the final cut of the program that was presented to US audiences. In this fragment, Donahue was shown addressing American correspondents in Moscow, asking whether they faced pressure "not to appear soft on the reds."[66] When the *Baltimore Sun* correspondent denied that there was editorial intervention in his work, Donahue pressed on: "So you're saying no, there's no pressure. I think there is. No one is forcing you to be harsh about the communists. I think such pressure exists. I think such pressure is very real, although it's difficult to perceive. They tell you that anything that looks a bit good in the Soviet Union is really only a screen behind which lurk problems. And if you talk about good things in your reports from Moscow, it means you sold your soul."[67]

American journalists vehemently denied Donahue's charge and insisted that this was not how their reporting worked. Donahue replied that he stood behind his statement, ending the segment on a rather acrimonious note.[68] The reasons for omitting this exchange from the final US edit are unclear. It is conceivable that either Phil Donahue or someone on his team judged that such a critical take on American reporting from Moscow would not go down well in a program aimed at a mainstream audience. Donahue's remarks struck at the heart of his audience's ideas about a free American press, which was central to their understanding of what the United States symbolized in the superpower contest.

The first journalists' spacebridge demonstrated how efforts to promote a candid Soviet-American conversation hit a dead end that had characterized discussions of the mass media throughout the Cold War, albeit with the added benefit of partially exposing audiences to the arguments and grievances of the other side. Participants on both sides defended and reproduced the well-established binary views of the American and Soviet press and cast doubts on each other's commitment to change by questioning the rival's journalistic practices. Despite repeated invitations, Soviet and American journalists refused to reflect on their own contribution to mutual misunderstandings, shifting the blame onto the rival's media instead.

The second journalists' spacebridge, recorded in April 1987, was a larger endeavor, linking journalists in four locations—Moscow, San Francisco, Tbilisi, and Boston—with students in fifty American universities watching the discussion live via a satellite link.[69] Vladimir Pozner and Tengiz Sulkhanishvili hosted in Moscow and Tbilisi, and Peter Jennings, a well-known ABC anchor, in the United States. The program was recorded in collaboration with the American Society of Newspaper Editors (ASNE) during its annual convention in San Francisco. The audience in the San Francisco studio consisted mostly of ASNE members from across the US. The audience in Moscow, Tbilisi, and Boston likewise came from the ranks of professional journalists and journalism students. The main discussion took place between a panel of journalists in Moscow and in San Francisco. Audience members in Moscow, Tbilisi, San Francisco, and Boston occasionally contributed questions or comments. Alongside Pozner, the Soviet panel in Moscow featured Aleksandr Shal'nev, who was an *Izvestiia* international commentator, a former TASS correspondent in the US, and the author of a 1984 book about American public's perception of Reagan's Strategic Defense Initiative. The third Soviet panelist was Yuri Shchekochikhin, the much-respected head of investigative reporting at *Literaturnaia Gazeta*. In addition to Peter Jennings, the panel in the United States featured old hands who had little recent experience in the Soviet Union. Seymour Topping, managing editor of the *New York Times*, had been its Moscow bureau chief from 1960 to 1963 and had gone on to a distinguished career at the *Times*. He had served as chief correspondent in Southeast Asia (his area of specialty) and as foreign editor and had held several senior editorial posts. The second panelist was Stuart Loory from CNN, who had worked as a Moscow correspondent between 1964 and 1966. The third participant, Elizabeth Tucker, was introduced as a staff writer for the *Washington Post* "known for writing on Soviet themes."[70]

Titled "The Role of the Media in Current Relations," the spacebridge aimed to investigate what journalists on both sides could do to improve mutual understanding. Once again, however, a few minutes into the program, it turned into a debate on the essence of American and Soviet journalism. After the initial introductions, audiences were invited to view a short video. Prepared by the Americans, the video presented a brief overview of journalism in the United States and in the Soviet Union. The narration positioned news media as representative of the respective political systems and channeled an American understanding of the differences between liberal and socialist journalism. The US press was introduced as a fiercely independent watchdog of democ-

*Figure 7.2.* Soviet hosts and audiences in the studio ready for the Moscow–San Francisco spacebridge, April 27, 1987. Soviet panel members in Moscow (*left to right*) are Yuri Shchekochikhin (*Literaturnaia Gazeta*), Aleksandr Shal'nev (*Izvestiia*), and Vladimir Pozner (Gosteleradio). (Photo: Roman Poderni/TASS photo archive.)

racy, whose role was to scrutinize the government, keep the public informed, and facilitate critical discussion of current affairs. The narration emphasized that freedom of speech was central both to American democracy and to American journalism. The Soviet press, in contrast, was represented as the handmaiden of the Soviet state whose main function was to express government positions, publicize government policies, and publish government speeches. The vague reference to the Union of Soviet Journalists implied that it existed to control journalists' work and that participation was mandatory. Toward the end of the clip, it was explained that, with the recent introduction of *glasnost*, Soviet journalists were allowed to express different opinions and no longer had to write in the same way.[71] *Glasnost* was thus presented as an exciting innovation that could bridge the gap between the free American and the unfree Soviet media for the first time in history.

In many ways, this exposition shaped the subsequent conversation between the panelists and the audience on both sides. Vladimir Pozner opened the discussion by asking the participants to think how they could work together to overcome their differences and improve mutual understanding. American panelists essentially ignored this invitation and instead plunged into pointed questions about *glasnost*. What does *glasnost* mean to you? Peter Jennings wanted to know. Is *glasnost* here to stay or might it be rolled back, like Khrush-chev's reforms? inquired Seymour Topping. Are you free to conduct journal-istic investigations? asked Elizabeth Tucker. Soviet participants replied that, while *glasnost* opened new professional opportunities, it had always been pos-sible to express personal viewpoints and different opinions in the Soviet press. Further, they explained that Soviet newspapers had been investigating corruption, exposing illegality, and doing their best to protect the "small in-dividual" long before the introduction of *glasnost*.[72]

Evaluating the Soviet press by the yardstick of US liberal media, American interlocutors did not appear to take Soviet assertions seriously. No journalis-tic investigation was deemed worthy unless it targeted the highest echelons of power; no journalist was expressing their real opinions unless they openly criticized the regime. American panelists pushed onward. Would you be able to investigate official corruption at the highest, all-union level? persisted Stu-art Loory. What are you doing to improve the human rights in your country? inquired an editor from Kansas who was sitting in the San Francisco studio. To this particular question, Vladimir Pozner replied with visible agitation that the Soviet Union and the United States understood human rights differently. For example, he said, the right to work, to study, and to be looked after in one's old age were considered fundamental rights in the Soviet Union but not in the US. The Soviet Union still had its problems, he admitted, but the press was doing a great deal to promote democratization.[73]

In contrast to the first journalists' spacebridge, the American side emerged as vigorous and assertive, while the Soviet panel appeared less energetic and rather subdued. The Soviet participants in the first spacebridge had spent years work-ing in the US and had grown accustomed to dynamic exchanges on American television. As a result, their statements were snappier and more forceful than those of the Moscow-based Soviet journalists who took part in the second pro-gram. With the exception of Pozner, who remained eloquent, sharp, and ani-mated, the Soviet panelists often appeared to be struggling for words.

Still, Soviet participants tried to steer the discussion back toward the orig-inal topic, or at least get the Americans to acknowledge that the US media could make a bigger contribution to promoting, in Pozner's words, "a truth-ful and objective" image of the Soviet Union.[74] What are you doing to improve the prevailing negative stereotypes of the USSR? inquired an audience mem-ber in Georgia. Why is it that most Americans visiting the USSR express dis-satisfaction with the information about the Soviet Union available in the US press? wondered an employee of the Levada Center for Public Opinion, a new sociological research organization set up during *perestroika*.[75] Briefly acknowledging that reporting may at times be imperfect, the American panelists refused to admit that the US press had anything to do with the American public's unfavorable view of the Soviet Union. At one point, Elizabeth Tucker charged that if the Soviet Union would become a more open society, Americans would be able to discard their old negative stereotypes and understand it better.[76] According to the American panelists, *Soviet* information policies were to blame for inadequate understanding of the adversary on *both* sides.

Soviet participants in the spacebridge treated American reporting on the USSR as a litmus test of US commitment to improving mutual understanding. In revisiting the topic of negative stereotypes and questioning the representations of the Soviet Union in the US media, Soviet journalists linked positive and well-informed coverage of their country with the establishment of a productive dialogue between the superpowers. In their view, such a dialogue was indispensable for improving international relations and reducing the nuclear threat. It appeared, however, that the American panelists refused to acknowledge their responsibility, let alone express a commitment to improving press coverage of the USSR. Such attitudes confirmed long-established Soviet perceptions of the American press and spelled an uncertain future.

The American participants' interest in *glasnost* was also rooted in well-established patterns of thinking about the Soviet Union. For several decades, American politicians, commentators, journalists, and the broader public held that the Soviet press was a government-controlled propaganda machine. In this context, *glasnost* and the idea that the Soviet people were finally allowed to speak up and criticize their government appeared novel, indeed almost inconceivable. Eager to discover whether the Soviets could change and "become like us," American panelists and audiences were determined to establish whether the USSR now had a "truly free" press. The American liberal understanding of news media dominated both the questions presented to Soviet participants and the engagement with their responses. Soviet assertions that journalistic investigations and individual opinions existed before *glasnost* were dismissed, for American participants believed that neither was possible in censored, government-owned media. The increasingly specific questions about what one could and could not write since the arrival of *glasnost* likewise sought to establish how close the Soviet media came to the normative (read: liberal, US) model of a free press. The answers to these questions had broader implications, especially given the Americans' tendency to see the Soviet press as emblematic of the system as a whole. Understanding the scope of freedom of the press in the Soviet Union became the key for gauging the effectiveness and the depth of Gorbachev's "new thinking."

Ultimately the spacebridges, including the ones featuring journalists, had very different impacts on both sides. In the Soviet Union, the spacebridges were aired in prime time on the First Channel—the most important nationwide channel on Soviet television. It has been estimated that more than 250 million Soviet viewers watched the first *Citizens Summit*.[77] Subsequent spacebridges also attracted large audiences and became closely associated with *glasnost* on television. US viewing figures were much more modest. According to Phil Donahue, of the 220 stations that carried his regular talk show, only 80 bought *Citizens Summit*.[78] The first journalists' spacebridge reached larger audiences because it was broadcast as an installment of *Donahue* on all the channels that usually carried that show. The second journalists' spacebridge was broadcast on PBS, and its viewing figures in the US were considerably lower than in the Soviet Union.[79] The contrast in the spacebridges' viewing figures on both sides preoccupied the Soviets from the onset, so much so that Gorbachev brought it up when he and Reagan discussed the free flow of information and Soviet-American cultural reciprocity at the Reykjavik summit in 1986.[80]

Vladimir Pozner, who also commented on the differences in viewership, believed that the lack of enthusiasm about the spacebridge in the US derived from the anti-Soviet bias of American television. Another reason, in his opinion, was that producers believed that a conversation between regular people across the Iron Curtain did not make exciting viewing and was therefore unlikely to attract audiences.[81] Phil Donahue was much harsher in his assessment in a 2001 interview: "We care less about them than they care about us. They [the Russians] have an enormous curiosity about us [America] and it is not reciprocated."[82] Other American participants were less critical in their reflections. The discrepancies between the number of viewers the program was likely to generate on each side came up in a question posed by a member of the Soviet audience to the American panel in the second journalists' spacebridge. Peter Jennings's reply (offered after prodding from Pozner) both channeled and reinforced the American perspective on the respective media. Audiences in the United States, Jennings said, had many programs competing for their attention and could freely choose their viewing material. What was not said, yet strongly implied, was that Soviet audiences had only three channels, with programming determined by the government, and thus had no choice but to watch what they were given.[83]

The question of the discrepancy between viewing figures became particularly important as Soviet and American participants came to see the space-bridges as an opportunity to expose the lies of the rival's propaganda and get the truth out to audiences on the other side. Soviet organizers and participants sought to show their American interlocutors that they had been systematically misinformed about the USSR and needed to learn the truth about a whole range of issues, from the nature of the Soviet disarmament proposals to what the Soviet people were really like. Hearing it from Soviet people in flesh and blood would underscore their basic, shared humanity and the importance of dialogue and collaboration.

The goals of the American participants were more ambitious and derived to a large extent from the tradition of viewing the Soviet Union as a closed society, hungry for information about the US. From American standpoint, the spacebridge became an unprecedented opportunity to bypass the lies of Soviet propaganda and impress upon millions of Soviet people the truth about the oppressive dictatorship they lived under and about the superiority of American freedoms, democratic values, and institutions. Peter Jennings, who moderated several of the spacebridges, including a series of links between US congressmen and members of the Supreme Soviet, reflected that most Soviet viewers were profoundly influenced by the sight of American journalists criticizing Soviet government policies, so much so that they "ended up [. . .] being on our side as well."[84] The spacebridges were to become collective classrooms where the entire population of the USSR would watch American journalists deliver a master class in democracy. That such "learning" was not to be reciprocal deeply troubled Soviet participants and organizers alike: as Vladimir Pozner wondered, why should the Soviet Union allow millions to watch scathing American comments on the USSR, knowing that only a few thousand US viewers would be exposed to a critical discussion of their country's behavior?[85]

It is impossible to say how many Americans would have watched the space-bridges had they been embraced and promoted by commercial broadcasters in the US. As it stands, however, by getting behind these programs, the government-controlled, "unfree" Soviet media emerged as more daring, innovative, and open to potential political risk than their American counterparts. The Soviet commitment to *glasnost* and *perestroika* goes a long way toward explaining why leaders, producers, and journalists opted to broadcast this challenging content.[86] Their decision becomes even clearer if situated in the long-term context of Soviet reporting from the United States after 1953, and especially after 1968. Encountering a worldview so entirely at odds with the socialist ideology was not new to Soviet audiences, for they had had access to such worldviews for years through the writing of Soviet foreign correspondents. The dialogue featured in the spacebridges was certainly more stimulating than the usual programming on Soviet television, and it touched on numerous topics hitherto considered taboo. Yet the extent of these programs' departure from pre-*perestroika* information practices may have been overstated by both contemporary participants and subsequent scholarship. The popularity of the spacebridges in the USSR and the subsequent casting of the programs as a triumph of "free information" over "government propaganda" suggest that the American liberal understanding of the media was gaining more and more ground with socialist practitioners and, more broadly, illustrate the gradual decline in the mobilizing power of socialist ideology.

## 1986–1991: Mr. Kondrashov Goes to Washington. And Mr. Smith Goes to Moscow.

Although Hedrick Smith and Stanislav Kondrashov knew of each other for many years, they first met only in the winter of 1982, when Kondrashov came to Washington, DC, on a short reporting assignment. Smith headed the *New York Times* bureau in the capital and was willing to share his insights into the current state of Soviet-American relations over lunch. Having finally met Smith in person, Kondrashov thought that it was thanks to the American journalist's charming and amicable manner that so many Soviet people were willing to open up to him.[87] Since the late 1970s both journalists had remained mostly home-based. Shortly after his Moscow assignment, Hedrick Smith was transferred to the *Times*'s prestigious Washington bureau, where he became the head of the bureau and chief correspondent. Stanislav Kondrashov completed his second five-year assignment as *Izvestiia*'s permanent Washington correspondent in 1976. Back in Moscow, he served as a senior international commentator, editor, and deputy head of a department. Their senior posts demanded that they keep up with the most recent developments on the other side and with Soviet-American relations overall.

In the final years of the Cold War, both correspondents returned to long-form journalism to explore the adversary. Stanislav Kondrashov's final original account about the United States, *The Americanist's Journey*, was published in 1986.[88] Hedrick Smith's second comprehensive account about the USSR, *The*

*New Russians,* was published in 1990. New developments in Soviet-American relations prompted each journalist to reflect on the rival superpower in new ways. When examined side by side, the books make visible how each journalist's thinking about "us" and "them" evolved during the last years of the superpower conflict and highlight the different universal categories each projected onto the adversary overseas.

### Stanislav Kondrashov: *The Americanist's Journey*

Stanislav Kondrashov wrote more than ten accounts about America, many of which were published in multiple editions. In most of these books, Kondrashov wrote about himself in first person, yet reduced his presence in the narrative to an absolute minimum. The focus of the accounts was not the journalist and his experiences, but American society, the people, and the events he witnessed. The narrative voice was that of a detached, dispassionate observer; the accounts were for the most part written in a realistic, documentary style. In contrast, *The Americanist's Journey* stood out both in the depth of its introspection and in its literary form. Written in the third person, the account followed "the Americanist"—a foreign correspondent and specialist on the United States—on a special, two-month reporting assignment in the US. Whereas the journalist's role as a mediator was almost transparent in Kondrashov's previous work, this account reflected on the ways that the Americanist mediated, interpreted, and dissected American society for his readers. Moreover, *The Americanist's Journey* openly explored how the journalist's insights and observations were related to, indeed derived from, his personal worldview and past experiences. Another unprecedented feature of the book was its commitment to introspection: as the narrative unfolded, it followed the Americanist as he gazed inward, reflecting on his experiences, his past, the meaning of his personal and professional life, and how they impacted one another.

*The Americanist's Journey* was not a fictional account. Based on Kondrashov's diary, it chronicled a special reporting assignment he undertook in November and December 1982.[89] At the time, *Izvestiia*'s permanent Washington correspondent, Melor Sturua, was not allowed to return to his post, in retaliation for the expulsion of *Newsweek*'s Andrew Nagorski from Moscow. Kondrashov made no effort to disguise the fact that "the Americanist" in the story was himself, yet he never explained why he chose this distancing technique to reflect on his career as a foreign correspondent. One possible explanation, suggested in the account, is that Kondrashov hoped that this particular narrative form would illustrate how his personal experience had a larger significance and could therefore be relevant for understanding the relationship between the Soviet Union and the United States.

Kondrashov completed *The Americanist's Journey* in 1984 and submitted it for publication in the popular literary journal *Novyi Mir*, where it was meant to appear in several installments. Publication, however, was canceled. Years later, Kondrashov revealed in an interview that Glavlit banned the text because the protagonist's loyalties appeared ambiguous, and it was unclear whether "the Americanist" supported the Soviet Union or the United States.[90] Kondrashov did not try to find a new home for the book. In 1985 he added a new segment, which chronicled his assignment to cover the presidential election of 1984. Another segment was added in December 1985 and included a brief account of two important assignments that Kondrashov undertook that year: Soviet correspondents' interview with Ronald Reagan at the White House and coverage of the Geneva Summit. Throughout these sections, Kondrashov continued to refer to himself in the third person, as "the Americanist." In 1986, merely two years after it was rejected on suspicion of divided loyalties, *The Americanist* was published as a stand-alone book—a vivid illustration of how Gorbachev's "new thinking" was pushing the conventional boundaries of writing about Soviet-American relations. In 1988 *The Americanist's Journey* was published again as part of a volume that collected Kondrashov's seminal reporting from the US. Its inclusion in this volume suggests that Kondrashov considered *The Americanist's Journey* among his most important works.[91]

The Americanist's life, Kondrashov told his readers, was dedicated to living in a foreign country and writing about it. He emphasized that he did not himself choose to connect his life with America but that it was his job, his professional duty.[92] Trying to pre-empt readers' envy and fascination with his life overseas, Kondrashov stressed how difficult it was to live abroad, especially because of the painful separation from his own country. Having spent many years in a place where he did not belong, the Americanist shared the experiences neither of his compatriots at home nor of the people among whom he lived as a foreigner.[93] As he sat in an empty terminal of a Canadian airport waiting for a plane that would take him to yet another assignment in the United States, the Americanist reflected on his past and feared that he did not live his life as a participant, but merely as an observer.[94] The word *inarticulacy* dominated Kondrashov's descriptions of the Americanist, suggesting that the urge to speak out and articulate the lessons he had learned during his life abroad were the motive behind this introspective account: "His inarticulacy [*nevyskazannost'*] threatened to explode, and it seemed to him that the abundance of impressions gained abroad by one of the soldiers of the ideological front must have social relevance and must be considered in our collective ideological economy."[95] Kondrashov's purpose for writing this book was therefore to articulate the meaning of his life's work and his relevance as a socialist writer. The most important thing the Americanist could offer his fellow countrymen was his knowledge about the United States. He stressed that his experiences were of particular relevance at the time of writing, when the relationship between the two countries reached a new nadir and the threat of nuclear war seemed more real than ever.

Upon his arrival in the United States, the Americanist plunged into work, trying to catch up on the most recent political developments and understand what motivated the anti-Soviet attitudes of Ronald Reagan and his supporters. As he did so, the Americanist found himself constantly revisiting his favorite topic: "us and them." He reflected that Soviet ideas about the brotherhood of men and the unwavering commitment to the interests of the working people were far superior to the petty capitalist instincts that animated the rival superpower. Yet the United States appeared to be gaining more and more supporters around the world, thanks, the Americanist reluctantly admitted, to the better quality of everyday life. Assuming the role of an educator and coach, Kondrashov laid out the flaws of American capitalism, where an exclusive focus on material success resulted in social atomization. At the same time he emphasized that in order to overcome capitalism and win the universal battle for hearts and minds, the superior ideas of socialism had to be backed by a higher standard of living:

> Our weaknesses and shortcomings, our lagging behind in the material world, the flaws of our everyday life breed the feeling of superiority on the other side of the ocean and, in turn, help our haters and give them ammunition against us. [...] The solution is historically determined; it's simple but difficult to achieve: work, work, and work. Better than them. To win the rounds of material and spiritual competition between socialism and capitalism. For the sake of our people and for the sake of showing to the entire world. Not with the power of weapons, but with the power of example.[96]

Only by triumphing on both the material and the ideological fronts would socialism inherit the future. Acknowledging the comparative advantages of capitalism, Kondrashov urged, was essential for realizing the socialist ideal: "You must fearlessly look into the face of the changing world, look truth in the eyes and accurately evaluate the position of your country vis-à-vis other countries and other peoples."[97] In this important task, the Americanist suggested, his vast knowledge and experience overseas would make a valuable contribution to his country.

Kondrashov stressed the utmost importance of peaceful coexistence with the United States. Despite their ideological differences, the nuclear age bound the two superpowers in a shared responsibility for the future of the world. Although throughout his visit the prospects for peaceful coexistence appeared particularly bleak, on his last day in the US the Americanist found hope in a surprising place: the cinema. After attending the screening of *E.T.: The Extra-Terrestrial* in New York, the Americanist concluded that the film boiled down to one simple message: "If you love your home and your country, you must respect the love of other people (and even of creatures from other planets) for their homes, their countries, their planets."[98] The Americanist found it encouraging that a film that stressed that mutual respect was the only way to overcome mutual destruction enjoyed such popularity with American viewers. Here Kondrashov revealed his second potential contribution as a socialist writer: to help Soviet people better understand the rival superpower and respect it. His years of experience living among the Americans and his vast knowledge of the other side would be crucial for the development of peaceful coexistence and essential for preventing nuclear holocaust.

In writing *The Americanist's Journey*, Stanislav Kondrashov sought to articulate the relevance of his experiences to his country and fellow citizens as they stood at an important historical crossroads. Kondrashov's mission also had deep personal meaning: he looked to writing as a way to reestablish his sense of belonging to socialist society, which he felt was lost after years of living in the US. In the passage that concluded the 1984 account, Kondrashov expressed the hope that articulating his thoughts would help restore clarity to his professional identity and his self-understanding:

> Your personal and your private [self], your life, fate, longings, nostalgia are exposed to the utmost. And with the utmost clarity, you sense the elements shared by two countries confronting one another in a shared nuclear age. You are both a private and a public man, through whom time flowed in a peculiar way. This is what was unsaid until now. And this is why you are burdened with inarticulacy and keep traveling there again and again, even though you are growing heavier and more cognizant of the contingencies of your life there. And this central thought, this explanation of your torments suddenly occurs to you

when, sitting alone at your desk, you begin yet another effort to settle the score with your readers.[99]

Kondrashov opened up to his readers and revealed his inner world: the sense of alienation, the desire to be relevant, and the melancholic feelings of a middle-aged man who wondered whether his youth had been wasted. Kondrashov sought articulation in order to reconnect the professional and personal aspects of his existence. His calls to his fellow Soviet people to work hard to overcome capitalism and realize the promise of socialism can be read as self-admonishing, a call to himself to overcome the impact of foreign life. Articulation would help Kondrashov become complete again; clarification of his contribution as a socialist writer would also restore his sense of coherence as a socialist person. In his last paragraph, Kondrashov showed that even these private anxieties were relevant to a larger cause, for his peculiar liminal position revealed with utmost clarity that the two sides of the Cold War divide were intimately connected.

Several features thus distinguished this account from Kondrashov's previous work and from the writings of his colleagues. In using an analysis of the Cold War adversary to reveal and work through his personal and professional uncertainties, Kondrashov pushed the established boundaries of the profession and the genre alike. Similarly unconventional was Kondrashov's willingness to admit the impact of life in America on his private self and to explore it openly. Kondrashov's discussion of the comparative advantages of capitalism, while not new in itself, exhibited unprecedented levels of self-criticism. Overall, *The Americanist's Journey* aligned with the responsibilities that *glasnost* entrusted to the Soviet media and demonstrated how Gorbachev's new policies resonated with Kondrashov's worldview. Indeed, the 1982 diary on which the book was based anticipated many of the ideas that would become staples of the "new thinking" and *glasnost*.[100] Kondrashov, too, put forward the idea of an interdependent world where the leading superpowers shared a responsibility to prevent nuclear war. Keenly aware of the large gaps separating Soviet and American cultures, ideologies, and national characters, Kondrashov sought to impress on his readers that both sides shared a basic humanity, aversion to war, and love for their homelands. At the same time, Kondrashov exhibited a passionate conviction in the moral and cultural superiority of the Soviet Union and was eager to see socialism enjoy the worldwide recognition it deserved. *The Americanist's Journey* combined an internationalist ethos with the profound commitment to socialist ideas—a blend that characterized Kondrashov and many other journalists of his generation, as well as Gorbachev's "new thinking."

## Hedrick Smith: *The New Russians*

When Hedrick Smith left Moscow in 1974, he thought it highly unlikely that he would return in the foreseeable future. His hunch became a certainty after *The Russians* was published in the United States and the Soviets caught word of its contents. Several copies made it into the Soviet Union, joining a long list of forbidden books. Smith's account was attacked in the Soviet press and he became persona non grata.[101] Smith did not return to Moscow until 1988, when he was in the press corps that covered President Reagan's summit meeting with Mikhail Gorbachev. Shortly after that, he resigned from the *Times* to start a new career as a writer and documentary producer for PBS, launching his own production company three years later. Between 1988 and 1991, as a major personal and professional transition in Smith's life overlapped with a historical transition in the USSR, he returned several times to report on new developments, to film a series of documentaries for PBS titled *Inside Gorbachev's USSR*, and to collect materials for a new book that would become a sequel to his 1976 bestseller.[102] *The New Russians* first appeared in 1990, offering an analysis of Gorbachev's reforms and the changes they had introduced into Soviet politics and society. Another edition, which included Smith's account of the failed coup of August 1991, was published a year later.

Hedrick Smith began his new account where he had ended *The Russians*.[103] When he left the country in 1974, he told his readers, it seemed impossible that Russia would undergo any fundamental change. Recapping the idea of Eternal Russia, Smith explained that after "five long centuries of absolutism," from Ivan the Terrible to Leonid Brezhnev, authoritarian rule became "firmly embedded in Russian society and ingrained in the Russian psyche."[104] The Soviet people were "submissive" and passive and showed no political initiative; they expected the state to take care of all their needs and "to tell them what to do."[105] Unlike Westerners, who strove for improvement and innovation, Soviets were held back by state dogma and by their own inertia. Smith recalled that everything that he knew about Russian history and the Russian national character, every experience he had had living in the USSR, told him that even modest, let alone fundamental, changes would be highly unlikely. Back in 1974, Smith concluded, "Soviet politics appeared as frozen as the Siberian tundra."[106]

Sure enough, Smith admitted, less than ten years later, it turned out that he was wrong. Since Mikhail Gorbachev had come to power in 1985, the new youthful leader had unleashed transformation on a scale no one had thought possible and had empowered the Soviet people "to begin taking their destinies in their own hands."[107] Smith conveyed his enthusiasm about *perestroika* through metaphors of awakening and renewal. "In the name of reforms that would modernize, humanize, and ultimately save Soviet socialism," he told his readers, Gorbachev had "summoned a democratic spirit that aroused the slumbering giant of Russia."[108] So much had changed in the Soviet Union that Smith was moved to proclaim 1985 as the dawn of "the world of the New Russians," and he was eager to explore it in greater depth.[109] The value of such an exploration, Smith explained, could not be overestimated. The reforms introduced by Gorbachev had worldwide, universal significance: "The transformation now under way in the Soviet Union [. . .] is a modern reenactment of one of the archetypal stories of human existence, the story of how people and societies transform themselves, grow and change. It's a story of the struggle from darkness to light, from poverty toward prosperity, from dictatorship toward democracy. [. . .] What is happening now to people in the Soviet Union has universal meaning. It is an affirmation of the human capacity for change, growth, renewal."[110]

Previously, Smith had argued that the Russian national character and traditions of absolutism excluded it from the universal processes that characterized the development of the West.[111] Now Smith inscribed the Soviet Union into the universal story of progress from the "darkness" of oppression, hardship, and denial to the "light" of freedom, democracy, and prosperity. With the reforms unleashing the Soviet people's true human potential, Russia was ready to cast off its eternal nature and join the West. Were the Soviets about to become like Americans then? Smith warned against setting hopes too high: "It is tempting for us in the West, especially Americans, to witness such sea changes in events and in people's psychology and then to interpret them through the prism of our own values, our own political framework. [. . .] Our framework is capitalism and multiparty democracy; our way of life seems so natural, so right to us, that we take for granted that once dictatorship is removed, Russians deep-down will feel and then assert our same values."[112]

In the successive chapters, as he explored changes in the Soviet media, economy, and politics, Smith introduced a diverse cast of Soviet characters who explained what *perestroika* meant to them in their own words. At the same time, the broader alternative framework, or how to make sense of the new developments without falling back on liberal values, remained unclear.

Smith's first stop was the world of media and Soviet information policies, with an emphasis on the changes brought by *glasnost*. Smith introduced readers to the Levada group—an innovative collective of sociologists who pioneered public opinion polling in the Soviet Union. He explained how, by asking bold questions in their polls and collaborating with Soviet newspapers, the Levada group contributed to the building of civil society and democracy in the Soviet Union.[113] Smith then moved on to examine how the Soviet press (labeled "the troubadours of truth") launched an open discussion of the country's problems, began to investigate corrupt officials, and introduced the public to previously forbidden books, such as *The Gulag Archipelago* and *Doctor Zhivago*.[114] The people' hunger for truth, Smith concluded, created genuine competition within the Soviet media. Given the choice, Soviet readers turned their backs on "propaganda peddlers" and embraced "real news" instead.[115] Soviet journalists now led the nation into a "classroom in democracy" with a range of television programs that explored the painful history of Stalinism, investigated party officials, staged candid debates, and discussed previously forbidden topics.[116]

As he examined the changes brought by *glasnost*, Smith situated the Soviet media in his overall narrative of a transition from oppression to freedom. Soviet journalists were depicted as shedding their ideological shackles and finally enjoying the freedom to speak up and express a broad range of opinions and viewpoints. The press came across as taking its rightful role as a watchdog that holds government officials accountable for their actions. Soviet media were depicted as creating an informed, politically engaged public, ready to participate in the democratic process. Smith made sure to remind his readers that "*glasnost* does not connote the full freedoms that American newspapers and television networks take for granted."[117] This caveat notwithstanding, Smith's overall portrayal of an emancipated Soviet media closely resembled the American ideal of a liberal press as the centerpiece of democracy. It appeared that *glasnost* was transforming the Soviet press into its American counterpart.

As Hedrick Smith explored the different facets of *perestroika*, his readiness to part with the idea of Eternal Russia showed its limits. At every stage of his journey through the worlds of information, economy, and politics, Smith stressed that the successful outcome of reforms was contingent on the Russians' willingness and ability to *overcome* their national character. Although Soviet people "were fed up with the degrading misery of their lives," many of them "recoiled from change, preferring the old, familiar hell."[118] Gorbachev's drive to revamp the economy was challenged by Russian "escapism," "impracticality," and "lackadaisical attitude towards work."[119] The dreams of self-determination harbored by the Soviet nationalities clashed with Russian nationalists' nostalgia for a strong ruler and their determination to preserve the empire at all costs.[120] Efforts to promote democracy ultimately faced a resistance that, Smith claimed, "has been embedded in the Russian psyche by a long history of absolutism under both czars and commissars."[121] Smith himself often appeared to waver between hopes for the Soviet Union's successful transformation and fears that "Mother Russia" would get the better of it. Repeated references to the challenges posed by the Russian character created the impression that the Soviet people participated in reforms as if *in spite of* themselves, underlining Smith's portrayal of *perestroika* as internal struggle of epic proportions. Even though Smith recognized and celebrated the changes sweeping through the Soviet Union, he did not altogether abandon the idea of Eternal Russia. Now it emerged, as if constantly undermining the efforts of the "New Russians" to shed the ballast of their past and catch up with the West.

Unlike Kondrashov, Smith rarely ventured into comparative contemplations about "us" and "them." And whereas Kondrashov's comparative reflections often led him to think critically about his own country, Smith's new experiences in the Soviet Union occasioned no critical reflections on the United States. When the United States featured in the introduction to the book, it appeared as both the inspiration and the model for Soviet reforms. According to Smith, the very existence of *perestroika* demonstrated that despite isolation, censorship, and indoctrination, the Soviets had finally recognized what many foreign observers had known all along: that the USSR failed to fulfill its promise to deliver a better life to its citizens and lagged behind the West in every sphere: "If America and the West played any role in provoking *perestroika*, it was not through any specific policy of the 1980s, but rather because of our long-term economic success. [...] by the early 1980s, the brightest people in the Soviet system could see the telling contrast between Soviet stagnation and Western progress. They could see that the world was passing them by—and that realization forced them to reexamine their own system, to try to find out what had failed and discover ways to shake their nation out of its despotic lethargy."[122]

Progress—equated by Smith with economic success, information age, and democratic institutions—appeared intrinsic to the Western way of life. Shedding the "despotic lethargy" imposed by socialist ideology and adopting the Western political and economic model was the only way the Soviet Union could catch up with the rest of the developed world. Although Smith used Gorbachev's term "stagnation" to discuss the imperative for reform, his idea of "stagnation" differed from the one featured in the Soviet rationale for *perestroika*. Gorbachev used the term "stagnation" to describe how the Soviet Union had fallen short of its own principles and its difficulties in meeting the goals of socialism.[123] Smith contrasted Soviet "stagnation" with Western "progress" and used the contrast to emphasize the bankruptcy of the socialist way of life, as he had done in the 1970s. Now that the Soviets themselves appeared to share Smith's view of Western progress and Soviet stagnation, he had even fewer reasons to acknowledge that in his own country, many people remained excluded from "long-term economic success." Although the United States was rarely mentioned in the book, binary categories—despotism versus freedom, stagnation versus progress—informed Smith's analysis of Soviet developments, as did the idea of the superiority of the American political and economic model. Hedrick Smith thus reiterated his previous ideas about the "natures" of Russia and the West and positioned *perestroika* as evidence of the latter's superiority.

Set side by side, Kondrashov's and Smith's books highlight both the changes and the continuities in the ways that Cold War correspondents reflected on their countries of expertise in the last years of the superpower confrontation. The binary between "truth" and "lies" continued to inform the professional understanding of both journalists, albeit in new ways. For Kondrashov, the new era brought forward the imperative to acknowledge the comparative shortcomings of the Soviet socialist project and to assess realistically the true state of socialism in the world. "Looking the truth in the eyes" meant seeing that the United States was winning hearts and minds, evaluating *both* systems critically, learning from Soviet shortcomings, and deducing what needed to be done. The Soviet journalist figured as the bearer of truth who would prompt his country to engage in honest, critical self-reflection and who could show his compatriots the way forward. Kondrashov remained convinced that the truth was on his side. In his view, socialist ideology was the only ideology committed to peace, equality, and fraternity, and the only one that appealed to humankind's true nature. For Hedrick Smith, the last years of the Cold War represented the triumph of truth over the centuries-long deception that autocracy, dogma, and censorship had imposed on the Russian people. In his account, truth was synonymous with the superiority of the US economic model and political freedoms. It was this universal truth, long known to the American journalist, that the Soviet people were now finally free to embrace.

Stanislav Kondrashov dedicated his professional life to chronicling, analyzing, and explaining the United States to Soviet readers. Though he was not naïve about the realities of daily life in the USSR, Kondrashov invited his readers to compare the Cold War adversary with an *ideal* version of their country, a version that would realize the socialist promise and combine a high quality of life with equality and social justice. In *The Americanist's Journey*, Kondrashov put forward a different conception of comparative thinking. *Glasnost* made it imperative to acknowledge, explicitly and publicly, that there was a gap between Soviet reality and the socialist ideal. At the same time, Kondrashov urged his readers to appreciate the ideal itself, to understand its comparative advantages, and to keep striving toward its realization. Hedrick Smith was a sharp and brilliant journalist with many years of experience reporting at home and abroad. In his subsequent journalistic work, he focused on interrogating the staples of the "American Dream" and exposed the gaps between the ideal and the reality that many Americans confronted in their everyday life. Smith's books and documentaries offered critical and often uncompromising assessments of US politics, economy, education, and science. Yet in his books dedicated to "Russia" and "the Russians," Smith invariably contrasted the USSR with an *ideal* United States, free from injustice or inequality, where the "American Dream" had been realized.

The persistent presence in the writing of both correspondents of the ideal state, in which the promises of a socialist utopia or an American Dream were available to all, demonstrates how immersed they were in the battle of ideas that characterized the Cold War. Each saw his country as the custodian of truth, his ideology as the only one that was consistent with human nature and that deserved to inherit the future. Stanislav Kondrashov trusted that only socialism could ensure a future free from war, where the "brotherhood of men" would rise above "petty instincts." Hedrick Smith suggested that liberal democracy and capitalism represented the only path to a future in which freedom would triumph over oppression. At the end of 1991, it appeared that readers on both sides where more inclined to side with Smith than with Kondrashov.

A comparative examination of these accounts also captures the place of the respective ideologies as they faced the end of the Cold War order. Soviet socialism reflected on its mistakes yet remained confident in its own ultimate triumph. The Soviet Union looked at its foreign "other" to understand how to be *not capitalist* and *triumph over capitalism* at the same time. Unprecedented levels of self-criticism on the one hand and a succession of failed solutions on the other eventually eroded the Soviet public's commitment to the Soviet project. The Cold War's final years prompted little comparable critical self-reflection in the United States. On the contrary, the disintegration of the

Soviet empire shortly after the end of the Cold War gave rise to a triumpha-list narrative that positioned the US as the "winner" of the superpower con-flict. Politicians, policy makers, pundits, scholars, and members of the public mistook the ideal America, which had emerged from comparisons with Soviet socialism, for reality. They presented the collapse of the Soviet empire as proof that US ideology was infallible.[124] Ultimately, this triumphalist approach obscured the experience of all those who felt excluded from the American dream, or threatened by it.

Stanislav Kondrashov continued to profess his commitment to socialist ideas until his death in 2006. In the final years of his life, he believed that his country's excessive faith in capitalist values and Western models had led it on a path to disaster.[125] In 2012 Hedrick Smith published a new book exploring how US corporations, banks, and politicians had robbed the middle class of its political power and its share of the nation's economic prosperity. Smith's book was entitled *Who Stole the American Dream?*

# Us and Them

In November 2017, the Russian television channel RT America registered as a foreign agent under the US Foreign Agents Registration Act (FARA).[1] Subsequently, the channel's congressional press credentials were revoked, and RT America lost access to the congressional press gallery. RT America's registration under FARA came amid a scandal surrounding allegations of Russia's intervention in the US presidential election campaign of 2016. During the preceding months, RT America and its mother network RT—an international multilingual television network backed by the Russian state—had become the objects of unwavering attention on part of US news media, politicians, government officials, and intelligence services.[2] American observers charged that RT journalists were not "real journalists" and that RT itself was not a real news service but a Russian government-controlled propaganda machine. RT was depicted as a major player in a broader Russian conspiracy to subvert American democracy by harnessing digital technology, abusing social media, and peddling "fake news."[3] The effort to bar RT America from the congressional galleries closely resembled the 1951 campaign against TASS. In contrast to 1951 though, those in favor of expelling had the upper hand.

Russian president Vladimir Putin called the attacks on RT America "ridiculous and undemocratic." Evoking the binary between truth and lies, Putin stated that the channel had been singled out because its truthful and courageous reporting challenged the media "monopoly" of the "Anglo-Saxon world." Putin portrayed RT as a plucky David facing the Goliath of British and US global news media outlets and accused the latter of interfering in the domestic affairs of "almost every country in the world." In his concluding remarks, the Russian president promised a "swift mirror response."[4] A few days later, Putin signed new legislation empowering the Russian Ministry of Justice to require that foreign mass media operating in Russia register as "agents of a foreign government" and disclose their finances.[5] A subsequently published list named the Voice of America, Radio Free Europe/Radio Liberty (RFE/RL), and their affiliate Russian-language or local-language news outlets as "foreign agents."[6]

Senator John McCain (R-AZ), chairman of the Senate Armed Services Committee and 2008 Republican nominee for president of the United States, issued a public statement condemning RT and Putin's actions: "As a champion for free speech and free press around the world, the United States must be very clear: there is no equivalence between RT and television networks such as Voice of America, Radio Free Europe/Radio Liberty, CNN, or the BBC. The journalists that work for these networks seek the truth, debunk lies, and hold governments accountable. RT's propagandists debunk the truth, spread lies, and seek to undermine democratic governments in order to further Vladimir Putin's agenda."[7] McCain's remarks placed the binaries between truth and lies and between democracy and tyranny at the foreground of the conflict around RT and, more broadly, at the heart of the dispute over Russia's alleged interference in the US elections. In McCain's view, American news media (and the BBC) were the custodians of truth, concerned with spreading democracy, and thus represented a direct opposite of RT—a mouthpiece of lies and hostile propaganda and an instrument of Russian dictatorship. Exposing RT as "a propaganda network," McCain concluded, was essential for defending American democracy.

The row over RT was but a small episode in a series of events that have cumulatively come to be known as the worst period in Russian-American relations since the end of the Cold War. This new confrontation unfolded on several fronts, including security, politics, economics, and human rights, and touched on developments in Ukraine, Western Europe, and the Middle East. Yet the biggest point of contention in American-Russian relations became the allegations of Russian interference in the US presidential election in 2016. The allegations—denied by Russian officials—sent shock waves throughout the American political system and the international news cycle.[8] In what struck many as a replay of Cold War scenarios, each side accused the other of subversion, the spreading of propaganda, and "fake news."[9] Each side insisted on the truthfulness of its own media and *their* accurate representations of reality in contrast with the other's lies. A shattering of the sense of national identity, the hopes and fears associated with new media and digital technology, and different interpretations of the end of the Cold War fueled a frenzy of mutual accusations.[10]

Anxieties about information—especially information emanating from hostile powers and hostile media outlets—dominated the conversation on both sides. Some of the principal actors involved in this episode—RT America, RT, Voice of America, and Radio Free Europe/Radio Liberty—were the direct descendants of Soviet and American international broadcasting services that had developed during the Cold War.[11] Now, as then, government officials and information specialists were trying to implement policies aimed at reducing the threat of enemy propaganda and adopting solutions that had little effect on information technology.[12] In the United States and in Russia, official rhetoric and public discussions established enemy disinformation as the single most important threat to the values each side held most dear: American democracy and the political stability of the Russian state, respectively. Of the many points of tension between Russia and the United States, the one revolving around information became the most resonant precisely *because* it evoked the threat of subversion and hostile propaganda, drawing the battle lines between truth and lies.

The story of foreign correspondents, and of Cold War mass media more broadly, helps to explain why information was—and remains to this day—a bone of contention in American-Russian relations. The Cold War gave birth to a political culture that was dominated by the binary between "truth" and "lies," and this culture remained at the heart of the superpowers' ideological conflict even as its contours shifted over the years.[13] Information emerged as the central arena where the ideological conflict played out: it was imagined as the problem at the origin of the Cold War and the solution that would ultimately end the superpower confrontation. Mass media became an object of analysis and a subject of concern, as leaders and pundits scrutinized the rival's press as key to understanding the enemy's nature, intentions, and policies. Mass media emerged as both a source of anxiety, as each side worried about the subversion and propaganda of the enemy press, and a source of hope that reporting could advance the cause of global democracy or prevent nuclear war. The press became the symbolic embodiment of political systems and national identities as both sides paraded their newspapers and their journalists as the custodians of truth and freedom, who would help their compatriots understand themselves in comparison with the adversary and who would safeguard the world's future.

In a recent pioneering study, historian Masuda Hajimu differentiated between the Cold War as an "elite discourse" generated by pundits and politicians, which emphasized the conflict between the superpowers, and as a "constructed reality" whereby individuals and groups actively participated in shaping the meaning of the Cold War and made it relevant to their lives and experiences.[14] Masuda's insight provides a useful framework for understanding the role of foreign correspondents as the *link* between the elite discourse and the constructed reality of the Cold War. The core principles of socialism on the one hand and of capitalism and liberal democracy on the other guided the observations of foreign correspondents and helped them make sense of their experiences. These subjective experiences were then translated into "objective knowledge," which was transmitted to the journalists' audiences and taught them how to think about themselves in comparison with the adversary. It was through the observations, the experience, and the writing of foreign correspondents that Cold War ideology and knowledge about the other were produced, elaborated, and became meaningful.

Although Soviet and American journalists became the symbols of the two opposing ideological systems, this book has demonstrated that they had more in common than is usually thought. Soviet and American foreign correspondents were firmly embedded within their countries' elites: they usually trained in their countries' prestigious institutions and had deep professional, cultural, and social ties with their respective political establishments. On both sides, foreign correspondents usually took a range of minor assignments abroad before their posting in the Soviet Union or the United States. In most cases, such an assignment served as a springboard to a successful career as an editor, commentator, or political adviser. Most Cold War correspondents were men. These factors explain the many similarities one finds in the reporting produced by the two respective press corps over the years, and they guided my own decision to examine the work of these correspondents as a corpus—indeed, as a *genre*.

Contemporary commentators in the Soviet Union and the United States noted the shared features in the reports of the adversary's correspondents and attributed these similarities to the workings of rival ideology. American observers often charged that all Soviet journalists were singing the same tune and that they were not doing any *real* reporting but merely repeating the Communist Party line. Soviet commentators frequently complained that there was a unanimously hostile tone emanating from the reports of the American journalists and accused them of purposefully misrepresenting the Soviet Union to please their bourgeois masters. These similarities in the reporting produced by the respective sets of correspondents over the years did not, however, derive from orders imposed from above. Rather, they occurred because journalists' personal and professional self-understanding was forged and fashioned by the foundational principles of Soviet state socialism or of American liberal democracy and market capitalism.

On both sides, the reporting of foreign correspondents was bound by a set of external and internal constraints, which in turn were shaped by their countries' respective ideologies of the press and by the ongoing developments in superpower relations. In Soviet international reporting, ideology operated *overtly*—through party and state officials, Glavlit censors, and editors, who determined the thematic boundaries of journalistic reports. Although Soviet correspondents wrote within these boundaries, there was still an opportunity for negotiation, as well as room for individual journalists' personal styles, approaches, and pursuit of topics they found interesting and important. Although American correspondents had greater room for maneuver than their Soviet colleagues, they too wrote within a certain system of editorial and official constraints. In US international reporting, ideology operated *covertly*—through editorial intervention, the framing of reports with headlines and runners, and informal discussions among journalists, editors, and government officials. The extent of the limitations and the consequences of crossing the boundaries obviously differed: Soviet journalists had fewer alternatives and more to lose than their American colleagues.

Acknowledging and understanding these differences does not diminish the importance of the parallels. Foreign correspondents on both sides were personally invested in their respective ideologies, and they animated them through their reports. They tasked their audiences with reading their reports comparatively and with inferring the superiority of the Soviet Union or the United States from descriptions of life on the other side. In this way, they helped their compatriots to fashion themselves as socialist or liberal subjects. International reporting on both sides tended to privilege certain types of stories or angles while suppressing or downplaying others, and was shaped by the reactions journalists anticipated from the official establishment and the reading public. American and Soviet journalists alike were bound by their own internalized assumptions regarding what one could and could not write about the adversary—an understanding that their readers, or the powers that be, would not welcome *all* truths and that telling *certain* truths could ruin one's professional standing and career. Nevertheless, Soviet and American correspondents alike claimed to be speaking the truth, and these claims should be taken seriously and interrogated.

Among the central questions explored in this book was what "truth" meant for American and Soviet correspondents and how their claims to speak the truth produced diametrically opposed narratives about what the Soviet Union and the United States were *really* like. Foreign correspondents on both sides adhered to truth-telling ethics and standards, yet their understandings of the truth were contingent on their respective political and professional cultures. The introduction to this book distinguished between the Soviet notion of an absolute truth and the Western notion of a relativist truth, or what Natalia Roudakova called the "truth of meaning" and the "truth of facts."[15] In the Soviet understanding, truth was singular, absolute, and tangible. The journalist's duty was to identify how the truth of socialism manifested itself in particular stories and to educate socialist readers by highlighting these stories' universal importance. Like their Western colleagues, Soviet journalists researched their stories, sought to establish the facts, interviewed their subjects, and endeavored to engage their readers. Unlike their Western counterparts, Soviet journalists relied on literary devices and narrative enhancements, and they often blurred the lines between facts and interpretations. The American journalists' truth-finding mission concentrated on uncovering the facts, accurately reporting multiple perspectives, and carefully separating reporting from analysis. The Western liberal understanding of journalism allowed for the coexistence of multiple truths, accommodating different interpretations, approaches, and perspectives on the same issue.[16] However, a comparative analysis of Cold War reporting reveals that American journalists also adhered to a certain "absolute truth"—one which held that liberal democracy and market capitalism were superior to all other forms of social arrangement and thus best suited for liberating human potential. Similarly, Soviet correspondents also often incorporated a certain degree of "relativist truth" in their work, at times acknowledging that different cultures and people had different values and could entertain different versions of truth, and that these truths could be irreconcilable. Both the "truth of meaning" and the "truth of facts" ultimately inspired journalists to look beyond the imperfections of their own societies and to contrast the other side with an ideal world where the promises of socialism or of liberal democracy would be realized in full.

Cold War correspondents were professionally and personally invested in the ethics of truth telling. They were also committed to understanding the other side's interpretation of the truth and endeavored to explain it to their compatriots. The dedication to understanding the adversary, despite the gulfs separating the two superpowers, allowed these journalists to develop a certain appreciation of the rival's culture and achievements. A close reading of their reporting reveals a persistent sympathy, and even empathy, toward the people on the other side. However critical foreign correspondents might have been in regard to the other country's politics, social structures, values, or basic aspects of daily life, however immersed they may have been in stereotypical views of the rival, they still made an effort to make the "other" more familiar and looked for shared human elements on both sides of the divide.

These aspects of Cold War correspondents' work become visible perhaps only in hindsight, in comparison with more recent reporting wherein the "othering" of Russia in American media and vice versa is more prevalent than efforts to make the "other" more intelligible. Although the end of the Cold War and the revolutions in travel and communications brought the two sides closer together, a contemporary consumer of Russian and American media may be forgiven for having the impression that they are further apart now than they were before 1991. Despite frequent assertions to the contrary, Russians' and Americans' mutual preoccupation remains as powerful as ever, and its effects are visible in politics, mainstream media, and popular culture. Even though the information world created and inhabited by Cold War correspondents is no more, this preoccupation testifies to the endurance of a peculiar historical phenomenon: Americans and Russians still seem to find it hard to understand themselves without the other.

Much like international reporting in the Cold War, this project involved a great deal of traveling across geographical and cultural boundaries. As the book arrives at its final destination, it is time to thank all those who guided, inspired, supported, encouraged, and made me feel at home every step of the way.

Jochen Hellbeck and David Foglesong have been the most encouraging and generous teachers and friends. It was David who first suggested that I check out the accounts of foreign correspondents, lent me two American journalists' books, and ignited my interest in this subject. And when my research hit an early roadblock, it was Jochen who made me realize this project's depth and breadth and how rewarding it was going to be. David's probing questions and meticulous comments reminded me to pay attention to details without losing sight of the bigger picture. Jochen's careful guidance helped me understand what was really important in, and about, my sources and inspired me to take my insights to places I never thought possible. Like good parents, my mentors were supportive, patient, demanding, encouraging, reassuring, and truly caring. They read many, many drafts and chapters, they were always available to hear about my triumphs and trials, and as they did, they imparted rigorous comments and sage advice. I will never be able to thank them enough for their hard work, for their generosity, and for their support. I hope both Jochen and David enjoy this book and see how much their guidance and their intellectual work inspired my own scholarship.

Each interaction with my dissertation committee at Rutgers taught me what kind of scholar and mentor I want to become. Ziva Galili has been a source of inspiration and original ideas as well as a most generous friend ever since we first met. Jackson Lears's seminars were an intellectual rollercoaster that taught me to think imaginatively and to think big and profoundly shaped my understanding of modernity and "the West." David Greenberg's seminars helped me find my way into the world of American journalism and provided a stimulating environment where I could engage my sources for the first time. Christopher Read projected his support all the way from Coventry to New Jersey, and I am grateful for his mentorship and expert guidance on the British academic system.

A splendid cohort of fellow scholars made my time at Rutgers a special experience that I will never forget. Paul Clemens, Melissa Feinberg, Paul Hanebrink, Allen Howard, Temma Kaplan, Seth Koven, and Yael Zerubavel provided ample encouragement, thoughtful comments, and helpful advice. I am grateful to Andrew Daily, Courtney Doucette, Matt Friedman, Alix Genter, Molly Giblin, Bridget Gurtler, Dennis Halpin, Yelena Kalinsky, Melanie Kiechle, Alissa Klots, Anita Kurimay, Yvette Lane, Rebecca Lubot, Amir Mane, Allison Miller, Nick Molnar, Svanur Pétursson, Kris Shields, and Dora Vargha for their brilliance, their friendship, and their emotional and intellectual generosity throughout graduate school and thereafter. The road to Rutgers and beyond would not have been the same without Tal Zalmanovich, whose compassion, humor, wisdom, intellect, and companionship have been comforting and empowering me for years. I thank Tal for her presence in my life and for being my friend.

My teachers at Tel Aviv University—Igal Halfin, Vera Kaplan, Eyal Naveh, Billie Mehlman, Irad Malkin, and the late Boaz Neumann—introduced me to the magic of studying history and nurtured my passion for it. Their lectures and seminars made me realize how exciting reading primary sources, thinking about big ideas, and engaging with the ideas of others could be and helped me discover that I wanted to become a scholar. My teachers' generosity and support helped me undertake this journey, and they inspire me and make me proud to this day.

I am truly fortunate to have amazing friends whose presence in my life makes all the difference. Artemy Kalinovsky read all the chapters, sometimes more than once and sometimes on very short notice, offered rigorous comments, and cheered at my progress. I am deeply grateful for Artemy's generous engagement with my work and for his friendship. My understanding of journalism would not have been the same without my friend Simon Huxtable, whose comradery, insight, thoughtful comments, and imaginative scholarship have shaped my work in immeasurable ways. I thank Miri Raphael, Michal Lee Sapir, Irit Klein, Leah Goldman, and Maike Lehman for always reminding me that true friendship defies time and space.

It is a great privilege to partake in a scholarly community that makes my professional life intellectually exciting and personally rewarding. Fellow scholars of Soviet journalism Thomas Wolfe, Natalia Roudakova, and Mary Catherine French have been always encouraging and generous with their ideas, and their scholarship had enriched my work in numerous ways. I am deeply grateful to Rachel Applebaum, Sari Autio-Sarasmo, Choi Chatterjee, Christine Evans, Juliane Fürst, Diane Koenker, Pia Koivunen, Rósa Magnúsdóttir, Margaret Peacock, Sudha Rajagopalan, Susan Reid, Kristin Roth-Ey, Andrey Shcherbenok, Yuri Slezkine, and Vladislav Zubok for their thoughtful comments, generous advice, and encouragement. Their insights and wisdom have benefited my work immensely over the years, and I feel fortunate whenever I get to spend time in their company. I am also indebted to Dayna Barnes, Lise Butler, Natalia Chernyshova, David Engerman, Jacob Feygin, Anna Fishzon, Kristy Ironside, Tom Junes, Simo Mikkonnen, Alex Oberländer, Mike Paulaskas, Anatoly Pinsky, Jan Plamper, Or Rosenboim, James Ryan, Daniel Strieff, Nimrod Tal, and Kirill Tomoff, as well as my colleagues at the University of Amsterdam and at City, University of London, for their kindness and comradely spirit.

A range of institutions provided financial support for my research and offered a nurturing intellectual home for developing my ideas. Generous funding from the Rutgers University History Department, the Rutgers University School of Arts and Social Sciences, the Andrew W. Mellon Foundation, and the Society for Historians of American Foreign Relations supported the research and writing of my doctoral dissertation. More recently, funding from my department at City, University of London allowed me to secure the permissions for images in this book.

In 2007–2008, I had the good fortune to be a graduate fellow at the Rutgers Center for Historical Analysis, which during that year explored "the Question of the West." The readings, seminar discussions, and participants' generous comments on my own work profoundly shaped this project in its early stages and enriched my thinking. I am grateful to Ann Fabian and Jackson Lears for this opportunity. In 2012 I had the pleasure to be affiliated with the Tamiment Library at New York University. A postdoctoral fellowship at the Center for the United States and the Cold War provided a supportive setting for turning the dissertation into a book and conducting additional research. I thank Kevyne Barr, Zuzanna Kobrzynski, Sam Lebovic, Mary Nolan, Ellen Schrecker, my cofellows at the center, and the participants in the Cold War seminars for their ideas, their generous insights, and their kindness. Marilyn B. Young was an intellectual tour de force and an amazingly warm person who enriched my work in numerous ways. I hope she would have liked the direction that her insights inspired me to take. Thanks to the Max Planck Society's Minerva Fellowship, I was able to spend a year at the Research Centre for East European Studies at the University of Bremen. I am indebted to Susanne Schattenberg, Olga Sveshnikova, Ulrike Huhn, Maria Klassen, and Nikolai Mitrokhin for welcoming me to Bremen and for helping to make my time there both enjoyable and intellectually productive. I also thank the participants in conferences and seminars where I presented my work-in-progress for their suggestions and comments.

This book would have looked different and taken longer without the help of many people who are really good at what they do. Francesca Pitaro and Valerie Komor at the Associated Press Corporate Archives provided expert guidance to the collections and helped me locate precious documents and images. Ralph Gibson at the London bureau of Sputnik Images and Tal Nadan at the New York Public Library helped me find images and secure permissions. Timur Mukhamatulin and Umayra Rashidova provided assistance with research and transcription. A big thank you goes to Brian Becker, Esther Blokbergen, and Alix Genter for their meticulous and expert editing of my prose. The editorial staff at Johns Hopkins University Press made my work on the book as enjoyable and as stress free as possible. I am grateful to Elizabeth Demers for commissioning this book and to Laura Davulis and Esther P. Rodriguez for responding to my million queries with cheer and calm and for their support and encouragement. I thank Juliana McCarthy for expertly chaperoning this book into production and Heidi Fritschel for her patient and careful work on copyediting the manuscript at its final stage. I also thank Margaret Peacock as well as the anonymous reviewers who read my book proposal and my manuscript for their thoughtful and generous engagement with my work and for recommending it for publication.

Meeting my protagonists was one of the great pleasures of working on this project. I thank the Cold War correspondents Mikhail Beglov, Genrikh Borovik, Susan Jacoby, Robert Kaiser, Andrew Nagorski, Peter Pringle, Jerrold Schecter, Hedrick Smith, Melor Sturua, and Valentin Zorin, as well as Zhores Medvedev, Natan Sharansky, and Ambassador Jack F. Matlock, for sharing with me their memories and experiences. Tatiana Strel'nikova and Vasily Strel'nikov kindly helped me to learn more about their father, Boris Strel'nikov, and allowed me access to some of his letters and photos. Natalia Beglova shared valuable information about Ivan Beglov and his family. I am deeply grateful to Nikolai Kondrashov for welcoming me into his family home and for trusting me with the treasure of his father's archive.

Several wonderful people made my time in Russia easy and pleasant. Natalia Skuratovskaia is an amazing friend who has been welcoming me into her home year after year. Each encounter with Mikhail Rozhansky is always full of warmth and intellectual excitement. Participating in the Baikal International School for Social Research has been one of the most meaningful experiences in my professional life, and I cannot wait to come back. Leonid Shinkarev's private tour of the old Izvestiia building brought its history to life. Nadezhda Azhgikhina from the Russian Union of Journalists and the late Professor Eduard Ivanian shared their memories and helped me get in touch with my Russian protagonists. Al'bert Pavlovich Nenarokov made my visits to RGASPI something to look forward to. I am grateful to Victoria Zhuravleva for being a mentor, a role model, and a true friend for many years.

Finally, I want to thank the most supportive family in the world—the Feinbergs, the Kucherenkos and the Aboukrats, the Manors, and the Tsitselyuks. Their endless supply of love, cheer, laughs, jokes, songs, compassion, encouragement, and delicious food has sustained me on this journey and throughout my life. I thank Miki and Nataly for everything and for always having my back. My parents taught me to make friends, to feel at home in new countries, and to love my Russian and Soviet heritage. It is thanks to their stories and their own arduous journey across borders that I became the person I am. Zohar has been an integral part of this journey from the beginning. Numerous international moves, uncertainty about the future, deadlines, endless discussions of journalism, history, Russian-American relations, and unceasing indoctrination into Soviet culture—he took it all in stride. I could not have asked for a better partner and a better friend and can never thank him enough for all his help and support. Barak came into our lives just a week before I signed the book contract. He makes me a better person and a better writer and turns everything into a glorious adventure. I am deeply grateful to both Zohar and Barak for being there, for making sure that I have my dinners and go to the park, and for showing me that life is about creativity, joy, and love.

## *Organizations*

### Russia

| | |
|---|---|
| APN | Novosti Press Agency |
| Agitprop | Agitation and Propaganda Department of the Central Committee of the CPSU |
| Glavlit | The Main Directorate for the Protection of State Secrets in the Press |
| Gosteleradio | USSR State Committee for Television and Radio Broadcasting |
| MID | Ministry of Foreign Affairs |
| MGIMO | Moscow State Institute of International Relations |
| MGU | Moscow State University |
| Sovinformburo | Soviet Information Bureau |
| TASS | Telegraph Agency of the Soviet Union |

### United States

| | |
|---|---|
| ABC | American Broadcasting Company |
| AP | Associated Press |
| ASNE | American Society for Newspaper Editors |
| CBS | Columbia Broadcasting System |
| INS | International News Service |
| IPI | International Press Institute |
| NBC | National Broadcasting Company |
| *NYRB* | *New York Review of Books* |
| PBS | Public Broadcasting Service |
| UPI | United Press International (until 1958 UP—United Press) |
| USIA | United States Information Agency |

## *Archives*

### Russia

| | |
|---|---|
| F. (fond) | collection |
| Op. (opis') | inventory |
| D. (delo; plural dd.) | file |
| ed. khr. (edinitsa khraneniia) | unit of preservation |
| L. (list; plural Ll.) | page |
| ob. (oborot) | over |

| GARF | State Archive of Russian Federation |
| F. R-4459 | TASS |
| F. R-9425 | Main Directorate for the Protection of State Secrets in the Press (Glavlit) |
| F. R-9587 | Novosti Press Agency (APN) |
| F. R-9613 | Editorial boards and publishing houses of trade union newspapers |
| F. R-1244 | Editorial board of the newspaper *Izvestiia* |
| | |
| RGANI | Russian State Archive of Contemporary History |
| F. 5 | Apparat of the Central Committee of the CPSU |
| F. 11 | Commission on the questions of ideology, culture, and international party relations of the Central Committee of the CPSU |
| | |
| RGASPI | Russian State Archive of Social and Political History |
| F. 17 | Central Committee of the CPSU |
| | |
| TsAGM | Central Archive of the City of Moscow |
| F. P-453 | Party organization of the newspaper *Izvestiia* |
| F. P-3226 | Party organization of the newspaper *Pravda* |
| | |
| Stanislav Kondrashov Archive | Stanislav Kondrashov personal archive, Pakhra, Russian Federation |
| Tatiana Strel'nikova Archive | Tatiana Strel'nikova Personal Archive, Moscow, Russian Federation |

United States

| APCA | AP02A.02, Foreign Bureau Correspondence, 1933–1967, The Associated Press Corporate Archives |
| | |
| NYT Foreign Desk | Foreign Desk Records, 1948–1993, New York Times Company Records, Manuscripts and Archives Division, New York Public Library |
| | |
| RG 59 | Record Group 59: General Records of the Department of State, National Archives and Records Administration II, College Park, Maryland |
| Entry 5552 | Bureau of European Affairs, Office of Soviet Union Affairs, Bilateral Political Relations, Special Collection Subject Files, 1950–1982 |
| Entry 5345 | Bureau of European Affairs, Office of Soviet Union Affairs, Bilateral Political Relations, Bilateral Political Relations Subject Files |
| | |
| RG 84 | Record Group 84: Records of the Foreign Service Posts of the Department of State |
| Entry 3313 | Union of Soviet Socialist Republics, US Embassy, Moscow, Classified General Records, 1941–1963 |
| Entry 3314 | Union of Soviet Socialist Republics, US Embassy, Moscow, Top Secret General Records, 1941–1948 |
| | |
| Salisbury Papers | Harrison E. Salisbury Papers, Rare Book and Manuscript Library, Columbia University Library |
| | |
| Smith Papers | Hedrick Smith Papers, Library of Congress, Manuscript Division, Washington, DC |

## Introduction • Battle of Words

1. Harrison Salisbury to Edwin L. James, September 22, 1949, Box 187, Salisbury Papers.

2. Ivan Beglov to Nikolai Pal'gunov, November 9, 1951, GARF, F. R-4459, Op. 38, D. 309, L. 90.

3. See, for example, Seeger, *Discovering Russia*; Eaton, *Daily Life in the Soviet Union*, 270–273; Shiraev and Zubok, *Anti-Americanism in Russia*, 21.

4. Following David Engerman, I define ideology as "explicit ideas and implicit assumptions that provided frameworks for understanding the world and defining action in it." Engerman, "Ideology," 20. Another definition that informed my use of the term "ideology" in this book is Terry Eagleton's broad definition of ideology as "the general material process of production of ideas, beliefs and values in social life." Eagleton, *Ideology*, 28.

5. Cultural histories of American-Russian relations have demonstrated that many ideas, tropes, and myths informing Cold War interactions predated the superpower confrontation and remained in place after the collapse of the Soviet Union. However, no other period rivaled the Cold War in terms of producing images of the foreign "other" for the purposes of self-definition. For excellent histories of Russian-American and American-Russian imaginations in the late nineteenth and twentieth centuries, see Rogger, "America in the Russian Mind," 27–51; Gleason, "Republic of Humbug," 1–23; Etkind, *Tolkovanie puteshestvii*; Tolz, *Russia*; Engerman, *Modernization from the Other Shore*; Ball, *Imagining America*; Kurilla, *Zaokeanskie partnery*; Foglesong, *American Mission*; Zhuravleva, *Ponimanie Rossii v S.Sh.A.*; Fedorova, *Yankees in Petrograd*; Hasty and Fusso, *America through Russian Eyes*.

6. Westad, "The Cold War," 1–19; Engerman, "Ideology," 20–43.

7. Engerman, "Ideology," 20, 21; Del Pero, "Incompatible Universalisms," 4–5.

8. Engerman, "Ideology," 23.

9. Engerman, "Ideology," 41.

10. Feinberg, *Curtain of Lies*, x.

11. Feinberg, *Curtain of Lies*, x.

12. Feinberg, *Curtain of Lies*; Bernhard, *U.S. Television News*; Krugler, *Voice of America*; Osgood, *Total Cold War*; Roth-Ey, *Moscow Prime Time*; Lovell, *Russia in the Microphone Age*; Evans, *Between Truth and Time*.

13. Reid, "Cold War in the Kitchen," 211–252; Cohen, *Consumers' Republic*; Johnston, *Being Soviet*, 127–209; Wolfe, *Governing*, 48–70; May, *Homeward Bound*.

14. I am grateful to Natalia Roudakova and Simon Huxatble for helping me think through these concepts.

15. Roudakova, *Losing Pravda*, 93.

16. Roudakova, *Losing Pravda*, 57, 60–64, 93.

17. Schudson, *Discovering the News*, 57–60, 141–149, 154–157; Mindich, *Just the Facts*, 113–117; Cater, *Fourth Branch of Government*; Frus, *Politics and Poetics*, 101.

18. Frus, *Politics and Poetics*, 106–107; Schudson, *Discovering the News*, 141–151.

19. Quotation is from Frus, *Politics and Poetics*, 111; see also Schudson, *Discovering the News*, 193, Frus, *Politics and Poetics*, 100–111.

20. Lebovic, *Free Speech and Unfree News*, 175–181.

21. Frus, *Politics and Poetics*, 113; Eagleton, *Criticism and Ideology*, 64; Hall, "Culture, the Media and the Ideological Effect," 340–346.

22. Roudakova, *Losing Pravda*, 57, 60–64, 93.

23. Roudakova, *Losing Pravda*, 61–61.

24. Roudakova, *Losing Pravda*, 47.

25. Polevoi, *Ocherk v gazete*, 26–30; Roudakova, *Losing Pravda*, 63–64.

26. Huxtable, "Compass in the Sea of Life," 56–98; Wolfe, *Governing*, 115–126; Roudakova, *Losing Pravda*, 65.

27. Roudakova, *Losing Pravda*, 64–65.

28. Kate Brown's comparative study of Soviet and American sealed-off atomic cities and Margaret Peacock's comparative study of the image of the child in Soviet and American international propaganda demonstrate that similarities also underlined other Soviet and American Cold War projects. Brown, *Plutopia*; Peacock, *Innocent Weapons*.

29. Cater, *Fourth Branch of Government*; Christians, *Normative Theories*; Siebert, Peterson, and Schramm, *Four Theories of the Press*; Eaton, *Daily Life in the Soviet Union*, 270–273.

30. Wolfe, *Governing*; Huxtable, "Compass in the Sea of Life"; Roudakova, *Losing Pravda*, 1–97; Schudson, *Discovering the News*, 56–70, 121–195; Aucoin, *Evolution of American Investigative Journalism*, 17–41.

31. Lebovic, *Free Speech and Unfree News*, 150, 162.

## Chapter 1 • Making "Soviet Restons"

1. Stalin's remark is mentioned in Bovin, *XX vek kak zhizn'*, 265, note 1.

2. Pechatnov, "Exercise in Frustration," 3.

3. GARF, F. R-4459, Op. 38, D. 203.

4. Pechatnov, "Exercise in Frustration," 3–4.

5. Yuri Zhukov, *Pravda* correspondent in France cited in Pechatnov, "Exercise in Frustration," 7–8.

6. "Stalin Interview with Pravda on Churchill," *New York Times*, March 14, 1946, p. 4.

7. Johnston, *Being Soviet*, 130.

8. Pechatnov, "Exercise in Frustration," 7.

9. On the use of writers in wartime propaganda, see Krylova, "'Healers of Wounded Souls,'" 312–313; Brooks, *Thank You, Comrade Stalin!*, 164–184; McReynolds, "Dateline Stalingrad," 28–43.

10. Simonov, *Glazami cheloveka*, 81.

11. Simonov, *Glazami cheloveka*, 82.

12. Lewis Wood, "Fight on Fascism Urged on Editors: At Annual Meeting of Newspaper Editors in Capital," *New York Times*, April 20, 1946, p. 5; Charles Yarbrough, "Red Journalists' Frank Words Win Applause of Editors Here," *Washington Post*, April 20, 1946, p. 1; Otto Zausmer, "Russian Says We Must Hate Fascism Together," *Daily Boston Globe*, May 5, 1946.

13. Erwin D. Canham, "Beyond Nationalism. Down the Middle of the Road," *Christian Science Monitor*, April 23, 1946, p. 18; Marquis Childs, "The Russian Journalists' Tour,"

*Washington Post*, April 29, 1946, p. 7. For more on the delegation's trip, see Caute, *Dancer Defects*, 89–91.

14. Childs, "The Russian Journalists' Tour," p. 8; "U.N. Chief Says Editors Must Help to Bar War: Trygve Lie Addresses Meeting at Capital; Russian Journalists Answer Questions in Forum," *Los Angeles Times*, April 21, 1946, p. 2.

15. Ehrenburg, *Liudi, gody, zhizn'*, vol. 3, 61–62.

16. Ilya Ehrenburg, "V Amerike," *Izvestiia*, August 9, 1946, p. 4.

17. Pechatnov, "Exercise in Frustration," 2.

18. Pechatnov, "Exercise in Frustration," 4.

19. RGASPI, F. 17, Op. 132, D. 26, Ll. 52–53, 57–58; RGASPI, F. 17, Op. 128, D. 1025, Ll. 1–46.

20. RGASPI, F. 17, Op. 128, D. 1025, Ll. 1–2.

21. RGASPI, F. 17, Op. 128, D. 1025, L. 4.

22. RGASPI, F. 17, Op. 128, D. 1064, L. 2.

23. RGASPI, F. 17, Op. 128, D. 1064, L. 2.

24. RGASPI, F. 17, Op. 128, D. 1064, L. 5

25. RGASPI, F. 17, Op. 128, D. 1025, L. 266.

26. RGASPI, F. 17, Op. 128, D. 1025, Ll. 261–270. Enclosed in one of the reports was a seventeen-page dossier on Columbia University's School of Journalism, which profiled the school and even included a list of courses and the professors who taught them; RGASPI, F. 17, Op. 128, D. 1025, Ll. 241–243.

27. Pechatnov, "Exercise in Frustration," 4.

28. A. Zhdanov, *Doklad o zhurnalakh "Zvezda" i "Leningrad,"* (Moscow: Gospolitizdat, 1952), p. 21. The phrase "ideological front" appeared in Zhdanov's speech eleven times.

29. Nadzhafov and Belousova, *Stalin i kosmopolitizm*, 44–46.

30. Cited in Nadzhafov and Belousova, *Stalin i kosmopolitizm*, 45.

31. "Povyshat' rol' pechati v khoziaistvennoi i politicheskoi zhizni strany," *Pravda*, October 18, 1946, p.1.

32. Konstantin Simonov, "Dramaturgiia, teatr, i zhizn," *Pravda*, November 22, 1946, p. 3.

33. Simonov, "Dramaturgiia, teatr, i zhizn.'"

34. Krugler, *Voice of America*, 74–77; Belmonte, *Selling the American Way*, 13–18; Smith, *Moscow Mission*, 161–168.

35. Belmonte, *Selling the American Way*, 21.

36. Krugler, *Voice of America*, 75–76.

37. Joshua Rubenstein, "Ilya Ehrenburg: Between East and West," 53.

38. The "bourgeois press" was the central topic of discussion in three articles that appeared in 1947, ten articles in 1948, fifteen articles in 1949, and twenty-nine in 1950. By contrast, the term was used only once in 1945 and once in 1946; both times it was used in a historical context—in an article on the "Whites" in the 1920s (1945) and one on pre-Soviet Estonia (1946).

39. For the entire duration of the Second World War, *Krokodil*'s venom was directed primarily at the Germans. The "bourgeois press" made its first postwar appearance in July 1945 as a rather comic depiction of Hearst newspapers. For the rest of 1945 and during 1946, *Krokodil* was easy on the foreign press, but 1947 saw a sharp increase in anti-American cartoons in general and derision toward the "bourgeois press" in particular.

40. In 1945, *Krokodil* carried two more cartoons targeting the American press (September 10 and December 30). In 1946, three cartoons attacked the press (August 20, September 10, and September 30). By contrast, in 1947 every issue carried an anti-American cartoon and about one-fourth of those issues carried an anti-American cartoon on the front page. Six cartoons in 1947 were dedicated specifically to the American press.

41. Simonov, *Glazami cheloveka*, 103.

42. Simonov, *Glazami cheloveka*, 103–104; Caute, *Dancer Defects*, 80.

43. Simonov, *Glazami cheloveka*, 147–148.
44. Konstantin Simonov, *Sobranie sochinenii v desiati tomakh*, vol. 3 (Moscow: Khudozhestvennaia literatura, 1980), 7–70.
45. M. Galaktionov, "'Russkii vopros,'" *Pravda*, March 2, 1947, p. 3.
46. Galaktionov, "'Russkii vopros,'" p. 3.
47. For other interpretations of the anti-American campaign, see Nadzhafov, "Beginning of the Cold War," 140–174; Pechatnov, "Exercise in Frustration"; Magnúsdóttir, *Enemy Number One*, 17–37.
48. RGASPI, F. 17, Op. 132, D. 224, L. 48.
49. Kenez, *History of the Soviet Union*, 182–183; Johnston, *Being Soviet*, 169–181; Brooks, *Thank You, Comrade Stalin!*, 209–232.
50. RGASPI, F. 17, Op. 132, D. 224, Ll. 48–52.
51. Etkind, *Tolkovanie puteshestvii*, 3; Kotkin, *Magnetic Mountain*, 152–153.
52. Ball, *Imagining America*, 119–140; Etkind, *Tolkovanie puteshestvii*, 142–165.
53. Il'f and Petrov, *Odnoetazhnaia Amerika*, Chapter 46.
54. RGASPI, F. 17, Op. 132, D. 224, Ll. 55–56.
55. RGASPI, F. 17, Op. 132, D. 224, L. 49.
56. RGASPI, F. 17, Op. 132, D. 224, L. 50.
57. RGASPI, F. 17, Op. 132, D. 224, L. 57.
58. RGASPI, F. 17, Op. 132, D. 117, L. 92.
59. GARF, F. R-4459, Op. 38, D. 203. TASS bulletins were ranked by degree of secrecy and distributed according to prospective readers' status in the hierarchy. As in any other hierarchical allocation of privilege in the USSR, one's status was partially determined by the level of secrecy of TASS bulletins one could access.
60. The practice of sending writers as Soviet spokespeople to international events continued. In the early 1950s, Ehrenburg, Simonov, Aleksandr Fadeev, Boris Polevoi, and Yuri Zhukov frequently traveled abroad as members of Soviet delegations to events such as the International Peace Congress and the International Youth Congress. The persistent selection of writers as Soviet spokespeople shows the importance that the state continued to attribute to the power of the writers' talent in delivering its message around the world.
61. GARF, F. R-1244, Op. 1, D. 70, L. 20.
62. RGASPI, F. 17, Op. 132, D. 122, Ll. 84–85; GARF, F. R-4459, Op. 38, D. 192, L. 26.
63. GARF, F. R-4459, Op. 38, D. 237, L. 182.
64. GARF, F. R-4459, Op. 38, D. 237, Ll. 182–183.
65. GARF, F. R-4459, Op. 38, D. 237, Ll. 173, 182.
66. GARF, F. R-4459, Op. 38, D. 237, L. 173; GARF, F. R-4459, Op. 38, D. 192, Ll. 27–29.
67. GARF, F. R-4459, Op. 38, D. 192, Ll. 5–7.
68. Knight, *How the Cold War Began*, Introduction.
69. Knight, *How the Cold War Began*, Chapter 3.
70. "Two Russian Envoys in Canada Are Leaving after Spy Report," *New York Times*, July 17, 1946, p. 1.
71. See, for example, "TASS," *Time*, July 29, 1946.
72. Manning, "Impact of Propaganda Materials," 146.
73. Manning, "Impact of Propaganda Materials," 147.
74. GARF, F. R-4459, Op. 38, D. 237, L. 123; GARF, F. R-4459, Op. 38, D. 531, Ll. 28–29.
"Foreign Correspondents under Foreign Agents Registration Act," July 27, 1951, Box 7: Soviet Correspondents, 1951–1960, Entry 5552, RG 59; "Regulations and Controls Governing Soviet Correspondents in the U.S.," September 6, 1963, Box 4: American Correspondents, 1963, Entry 5552, RG 59.

75. GARF, F. R-4459, Op. 38, D. 531, Ll. 28–29.
76. GARF, F. R-4459, Op. 38, D. 531, Ll. 28–29.
77. Robert K. Bingham, "The Man from TASS," *The Reporter*, October 10, 1950, p. 39; "Freedom to Libel," *Time*, July 11, 1949; "Moscow's Pen Pal," *Time*, May 15, 1950.
78. Edwin L. James, "Watch Is Kept on Role of Local Communists," *New York Times*, May 23, 1948.
79. GARF, F. R-4459, Op. 38, D. 192, Ll. 10–12. For a detailed account of the anti-TASS campaign, see Fainberg, "Unmasking the Wolf in Sheep's Clothing," 166–170.
80. GARF, F. R-4459, Op. 38, D. 192, Ll. 22, 53, 58–59.
81. GARF, F. R-4459, Op. 38, D. 192, Ll. 58–60, 62–63.
82. GARF, F. R-4459, Op. 38, D. 237, Ll. 209–211.
83. GARF, F. R-4459, Op. 38, D. 237, Ll. 213–216.
84. GARF, F. R-4459, Op. 38, D. 237, Ll. 214–215.
85. GARF, F. R-4459, Op. 38, D. 237, Ll. 279–281; GARF, F. R-4459, Op. 38, D. 255, Ll. 65–66, 74–77, 117–120.
86. RGASPI, F. 17, Op. 128, D. 1064, Ll. 3–4; RGASPI, F. 17, Op. 132, D. 122, Ll. 84–85.
87. RGASPI, F. 17, Op. 132, D. 122, Ll. 84–85.
88. RGASPI, F. 17, Op. 132, D. 122, Ll. 84–85.
89. GARF, F. R-4459, Op. 38, D. 237, L. 190.
90. GARF, F. R-4459, Op. 38, D. 237, Ll. 230–231.
91. GARF, F. R-4459, Op. 38, D. 237, Ll. 244–252, 270–273, 274–275.
92. GARF, F. R-4459, Op. 38, D. 255, Ll. 65–66, 68–72, 74–77, 117–120.
93. Beglova, *Moskovskaia sem'ia riazanskogo razliva*, 19–21.
94. GARF, F. R-4459, Op. 38, D. 255, Ll. 117–124; GARF, F. R-4459, Op. 38, D. 309, Ll. 11–13.
95. GARF, F. R-4459, Op. 38, D. 309, Ll. 53–54.
96. GARF, F. R-4459, Op. 38, D. 309, Ll. 53–54.
97. "Tass Washington Bureau Chief No Newsman, Says ASNE Head," *Washington Post*, July 25, 1951, p. 3; "TASS Correspondent Hit: Editor Charges Its Man in Washington Has No Training," *New York Times*, July 25, 1951, p. 12.
98. "Red Head"; "Moscow's Pen Pal"; Paul F. Healy, "Stalin's American Snoops," *Saturday Evening Post*, January 20, 1951, p. 47.
99. "TASS Correspondent Hit."
100. GARF, F. R-4459, Op. 38, D. 309, L. 67.
101. GARF, F. R-4459. Op. 38, D. 309, Ll. 67–71.
102. GARF, F. R-4459. Op. 38, D. 309, Ll. 60, 69–71.
103. "TASS Accreditation Halted During Official Spy Check," *Editor and Publisher*, September 8, 1951, pp. 7–8.
104. Fainberg, "Unmasking the Wolf in Sheep's Clothing," 170–176.
105. GARF, F. R-4459, Op. 38, D. 309, Ll. 75–76.
106. GARF, F. R-4459, Op. 38, D. 309, Ll. 77–78.
107. GARF, F. R-4459, Op. 38, D. 309, L. 85.
108. GARF, F. R-4459, Op. 38, D. 309, Ll. 85–89.
109. GARF, F. R-4459, Op. 38, D. 309, Ll. 75–76.
110. Memorandum on "Communist Correspondents in the U.S.," July 30, 1951, Box 7: Soviet Correspondents, 1951–1960, Entry 5552, RG 59.
111. GARF, F. R-4459, Op. 38, D. 309, L. 90.
112. GARF, F. R-4459, Op. 38, D. 309, L. 90.
113. GARF, F. R-4459, Op. 38, D. 309, L. 90.
114. GARF, F. R-4459, Op. 38, D. 309, L. 75.

115. RGASPI, F. 17, Op. 132, D. 15, Ll. 100–101, 107, 109; RGASPI, F. 17, Op. 132, D. 294, Ll. 30–34; GARF, F. R-4459, Op. 38, D. 381, Ll. 40–41.
116. GARF, F. R-4459, Op. 38, D. 381, L. 41.
117. RGASPI, F. 17, Op. 132, D. 294, L. 32.
118. RGASPI, F. 17, Op. 132, D. 294, Ll. 32–34.
119. RGASPI, F. 17, Op. 132, D. 294, L. 31; RGASPI, F. 17, Op. 132, D. 522, Ll. 230–250.
120. Melor Georgievich Sturua, interview by the author, February 4, 2011, Moscow.
121. RGASPI, F. 17, Op. 132, D. 522, L. 245.
122. Ovchinnikov, *Kaleidoskop zhizni*.
123. Hough, "Foreign Policy Establishment," 146–150.
124. Genrikh Aviezerovich Borovik, interview by Ksenia Larina on *Echo Moskvy*, November 8, 2009, last accessed August 2019, http://www.echo.msk.ru/programs/ dithyramb/631768-echo/.
125. R. A. Sergeev, "Na chasakh vozle Krymskogo mosta."
126. Borovik, interview, November 8, 2009.
127. Sturua, interview, February 4, 2011.
128. Borovik, interview, November 8, 2009.
129. Sturua, interview, February 4, 2011.
130. Sturua, interview, February 4, 2011.
131. Sturua, interview, February 4, 2011.
132. Sturua, interview, February 4, 2011.
133. Sturua, interview, February 4, 2011. The practice was discontinued after Stalin's death.
134. Sturua, interview, February 4, 2011.
135. Sturua, interview, February 4, 2011.
136. This practice, too, was discontinued after Stalin's death.
137. Stanislav Kondrashov's unpublished memoir, Stanislav Kondrashov Archive.

## Chapter 2 • *The Heralds of Truth*

1. Eddy Gilmore to Alan J. Gould, Assistant General Manager of the Associated Press, November 10, 1945, Box 4: Moscow Bureau 1945, APCA.
2. Gilmore to Gould, November 10, 1945, Box 4: Moscow Bureau 1945, APCA.
3. Khlevniuk et al., *Politburo TsK Vkp(b)*, 195.
4. Khlevniuk et al., *Politburo TsK Vkp(b)*, 195–196.
5. Khlevniuk et al., *Politburo TsK Vkp(b)*, 195–202.
6. Khlevniuk et al., *Politburo TsK Vkp(b)*, 201–202.
7. Bassow, *Moscow Correspondents*, 63–64, 68–69, 75–76, 98–99, 122.
8. "Resolution of Politburo TsK VKP(b) on censorship of outgoing information from the Soviet Union," 25.02.1946, RGASPI, F. 17, Op. 3, D. 1056, Ll. 25–26, accessed August 2019 via the Alexander Yakovlev Foundation Digital Archive, http://www.alexanderyakovlev.org /fond/issues-doc/69274.
9. Bassow, *Moscow Correspondents*, 123. According to the original provisions, adopted in February 1946, the journalists were not allowed to revisit their dispatches after the censors' interventions and had no way of knowing whether and how the items were altered, nor were the censors required to notify the journalists that the dispatch was blocked entirely and not transmitted at all. The Politburo updated the rules in March 1946. The new additions permitted the journalists to see the censors' interventions and allowed the journalists to decide whether or not to file their dispatches in an altered form. With the introduction of the new rules, the journalists were also notified when the entire dispatch was blocked. RGASPI, F. 17, Op. 3, D. 1057, L. 18, accessed August 2019 via the Alexander Yakovlev Foundation Digital Archive, http://www.alexanderyakovlev.org/fond/issues-doc/69274.

10. Telegram #641 to Secretary of State, March 4, 1946; Telegram #666 to Secretary of State, March 5, 1946; Telegram #840 to Secretary of State, March 17, 1946, Box 126, 1946:891, Entry 3313, RG 84.

11. Bassow, *Moscow Correspondents*, 123–124; RGASPI, F. 17, Op. 3, D. 1057, L. 18.

12. Bassow, *Moscow Correspondents*, 123–130; Telegram #686 to Secretary of State, March 6, 1946; Smith to Secretary of State, July 25, 1946; Smith to Secretary of State, November 26, 1946, Box 126, 1946:891, Entry 3313, RG 84.

13. Journalists could use the diplomatic pouch to send and receive personal and professional correspondence because it was widely known that anything arriving by regular mail would be opened, read, and occasionally held by the Soviet authorities. The letters in the diplomatic pouch traveled to the US Embassy in Helsinki, where they were sealed in a specially marked bag and sent to Moscow. Although international conventions prohibited Soviet authorities from scrutinizing the contents of these bags, they were sometimes reported as lost or mislabeled, which made their use for transfer of copy rather risky.

14. At times, journalists used the pouch to alert editors to important news that they did not want to try to send through official channels, fearing repercussions for themselves or their sources. In such cases, the information would be published under a different dateline and byline, without any mention of the Moscow correspondent. Permission to use the diplomatic pouch to send news depended on the ambassador. Bassow, *Moscow Correspondents*, 127; Seeger, *Discovering Russia*, 336.

15. "Treatment of U.S. Personnel in the Soviet Union," May 26, 1950, Box 8: 1620: American Representation in the USSR, 1933–1967, Entry 5345, RG 59.

16. Ukaz prezidiuma Verkhovnogo Soveta SSSR "Ob otvetstvennosti za razglashenie gosudarstvennoi tainy i utratu dokumentov soderzhashchikh gosudarstvennuiu tainu" [Directive of the Supreme Soviet of the USSR "on the responsibility for revealing state secrets and losing documents, containing state secrets"], *Vedomosti Verkhovnogo Sovieta Soiuza Sovetskikh Sotsialisticheskikh Respublik*. No. 20 (474), June 16, 1947, in Nadzhafov and Belousova, *Stalin i kosmopolitizm*, 118–119. For American interpretations of the law, see The Chargé in the Soviet Union (Durbrow) to the Secretary of State, November 29, 1947, *FRUS, 1947*, Vol. IV, Document 427, https://history.state.gov/historicaldocuments/frus1947v04/d427.

17. Kenez, *Birth of the Propaganda State*, 4–14.

18. Zhirkov, *Istoriia tsenzury*, Part II: Evoliutsiia sovetskoi tsenzury: Glavlit—kak ee ofitsial'noe ucherezhdenie (1922–1927), http://evartist.narod.ru/text9/38.htm#3_09.

19. Zhirkov, *Istoriia tsenzury*, Part II; Nevzhin, "*Esli zavtra v pokhod . . .*," 55–57.

20. On censorship and Glavlit during the Second World War and in the postwar years, see Goriaeva, *Politicheskaia tsenzura v SSSR*, 284–311.

21. Bassow, *Moscow Correspondents*, 129.

22. Eddy Gilmore to Alan J. Gould, July 18, 1949, Box 14: Moscow Bureau 1949, APCA.

23. Bassow, *Moscow Correspondents*, 253–254.

24. Bassow, *Moscow Correspondents*, 124; "Expelled Reporter Quits Russia; Spy Charge Trumped Up, He Says," *New York Times*, April 19, 1948, p. 8.

25. Bassow, *Moscow Correspondents*, 124; Seeger, *Discovering Russia*, 336; "Soviet Ousts NBC Reporter; Russian Aide Calls Him Spy," *New York Times*, April 16, 1948, p. 1.

26. In his interview with the American press in Berlin, Magidoff stated that before the publication of Nelson's accusation, he and his wife were constantly followed by the secret police; "Expelled Reporter Quits Russia."

27. Carruthers, *Cold War Captives*, 46–48. Bucar's series was first published in *Pravda* on February 27, February 28, and March 1, 1949. The Russian-language version of Bucar's book was published as Annabella Biukar, *Pravda ob amerikanskikh diplomatakh* (Moscow: Izdanie Literaturnoi Gazety, 1949).

28. Edmund Stevens, "Triple Squeeze Ousts Foreign Reporters," *Christian Science Monitor*, January 24, 1950, p. 1. Robert Magidoff wrote that long before his own case broke up, he had foreseen that there would be intimidations or frame-ups involving American or British journalists; Magidoff, *In Anger and Pity*, 47–49, 57.

29. Smith to Secretary of State, October 9, 1946; Durbrow to Secretary of State, October 25, 1946, Box 126, 1946:891, Entry 3313, RG 84; The Acting Secretary of State to the Chargé in the Soviet Union (Durbrow), November 8, 1946, in *FRUS, 1946*, Vol. VI, Document 552.

30. Newman had worked in the Soviet Union since 1946. Bassow, *Moscow Correspondents*, 125, 133.

31. The *Daily Worker* sent a new Moscow correspondent in 1952. The political allegiances of the *Daily Worker*, and the privileged treatment it was given by the Soviet authorities, set its correspondent apart from the rest.

32. Bassow, *Moscow Correspondents*, 124–125.

33. Harrison Salisbury to Edwin L. James, September 22, 1949, Salisbury Papers, Box 187; Bassow, *Moscow Correspondents*, 138–141.

34. In response to Salisbury's pleas to leave for vacation, the editors reminded him that if he failed to get a reentry visa, they would not be able to find a new assignment for him, and his employment with the *Times* would effectively cease. Salisbury was able to leave without the threat of losing his job in June 1950. Harrison Salisbury to Edwin L. James and to C. L. Sulzberger, November 19, 1949; Edwin L. James to Harrison Salisbury, March 10, 1950, Salisbury Papers, Box 187.

35. Harrison Salisbury to C. L. Sulzberger, May 23, 1949, Salisbury Papers, Box 187.

36. Salisbury to James, September 22, 1949, Salisbury Papers, Box 187.

37. Salisbury to James, September 22, 1949, Salisbury Papers, Box 187.

38. Magidoff, *In Anger and Pity*, 53–54. The US Embassy version of the events pointed out that Bucar's and McMillin's love interests were explicitly instructed to fraternize with foreigners and to try to lure any embassy worker into a romantic attachment. Carruthers, *Cold War Captives*, 46–47.

39. Harrison Salisbury to A. H. Sulzberger, April 15, 1949, Salisbury Papers, Box 187.

40. Gilmore, *Me and My Russian Wife*, Chapter 29.

41. Airgram A-559, Durbrow to Secretary of State, August 31, 1946; Airgram A-682, Durbrow to Secretary of State, October 17, 1946, Box 114, 1946:800, Entry 3313, RG 84.

42. Department of State, Office of Intelligence Research, Eastern European Branch, "Countering Soviet Propaganda," April 21, 1950, Box 3: 1210 (f) Status of Women in USSR, Entry 5345, RG 59.

43. The Ambassador in the Soviet Union (Smith) to the Secretary of State, March 1, 1947, *FRUS, 1947*, Vol. IV, Document 371.

44. Edmund Stevens, "U.S. 'Voice' Haunts Red War Planners," *Christian Science Monitor*, January 31, 1950, p. 1; Magidoff, *In Anger and Pity*, 268.

45. Eddy Gilmore to Alan Gould, August 17, 1949, Box 14: Moscow Bureau 1949, APCA.

46. Eddy Gilmore to Alan Gould, January 21, 1950, Box 16: Moscow Bureau 1950, APCA.

47. Occasionally, both journalists and embassy employees were reluctant to cooperate with each other or share information. For example, in December 1946, US Under Secretary of State Dean Acheson asked the embassy to compile a list of every question presented by American correspondents to Soviet officials and the answers they received. The embassy replied that correspondents reported with "considerable reluctance" and in some cases with special restrictive conditions. Telegram 2115 from Secretary of State, December 11, 1946; Willis to Durbrow, December 11, 1946, Box 126, 1946:891, Entry 3313, RG 84.

48. Davies, *Postwar Decline*, 39–40; Halberstam, *Powers That Be*, 33–40, 343; Alterman, *Sound and Fury*, 39–41.

49. Bassow, *Moscow Correspondents*, 127.

50. Lebovic, *Free Speech and Unfree News*, 157–160.

51. See, for example, "Passed by Censor," *Time*, June 19, 1950, p. 76; "Censored," *Time*, February 27, 1950, p. 28. "Does Stalin Mean It?" *New Leader*, January 5, 1953, p. 30; *Counterattack* (newsletter), undated, NYT Foreign Desk, Box 82, Folder 3.

52. Alan J. Gould to Eddy Gilmore, December 30, 1948, Box 14: Moscow Bureau 1949, APCA.

53. Will Lissner to Edwin L. James, December 21, 1948, Box 14: Moscow Bureau 1949, APCA.

54. Tom Whitney to Alan J. Gould, January 26, 1949, Box 14: Moscow Bureau 1949, APCA.

55. Will Lissner to Edwin James, February 5, 1949, Box 14: Moscow Bureau 1949, APCA. Before Harrison Salisbury left for Moscow, the *Times* publisher asked him to assess whether the AP correspondents in Moscow toned down their copy and avoided criticizing the USSR in order to protect their Russian spouses. Harrison Salisbury to A. H. Sulzberger, April 15, 1949, Salisbury Papers, Box 187.

56. T. G. Bagration to the editors, *New York Times*, June 15, 1951.

57. Durbrow to the Secretary of State, June 10, 1947, *FRUS, 1947*, Vol. IV, Document 392; Arthur Hays Sulzberger to Edwin L. James, April 21, 1949, Salisbury Papers, Box 188; Harrison Salisbury to Edwin L. James, March 28, 1949, Salisbury Papers, Box 187; Harrison Salisbury to Turner Catledge, November 15, 1951, Salisbury Papers, Box 188.

58. Salisbury to James, March 28, 1949, Salisbury Papers, Box 187; Harrison Salisbury to Edwin L. James, June 7, 1949, Salisbury Papers, Box 187.

59. A. H. Sulzberger to C. L. Sulzberger, November 7, 1950, Salisbury Papers, Box 12.

60. The published installments of Harrison Salisbury's series appeared in the *New York Times* as follows: "Moscow Is in Midst of Building Effort," October 11, 1950, p. 18; "Domestic Matters Intrigue Russians," October 12, 1950, p. 19; "No 'Scare Buying' in Moscow Stores," October 13, 1950, p. 13; "Russian Citizens Blame U.S. in Korea," October 14, 1950, p. 6.

61. "Russian Citizens Blame U.S. in Korea," *New York Times*, October 14, 1950, p. 6.

62. "Russian Citizens Blame U.S. in Korea."

63. "Russian Citizens Blame U.S. in Korea."

64. "Russian Citizens Blame U.S. in Korea."

65. Foglesong, *American Mission*, 109–11; Belmonte, *Selling the American Way*, 42–43, 61–62. On Soviet reactions to American broadcasting, see Mikkonen, "Stealing the Monopoly," 771–805.

66. The Ambassador in the Soviet Union (Harriman) to the Secretary of State, January 20, 1946, *FRUS, 1946*, Vol. VI, Document 463; The Charge in the Soviet Union (Durbrow) to the Secretary of State, May 22, 1947, *FRUS, 1947*, Vol. IV, Document 389; The Ambassador in the Soviet Union (Smith) to the Secretary of State, December 27, 1947, *FRUS, 1947*, Vol. IV, Document 445. Also see Stevens, "U.S. 'Voice' Haunts"; Magidoff, *In Anger and Pity*, 268; Smith, *Moscow Mission*, 169–17?

67. Salisbury, *Journey for Our Times*, 373–375; Turner Catledge to Harrison Salisbury, October 19, 1950, Salisbury Papers, Box 188.

68. Salisbury, *Journey for Our Times*, 373–374; A. H. Sulzberger to C. L. Sulzberger, November 7, 1950, Salisbury Papers, Box 12; Turner Catledge to Harrison Salisbury, October 19, 1950, Salisbury Papers, Box 188; Lester Markel to A. H. Sulzberger, October 25, 1950, Salisbury Papers, Box 188.

69. Walworth Barbour to Frederick Reinhardt, October 9, 1950, Box 154: Correspondents - General 631.3, Entry 3313, RG 84.

70. Salisbury, *Journey for Our Times*, 375.

71. A. H. Sulzberger to C. L. Sulzberger, November 7, 1950, Salisbury Papers, Box 12.

72. Harrison Salisbury to Turner Catledge, October 31, 1950, Salisbury Papers, Box 188.

73. "Russian Citizens Blame U.S. in Korea."

74. A. H. Sulzberger to C. L. Sulzberger, November 7, 1950, Salisbury Papers, Box 12.

75. Halberstam, *Powers That Be*, 33–40, 343; Alterman, *Sound and Fury*, 39–41; Davies, *Postwar Decline*, 39–40.

76. A. H. Sulzberger to Turner Catledge, October 9, 1950, Salisbury Papers, Box 188; A. H. Sulzberger to Lester Markel, October 25, 1950, Salisbury Papers, Box 188.

77. "Did 'Times' Try to Suppress Series on USSR?" *Daily Worker*, October 20, 1950, p. 4.

78. "Worker Windfall," *Time*, October 30, 1950, p. 87.

79. Eugene Lyons to the editors, *New York Times*, October 23, 1950, p. 22. Lyons began his career as a socialist and a fellow traveler but was eventually disappointed with the Soviet regime and became one of its harshest critics.

80. Yedidia Hamburg to the editors, *New York Times*, November 14, 1950, p. 30.

81. Harrison Salisbury to C. L. Sulzberger, November 22, 1950, Salisbury Papers, Box 187.

82. Emanuel Freedman to Harrison Salisbury, January 4, 1951, Salisbury Papers, Box 187.

83. "Dateline Moscow," *New Leader*, November 12, 1951, p. 8.

84. "Dateline Moscow," p. 7.

85. "Dateline Moscow," p. 8.

86. Russell F. Anderson, "News from Nowhere: Our Disappearing Foreign Correspondents," *Saturday Review of Literature*, November 17, 1951, p. 12.

87. Anderson, "News from Nowhere," p. 81.

88. "History of the IPI (1950–1959)," International Press Institute website, last accessed August 2019, https://ipi.media/about/history/; The AP Weekly Log, October 2–8, 1952, AP02A, Box 18, Moscow Bureau 1952, APCA; Sloan, *American Journalism*, 253.

89. International Press Institute, *The News from Russia* (Zurich: International Press Institute, 1952), 5.

90. International Press Institute, *News from Russia*, 8–18, 26.

91. International Press Institute, *News from Russia*, 29–44.

92. International Press Institute, *News from Russia*, 50.

93. International Press Institute, *News from Russia*, 50.

94. Schudson, *Discovering the News*, 144–149; Davies, *Postwar Decline*, 18–21.

95. Arthur Hays Sulzberger, "Keynote: Get Facts and Interpret Them," *Editor and Publisher*, August 30, 1952, p. 9.

96. Eddy Gilmore to Alan J. Gould, October 20, 1952, Box 18: Moscow Bureau 1952, APCA; Salisbury to Lester Markel, October 17, 1952, NYT Foreign Desk, Box 132, Folder 12.

97. Gilmore to Gould, October 20, 1952, Box 18: Moscow Bureau 1952, APCA.

98. Gilmore to Gould, October 20, 1952, Box 18: Moscow Bureau 1952, APCA; Salisbury, *Journey for Our Times*, 248–249.

99. Gilmore to Gould, October 20, 1952, Box 18: Moscow Bureau 1952, APCA.

100. Harrison Salisbury to the *New York Times*, June 27, 1951, NYT Foreign Desk, Box 82, Folder 1.

101. American foreign correspondents (as well as their editors and readers) often referred to the Soviet Union as "Russia" and used the two terms interchangeably. Therefore in my descriptions or paraphrasing of the journalists' writing, the two terms—"Russian" and "Soviet"—appear interchangeably.

102. Stevens, *This Is Russia*.

103. The published installments of the series appeared in the *Washington Post* between November 2 and November 20, 1949.

104. Newman, *Report from Russia*.

105. The title of Magidoff's book came from an interview he gave to American journalists after his expulsion. Referring to the secretary who denounced him, Magidoff said that that he thinks about her "more in pity than in anger." "Expelled Reporter Quits Russia," p. 8.

106. The Ambassador in the Soviet Union (Smith) to the Secretary of State, "Evaluation of Present Kremlin International Policies," November 5, 1947, *FRUS, 1947*, Vol. IV, Document 421; The Ambassador in the Soviet Union (Smith) to the Secretary of State, November 15, 1947, *FRUS, 1947*, Vol. IV, Document 426. See also Foglesong, *American Mission*, 109–111; Belmonte, *Selling the American Way*, 30–31, 45.

107. Magidoff, *In Anger and Pity*, 94–97, 241–248, 260–268; Edmund Stevens, "Hemline Scorns the Party Line," *Christian Science Monitor*, October 27, 1949, p. 1; Edmund Stevens, "The Free Market and How It's Broken," *Christian Science Monitor*, October 29, 1949, p. 1; Edmund Stevens, "The Great Hush-Hush: Figures Don't Tell Facts," *Christian Science Monitor*, November 5, 1949, p. 1; Edmund Stevens, "Soviet Capitalizes on Fettered Labor," *Christian Science Monitor*, January 26, 1950, p. 1; Joseph Newman, "Soviet Zealously Conceals Economy Flaws to Save Official Story of Worker's Heaven," *Washington Post*, November 3, 1949, p. 10; Joseph Newman, "Russian Lot Has Improved since 1947, but Remains Low," *Washington Post*, November 6, 1949, p. M4; Joseph Newman, "Russia, with Wealth and Broad Lands, Offers Riddle of Low Standard for Worker," *Washington Post*, November 18, 1949, p. 16.

108. Magidoff, *In Anger and Pity*, 260–268; Stevens, "The Free Market"; Edmund Stevens, "Graft Grafts Itself to Roots of Business," *Christian Science Monitor*, November 1, 1949, p. 1; Newman, "Soviet Zealously Conceals Economy Flaws."

109. Newman, "Soviet Zealously Conceals Economy Flaws."

110. Stevens, "Graft Grafts Itself."

111. Americans' interest in Soviet treatment of religious worship predated the Cold War. As David Foglesong demonstrated, Americans had shown great interest in the status of religion in the Soviet state since the state's inception. Many American observers viewed "godlessness" as one of the most terrifying features of the Bolshevik state. During the Second World War, the American press applauded the restoration of the Orthodox Church and saw it as a hopeful harbinger of postwar reform in Russia. Foglesong, *American Mission*, 57, 82–84.

112. Joseph Newman, "Bolsheviks Help Church to Resume Role," *Washington Post*, November 13, 1949, p. M3.

113. Edmund Stevens, "Noose for Religion Tested in Baltics," *Christian Science Monitor*, January 19, 1950, p. 1.

114. Edmund Stevens, "Jews Denied Jobs or Exit Visa to Israel," *Christian Science Monitor*, January 10, 1950, p. 1; Edmund Stevens, "Zionism Jolts Soviet: Profile of New Purge," *Christian Science Monitor*, January 12, 1950, p. 1; Joseph Newman, "Swift Retaliation against Moscow Jews Followed Demonstration at Israel Legation," *Washington Post*, November 8, 1949, p. 2; Joseph Newman, "Australian Couple Flees Soviet's State for Jews," *Washington Post*, November 10, 1949, p. 4.

115. Edmund Stevens, "Soviet Wives of Aliens Wedded to Tragedy," *Christian Science Monitor*, November 10, 1949, p. 1; Edmund Stevens, "'Citizens' Trapped: No Visa, No Way Out,'" *Christian Science Monitor*, November 12, 1949, p. 1; Joseph Newman, "Soviet Visa Denial Keeps Missions Out," *Washington Post*, November 15, 1949, p. 3; Joseph Newman, "Soviet Withholds Passports for Citizens to Visit Outer World, See Its Superiority," *Washington Post*, November 16, 1949, p. 9.

116. Edmund Stevens, "Peasant Is Squeezed 'Twixt Quota and Cow,'" *Christian Science Monitor*, October 25, 1949, p. 1.

117. Franklin D. Roosevelt, *Annual Message to Congress on the State of the Union*, January 6, 1941, Franklin D. Roosevelt Presidential Library and Museum website, http://www.fdrlibrary.marist.edu/pdfs/fftext.pdf.

118. Roosevelt, *State of the Union*; Rodgers, *Contested Truths*, 215.

119. Rodgers, *Contested Truths*, 215.

120. Edmund Stevens, "Collective Slavery Is Seed for Revolt," *Christian Science Monitor*, January 28, 1950, p. 1.

121. Joseph Newman, "Two Years' Residence Reveals Two Russias," *Washington Post*, November 20, 1949, p. M5.

122. Stevens, "Collective Slavery," p. 1.

123. For more on this theme, see Hendershot, *Anti-Communism and Popular Culture*, 9–40; Shcherbenok, "Asymmetric Warfare," http://www.kinokultura.com/2010/28-shcherbenok .shtml.

124. Newman, "Two Years' Residence," p. M5.

125. Magidoff, *In Anger and Pity*, 59.

126. See Parry-Giles, "Militarizing America's Propaganda Program," 95–133; Bernhard, *U.S. Television News.*

127. Harry S. Truman, "Address on Foreign Policy at a Luncheon of the American Society of Newspaper Editors," Washington, DC, April 20, 1950; Harry S. Truman Library and Museum website, https://www.trumanlibrary.gov/library/public-papers/92/address-foreign -policy-luncheon-american-society-newspaper-editors.

128. Truman, "Address on Foreign Policy," April 20, 1950.

129. David Greenberg, "Brainwashing, Psywar, and Hidden Persuasion: Propaganda Anxieties in the Early Cold War," paper presented at New York University–Tamiment Library Center for the United States and the Cold War, March 26, 2015; Krugler, *Voice of America*, 76–77; Belmonte, *Selling the American Way*, 12–14.

130. For a broader discussion of the news media's participation in the US government's information programs, see Parry-Giles, "Militarizing America's Propaganda Program"; Bernhard, *U.S. Television News*; Alterman, *Sound and Fury*; Davies, *Postwar Decline*.

131. The Ambassador to the Secretary of State, November 15, 1947, *FRUS, 1947*, Vol. IV, Document 426.

132. The Ambassador to the Secretary of State, November 15, 1947, *FRUS, 1947*, Vol. IV, Document 426.

133. The Ambassador in the Soviet Union (Smith) to the Secretary of State, March 1, 1947, *FRUS, 1947*, Vol. IV, Document 371.

134. Belmonte, *Selling the American Way*, 32.

## Chapter 3 • Overtake America

1. The Grand Prix was shared by Gerasimov's *The Journalist* and István Szabó's *Father* (1966).

2. Magnúsdóttir, *Enemy Number One*, 78–79. The official agreement on cultural and educational exchanges between the USSR and the US was signed in January 1958; Gilburd, *To See Paris*, 27–28, 42–52.

3. Polevoi, *Amerikanskii dnevnik*; Adzhubei, "*Serebrianaia koshka*"; Gribachev, *Semero v Amerike*. For an insightful analysis of Polevoi's *American Diary*, see Gilburd, *To See Paris*, 303–307.

4. RGANI, F. 5, Op. 16, D. 734, Ll. 131–146. Rósa Magnúsdóttir offers an excellent discussion of the Polevoi report's impact on Soviet cultural exchanges and attitudes toward the US more broadly. See Magnúsdóttir, *Enemy Number One*, 86–95.

5. RGANI, F. 5, Op. 16, D. 734, Ll. 133–134, 136.

6. RGANI, F. 5, Op. 16, D. 734, L. 138.

7. RGANI, F. 5, Op. 16, D. 738, Ll. 96–97, 105, 135.

8. RGANI, F. 5, Op. 16, D. 734, Ll. 140–144.

9. RGANI, F. 5, Op. 16, D. 734, Ll. 134–135.

10. RGANI, F. 5, Op. 16, D. 734, L. 149. The delegation produced two separate reports dedicated to TASS in the US: RGANI, F. 5, Op. 16, D. 734, Ll. 148–149, and RGANI, F. 5, Op. 16, D. 738, Ll. 109–112.

11. RGANI, F. 5, Op. 16, D. 738, L.110.

12. RGANI, F. 5, Op. 16, D. 734, Ll. 148–149

13. RGANI, F. 5, Op. 16, D. 738, L. 110.

14. RGANI, F. 5, Op. 16, D. 738, L. 100.

15. RGANI, F. 5, Op. 16, D. 734, L.149; RGANI, F. 5, Op. 16, D. 738, L.111.

16. RGANI, F. 5, Op. 16, D. 738, L. 110.

17. RGANI, F. 5, Op. 16, D. 734, Ll. 149–149; RGANI, F. 5, Op. 16, D. 738, Ll. 110–111.

18. RGANI, F. 5, Op. 16, D. 734, L. 138.

19. RGANI, F. 5, Op. 16, D. 734, L. 135.

20. The other members of the delegation were Boris Izakov, who represented *Mezhdunarodnaia Zhizn'*, a new journal on international affairs founded by Molotov only a year before the tour, and Viktor Poltoratskii, a senior editor at *Izvestiia*'s international department, also a Stalin Prize laureate.

21. RGANI, F. 5, Op. 16, D. 734, Ll. 147, 150–153; RGANI, F. 5, Op. 16, D. 738, Ll. 96–119.

22. Zubok, *Failed Empire*, 101–105; Magnúsdóttir, *Enemy Number One*, 77–81.

23. Eimermacher et al., *Doklad N. S. Khrushcheva*, 51–119.

24. Eimermacher et al., *Doklad N. S. Khrushcheva*, 406–407, 409–411, 414–416, 418–425, 429–431.

25. There are several excellent studies dedicated to the 1960s generation. See especially Zubok, *Zhivago's Children*; Vail' and Genis, *60-ye*; English, *Russia and the Idea of the West*; Raleigh, *Soviet Baby Boomers*; Zubkova, *Obshchestvo i reformy*.

26. Zubok, *Failed Empire*, 176–181; Zubkova, *Obshchestvo i reformy*, 137–145, 167–169.

27. Wolfe, *Governing*, 31–38.

28. Wolfe, *Governing*, 18–34; Huxtable, "Compass in the Sea of Life," 61–73.

29. Huxtable, "Compass in the Sea of Life," 62–65, 143–180; Eduard Polianovskii, "Piat' printsipov Alekseia Adzhubeia," *Izvestiia*, January 6, 2004, http://www.izvestia.ru/news /285551; Iurii Feofanov, "Pervaia Planerka," in Mamleev, *Aleksei Adzhubei*, 109–110.

30. Wolfe, *Governing*, 34–36.

31. Huxtable, "Compass in the Sea of Life," 14–16, 21–25; Volkovskii, *Otechestvennaia zhurnalistika*, 84–85, 140–149; Polevoi, *Ocherk v gazete*, 26–30.

32. Quoted in Volkovskii, *Otechestvennaia zhurnalistika*, 80–81.

33. Vail' and Genis, *60-ye*, 15; Zubkova, *Obshchestvo i reformy*, 157–167; Gilburd, "The Revival of Soviet Internationalism," 362–401; Koivunen, "Performing Peace and Friendship"; Magnúsdóttir, *Enemy Number One*, 122–151; Gilburd, *To See Paris*, 19–102.

34. Vail' and Genis, *60-ye*, 15.

35. Wolfe, *Governing*, 58–61.

36. "My peregonim Ameriku! Rech Predsedatelia Soveta ministrov SSSR N. S. Khrushcheva pri otkrytii vystavki Soedinennykh Shtatov Ameriki v Moskve," *Trud*, July 25, 1959. Quoted in Reid, "Who Will Beat Whom?" 863–864.

37. Reid, "Who Will Beat Whom?" 864; Wolfe, *Governing*, 48–70.

38. GARF, F. R-1244, Op. 1, D. 170, L. 83.

39. GARF, F. R-1244, Op. 1, D. 170, Ll. 177–178.

40. GARF, F. R-1244, Op. 1, D. 166, L. 177.

41. GARF, F. R-1244, Op. 1, D. 165, Ll. 151–152; GARF, F. R-1244, Op. 1, D. 169, L. 15.

42. GARF, F. R-1244, Op. 1, D. 172, Ll. 203–204.

43. GARF, F. R-1244, Op. 1, D. 172, Ll. 204, 213; GARF, F. R-1244, Op. 1, D. 174, L. 203.

44. GARF, F. R-1244, Op. 1, D. 174, Ll. 98, 102–103; GARF, F. R-1244, Op. 1, D. 176, L. 7.

45. GARF, F. R-1244, Op. 1, D. 172, Ll. 204, 213; GARF, F. R-1244, Op. 1, D. 174, L. 203.

46. GARF, F. R-1244, Op. 1, D. 165, Ll. 48, 180.

47. Polianovskii, "Piat' printsipov."

48. Adzhubei, *Te desiat' let*, 9.

49. GARF, F. R-4459, Op. 38, D. 658, Ll. 39–46.

50. GARF, F. R-1244, Op. 1, D. 172, L. 203.

51. TsAGM, F. P-3226, Op. 1, D. 70, L. 111.

52. GARF, F. R-1244, Op. 1, D. 170, L. 67; GARF, F. R-1244, Op. 1, D. 165, L. 48; GARF, F. R-1244, Op. 1, D. 166, Ll. 163, 177, 185; GARF, F. R-1244, Op. 1, D. 180, L. 218.

53. For example, during an editorial board meeting one journalist referred to a common practice of receiving "a phone call from Smolenskaia square" [the location of Soviet Ministry of Foreign Affairs]. GARF, F. R-1244, Op. 1, D. 180, L. 67.

54. GARF, F. R-1244, Op. 1, D. 177, Ll. 101–105, 116–117, 130–131.

55. I am grateful to Mary Catherine French and Simon Huxtable, whose dissertations and insights helped me think about these developments. French, "Reporting Socialism," 113–127; Huxtable, "Compass in the Sea of Life," 72–76.

56. GARF, F. R-1244, Op. 1, D. 177, Ll. 101–105, 116–117, 130–131, 137, 149–160; GARF, F. R-1244, Op. 1, D. 182, L. 251; TsAGM, F. P-3226, Op. 1, D. 54, Ll. 111–112.

57. On the concept of Marxist consciousness, see Halfin, *From Darkness to Light*. On the debates about the public's ideological maturity and consciousness, see Dobson, "'Show the Bandit-Enemies No Mercy!,'" 21–40; Jones, "From the Secret Speech to the Burial of Stalin," 41–63.

58. French, "Reporting Socialism," 181.

59. GARF, F. R-1244, Op. 1, D. 175, L. 146.

60. GARF, F. R-1244, Op. 1, D. 175, L. 147.

61. For Begicheva's contribution to the anti-cosmopolitan campaign in 1948, see A. Begicheva to I. V. Stalin on the dominant influence of "enemy-cosmopolitans" in the arts, December 8, 1948, RGASPI, F. 17, Op. 132, D. 237, Ll. 75–81, accessed June 2018 via the Aleksander Yakovlev Foundation Digital Archive, http://www.alexanderyakovlev.org/fond/issues-doc/69477.

62. GARF, F. R-1244, Op. 1, D. 177, Ll. 76–77.

63. TsAGM, F. P-3226, Op. 1, D. 56, Ll. 75–86.

64. TsAGM, F. P-3226, Op. 1, D. 70, Ll. 75–76.

65. GARF, F. R-4459, Op. 38, D. 834, Ll. 15–17.

66. GARF, F. R-4459, Op. 38, D. 834, Ll. 15–17.

67. GARF, F. R-4459, Op. 38, D. 834, L. 15.

68. GARF, F. R-4459, Op. 38, D. 834, Ll. 16–17.

69. GARF, F. R-4459, Op. 38, D. 834, Ll. 1–7, 15–17.

70. GARF, F. R-4459, Op. 38, D. 834, Ll. 1–7.

71. GARF, F. R-4459, Op. 38, D. 978, Ll. 2–3.

72. GARF, F. R-4459, Op. 38, D. 978, L. 1.

73. GARF, F. R-4459, Op. 38, D. 531, Ll. 57–59.

74. GARF, F. R-4459, Op. 38, D. 531, L. 59.

75. GARF, F. R-4459, Op. 38, D. 740, Ll. 1–3.

76. GARF, F. R-4459, Op. 38, D. 740, Ll. 1–3.

77. GARF, F. R-4459, Op. 38, D. 978, Ll. 14–15.

78. GARF, F. R-4459, Op. 38, D. 978, Ll. 16–18.

79. GARF, F. R-4459, Op. 38, D. 978, Ll. 14–20, 22–24; GARF, F. R-4459, Op. 38, D. 1105, Ll. 61–64; Memorandum of Conversation, "US-Soviet Relations," March 7, 1961, Box 7: Soviet

Correspondents, 1961, Entry 5552, RG 59; Airgram A-771 from American Embassy in Moscow, April 3, 1962, Box 7: Soviet Correspondents, 1962, Entry 5552, RG 59; "Transfer to Moscow of New York TASS Correspondent," March 15, 1963; Airgram A-625, "Izvestiia Correspondent Sturua," November 6, 1963, Box 7: Soviet Correspondents, 1963, Entry 5552, RG 59.

80.  Walter J. Stoessel Jr. to David Henry, August 30, 1963, Box 7: Soviet Correspondents, 1963, Entry 5552, RG 59.

81.  Stoessel Jr. to Henry, August 30, 1963, Box 7: Soviet Correspondents, 1963, Entry 5552, RG 59.

82.  Boris Strel'nikov interviewed by Grigorii Sagal, "Korrespondent v SShA," in Sagal, *Dvadtsat' piat' interv'iu*, 249–259.

83.  Kondrashov's unpublished memoir, Stanislav Kondrashov Private Archive.

84.  Genrikh Borovik, interviewed by Sergei Korzun, *Echo Moskvy*, April 14, 2013, last accessed April 2020, https://echo.msk.ru/programs/korzun/1051820-echo/; Valentin Sergeevich Zorin, interview by the author, October 12, 2009, Moscow; Sagal, "Korrespondent v SShA, 249–259; Yuri Zhukov interviewed by Grigorii Sagal, "Iasnost', posledovatel'nost' mysli," in Sagal, *Dvadtsat' piat' interv'iu*, 215–222; Melor Sturua interviewed by Grigorii Sagal, "Ty pishesh' o liudiakh interesuiushchikh tebia," in Sagal, *Dvadtsat' piat' interv'iu*, 261–271.

85.  GARF, F. R-1244, Op. 1, D. 166, Ll. 163–164, 177, 185; GARF, F. R-1244, Op. 1, D. 168, Ll. 3, 81; GARF, F. R-1244, Op. 1, D. 177, Ll. 136–138.

86.  Tatiana Strel'nikova Private Archive.

87.  Sturua, interview, February 4, 2011.

88.  "Izvestiia Correspondent Sturua," November 6, 1963, Box 7: Soviet Correspondents, 1963, Entry 5552, RG 59.

89.  Airgram #A-368, "Biographic Data on New Izvestiia Correspondent Andrei Itskov," September 17, 1963; "Izvestiia Correspondent Sturua," November 6, 1963, Box 7: Soviet Correspondents, 1963, Entry 5552, RG 59; State Department's profile on Zhukov, April 14, 1967, Box 8: Soviet Correspondents, 1967, Entry 5552, RG 59; Robert L. Stevenson, "Luncheon with Victor Kopytin, TASS correspondent," January 11, 1967, Box 8: Soviet Correspondents, 1968, Entry 5552, RG 59.

90.  Memorandum from the Assistant Secretary of State for Public Affairs (Tubby) to the President's Press Secretary (Salinger), Washington, February 6, 1961, *FRUS, 1961–1963*, Vol. V, Document 23, https://history.state.gov/historicaldocuments/frus1961-63v05/d23.

91.  From American Embassy in Moscow (Thompson) to Secretary of State, March 21, 1961, Box 7: Soviet Correspondents, 1961, Entry 5552, RG 59.

92.  Memorandum from the Assistant Secretary of State for Public Affairs to the President's Press Secretary, February 6, 1961, *FRUS, 1961–1963*, Vol. V, Document 23.

93.  "Regulations and Controls Governing Soviet Correspondents in the US," September 6, 1963, Box 4: American Correspondents, 1963, Entry 5552, RG 59.

94.  Memorandum from Secretary of State Rusk to President Kennedy, Washington, April 25, 1962, *FRUS, 1961–1963*, Vol. V, Document 184, https://history.state.gov/historicaldocuments/frus1961-63v05/d184; "Regulations and Controls," September 6, 1963, Box 4: American Correspondents, 1963, Entry 5552, RG 59.

95.  "Regulations and Controls," September 6, 1963, Box 4: American Correspondents, 1963, Entry 5552, RG 59.

96.  Memorandum for SOV file, "Department turns down trip by two Soviet journalists," April 14, 1964; "'Izvestiia' correspondent asks why trip was turned down," April 17, 1964, Box 8: Soviet Correspondents, 1964, Entry 5552, RG 59.

97.  "Regulations and Controls," September 6, 1963, Box 4: American Correspondents, 1963, Entry 5552, RG 59.

98. "'Izvestiia' correspondent," April 17, 1964, Box 8: Soviet Correspondents, 1964, Entry 5552, RG 59.

99. "Soviet Embassy Complains on Travel Restrictions on Izvestiia Correspondent," January 29, 1968, Box 8: Soviet Correspondents, 1968, Entry 5552, RG 59.

100. State Department transcripts of reports on burglaries in the apartments of Soviet correspondents in New York mention TASS European service English-language broadcast on September 14, 1963; Moscow domestic service report on September 23, 1963, Box 7: Soviet Correspondents, 1963, Entry 5552, RG 59; "Izvestiia Man Here Reports Burglary," *New York Times*, September 16, 1963.

101. Sturua, interview, February 4, 2011.

102. Vasily Strel'nikov, interview by the author, June 21, 2010, Moscow.

103. Sagal, "Korrespondent v SShA," 249–259.

104. "Freedom 'Lesson' Barred to Soviet," *New York Times*, March 7, 1961, p. 12.

105. See David Klein to Earl Heuer, April 25, 1961, Box 7: Soviet Correspondents, 1961, Entry 5552, RG 59; Robert I. Owen to Dorothy D. Bartholomew, May 7, 1964; Carroll H. Woods to Henry C. Ruddy, November 6, 1964, Box 8: Soviet Correspondents, 1964, Entry 5552, RG 59; Glenn O. Young to the Secretary of State, March 28, 1969, Box 8: Soviet Correspondents, 1969, Entry 5552, RG 59.

106. "TASS participation in a US tour for foreign newsmen," April 10, 1961, Box 7: Soviet Correspondents, 1961, Entry 5552, RG 59; "White House sponsored tours for foreign correspondents," February 19, 1962, Box 7: Soviet Correspondents, 1962, Entry 5552, RG 59.

107. "White House sponsored tours," February 19, 1962, Box 7: Soviet Correspondents, 1962, Entry 5552, RG 59.

108. Airgram #1072 from American Embassy in Moscow, "Reports by Soviet Correspondents in the U.S. on Vietnam," March 4, 1965; "Possible Call by Soviet Embassy Officials regarding Visas for Soviet Correspondents," December 6, 1965, Box 8: Soviet Correspondents, 1965, Entry 5552, RG 59; From Carroll H. Woods to Ernest G. Wiener, February 21, 1966; Memorandum to the Files, March 31, 1966; Memorandum of Conversation, "U.S.–USSR relations," April 27, 1966; Airgram #A-386, "Soviet Journalist Seeks Invitation to Visit Cape Kennedy," September 2, 1966, Box 8: Soviet Correspondents, 1966, Entry 5552, RG 59; Memorandum of Conversation, Pravda Offices, Moscow, August 1967; "Future of Soviet-American Relations: Mr. Brzezinski 'interviewed' by Yuri Zhukov of Pravda," April 13, 1967; Alexander G. Barmine, "Lunch with TASS Correspondent Victor Kopytin," October 6, 1967; Memorandum to the Secretary of State, "Your Meeting with Pravda Correspondent Sergei N. Vishnevskiy," November 20, 1967, Box 8: Soviet Correspondents, 1967, Entry 5552, RG 59; Stevenson, "Luncheon with Kopytin," January 11, 1967, Box 8: Soviet Correspondents, 1968, Entry 5552, RG 59.

109. "Agency History," website of RIA Novosti (APN's successor), https://xn--c1acbl 2abdlkab1og.xn--p1ai/about_us/.

110. Kalugin, *Spymaster*, 33.

111. Memorandum to Foy D. Kohler, "The Role of 'APN–Press News Agency' in the Soviet Cultural and Political Offensive," August 8, 1962, Box 7: Soviet Correspondents, 1962, Entry 5552, RG 59.

112. Kondrashov's unpublished memoir, Stanislav Kondrashov Private Archive.

113. Salinger, *With Kennedy*, 205–206; Memorandum from the President's Press Secretary (Salinger) to Secretary of State Rusk, Washington, November 28, 1961, *FRUS, 1961–1963*, Vol. V, Document 135, https://history.state.gov/historicaldocuments/frus1961-63v05/d135.

114. Airgram #A-462, "Meeting at MFA Press Section," September 7, 1965, Box 8: Soviet Correspondents, 1965, Entry 5552, RG 59.

115. See State Department reports on Zhukov's meetings with US officials in Box 3: Yuri Zhukov Visit 1958 -1960, Entry 5552, RG 59; Memorandum from the President's Press

Secretary (Salinger) to President Kennedy, October 31, 1962, *FRUS, 1961–1963*, Vol. V, Document 258, https://history.state.gov/historicaldocuments/frus1961-63v05/d258.

116.  Pierre E. G. Salinger, recorded interview by Theodore H. White, August 10, 1965, pp. 169–205, John F. Kennedy Library Oral History Program, John F. Kennedy Presidential Library Digital Archives, https://www.jfklibrary.org/Asset-Viewer/Archives/JFKOH-PES-02.aspx.

117.  Memorandum to President Kennedy, October 31, 1962, *FRUS, 1961–1963*, Vol. V, Document 258.

118.  Memorandum of Conversation, "US-Soviet Relations," March 7, 1961, Box 7: Soviet Correspondents, 1961, Entry 5552, RG 59; "Izvestiia Columnist N. Polyanov," June 26, 1962, Box 7: Soviet Correspondents, 1962, Entry 5552, RG 59; Memorandum of Conversation, "U.S.–USSR relations," April 27, 1966, Box 8: Soviet Correspondents, 1966, Entry 5552, RG 59; Barmine, "Lunch with Kopytin," October 6, 1967; Memorandum to the Secretary of State, "Your Meeting with Pravda Correspondent Sergei N. Vishnevskiy," November 20, 1967, Box 8: Soviet Correspondents, 1967, Entry 5552, RG 59; Memorandum from the President's Press Secretary (Salinger) to the President's Special Assistant for National Security Affairs (Bundy), June 25, 1962, *FRUS, 1961–1963*, Vol. XV, Document 70, https://history.state.gov/historical documents/frus1961-63v15/d70; Stevenson, "Luncheon with Kopytin," January 11, 1967, Box 8: Soviet Correspondents, 1968, Entry 5552, RG 59.

## Chapter 4 • *In Sputnik's Shadow*

1.  Harrison Salisbury to Arthur Hays Sulzberger, March 16, 1953, Salisbury Papers, Box 187, Folder 39.

2.  Harrison Salisbury to Emmanuel Freedman, April 6, 1953, Salisbury Papers, Box 187, Folder 40. Emphasis in the original.

3.  Harrison Salisbury to C. L. Sulzberger March 18, 1953, Salisbury Papers, Box 9, Folder 9.

4.  Eddy Gilmore to Alan J. Gould, April 7, 1953, Box 18: Moscow Bureau 1953, APCA.

5.  On the Soviet "peace offensive," see Brooks, *When the Cold War Did Not End.*

6.  Ray Erwin, "News Runs Slightly Easier in Moscow," *Editor and Publisher*, August 8, 1953, p. 8. The head of Reuters proclaimed that Soviet censorship of foreign correspondents had been significantly reduced as early as April. "Reuters Chief Says Censorship Eased by Soviet," *Editor and Publisher*, April 18, 1953, p. 12.

7.  Gilmore to Gould, April 7, 1953, Box 18: Moscow Bureau 1953, APCA.

8.  Daniel Schwarz to Harrison Salisbury, April 15, 1953, Salisbury Papers, Box 187, Folder 40; Harrison Salisbury to Daniel Schwarz, May 7, 1953, Salisbury Papers, Box 187, Folder 41; Eddy Gilmore to Alan J. Gould, "New Stories from USSR," June 3, 1954, Box 18: Moscow Bureau 1954, APCA; Schorr, *Staying Tuned,* Chapter 5.

9.  Bassow, *Moscow Correspondents*, 144–145.

10.  RGANI, F. 5, Op. 16, D. 740, Ll. 1–4.

11.  Edward L. Freers to Joseph A. Frank, August 31, 1956, Box 3: PPB 9-7 American Correspondents, 1956–1957, Entry 5552, RG 59.

12.  RGANI, F. 5, Op. 16, D. 748, Ll. 96–97.

13.  RGANI, F. 5, Op. 16, D. 748, Ll. 96–97, 135–136; RGANI, F. 5, Op. 33, D. 203, Ll. 46–47.

14.  RGANI, F. 5, Op. 16, D. 748, Ll. 96–97, 135–136.

15.  RGANI, F. 5, Op. 16, D. 748, Ll. 96–97, 135–136.

16.  Clifton Daniel to Nathaniel Gerstenzang, June 14, 1955, NYT Foreign Desk, Box 23, Folder 7.

17.  Preston Grover to Alan J. Gould, April 13, 1961, Box 29: USSR, APCA.

18.  Clifton Daniel to Turner Catledge, February 13, 1955, NYT Foreign Desk, Box 23, Folder 7. See also Hamilton, *Journalism's Roving Eye*, 435.

19.  Fischer and Fischer, *International Reporting*, 158.

20. Fischer and Fischer, *International Reporting*, 158.

21. "Text of Khrushchev Interview on Wide Range of Issues between East and West," *New York Times*, October 10, 1957, p. 10; Turner Catledge, "Khrushchev, in Interview, Asserts U.S.-Soviet Accord Is the Way to Avert a War," *New York Times*, May 11, 1957, p. 1.

22. Schorr, *Staying Tuned*, Chapter 7.

23. Schorr, *Staying Tuned*, Chapter 7.

24. Harrison Salisbury to Emanuel Freedman, January 23, 1956, NYT Foreign Desk, Box 82, Folder 5.

25. Salisbury to Freedman, January 23, 1956, NYT Foreign Desk, Box 82, Folder 5.

26. Coleman Harvel to Alan J. Gould, October 8, 1955, Box 18: Moscow Bureau 1955, APCA.

27. William J. Jorden, "The People of Russia: A Bus Driver in Moscow Gives His Views on Life in the Soviet Union," *New York Times*, August 18, 1957, p. 1; William J. Jorden, "The People of Russia: A School Teacher in Soviet Armenia Mingles Family Life and Work," *New York Times*, August 21, 1957, p. 1.

28. Turner Catledge to Max Frankel, July 26, 1957, NYT Foreign Desk, Box 34, Folder 8.

29. Schorr, *Staying Tuned*, Chapter 5.

30. Levine, *Main Street*, ii.

31. Mosby, *View from No. 13*, ix.

32. Each book in the *Inside* series presented the results of Gunther's extensive exploration of a continent or a country, including history and an assessment of current political affairs, information about the daily lives of regular people, interviews with professionals and citizens, statistics, and Gunther's own analysis of what he'd learned from extensive travel.

33. Gunther, *Inside Russia*. In 1962, Gunther published another Russia book; two volumes of *Meet Soviet Russia* were accompanied by a TV series documenting his travels.

34. Levine, *Main Street*, 32, 207–218; Aline Mosby's account blends her observations of Russia with stories about her experiences as an American woman in Moscow. See especially Mosby, *View from No. 13*, Chapters 4–7.

35. Levine, *Main Street*, 57–64, 86–88; Gunther, *Inside Russia*, 194–204, 356–362.

36. The only exception was Harrison Salisbury, who stressed the cultural and historical differences that separated Russia and the United States. Fainberg, "Portrait of a Journalist," 153–164.

37. Levine, *Main Street*, 27–28, 399–400; Gunther, *Inside Russia*, 500–501; Mosby, *View from No. 13*, 77, 87–88, 199, 202, 300–301.

38. Levine, *Main Street*, 65–67, 131–132; Gunther, *Inside Russia*, xxiv, 209–211, 263, 351–352, 501, 505; Mosby, *View from No. 13*, 300–301.

39. Levine, *Main Street*, 27–28, 399–400; Mosby, *View from No. 13*, 198–199, 202, 298–301.

40. Foglesong, *American Mission*, 129–139.

41. Gunther, *Inside Russia*, 25.

42. Gunther, *Inside Russia*, 212–236, 501–502.

43. Levine, *Main Street*, 15.

44. Zelizer, *Arsenal of Democracy*, 138–140; Divine, *Sputnik Challenge*, xvi–xxiii.

45. Gunther, *Inside Russia*, xxiii. For Gunther's overall take on Soviet science and technology, see Gunther, *Inside Russia*, xxii–xxiii, 253–283.

46. Gunther, *Inside Russia*, 263–264, 283.

47. Max Frankel, "Four Siberian Centers Typify Soviet Efforts to Overtake U.S.," *New York Times*, April 28, 1959, p. 1.

48. Max Frankel, "Soviet Building a New World in Siberia," *New York Times*, April 27, 1959, p. 1.

49. "To the editors of the New York Times," April 28, 1959, NYT Foreign Desk, Box 34, Folder 10.

50. On post-Sputnik concerns with Soviet superiority, see Zelizer, *Arsenal of Democracy*, 138–139.

51. Levine, *Main Street*, 24. See also Mosby, *View from No. 13*, 56–74, 166–167, 201.

52. Frankel, *Times of My Life*, 181.

53. Max Frankel to Emmanuel Freedman, June 16, 1959, NYT Foreign Desk, Box 34, Folder 10.

54. Hendershot, *Anti-Communism*, 13–16; Osgood, *Total Cold War*, 253–274.

55. Leonid Il'ichev from the Foreign Ministry's Press Department argued that censorship was the "only means to exercise timely intervention" in case foreign correspondents submitted "rude slanderous dispatches" or "severely distorted the announcements or the actions of Soviet leaders." RGANI, F. 5, Op. 16, D. 748, Ll. 96–97. The Soviet ambassador to the US used roughly the same explanation: "From text of Menshikov's appearance before Radio and TV Executives Society, November 19, 1958," Box 4: PPB 9-7 American Correspondents, 1958–1959, Entry 5552, RG 59. On Glavlit's perception of the censorship of foreign correspondents, see GARF, F. R-9425, Op. 1, D. 1057, Ll. 65, 69–72; GARF, F. R-9425, Op. 1, D. 1014, Ll. 9, 52–61.

56. Catledge, "Khrushchev, in Interview, Asserts U.S.-Soviet Accord Is the Way to Avert a War," p. 1.

57. GARF, F. R-9425, Op. 1, D. 1014, Ll. 52–53.

58. GARF, F. R-9425, Op. 1, D. 1014, Ll. 56, 58.

59. GARF, F. R-9425, Op. 1, D. 1014, Ll. 52–60; GARF, F. R-9425, Op. 1, D. 1015, Ll. 101–104.

60. GARF, F. R-9425, Op. 1, D. 1014, L. 56.

61. GARF, F. R-9425, Op. 1, D. 1014, L. 58.

62. GARF, F. R-9425, Op. 1, D. 1014, L. 52.

63. GARF, F. R-9425, Op. 1, D. 1056, Ll. 1–4; GARF, F. R-9425, Op. 1, D. 1015, Ll. 121–124, 160–161. See also Sherry, *Discourses of Regulation*, 47–50.

64. Telegram #645 from Moscow to the Secretary of State, September 20, 1958, Box 4: PPB 9-7 American Correspondents, 1963, Entry 5552, RG 59; Ben Basset to Turner Catledge, August 21, 1958; Harold K. Milks to Ben Basset, September 13, 1958, Box 25: USSR/Moscow 1959, APCA.

65. GARF, F. R-9425, Op. 1, D. 1015, L. 70.

66. "US Correspondents expelled by the Soviet Government since 1956," January 6, 1966, Box 4: PPB 9-7 American Correspondents, 1966, Entry 5552, RG 59; Preston Grover to Frank J. Starzel, April 6, 1959, Box 26: USSR 1959, APCA; From Moscow to Secretary of State, February 12, 1963, Box 4: PPB 9-7 American Correspondents, 1963, Entry 5552, RG 59.

67. "US Correspondents expelled," January 6, 1966, Box 4: PPB 9-7 American Correspondents, 1966, Entry 5552, RG 59; Schorr, *Staying Tuned*, Chapter 7.

68. Telegram #2820 from Moscow to Secretary of State, June 29, 1957, Box 3: PPB 9-7 American Correspondents, 1956–1957, Entry 5552, RG 59; Telegram #2094 from Moscow to Secretary of State, May 27, 1958; Telegram #2216 from Moscow to Secretary of State, June 14, 1958; Telegram #1581 from Moscow to Secretary of State, February 9, 1959, Box 4: PPB 9-7 American Correspondents, 1963, Entry 5552, RG 59.

69. Khrushchev, *Vremia*, Book IV, Part IV.

70. Harrison Salisbury to Emmanuel Freedman, January 13, 1959, NYT Foreign Desk, Box 83, Folder 1.

71. Schorr, *Staying Tuned*, Chapter 7.

72. "From text of Menshikov's appearance," Box 4: PPB 9-7 American Correspondents, 1958–1959, Entry 5552, RG 59.

73. Telegram #3221 From Moscow to the Secretary of State, June 22, 1960, Box 4: PPB 9-7 American Correspondents, 1960, Entry 5552, RG 59.

74. GARF, F. R-9425, Op. 1, D. 1014, Ll. 25, 60–61; "Meet the Press: First Deputy Premier of the Soviet Union, Anastas Mikoyan," produced by Lawrence E. Spivak, broadcast January 18, 1959, NBC. For the transcript of Mikoyan's interview on "Meet the Press," see "Text of the Panel Interview with Mikoyan on Television Broadcast," *New York Times*, January 19, 1959, p. 10. See also Memorandum of Visit, January 19, 1959, *FRUS, 1958–1960*, Vol. X, Part 1, Document 66, https://history.state.gov/historicaldocuments/frus1958-60v10p1/d66.

75. Telegram #132 from Moscow to Secretary of State, July 18, 1956, Box 3: PPB 9-7 American Correspondents, 1956–1957, Entry 5552, RG 59.

76. For example, internal correspondence between Glavlit and the Foreign Ministry's Press Department pointed out that under the leadership of Preston Grover, the Moscow bureau of the Associated Press had become more anti-Soviet. GARF, F. R-9425, Op. 1, D. 1015, Ll. 101–104.

77. "U.S. Correspondents in Moscow and the Christian Science Monitor," September 21, 1965, Box 4: PPB 9-7 American Correspondents, 1965, Entry 5552, RG 59.

78. Henry Bradsher to Wes Gallagher, July 29, 1964, Box 32: USSR, APCA.

79. "US Correspondents expelled," January 6, 1966, Box 4: PPB 9-7 American Correspondents, 1966, Entry 5552, RG 59.

80. "Address by the Honorable Andrew H. Berding Assistant Secretary of State for Public Affairs before the Annual Convention of Civitan International, Roosevelt Hotel, New Orleans, Louisiana, June 24, 1958," Box 4: PPB 9-7 American Correspondents, 1963, Entry 5552, RG 59.

81. "Address by Andrew H. Berding, June 24, 1958," Box 4: PPB 9-7 American Correspondents, 1963, Entry 5552, RG 59.

82. Foglesong, *American Mission*, 133–134; Divine, *Sputnik Challenge*, xvi–xvii; Zelizer, *Arsenal of Democracy*, 138–139.

83. Lebovic, *Free Speech and Unfree News*, 164–166.

84. Davies, *Postwar Decline*, 33–38, 95–96; Lebovic, *Free Speech and Unfree News*, 164–185, especially 175–181.

85. "Memo on a 50-minute conversation and discussion with Assistant Secretary of State Andrew Berding on the problem of maintaining American correspondents in Moscow," April 10, 1959, Box 26: USSR 1959, APCA; Telegram #2216 from Moscow to Secretary of State, June 14, 1958; Telegram #827 from Moscow to Secretary of State, October 13, 1958; William R. Tyler to Robert Manning, "Situation of U.S. Correspondents in the USSR," April 19, 1963, Box 4: PPB 9-7 American Correspondents, 1963, Entry 5552, RG 59; To American Embassy in Moscow, January 5, 1966; "Response to Soviet Actions against U.S. Correspondents," January 6, 1966; "Accreditation of Soviet Correspondents," November 28, 1966; John A. Armitage to Carroll H. Woods, October 31, 1966, Box 4: PPB 9-7 American Correspondents, 1966, Entry 5552, RG 59.

86. "Memo on conversation with Berding," April 10, 1959, Box 26: USSR 1959, APCA.

87. "Memo on conversation with Berding," April 10, 1959, Box 26: USSR 1959, APCA.

88. Frank Starzel to Andrew H. Berding, April 17, 1959; Frank Starzel to Preston Grover, April 24, 1959, Box 26: USSR 1959, APCA; Telegram #827 from Moscow to Secretary of State, October 13, 1958, Box 4: PPB 9-7 American Correspondents, 1963, Entry 5552, RG 59; Peter Grose to Ambassador Kohler, March 1, 1966, Box 4: PPB 9-7 American Correspondents, 1966, Entry 5552, RG 59.

89. "Memo on conversation with Berding," April 10, 1959, Box 26: USSR 1959, APCA; Robert Owen to Samuel G. Wise, Jr., October 10, 1962, Box 4: PPB 9-7 American Correspondents, 1962, Entry 5552, RG 59; Tyler to Manning, "Situation of U.S. Correspondents in the USSR," April 19, 1963; Memorandum on conversation with Marvin Kalb, April 4, 1963; Preston Grover to Wes Gallagher, March 29, 1963; Pat McGrady to Jim Greenfield, Assistant Secretary of State, August 8, 1963, Box 4: PPB 9-7 American Correspondents, 1963, Entry 5552, RG 59; Grose to Kohler, March 1, 1966, Box 4: PPB 9-7 American Correspondents, 1966, Entry 5552, RG 59.

90. "Situation of U.S. Correspondents in the USSR," April 19, 1963, Box 4: PPB 9-7 American Correspondents, 1963, Entry 5552, RG 59.

91. Telegram #3045 from Moscow to Secretary of State, June 7, 1961; Richard E. Snyder, "Incident Involving UPI Correspondent Aline Mosby," June 7, 1961, Box 4: PPB 9-7 American Correspondents, 1961, Entry 5552, RG 59. Aline Mosby, interview by Kathleen Currie, May 9, 1991, pp. 62–65, Washington Press Club Foundation Oral History Project, last accessed July 13, 2019, http://beta.wpcf.org/oralhistory/mosby.html.

92. "Gospozha Mosby v vytrezvitele," *Izvestiia*, June 7, 1961.

93. "Gospozha Mosby v vytrezvitele."

94. Secretary of State to American Embassy in Moscow, June 8, 1961; Telegram #3087 from Moscow to Secretary of State, June 10, 1961; From Secretary of State to American Embassy in Moscow, June 12, 1961; Telegram #3111 from Moscow to Secretary of State, June 13, 1961, Box 4: PPB 9-7 American Correspondents, 1961, Entry 5552, RG 59.

95. Preston Grover to Ben Bassett, June 7, 1961, Box 29: USSR, APCA.

96. Grover to Bassett, June 7, 1961, Box 29: USSR, APCA.

97. Mosby interviewed by Currie, p. 65.

98. "Gospozha Mosby v vytrezvitele."

99. Grover to Bassett, June 7, 1961, Box 29: USSR, APCA.

100. Grover to Gallagher, March 29, 1963, Box 31: USSR, APCA.

101. John C. Guthrie to John M. McSweeney, August 22, 1962, Box 4: PPB 9-7 American Correspondents, 1962, Entry 5552, RG 59. Two years later, a similar explanation was offered for the expulsion of Peter Johnson of Reuters. Airgram #1111, "Expulsion of Reuters Correspondent," February 7, 1964, Box 4: PPB 9-7 American Correspondents, 1964, Entry 5552, RG 59.

102. "Expulsion of Reuters Correspondent," February 7, 1964, Box 4: PPB 9-7 American Correspondents, 1964, Entry 5552, RG 59.

103. Telegram #1559, From Moscow to Secretary of State, December 1, 1959, Box 4: PPB 9-7 American Correspondents, 1958–1959, Entry 5552, RG 59.

104. See, for example, Telegram # 2253, From Moscow to Secretary of State, March 12, 1963; Airgram # A-1363, "Notes on Edmund Stevens' trip to Cuba," March 20, 1963, Box 4: PPB 9-7 American Correspondents, 1963, Entry 5552, RG 59.

105. USSR Affairs Contacts with Newsmen, March 7, 1958, Box 4: PPB 9-7 American Correspondents, 1958–1959, Entry 5552, RG 59.

106. Memorandum for the Secretary from Andrew H. Berding, February 25, 1958, Box 4: PPB 9-7 American Correspondents, 1958–1959, Entry 5552, RG 59.

107. Max Frankel to Emmanuel Freedman, October 23, 1959, NYT Foreign Desk, Box 34, Folder 12.

108. McGrady to Greenfield, August 8, 1963, Box 4: PPB 9-7 American Correspondents, 1963, Entry 5552, RG 59.

109. "U.S. Correspondents in Moscow," December 6, 1966, Box 4: PPB 9-7 American Correspondents, 1966, Entry 5552, RG 59; "Lifting of Soviet Ban on Washington Post," February 11, 1967, Box 4. PPB 9-7 American Correspondents, 1967, Entry 5552, RG 59.

110. To American Embassy in Moscow, January 5, 1966; "Response to Soviet Actions against U.S. Correspondents," January 6, 1966; "Accreditation of Soviet Correspondents," November 28, 1966; Armitage to Woods, October 31, 1966, Box 4: PPB 9-7 American Correspondents, 1966, Entry 5552, RG 59.

111. "Accreditation of Soviet correspondents," November 28, 1966, Box 4: PPB 9-7 American Correspondents, 1966, Entry 5552, RG 59.

112. Carroll H. Woods to John Armitage, October 24, 1966, Box 4: PPB 9-7 American Correspondents, 1966, Entry 5552, RG 59.

113. Grose to Kohler, March 1, 1966, Box 4: PPB 9-7 American Correspondents, 1966, Entry 5552, RG 59.

114. Seymour Topping to Emmanuel Freedman, March 8, 1961, NYT Foreign Desk, Box 118, Folder 8.

## Part 3 • *Your Fight Is Our Fight, 1965–1985*

1. *Human Rights: A Soviet-American Debate*, NBC (WRC-TV, Washington, DC), June 12, 1977.

2. Zubok, *Failed Empire*, 193–201, 215–226, 229–264, 271–278; Foglesong, *American Mission*, 153–173, 177–184; Roberts, *Soviet Union in World Politics*, 63–88.

## Chapter 5 • *Notes from the Rotten West*

1. Diary entry for January 31, 1968, Stanislav Kondrashov's Diary 1968, notebook 1, p. 11, Stanislav Kondrashov Private Archive.

2. Kondrashov, *Perekrestki Ameriki*; Kondrashov, *Zhizn' i smert'*; Sturua, *Brozhenie*; Borovik, *Odin God*.

3. For a good analysis of pre–Cold War writings see Ball, *Imagining America*, 1–173; Etkind, *Tolkovanie Puteshestvii*; Fedorova, *Yankees in Petrograd*; Hasty and Fusso, *America through Russian Eyes*; Gleason, "Republic of Humbug"; Rogger, "America in the Russian Mind"; Roman, *Opposing Jim Crow*, 81–89; Ryan, "Imagining America."

4. For example, Eaton, *Daily Life*, 273; Shiraev and Zubok, *Anti-Americanism*, 21.

5. For examples of scholarship using Soviet travelogues in analyses of Soviet transnational interactions, see Gilburd, "Books and Borders"; Applebaum, "Test of Friendship"; Gorsuch, "'Cuba, My Love'"; Gorsuch, *All This Is Your World*, 87–93, 140–167; Rupprecht, *Soviet Internationalism*, 73–110; Gilburd, *To See Paris*, 268–317; Applebaum, *Empire of Friends*, 81–101. On the transnational turn in Russian and Soviet history, see David-Fox, "The Implications of Transnationalism."

6. Magnúsdóttir, *Enemy Number One*, 90–94; Gilburd, *To See Paris*, 314–315, specifically on Melor Sturua.

7. Borovik, interview, April 14, 2013.

8. Sturua, interview, February 4, 2011.

9. Stanislav Kondrashov, interview by Aleksandr Pumpianskii, January 1999, in Grabel'nikov et al., *Zhurnalisty XX veka*, 444.

10. Strel'nikov was the first Soviet journalist to repeat Ilya Il'f and Evgeny Petrov's epic coast-to-coast journey; many of his books and article series were based on his road trips.

11. See also Gilburd, *To See Paris*, 304–305, 308, on the influences of early Soviet travelogues on the accounts of postwar visitors.

12. On Soviet censorship of the press, see Losev, *Zakrytyi Raspredelitel'*, 98–138; Blium, *Kak eto delalos'*. Eleonory Gilburd's discussion of Victor Nekrasov's travelogue and the aftermath of its publication illustrates the consequences of Soviet information policies. Gilburd, *To See Paris*, 311–314.

13. Yurchak, *Everything Was Forever*, 160–165; Roth-Ey, *Moscow Prime Time*, 9–10; Raleigh, *Soviet Baby Boomers*, 158–161; Chernyshova, *Soviet Consumer Culture*, 117–119.

14. Zubok, *Failed Empire*, 193–196; Wolfe, *Governing*, 110–111; Evans, "Decline of Developed Socialism?", 1–2.

15. English, *Russia and the Idea of the West*, 109, 118.

16. Wolfe, *Governing*, 111.

17. Zubok, *Zhivago's Children*, 283–286.

18. Vail' and Genis, *60-ye*, 284–285, 291; English, *Russia and the Idea of the West*, 118; Zubok, *Failed Empire*, 209.

19.  Sergeev, *Izvestiia*, Vol. 1, 114; Tolkunova, *Dvazhdy glavnyi*, 101, 145.

20.  English, *Russia and the Idea of the West*, 135.

21.  Bovin, *XX vek*, 145–146; Arbatov, *Zatianuvsheesia vyzdorovlenie*, 125–126; Zubok, *Failed Empire*, 214.

22.  Huxtable, "Compass in the Sea of Life," 93.

23.  Sturua, interview, February 4, 2011; Zorin, interview, October 12, 2009. See also Losev, *Zakrytyi Raspredelitel'*, 137.

24.  Stanislav Kondrashov to the editorial board of *Nedelia*, April 11, 1975, Stanislav Kondrashov Private Archive.

25.  Wolfe, *Governing*, 112–124; Huxtable, "Compass in the Sea of Life," 93, Roudakova, *Loosing Pravda*, 57–62, 81–93; Koltsova, *News Media*, 25–28; Huxtable, "Life and Death of Brezhnev's Thaw," 38–39.

26.  Borovik, interview, April 14, 2013; "Spravka Glavlita o zamechaniiakh k materialam, podgotovlennym k opublikovaniiu v 1966 g.," in Goriaeva and Vodop'ianova, *Istoriia sovetskoi politicheskoi tsenzury*, 556–559.

27.  Diary entry for April 11, 1968, Stanislav Kondrashov's Diary 1968, notebook 1, p. 11, Stanislav Kondrashov Private Archive; Sturua, interview, February 4, 2011; Zorin, interview, October 12, 2009. See also Bovin, *XX vek*, 265–268; Wolfe, *Governing*, 105, 125; Zorin, *Neizvestnoe ob izvestnom*, 148–149.

28.  For an excellent analysis of Soviet efforts to grapple with the challenge of foreign broadcasting, see Roth-Ey, *Moscow Prime Time*, 131–175.

29.  Roth-Ey, *Moscow Prime Time*, 131–146; Raleigh, *Soviet Baby Boomers*, 147–150; Lovell, *Russia in the Microphone Age*, 151–158, 175–181; Yurchak, *Everything Was Forever*, 175–181; Nathans, *To the Success*, Chapter 6.

30.  TsGAM, F. 3226, Op. 1, D. 70, Ll. 75–76.

31.  TsGAM, F. 3226, Op. 1, D. 70, L. 137.

32.  TsGAM, F. 3226, Op. 1, D. 70, Ll. 137–138.

33.  RGANI, F. 5, Op. 62, ed. khr. 39, 237. Quoted in Wolfe, *Governing*, 129–130.

34.  RGANI, F. 5, Op. 62, ed. khr. 39, 237. Quoted in Wolfe, *Governing*, 132.

35.  Roth-Ey, *Moscow Primetime*, 162.

36.  L. I. Brezhnev, "Vystuplenie na Plenume TsK KPSS," November 27, 1978, in Brezhnev, *Leninskim kursom*, Vol. 7, 541.

37.  Wolfe, *Governing*, 41–48; Huxtable, "Compass in the Sea of Life," 189–207, 216–230, 255; Roudakova, *Losing Pravda*, 80.

38.  English, *Russia and the Idea of the West*, 119–123; Zubok, *Failed Empire*, 194–222.

39.  Yurchak, *Everything Was Forever*, 165–169.

40.  Mitrokhin, "Elite of 'Closed Society,'" 145–185.

41.  Zubok, *Failed Empire*, 205–206; Mitrokhin, "Elite of 'Closed Society.'"

42.  Mitrokhin, "Elite of 'Closed Society.'"

43.  Kondrashov, *Amerikantsy v Amerike*, 1.

44.  Sturua, interview, February 4, 2011.

45.  Berlin, *Russian Thinkers*; Paperno, *Chernyshevsky and the Age of Realism*.

46.  Strel'nikov, *Tysiacha mil'*, 76–77.

47.  Strel'nikov, *Tysiacha mil'*, 76–77.

48.  Strel'nikov, *Tysiacha mil'*, 77

49.  Strel'nikov, *Tysiacha mil'*, 77

50.  Strel'nikov, *Tysiacha mil'*, 78.

51.  Kondrashov, *Svidanie s Kaliforniei*, 26.

52.  Strel'nikov, *Tysiacha mil'*, 325–326.

53.  Strel'nikov, *Tysiacha mil'*, 166.

54. Borovik, *Prolog*, 309–310.

55. For more on this topic, see Baldwin, *Beyond the Color Line*, 1–24, 202–263; Borstelmann, *Cold War and the Color Line*; Carew, *Blacks, Reds, and Russians*.

56. My analysis here is indebted to discussions with Andrey Shcherbenok and his insightful article in *KinoKultura*: Shcherbenok, "Asymmetric Warfare."

57. In his analysis of Marx's concept of alienation, the philosopher Bertell Ollman explains that its meaning reached beyond a separation between the worker and his product. In Marx's writings, alienation also occurs between people when "competition and class hostility made cooperation impossible." Alienation is experienced by members of the same class as well as by members of antagonistic classes. Thus, in capitalism, a worker was alienated both from fellow workers and from members of other classes. Ollman, *Alienation*, 133–134.

58. See, for example, Strel'nikov and Shatunovskii, *Amerika sprava i sleva*, 233–247.

59. Sturua, interview, February 4, 2011.

60. For example, Boris Strel'nikov's last collection of essays was titled *One Thousand Miles in Search of a Soul*.

61. Kondrashov, *Liudi za okeanom*, 32–33.

62. Reid, "Who Will Beat Whom?", 865; Chernyshova, *Soviet Consumer Culture*, 113–119; Yurchak, *Everything Was Forever*, 164–170.

63. Reid, "Cold War in the Kitchen," 219–220.

64. Chernyshova, *Soviet Consumer Culture*, 43–79, 113–119; Reid, "Who Will Beat Whom?", 865; Reid, "Cold War in the Kitchen," 219–220; Yurchak, *Everything Was Forever*, 164–170, 190–202; Zubok, *Zhivago's Children*, 42.

65. For an excellent discussion on the efforts to promote responsible socialist consumers, see Reid, "Cold War in the Kitchen," 219–220.

66. Yurchak, *Everything Was Forever*, 164–170, 190–202.

67. See, for example, Sturua, *Brozhenie*, 106.

68. Kondrashov, *Svidanie s Kaliforniei*, 103–104.

69. This was not in itself surprising, for in Soviet and American Cold War discourse, consumption was represented as primarily a female domain. See Reid, "Cold War in the Kitchen," 212–214; Chernyshova, *Soviet Consumer Culture*, 64–66, 73–74.

70. See for example, Sturua, *Brozhenie*, 105–106.

71. Discussions of this topic occasionally pop up in the Russian blogosphere. See, for example, Denis Dragunskii, "Nezadacha," *LiveJournal*, August 9, 2011, https://clear-text .livejournal.com/281818.html. The hundreds of comments on Dragunskii's post illustrate the controversies surrounding Soviet foreign correspondents and consumer products to this day and informed my analysis here.

72. Willis, *Klass*, 274.

73. This is how Stanislav Kondrashov reflected on the privileged access to foreign goods that his profession allowed. He did so in an account written before, and published after, *perestroika* began. Kondrashov, *Puteshevstvie Amerikanista*, 390–392. On Soviet notion of responsible consumers see, Reid, "Cold War in the Kitchen," 219–220.

74. Borovik, *Prolog*, 24. On the impact of Borovik's essay on the Soviet hippies, see Fürst, "Soviet Hippie 'Sistema,'" 123–146.

75. Sturua, *Brozhenie*, 93. Sturua dedicated the first two chapters of his book to the student movements and the riots at Harvard and Kent State Universities and two other chapters to the events at the 1968 Democratic Convention in Chicago.

76. Roman, *Opposing Jim Crow*, 25–90; Peacock, *Innocent Weapons*, 46–50.

77. Byrne, "Cold War in Africa," 149–163.

78. Peacock, *Innocent Weapons*, 46–50; Ball, *Liberty's Tears*, 107–110, 131–137, 155, 159–194.

79. Borovik, *Prolog*, 32–40, 113–119; Kondrashov, *Amerikantsy v Amerike*, 158–165. Kondrashov later revisited Dr. Spock in his trips to the US and his writings about Soviet-American relations. An updated version of his 1968 sketch on Dr. Spock appeared in his collections of American reports published in 1987 and 1988.

80. Kelly, *Refining Russia*, 399; Raleigh, *Soviet Baby Boomers*, 206.

81. Sturua, *Brozhenie*, 15.

82. Fürst, "Soviet Hippie 'Sistema,'" 123–146; Yurchak, *Everything Was Forever*, 158–238; Zubok, *Zhivago's Children*, 44.

83. Kondrashov, *Svidanie s Kaliforniei*, 203–204.

84. Kondrashov, *Svidanie s Kaliforniei*, 222.

85. Fürst, "Soviet Hippie 'Sistema,'"126–129.

86. Kondrashov, *Svidanie s Kaliforniei*, 237.

87. Kondrashov, *Svidanie s Kaliforniei*, 243–244.

88. Yurchak, *Everything Was Forever*, 34–35, 115; Raleigh, *Soviet Baby Boomers*, 222.

89. Strel'nikov and Shatunovskii, *Amerika sprava i sleva*, 233–247.

90. Raleigh, *Soviet Baby Boomers*, 222.

91. Raleigh, *Soviet Baby Boomers*, 157. See also the film *My Perestroika* (dir. Robin Hessman, USA, 2010).

92. Bovin, *XX vek*, 327.

93. Makarevich, *Sam ovtsa*, Ch.2. "Vse ochen' prosto."

94. Fürst, "Soviet Hippie 'Sistema,'" 142.

95. Zorin, interview, October 12, 2009; Sturua, interview, February 4, 2011.

96. Yurchak, *Everything Was Forever*, 170.

97. Aksyonov, *Melancholy Baby*, 30–31.

98. Losev, *On the Beneficence of Censorship*, x.

99. Losev, *On the Beneficence of Censorship*, 2–4.

100. Losev, *On the Beneficence of Censorship*, 17.

101. Losev, *On the Beneficence of Censorship*, 56–57. Among Losev's examples are "a bloody reign of terror is termed 'a personality cult,' the military occupation of a neighboring state 'brotherly assistance,' and economic collapse 'occasional failings.'"

102. For examples of the cultivation of nuances in official language by Central Committee members, see Yurchak, *Everything Was Forever*, 37–76. See also Dovlatov, *Kompromiss*.

103. See, for example, Dovlatov, *Kompromiss*; Losev, *Zakrytyi Raspredelitel'*.

104. Losev, *On the Beneficence of Censorship*, 60, 64.

105. Burlatskii, *Vozhdi i sovetniki*, 326.

106. Mikhail Barshchevskii, *Osoboe Mnenie*, Radio Ekho Moskvy, October 18, 2011, accessed August 2019, http://www.echo.msk.ru/programs/personalno/821419-echo/#element -text.

107. "Pochemu besnuetsia mezhdunarodnaia reaktsiia," *Izvestiia*, August 29, 1968, p. 1; Melor Sturua, "S'ezd v Chikago golosuet," *Izvestiia*, August 29, 1968, p. 1.

108. Borovik, *Prolog*, 121–124.

109. Fürst, "Soviet Hippie 'Sistema,'" 131–134.

110. It is important to note that Aesopian readership was practiced mostly among certain segments of the population—most often the intelligentsia, who frequently had access to other sources of information that could enable these comparisons. Such a reading would require a familiarity with the dissident milieu or with the fate of attempts to stage public protests in the USSR.

111. "Correspondent's Visa—Zorin," August 5, 1971, Box 8: PPB 9-7 Soviet Correspon-dents, 1971, Entry 5552, RG 59.

112. Airgram #1570, "Strel'nikov - Shatunovskii Series in Pravda: Articles 7 and 8," December 8, 1969, Box 8: PPB 9-7 Soviet Correspondents, 1969, Entry 5552, RG 59.

113. "Visa—Zorin," August 5, 1971, Box 8: PPB 9-7 Soviet Correspondents, 1971, Entry 5552, RG 59.

114. "Reports by Soviet Correspondents in the U.S. on Vietnam," March 4, 1965, Box 8: PPB 9-7 Soviet Correspondents, 1965, Entry 5552, RG 59; Telegram from the Embassy in the Soviet Union to the Department of State, "Vietnam and Soviet-American Relations," Moscow, April 5, 1965, *FRUS, 1964–1968*, Vol. XIV, Document 105, https://history.state.gov /historicaldocuments/frus1964-68v14/d105; Telegram from the Embassy in the Soviet Union to the Department of State, "Vietnam and Soviet-American Relations II," Moscow, August 20, 1965, *FRUS, 1964–1968*, Vol. XIV, Document 121, https://history.state.gov/historicaldocuments /frus1964-68v14/d121; Memorandum of Conversation, "U.S.-U.S.S.R. Relations," Moscow September 9, 1965, *FRUS, 1964–1968*, Vol. XIV, Document 125, https://history.state.gov /historicaldocuments/frus1964-68v14/d125; Telegram from the Embassy in the Soviet Union to the Department of State, Moscow, July 12, 1966, *FRUS, 1964–1968*, Vol. XIV, Document 165, https://history.state.gov/historicaldocuments/frus1964-68v14/d165/.

115. "Pravda on one day in the life of America," June 6, 1971, Box 8: PPB 9-7 Soviet Correspondents, 1971, Entry 5552, RG 59.

116. Box 8: PPB 9-7 Soviet Correspondents, 1969, Entry 5552, RG 59.

117. V. Matveev, "Ob odnoi diskussii za okeanom," *Izvestiia*, November 28, 1968, p. 4.

118. "Soviet Journalists on US-Soviet relations," January 1969, Box 8: PPB 9-7 Soviet Correspondents, 1969, Entry 5552, RG 59.

119. "Zhukov Answers Listeners' Questions," November 22, 1972; "Call on Pravda's Editor in Chief," November 29, 1972, Box 8: PPB 9-7 Soviet Correspondents, 1972, Entry 5552, RG 59; "Ogonek Magazine Takes on the U.S.," December 29, 1973, Box 10: PPB 9-7 Soviet Correspondents, 1973, Entry 5552, RG 59; "Pravda Continues to Explore U.S. Senate," January 1974, Box 10: PPB 9-7 Soviet Correspondents, 1974, Entry 5552, RG 59.

120. On personal diplomacy during the détente, see Zubok, *Failed Empire*, 204–208, 238.

121. Barmine, "Lunch with Kopytin," October 6, 1967, Box 8: Soviet Correspondents, 1967, Entry 5552, RG 59; Stevenson, "Luncheon with Kopytin," January 11, 1967; Paul McNichol to Simon Bourgin, "Visit by Soviet Correspondent," July 22, 1968; Alexander G. Barmine, "Visit of TASS Correspondent Kopytin," October 9, 1968, Box 8: PPB 9-7 Soviet Correspondents, 1968, Entry 5552, RG 59; Philip C. Brown to Eli Flam, January 3, 1974, Box 10: PPB 9-7 Soviet Correspondents, 1974, Entry 5552, RG 59.

122. "On Conversation with Soviet Journalist," August 5, 1968; Airgram #2146 from American Embassy, "Meeting with Ekonomicheskaia Gazeta Correspondents," November 8, 1968, Box 8: PPB 9-7 Soviet Correspondents, 1968, Entry 5552, RG 59; "Soviet Journalists on US-Soviet Relations," January 2, 1969; "Soviet Journalists Views on Chinese Situation," March 2, 1969; "Conversation with Soviet Journalists on Asian and Middle Eastern Subjects," April 5, 1969, Box 8: PPB 9-7 Soviet Correspondents, 1969, Entry 5552, RG 59; Airgram #A-35 from American Embassy to Department of State, "Conversation with Pravda Journalists about Latin America," January 14, 1972, Box 8: PPB 9-7 Soviet Correspondents, 1972, Entry 5552, RG 59.

123. McNichol to Bourgin, "Visit by Soviet Correspondent," July 22, 1968, Box 8: PPB 9-7 Soviet Correspondents, 1968, Entry 5552, RG 59.

124. Stevenson, "Luncheon with Kopytin," January 11, 1967; Barmine, "Luncheon with Kopytin," August 7, 1968, Box 8: PPB 9-7 Soviet Correspondents, 1968, Entry 5552, RG 59.

125. Airgram #A-46, "Meeting with Ekonomicheskaia Gazeta Correspondents," January 14, 1969, Box 8: PPB 9-7 Soviet Correspondents, 1969, Entry 5552, RG 59.

126. Zubok, *Failed Empire*, 276; Foglesong, *American Mission*, 182–184.

127. See, for example, "Zheleznaia ruka presidenta," *Literaturnaia Gazeta,* October 30, 1981, p. 9; Vitalii Kobysh, "Razgovor o glavnom," *Literaturnaia Gazeta,* November 11, 1981, p. 9.

128. Stanislav Kondrashov's Diary of the Trip to the USA in October-December, 1982, Stanislav Kondrashov Private Archive.

## Chapter 6 · Reports from the Backward East

1. Harrison E. Salisbury, "Russia: A Continent from Cover to Cover," *Los Angeles Times,* January 25, 1976, p. 6.

2. Hedrick L. Smith, interview, by the author, December 11, 2008, Bethesda, MD.

3. Hedrick Smith to James Greenfield, Richard Mooney, and Peter Millones, September 21, 1971, NYT Foreign Desk, Box 86, Folder 10.

4. Robert G. Kaiser, interview, by the author, December 6, 2010, Washington, DC.

5. Because of the fluidity of the international press corps, newspapers rarely invested in giving their correspondents Russian language training, preferring to recruit candidates who already spoke Russian (Russian specialists or native speakers) or to rely on the services of local translators. In most cases, Russian-speaking journalists were first- or second-generation native speakers. Few of the non-native speaking correspondents—like Salisbury, Gilmore, or Stevens, all of whom spent many years in Moscow—learned the language.

6. See, for example, Philip Knightley, "Reports from the Moscow Bureaus," *New York Times,* January 25, 1976, p. 5; Max J. Freidman, "Illuminating the Dark Pall That Has Hung over Russia," *Chicago Tribune,* January 25, 1976, p. F3; Salisbury, "A Continent," F. D. Reeve, "Our Men in Moscow," *The Washington Post,* February 29, 1976, F3.

7. For example, *Time* correspondent Jerrold Schecter and his wife, Leona, had five children, ages five to thirteen, all of whom accompanied their parents to Moscow and attended regular Soviet schools. These experiences often became the subject of Schechter's features. See Schecter and Schecter, *An American Family in Moscow.* See also Bassow, *Moscow Correspondents,* 289–292.

8. Bassow, *Moscow Correspondents,* 211–212, 266–268.

9. "Correspondents at New Year's," January 6, 1974, Box 6: PPB 9-7 American Correspondents, 1974, Entry 5552, RG 59.

10. Aucoin, *Evolution,* 48–49, 52–57; Schudson, *Discovering the News,* 162–163, 179–181.

11. Aucoin, *Evolution,* 53; Schorr, *Staying Tuned,* Chapter 7; Daniloff, *Of Spies and Spokesmen,* 45.

12. Aucoin, *Evolution,* 56; Hamilton, *Journalism's Roving Eye,* 393–403. On the American press in the Vietnam War, see Hamilton, *Journalism's Roving Eye,* 382–417; Hammond, *Reporting Vietnam*; Hallin, *"Uncensored War"*; Wyatt, *Paper Soldiers.*

13. Aucoin, *Evolution,* 56.

14. Kaiser, interview, December 6, 2010.

15. Kaiser, interview, December 6, 2010.

16. Smith, interview, December 11, 2008; Kaiser, interview, December 6, 2010.

17. David K. Shipler, "Reporters Find Hospitality in Soviet but Little News," *New York Times,* June 11, 1976, p. 8. See also Anatole Shub, "Alien is Lonely in Today's Moscow," *Washington Post,* July 7, 1968, P. B1; Jacoby, *Friendship Barrier,* 9-23; Shub, *Russian Tragedy,* 25-35; Dornberg, *New Tsars,* 7-17; "Policy Toward Soviet Correspondents," February 17, 1969, Box 5: PPB 9-7 American Correspondents, 1969, Entry 5552, RG 59; "Correspondents at New Year's," January 6, 1974, Box 6: PPB 9-7 American Correspondents, 1974, Entry 5552, RG 59.

18. "Policy toward Soviet Correspondents," February 17, 1969; "Travel Restrictions for US Correspondents," April 28, 1969; "Travel Restrictions for US Correspondents," April 29, 1969; "Travel Restrictions for US Correspondents," April 30, 1969, Box 5: PPB 9-7 American

Correspondents, 1969, Entry 5552, RG 59; "LA Times Correspondent," December 18, 1971; "Soviet Efforts to Influence Foreign Correspondents' Reporting," March 19, 1971, Box 5: PPB 9-7 American Correspondents, 1971, Entry 5552, RG 59; "Treatment of American Journalists," September 26, 1972, Box 5: PPB 9-7 American Correspondents, 1972, Entry 5552, RG 59.

19. Shipler, "Reporters Find Hospitality."

20. Panchenko, "Potemkinskie derevni," 93–95.

21. David-Fox, *Showcasing the Great Experiment*, 8.

22. Dornberg, *New Tsars*, 439; See also: Kaiser, *Russia*, 22, 138–141, 160–161, 328, 379; Shub, *New Russian Tragedy*, 20; Shipler, *Russia*, 20–27; Kevin Klose, "Siberian State Farm: Uniquely Russian," *Washington Post,* February 20, 1978, p. A17; Murray Seeger, "Seeing Soviet Union Through Eyes of Intourist: Puzzling Game of 'Ivan Says'," *Los Angeles Times*, July 9, 1972, p. H1.

23. David-Fox, *Showcasing the Great Experiment*.

24. Quoted in Shipler, "Reporters Find Hospitality."

25. "Policy Toward Soviet Correspondents," February 17, 1969; "Travel Restrictions," April 28, 1969, Box 5: PPB 9-7 American Correspondents, 1969, Entry 5552, RG 59; "Soviet Pressure on ABC Correspondent," March 27, 1971; "LA Times Correspondent," December 18, 1971, Box 5: PPB 9-7 American Correspondents, 1971, Entry 5552, RG 59; "Correspondents at New Year's," January 6, 1974, Box 6: PPB 9-7 American Correspondents, 1974, Entry 5552, RG 59.

26. See for example Murray Seeger, "Russians Who Talk to Foreigners Take Risk," *Los Angeles Times*, May 14, 1972, p. 2; Murray Seeger, "Americans in Russia: Rise in Harassment," *Los Angeles Times*, January 16, 1973, p. 10; Jacoby, *Friendship Barrier*, 13–21; Dornberg, *New Tsars*, 7–15; Klose, *Russia*, 10-26, 34–37; Nagorski, *Reluctant Farewell*, 29–51; Shipler, *Russia*, 26–50.

27. Quoted in Shipler, "Reporters Find Hospitality."

28. Foglesong, *American Mission*, 7–33.

29. Charlotte Saikowski, "Russians Rarely Worry about Losing Their Jobs: How Russians Live," *Christian Science Monitor*, May 8, 1972, p. 7.

30. Saikowski, "Russians Rarely Worry."

31. Saikowski's series appeared in the *Christian Science Monitor* from May 8 to May 12, 1972. In addition to the *Monitor*, the series (or excerpts from the series) were published in nineteen newspapers in twelve different states. In some cases, the headlines of Saikowski's articles in regional press differed from the original ones in the *Monitor*. For example, whereas in the *Monitor* the second instalment was entitled "The Question of 'Freedom' is Irrelevant to Most Russians," the *Arizona Daily Star* published the same article with the headline "Soviets Willing to Accept Totalitarian Government." See: The *Arizona Daily Star*, May 23, 1972, p. 13.

32. Kevin Klose, "Soviet Pensioners Lead Impoverished Lives at the Edge of Despair," *Washington Post*, January 31, 1981, p. A10.

33. "Life in Donetsk," *Washington Post*, February 10, 1981, p. A14. Klose's Donetsk series was published in the Washington Post on January 30, January 31, and February 1, 1981.

34. Chernyshova, "Consumers as Citizens."

35. Gunther, *Inside Russia Today*, 209–211, 354–377; William J. Jorden, "The People of Russia," *New York Times*, August 25, 1957, p. 38.

36. Smith, *The Russians*, 104–105; Nagorski, *Reluctant Farewell*, 91–98; Dornberg, *New Tsars*, 17–18; Klose, Russia, 197–198.

37. Dornberg, *New Tsars*, 262–266; Shub, *Empire*, 283–293; Smith, *The Russians*, 666–667; Kaiser, *Russia*, 132–133, 284, 445–447; Klose, *Russia*, 37–51; 121–122; Nagorski, *Reluctant Farewell*, 22-25; Shipler, *Russia,* 5, 261–265; Daniloff, *Two Lives,* 74.

38. Dornberg, *New Tsars*, 308–345; Kaiser, *Russia*, 47–48, 125–129; Klose, *Russia*, 29–51; Nagorski, *Reluctant Farewell*, 81–105; Shipler, *Russia*, 216–223.

39. Willis, *Klass*, 19–20.

40. Willis, *Klass*, 30.

41. Shub, *Russian Tragedy*, 69–75; Jacoby, *Friendship Barrier*, 31; Dornberg, *New Tsars*, 315–322; Murray Seeger, "Phase 2 Begins in Russian Revolution," *Los Angeles Times*, February 27, 1972, p. 1; Nagorski, *Reluctant Farewell*, 89–90; Shipler, *Russia*, 171–175.

42. Smith, *The Russians*, 76. See also, Dornberg, *New Tsars*, 287; Willis, *Klass*, 30.

43. Cohen, *Consumers' Republic*, 112–165; Osgood, *Total Cold War*, 253–274; Belmonte, *Selling the American Way*, 116–159; Hendershot, *Anti-Communism*, 13–16.

44. Potter, *People of Plenty*; Lears, *Fables of Abundance*, 17–40; Cohen, *Consumers' Republic*, 19; James T. Adams, *The Epic of America* (Boston: Little Brown, 1959), 374–386.

45. Patterson, *Grand Expectations*, Chapter 25.

46. Smith, *The Russians*, 667.

47. See for example Murray Seeger, "Soviet Youths Prefer West's Dress, Music," *Los Angeles Times*, July 4, 1972, p. D1; Murray Seeger, "US Jeans: The Hottest Thing Going in Russia," *Los Angeles Times*, November 20, 1973. Kaiser, *Russia*, 36–37; Shipler, *Russia*, 349–354.

48. Willis, *Klass*, 2. For other discussions of "the gap," see Dornberg, *New Tsars*, 27–28; Seeger, "Phase 2"; Shub, *Russian Tragedy*, 69–75.

49. Dornberg, *New Tsars*, 27.

50. Kaiser, interview, December 6, 2010.

51. Kaiser, *Russia*, 452–453.

52. For example, Anatole Shub's article series *Russia Turns Back the Clock* was put into the Congressional Record; Cong. Rec., S7055–S7062 (June 24, 1969); Kaiser, interview, December 6, 2010.

53. Sanders, *Peddlers of Crisis*, 198–202.

54. Sanders, *Peddlers of Crisis*, 283.

55. Smith, *The Russians*, 676–680; Dornberg, *New Tsars*, 7–30, 433–448; Shub, *Empire*, 34–36, 287; Kaiser, *Russia*, 193–194, 269–278; Shipler, *Russia*, 249–289, 346–349.

56. Dornberg, *New Tsars*, 433.

57. Dornberg, *New Tsars*, 433–438; 7–30; Shub, *Empire*, 420–421; Kaiser, Russia, 263, 339; Shipler, *Russia*, 5–6, 18; Anatole Shub, "Amid the Soviets an Eternal Russia," *The Washington Post*, August 1, 1967, p. A12.

58. Smith, *The Russians*, 678–679.

59. Smith, *The Russians*, 679.

60. Smith, *The Russians*, 679–680.

61. Kaiser, *Russia*, 277.

62. Foglesong, *American Mission*.

63. Cited in Foglesong, *American Mission*, 167.

64. See Dornberg, *New Tsars*, 7–30; 433–448; Shipler, *Russia*, 5–6, 348; Daniloff, *Two Lives*, 36, 72–74.

65. Dornberg, *New Tsars*, 436.

66. Dornberg, *New Tsars*, 436.

67. Custine, *Empire of the Czar* (1843).

68. For examples of references to de Custine in the accounts of correspondents, see Pond, *From the Yaroslavsky Station*, 24, 89–90, 177; Kaiser, *Russia*, 139–143; Shipler, *Russia*, 3, 18; Nagorski, *Reluctant Farewell*, 107–108; Dornberg, *New Tsars*, 433–448.

69. Dornberg, *New Tsars*, 444. A quote from de Custine was also the epigraph to Nicholas Daniloff's books and to Shipler's introduction to his book.

70. Peris, "Custiniana."

71. Custine, *Journey for Our Time*.

72. Walter Bedell Smith, "Introduction," in Custine, *Journey for Our Time*, 7.

73. Smith, "Introduction," 8–9.

74. Smith, "Introduction," 8.

75. Fainberg, "Portrait of a Journalist."

76. Smith, *Moscow Mission*. On the precedent of US envoys to Russia "recycling" the accounts published by their earlier predecessors, see Kurilla, *Zakliatye druz'ia*, 88–95.

77. Custine, *Empire of the Czar* (1989).

78. Patterson, *Restless Giant*, 13–107; see also Perlstein, *Invisible Bridge*.

79. Patterson, *Restless Giant*, 15–18.

80. Zubok, *Zhivago's Children*, 262–273; Nathans, *To the Success of Our Hopeless Cause*, Chapter 6; Walker, "Moscow Human Rights Defenders," 913  914.

81. Kaiser, interview, December 6, 2010.

82. Kaiser, interview, December 6, 2010; Zhores Medvedev, interview, by the author, May 9, 2011, London, UK; Natan Sharansky, interview, by the author, May 5, 2013, Jerusalem, Israel; Jacoby; *Friendship Barrier*, 113, 126; Klose, *Russia*, 218–223; Bassow, *Moscow Correspondents*, 257–258. My thinking about journalists' relations with the dissidents is indebted to Barbara Walker's excellent scholarship on this subject. See: Walker, "Moscow Human Rights Defenders"; Walker, "Moscow Correspondents."

83. Klose, *Russia*, 218–223; Bassow, *Moscow Correspondents*, 257–258; Peter Osnos, "Soviet Dissidents and the American Press," *Columbia Journalism Review* 16, no. 4 (November/December 1977): 32–36. See also: Walker, "Moscow Human Rights Defenders," 917–919.

84. See for example "Dissident Soviet Voice: Pyotr Grigoryevich Grigorenko," *New York Times*, November 16, 1968, p. 2; "A Soviet Dissident Tells of Reprisals," *New York Times*, November 27, 1968, p. 10; Anatole Shub, "Dissident Couple Feels Constant KGB Pressure," *Washington Post*, June 15, 1969, p. 1; Anatole Shub, "New Stalinists Fail to Break the Spirit of Soviet Liberals," *Washington Post*, June 16, 1969, p. 1; Harry Trimborn, "Writer Who Predicted Soviet Collapse Seized," *Los Angeles Times*, May 22, 1970, p. 5; The Associated Press, "Dissidents in the Soviet Union Are Facing a Crackdown," *New York Times*, December 18, 1970, p. 1; "Soviet Union: Crackdown," *Newsweek*, December 28, 1970, p. 24; Theodore Shabad, "Soviet Dissident Convicted; Gets 7 Years and 5 in Exile," *New York Times*, January 6, 1972, p. 3; Leo Gruliow, "Soviet Dissent on Trial," *Christian Science Monitor*, September 1, 1973, p. 10; Christopher Wren, "Dissident Warns Against Hope of a Liberalized Soviet Society," *New York Times*, November 24, 1973, p. 9. See also: Dornberg, *New Tsars*, 30; Shub, *Russian Tragedy*, 37–59, 62–66; Kaiser, *Russia*, 400–443; Smith, *The Russians*, 587–620; Klose, *Russia*, 53–248.

85. Zubok, *Zhivago's Children*, 261–273, 299–310; Nathans, "Talking Fish," 603; Walker, "Moscow Human Rights Defenders," 908–909.

86. Medvedev, interview, May 9, 2011; Sharansky, interview, May 5, 2013; From American Embassy to the Secretary of State, "AP Correspondent's Plan for New Coverage of Soviet Dissidence," March 25, 1971, Box 5: PPB 9-7 American Correspondents, 1971, Entry 5552, RG 59; Walker, "Moscow Human Rights Defenders," 913–919.

87. Anatole Shub, "The Slow Torture of Larissa Daniel," *Sunday Times*, May 25, 1969, p. 8; Walker, "Moscow Human Rights Defenders," 913–919.

88. "Involvement of US Correspondents in Arrest of Dissidents," May 9, 1969, Box 5: PPB 9-7 American Correspondents, 1969, Entry 5552, RG 59; "Detention of Los Angeles Times Correspondent Toth," June 2, 1977; Richard D. Vine to the Deputy Secretary of State, "Toth Case," June 14, 1977; From Marshall Shulman to the Acting Secretary, "Report of Working Group on Toth Case," June 16, 1977, Box 6: PPB 9-7 American Correspondents in USSR, 1976–1977, Entry 5552, RG 59; Sharansky, *Ne uboius' zla*, Chapters 6, 8, 10, 13, 14, and 16.

89. For example, Fredrick Forsyth, *The Odessa File* (Hutchinson, 1972), Amazon Video; Alan J. Pakula, *The Parallax View* (1974, Paramount Pictures), Amazon Video; Robert Ellis Miller, *The Girl from Petrovka* (Universal Pictures, 1974), Amazon Video; Alan J. Pakula, *All*

*the President's Men* (1976, Warner Brothers), Amazon Video. See also Cozma and Hamilton, "Film Portrayals of Foreign Correspondents," 497–500; Ehrlich and Saltzman, *Heroes and Scoundrels*, 12, 44–46, 129–130.

90. Sharansky, interview, May 5, 2013; Bassow, *Moscow Correspondents*, 240–241; Kaiser, interview, December 6, 2010.

91. Klose, *Russia*, 25–26.

92. Nathans, *To the Success of Our Hopeless Cause*, Chapter 6; Sharansky, interview, May 5, 2013; Walker, "Moscow Human Rights Defenders," 914.

93. Henry Kamm to Seymour Topping, November 28, 1968, NYT Foreign Desk, Box 2, Folder 9.

94. Kamm to Topping, November 28, 1968, NYT Foreign Desk, Box 2, Folder 9. "N.Y. Times Correspondent Henry Kamm Given Warning by Zamyatin," December 6, 1968, Box 5: PPB 9-7 American Correspondents, 1968, Entry 5552, RG 59; "MFA Press Department on Shub and Kamm," May 12, 1969; "Travel Restrictions," April 29, 1969; "Travel Restrictions," April 30, 1969, Box 5: PPB 9-7 American Correspondents, 1969, Entry 5552, RG 59; "MFA Press Chief on 'Visa War,'" November 7, 1970; "MFA warns Washington Post Correspondent," November 7, 1970; "MFA section warns Newsweek," December 16, 1970, Box 5: PPB 9-7 American Correspondents, 1970, Entry 5552, RG 59.

95. "Difficulties Recently Experienced by US Newsmen in Moscow," March 1968; Box 5: PPB 9-7 American Correspondents, 1968, Entry 5552, RG 59; "Intimidation of American Correspondent," January 23, 1971; "Correspondents—James Peipert," September 15, 1971; "Confidential Moscow 6904," September 17, 1971; "Public Arrest of Jews Contacting Correspondents," July 29, 1971; "Soviet Efforts to Influence," March 19, 1971, Box 5: PPB 9-7 American Correspondents, 1971, Entry 5552, RG 59; "Recent Incidents Involving American Correspondents in Moscow," October, 1973, Box 6: PPB 9-7 American Correspondents, 1973, Entry 5552, RG 59.

96. "Kamm Given Warning," December 6, 1968, Box 5: PPB 9-7 American Correspondents, 1968, Entry 5552, RG 59; "MFA warns Washington Post," November 7, 1970; "MFA warns Newsweek," December 16, 1970, Box 5: PPB 9-7 American Correspondents, 1970, Entry 5552, RG 59; "LA Times Correspondent," December 18, 1971, Box 5: PPB 9-7 American Correspondents, 1971, Entry 5552, RG 59; "Lguny vcherashnego dnia," *Literaturnaia Gazeta*, August 20, 1969, p. 9; I. Aleksandrov, "Nishcheta antikommunizma," *Pravda*, December 17, 1970, p. 4; A. Martynova, "Bednyi mister Siger," *Literaturnaia Gazeta*, December 24, 1972, p. 9; Iu. Kornilov, "Chego zhe dobivalsia g-n Shou," *Literaturnaia Gazeta*, August 15, 1973, p. 9; A. Ivanov, "Trudnaia zhizn' Rodzhera Leddingtona," *Literaturnaia Gazeta*, November 14, 1973, p. 9; E. Eligulashvili, "Fantomy vmesto faktov," *Literaturnaia Gazeta*, August 11, 1976, p. 10; V. Valentinov, "Pod flagom informatsionnogo agentstva," *Literaturnaia Gazeta*, February 2, 1977, p. 9.

97. "MFA on 'Visa War,'" November 7, 1970, Box 5: PPB 9-7 American Correspondents, 1970, Entry 5552, RG 59; "Chernyakov on Time and Newsweek Accreditation," April 16, 1971; "Time Bureau Threatened," April 12, 1971, Box 5: PPB 9-7 American Correspondents, 1971, Entry 5552, RG 59.

98. "MFA on 'Visa War,'" November 7, 1970, Box 5: PPB 9-7 American Correspondents, 1970, Entry 5552, RG 59.

99. "Policy toward Soviet Correspondents," February 17, 1969; "Travel Restrictions," April 28, 1969; "Travel Restrictions," April 29, 1969; "Travel Restrictions," April 30, 1969, Box 5: PPB 9-7 American Correspondents, 1969, Entry 5552, RG 59; "Soviet Efforts to Influence," March 19, 1971, "LA Times Correspondent," Box 5: PPB 9-7 American Correspondents, 1971, Entry 5552, RG 59; "Treatment of American Journalists," September 26, 1972, Box 5: PPB 9-7 American Correspondents, 1972, Entry 5552, RG 59.

100. "Kamm Given Warning," December 6, 1968, Box 5: PPB 9-7 American Correspondents, 1968, Entry 5552, RG 59; "Travel Restrictions," April 29, 1969, Box 5: American Correspondents, 1969, Entry 5552, RG 59.

101. Henry Bradsher, interview, by Soomin Seo, July 16, 2012, AP Headquarters, New York City, The Associated Press Oral History Program, Associated Press Corporate Archive; From American Embassy Moscow to Secretary of State, "Bombing AP Bureau Chief's Car," December 26, 1967; From American Embassy Moscow to Secretary of State, "Developments Bradsher Car Bombing," December 27, 1967, Box 4: PPB 9-7 American Correspondents, 1967, Entry 5552, RG 59.

102. Jacoby, *Friendship Barrier*, 16–19; Nagorski, *Reluctant Farewell*, 263–269; Bradsher, interview, July 16, 2012. George Krimsky, interviewed by Larry Heinzerling, October 24, 2009, Washington, CT, The Associated Press Oral History Program, Associated Press Corporate Archive. See also: "Foreign Ministry Informs Embassy of Two Correspondents' Misdemeanors," April 13, 1970, Box 5: PPB 9-7 American Correspondents, 1970, Entry 5552, RG 59.

103. Daniloff, *Spies and Spokesmen*, 69–70; Bassow, *Moscow Correspondents*, 248–250, 252; Bradsher, interview, July 16, 2012.

104. Ray Anderson to the New York Times, January 18, 1968, NYT Foreign Desk, Box 66, Folder 9; Bassow, *Moscow Correspondents*, 236–237.

105. Clifton Daniel to Raymond Anderson, January 18, 1968, NYT Foreign Desk, Box 66, Folder 9; McKinney H. Russell to Kempton B. Jenkins, December 18, 1970, Box 5: PPB 9-7 American Correspondents, 1970, Entry 5552, RG 59; Thompson R. Buchanan to Adolph Dubs, February 2, 1971, Box 5: PPB 9-7 American Correspondents, 1971, Entry 5552, RG 59.

106. From American Embassy Moscow to Secretary of State, "Auto Accident: Associated Press Correspondent Holger G. Jensen," July 9, 1970; From American Embassy Moscow to Secretary of State, "AP Correspondent Holger Jensen," July 9, 1970; From American Embassy Moscow to Secretary of State, "Jensen Case," July 14, 1970; From American Embassy Moscow to Secretary of State, "Harassment of AP Correspondent Jensen," July 24, 1970, Box 5: PPB 9-7 American Correspondents, 1970, Entry 5552, RG 59; Bassow, *Moscow Correspondents*, 248–249.

107. See for example From John M. Leddy to Dixon Donnelley, "Your Trip to Moscow—Briefing Memorandum," July 12, 1968, Box 5: PPB 9-7 American Correspondents, 1968, Entry 5552, RG 59; "Travel Restrictions," April 29, 1969; "Travel Restrictions," April 30, 1969; Handout to Mr. Evstafiev from Mr. Debs, April 30, 1969; "MFA on Shub and Kamm," May 12, 1969, Box 5: PPB 9-7 American Correspondents, 1969, Entry 5552, RG 59; "Harassment of American Correspondents in Moscow," January 30, 1971; Memorandum, "Correspondents," February 11, 1971; Adolph Dubs to R.T. Davies, "Your Meeting with Murray Gart, Time Chief of Correspondents," March 11, 1971; "Chernyakov on Time and Newsweek," April 16, 1971; R.T. Davies to Adolph Dubs, "Time Bureau in Moscow," April 17, 1971, Box 5: PPB 9-7 American Correspondents, 1971, Entry 5552, RG 59; McCloskey to Matlock, May 24, 1972; Memorandum of Conversation, "Reciprocal Treatment of Journalists," October 6, 1972; Ronald Ziegler to Robert McCloskey, December 5, 1972, Box 5: PPB 9-7 American Correspondents, 1972, Entry 5552, RG 59; From William J. Dyess to William H. Luers, "Your Meeting with Press Counselor Yevstafyev," November 16, 1973; "Treatment of US Journalists in Moscow," July 31, 1973; Box 6: PPB 9-7 American Correspondents, 1973, Entry 5552, RG 59; "Demarche with Soviet Embassy about US Correspondents," January 25, 1977, Box 6: PPB 9-7 American Correspondents in USSR, 1976-1977, Entry 5552, RG 59.

108. "Policy Toward Soviet Correspondents," February 17, 1969; "Travel Restrictions," April 28, 1969 Box 5: PPB 9-7 American Correspondents, 1969, Entry 5552, RG 59; "MFA Warns Washington Post," November 7, 1970; "MFA Warns Newsweek," December 16, 1970,

Box 5: PPB 9-7 American Correspondents, 1970, Entry 5552, RG 59; "Astrachan Chastised," January 29, 1971; "Soviet Efforts to Influence," March 19, 1971; "AP Correspondent's Plans," March 25, 1971; "Pressure on ABC Correspondent," March 27, 1971; "James Peipert," September 15, 1971; "Confidential Moscow 6904," September 17, 1971, Box 5: PPB 9-7 American Correspondents, 1971, Entry 5552, RG 59; Murray Seeger to Ronald Ziegler, September 28, 1972; Murray Seeger to Ronald Ziegler, November 22, 1972, Box 5: PPB 9-7 American Correspondents, 1972, Entry 5552, RG 59; "Meeting with Yevstafyev," November 16, 1973; "Memorandum of Telephone Conversation," August 6, 1973; "Treatment of US Journalists," July 31, 1973; Box 6: PPB 9-7 American Correspondents, 1973, Entry 5552, RG 59; "Protest on Roughing Up," September 16, 1974; "Correspondents at New Year's," January 6, 1974, Box 6: PPB 9-7 American Correspondents, 1974, Entry 5552, RG 59; "Continuation of Soviet Charges against AP Correspondent," February 2, 1977, Box 6: PPB 9-7 American Correspondents in USSR, 1976-1977, Entry 5552, RG 59.

109. "Amalryks Still at Liberty," May 8, 1969; "Anatole Shub Writes of Repression in USSR," May 28, 1969, Box 5: PPB 9-7 American Correspondents, 1969, Entry 5552, RG 59; "MFA Warns Newsweek," December 16, 1970, Box 5: PPB 9-7 American Correspondents, 1970, Entry 5552, RG 59; "Soviet Efforts to Influence," March 19, 1971; "Public Arrest of Jews," July 29, 1971; "AP Correspondent's Plans," March 25, 1971; "James Peipert," September 15, 1971; "Confidential Moscow 6904," September 17, 1971, Box 5: PPB 9-7 American Correspondents, 1971, Entry 5552, RG 59; "Issue for Decision," 1977, Box 6: PPB 9-7 American Correspondents in USSR, 1976-1977, Entry 5552, RG 59.

110. "Travel Restrictions," April 29, 1969; "MFA on Shub and Kamm," May 12, 1969, Box 5: PPB 9-7 American Correspondents, 1969, Entry 5552, RG 59; "MFA on 'Visa War,'" November 7, 1970, "MFA Warns Newsweek," December 16, 1970, Box 5: PPB 9-7 American Correspondents, 1970, Entry 5552, RG 59; "Astrachan Chastised," January 29, 1971; "Soviet Efforts to Influence," March 19, 1971, Box 5: PPB 9-7 American Correspondents, 1971, Entry 5552, RG 59; "Correspondents at New Year's," January 6, 1974, Box 6: PPB 9-7 American Correspondents, 1974, Entry 5552, RG 59.

111. "Handout to Mr. Evstafiev," April 30, 1969; "Correspondents," June 26, 1969, Box 5: PPB 9-7 American Correspondents, 1969, Entry 5552, RG 59; "Anti-American Propaganda," August 5, 1971, Box 5: PPB 9-7 American Correspondents, 1971, Entry 5552, RG 59; "Reciprocal Treatment," October 6, 1972, Box 5: PPB 9-7 American Correspondents, 1972, Entry 5552, RG 59; "Press Harassment," September, 1973; "Meeting with Yevstafyev," November 16, 1973, Box 6: PPB 9-7 American Correspondents, 1973, Entry 5552, RG 59.

112. "Kamm Given Warning," December 6, 1968, Box 5: PPB 9-7 American Correspondents, 1968, Entry 5552, RG 59; Draft memo, "Policy Toward Soviet Journalists," undated, 1969; Yale Richmond to Thompson R. Buchanan, May 3, 1969, Box 5: PPB 9-7 American Correspondents, 1969, Entry 5552, RG 59; "AP Warning to TASS: Astrachan and Axelbank," March 6, 1971, Box 5: PPB 9-7 American Correspondents, 1971, Entry 5552, RG 59; Seeger to Ziegler, November 22, 1972, Box 5: PPB 9-7 American Correspondents, 1972, Entry 5552, RG 59; "American Correspondents in Moscow," January 25, 1973; "Telephone Conversation," August 6, 1973, Box 6: PPB 9-7 American Correspondents, 1973, Entry 5552, RG 59; "Issue for Decision," 1977, Box 6: PPB 9-7 American Correspondents in USSR, 1976-1977, Entry 5552, RG 59.

113. "Travel Restrictions," April 29, 1969; Thompson R. Buchannan to Yale W. Richmond, May 29, 1969; "Reciprocal Travel Limitations on Correspondents," May 26, 1969, Box 5: PPB 9-7 American Correspondents, 1969, Entry 5552, RG 59; "US Confirms Its Decision to Expel a Pravda Reporter," *New York Times*, June 27, 1970, p. 20.

114. See for example "American Correspondents in Moscow," January 25, 1973; Robert J. McCloskey to James L. Yuenger, February 20, 1973; Murray J. Gart to William P. Rogers,

May 30, 1973, Box 6: PPB 9-7 American Correspondents, 1973, Entry 5552, RG 59; On the relationship between the press and US establishment in those years, see Aucoin, *The Evolution*, 56–90, 108; McPherson, *Journalism at the End of the American Century*, 58–59.

115. Smith, *The Russians*, 558; Kaiser, *Russia*, 428–429; Medvedev, interview, May 9, 2011.

116. Smith, *The Russians*, 562–565; Kaiser, *Russia*, 429–431.

117. Smith, *The Russians*, 562.

118. Smith, *The Russians*, 563–565; Kaiser, *Russia*, 430–431.

119. Smith, *The Russians*, 566–567.

120. Alexander Solzhenitsyn to Hedrick Smith, April 15, 1972, Box 82, Folder 5, Smith Papers. Italics and underlining in the original.

121. Smith, *The Russians*, 563. Reflecting on this experience in hindsight, Smith believed that contrary to Solzhenitsyn's fears, New York Times readers focused not on the questions, but on the writer's words, which remained unaltered. "The problem," thought Smith, "was in his mind. As a great writer, he wanted to stage the whole interview, like a scene from one of his novels." Hedrick Smith, private communication with the author, May 5, 2020.

122. Smith, *The Russians*, 567.

123. Sakharov, *Vospominaniia*, Chapter 14; Walker, "Moscow Human Rights Defenders," 919–920. See also: Sakharov, *Vospominaniia*, Chapter 10; Solzhenitsyn, *Bodalsia telenok s dubom*, "Nobeliana." For a more realistic view of the relationship between Soviet dissidents and American journalists, see Sharansky, *Ne uboius' zla*, Chapter 6.

124. Andrei Amalrik, "News from Moscow," *New York Review of Books*, March 25, 1971. The *New York Review of Books* blacked out Shapiro's name throughout the entire article and wrote that "the name of this well-known foreign correspondent for a Western news agency is known to the editors, but has been omitted here." Yet, as Barbara Walker pointed out, it was well known that the correspondent in question was Shapiro because before its publication Amalrik's article circulated in samizdat and among Moscow correspondents, with Shapiro's name explicitly mentioned. For an excellent analysis of Amalrik's article, see Walker, "Moscow Human Rights Defenders," 924–927.

125. Bernard Gwertzman, "News from Moscow," *New York Review of Books*, May 20, 1971.

126. Kaiser, interview, December 6, 2010.

127. Quoted in Shipler, "Reporters Find Hospitality."

128. Osnos, "Soviet Dissidents," 32.

129. Osnos, "Soviet Dissidents," 34.

130. Osnos, "Soviet Dissidents," 36.

131. Salisbury, "A Continent from Cover to Cover," p. 6; Ann Hall, "Behind the Soviet Monolith," *Hartford Courant*, February 22, 1976, p. 7F; Malcolm Boyd, "Inside View from over the Forbidden Border," *Los Angeles Times*, January 1, 1984, p. L3; F. D. Reeve, "Our Men in Moscow," *Washington Post*, February 29, 1976, pp. F3, F7. Freidman, "Illuminating the Dark Pall," p. F3; S. Frederick Starr, "A Reporter in Russia: Pushing the Limits," *Washington Post*, December 29, 1985, p. BW4; Howard A. Tyner, "Russian Dissidents: Profiles in Courage," *Chicago Tribune*, May 13, 1984, p. L44; R. C. Longworth, "Dark, Basic Changes Set in Motion by the Russian Character," *Chicago Tribune*, February 19, 1984, p. K37; Harry Trimborn, "Russia and the Russians: Inside the Closed Society by Kevin Klose," *Los Angeles Times*, May 20, 1984, p. T2; Marshall D. Shulman, "Probing Soviet Society," *New York Times*, November 20, 1983, p. BR1.

132. For example, Robert Kaiser's and Hedrick Smith's books were reviewed in scores of newspapers around the US. Harrison Salisbury's *Los Angeles Times* review alone, was published in three additional newspapers as: "Two Excellent, Revealing Reports on Russia, détente," *The Salt Lake Tribune*, February 1, 1976, p. 62; "Russian Enigma: The People's View," *Asbury Park Press*, February 29, 1976, p. 51; "Two Reporters Crack the Famous Russian

Enigma," *The San Francisco Examiner*, February 8, 1976, p. 204. See also: "Philadelphia bestsellers," *The Philadelphia Inquirer*, April 11, 1976; "Book Talk to Focus on Russia," *The Palm Beach Post*, October 29, 1976, p. 81. In January 1976 Smith and Kaiser appeared separately on the Firing Line and together on the Today Show (NBC) and Kup's Show.

133. Walter Martin to Hedrick Smith, March 22, 1976, Box 3, Folder 5, Smith Papers.

134. Ellen Lebow to *Atlantic Monthly*, November 22, 1975, Box 2, Folder 9, Smith Papers.

135. Harold Finkel to Hedrick Smith, May 21, 1976, Box 3, Folder 9, Smith Papers.

136. Michael B. Shirley to Hedrick Smith, February 5, 1976, Box 2, Folder 11, Smith Papers.

137. Ida Chaban to Hedrick Smith, April 21, 1976, Box 4, Folder 2, Smith Papers.

138. Vladimir Ashekanzi to Hedrick Smith, March 12, 1979, Box 3, Folder 5, Smith Papers.

139. Bassow, *Moscow Correspondents*, 348.

140. Bassow, *Moscow Correspondents*, 349

141. Bassow, *Moscow Correspondents*, 350.

142. Doder, *Shadows and Whispers*, 2.

## Part 4 • A Moment of Truth? 1985–1991

1. "Special Report: An Exclusive Interview with the Leader of the Soviet Union," *Time*, September 9, 1985, p. 1.

2. George L. Church, David Aikman, Erik Amfitheatrof, and James O. Jackson, "Moscow's Vigorous Leader," *Time*, September 9, 1985, p. 16.

3. Diary entry for November 1, 1985, Washington, DC, Stanislav Kondrashov Diary of Foreign Trips, 1984–1986, Stanislav Kondrashov Private Archive; see also Ovchinnikov, *Kaleidoskop*, "Interv'iu v Belom Dome."

4. Church et al., "Moscow's Vigorous Leader," 20–21.

5. G. Shishkin, V. Ovchinnikov, S. Kondrashov, and G. Borovik, "Po povodu interv'iu R. Reigana," *Izvestiia*, November 5, 1985, p. 5.

6. Shishkin et al., "Po povodu interv'iu R. Reigana."

## Chapter 7 • Cold War Correspondents Confront Old and New Thinking

1. Zubok, *Failed Empire*, 285; Tsygankov, *Russia's Foreign Policy*, 34–35.

2. Zubok, *Failed Empire*, 288–301; Gorbachev, *Zhizn' i Reformy*, Vol. 2, 11.

3. Taubman, *Gorbachev*, Chapter 6; English, *Russia and the Idea of the West*, 207; Wolfe, *Governing*, 153–156.

4. Wolfe, *Governing*, 145, 153–156.

5. Mikhail Gorbachev, "Ob itogakh Plenuma TsK," Politburo meeting on 1 July, 1987, in Chernyaev et al., *V Politburo TsK KPSS*, 199; Zubok, *Failed Empire*, 298.

6. Wolfe, *Governing*, 145.

7. For example, in 1984, Genrikh Borovik's *One Year of a Restless Sun* became the first part of *Prologue*—a new collection of Borovik's American writing. *Prologue* was published again as a book in 1985 and was awarded the USSR State Prize in 1986. In 1988 it was reprinted in *Roman-Gazeta*, a literary monthly magazine with a circulation of over 2 million. Stanislav Kondrashov's American essays from the 1960s and the 1970s also appeared in several new editions, supplemented by new materials. Borovik, *Prolog*; Kondrashov, *Liudi za okeanom*; Kondrashov, *Dolgii vzgliad na Ameriku*.

8. Gorbachev, "Ob itogakh Plenuma TsK," 236.

9. Zubok, *Failed Empire*, 316–318.

10. The title of "Great Communicator" conveyed not only praise but also scorn for the White House Office of Communication and for the US press. Several contemporary commentators questioned Reagan's media management throughout his time in office and

criticized the press for buying into Reagan's "media magic" and failing to scrutinize him properly. William Greider, "Reagan's Re-election: How the Media Became All the President's Men," *Rolling Stone*, December 20, 1984, http://www.rollingstone.com/politics/news/terms-of -endearment-19841220; Hertsgaard, *On Bended Knee*, 4–7; Kellner, *Media Spectacle*, 166.

11. Maltese, *Spin Control*, Chapter 7.

12. Alterman, *Sound and Fury*, 14, 96–97 on Reagan's relationship with George Will, and 137–141 on Reagan's relationship with William Safire.

13. Taubman, *Gorbachev*, Chapter 7; Matlock, *Reagan and Gorbachev*, iv, v; Dobrynin, *In Confidence*, 602.

14. Foglesong, *American Mission*, 177.

15. Foglesong, *American Mission*, 183–188.

16. Cited in Foglesong, *American Mission*, 191.

17. See, for example, Gorbachev, *Zhizn' i reformy*, Vol. 2, 22–26; Dobrynin, *In Confidence*, 577–578; Taubman, *Gorbachev*, Chapters 12 and 13; Matlock, *Reagan and Gorbachev*, vii.

18. Daniloff, *Two Lives*, 15–17, 19–36.

19. Daniloff, *Two Lives*, 2–15, 72–87.

20. Zubok, *Failed Empire*, 286–290

21. Zubok, *Failed Empire*, 291; Matlock, *Reagan and Gorbachev*, ix.

22. Matlock, *Reagan and Gorbachev*, ix; Shultz, *Turmoil and Triumph*, Chapter 35; Brands, *Reagan*, Chapter 87.

23. "'Red Handed,'" *Washington Post*, September 1, 1986, p. A14; "Fig Leaf?" *Los Angeles Times*, September 9, 1986, p. 4; "Not a Spy, a Hostage," *New York Times*, September 9, 1986, p. A26; "An Occupational Hazard," *Time*, September 15, 1986; "Moscow's Hostage," *Newsweek*, September 15, 1986, p. 38; "Working the Kremlin: Journalists Beware," *U.S. News and World Report*, September 15, 1986, p. 28; "A Frame-Up in Moscow," *U.S. News and World Report*, September 15, 1986, p. 18; "Threatening the Moscow Press," *Washington Post*, September 16, 1986, p. A14; "Still a Prisoner," *Washington Post*, September 22, 1986, p. A16; "Reporters and the CIA," *Newsweek*, September 22, 1986, p. 31; "Blowing Hot and Cold with Moscow," *New York Times*, September 23, 1986, p. A34.

24. "An Arrest That Is Act of Politics," *Chicago Tribune*, September 3, 1986, p. 16. See also "Tackling a Roadblock . . . and Leaving the Fear," *Los Angeles Times*, September 14, 1986, p. G4; "Ominous Ghosts in Moscow," *New York Times*, September 3, 1986, p. A26.

25. "From Russia: Faces," *New York Times*, September 2, 1986, p. A18; "Ominous Ghosts"; "Not a Spy"; David K. Shipler, "Mr. Shevardnadze Goes to Washington," *New York Times*, September 21, 1986, p. E1.

26. "Fig Leaf?"

27. "From Russia: Faces"; "Ominous Ghosts"; "The Developing Daniloff Affair," *Washington Post*, September 9, 1986, p. A24; "Partner—or Tool?" *Newsweek*, September 15, 1986, p. 40; "The KGB's New Muscle," *U.S. News and World Report*, September 15, 1986, p. 25; Morton Kondracke, "Champagne for the KGB," *Newsweek*, September 22, 1986, p. 24; Mortimer B. Zuckerman, "A Modicum of Trust," *U.S. News and World Report*, September 22, 1986, p. 92; Dimitri K. Simes, "There's Profit to Be Had in Iceland: Reagan's in a Strong Position to Soothe Critics on All Sides," *Los Angeles Times*, October 8, 1986, p. B5; Serge Schmemann, "Gorbachev Puts Russia's Best Face Forward," *New York Times*, October 12, 1986.

28. "Reporters and the CIA." See also "The Lefortova Hostage," *Wall Street Journal*, September 4, 1986, p. 26; "War in the Shadows," *Wall Street Journal*, September 9, 1986, p. 28; "What Price a Summit?" *Wall Street Journal*, September 12, 1986, p. 32; "After Daniloff," *Wall Street Journal*, October 1, 1986, p. 32; "Were 'Rules' Broken in Zakharov Case? In Moscow's Game of Spies, It's Always Tit for Tat," *U.S. News and World Report*, September 22, 1986, p. 16.

29. "The KGB's New Muscle"; "A Chill in the Air," *Newsweek*, September 22, 1986, p. 20; Zuckerman, "A Modicum of Trust"; Seweryn Bialer, "A Test of Soviet Intentions," *U.S. News and World Report*, September 29, 1986, p. 27.

30. "Threatening the Moscow Press."

31. Diary entry for September 7, 1986, in Reagan, *Reagan Diaries*, 435–436.

32. Reagan mentioned the press campaign for Daniloff in his diary: "The press is obsessed with the Daniloff affair & determined to paint all of us as caving in to the Soviets which they of course say is the worst way to deal with them." Diary entry for September 17, 1986, Reagan, *Reagan Diaries*, 438.

33. Diary entry for September 19, 1986, Reagan, *Reagan Diaries*, 439.

34. Diary entry for September 25, 1986, Reagan, *Reagan Diaries*, 440; diary entry for September 29, 1986, Reagan, *Reagan Diaries*, 441; Shultz, *Turmoil and Triumph*, Chapter 35.

35. Diary entry for September 25, 1986, Reagan, *Reagan Diaries*, 440. Reagan reiterated these concerns a few days later, writing "Already it's plain the press is going to declare that I gave in & the trade was Daniloff for Zakharov." Diary entry for September 30, 1986, Reagan, *Reagan Diaries*, 441–442.

36. "Tackling a Roadblock."

37. "An Arrest That Is Act of Politics"; "Fig Leaf?"; "Not a Spy"; "The Developing Daniloff Affair"; "Still a Prisoner."

38. Zuckerman, "A Modicum of Trust."

39. Zuckerman, "A Modicum of Trust."

40. "Press-conferentsia E. A. Shevardnadze," *Pravda*, October 1, 1986, p. 5.

41. V. Men'shikov, "Kogda gorit shapka," *Pravda*, September 7, 1986, p. 5.

42. Men'shikov, "Kogda gorit shapka."

43. V. Andreev, "Ishchut predlog?," *Pravda*, September 12, 1986, p. 5; "V press tsentre MID SSSR," *Izvestiia*, September 15, p. 4; "V press tsentre MID SSSR," *Pravda*, September 19, p. 5; L. Koriavin, "Rastopit' l'dy nedoveriia," *Izvestiia*, September 23, 1986, p. 5; N. Prozhogin and V. Sukhoi, "Zhguchie problemy," *Pravda*, September 24, 1986, p. 5.

44. A. Shal'nev, "Posle zvonka iz TsRU," *Izvestiia*, August 31, 1986, p. 4; "Shpionazh i zhurnalisty," *Izvestiia*, September 10, 1986, p. 4; "Amerikanskie zhurnalisty na sluzhbe TsRU," *Izvestiia*, September 23, 1986, p. 4; Melor Sturua, "Shpiony protiv lzhetsov," *Izvestiia*, September 27, 1986, p. 5.

45. Stanislav Kondrashov, "Ne upustit' shans . . . razmyshleniia o starom i novom myshlenii," *Izvestiia*, September 18, 1986, p. 5; Koriavin, "Rastopit' l'dy nedoveriia"; Vsevolod Ovchinnikov, "Ot Pauersa do Daniloffa," *Pravda*, September 20, 1986, p. 5; Yuri Zhukov, "Dve filosofii," *Pravda*, September 28, 1986, p. 4.

46. Kondrashov, "Ne upustit' shans"; Ovchinnikov, "Ot Pauersa do Daniloffa"; Zhukov, "Dve filosofii."

47. Phil Donahue, interview by James Moll, New York City, May 9, 2001, Parts 5 and 8, "The Interviews: An Oral History of Television," Archive of American Television, Emmy Foundation, http://emmytvlegends.org/interviews/people/phil-donahue.

48. *Encyclopaedia Britannica Online*, s.v. "Phil Donahue," by Patricia Bauer, accessed August 2019, https://www.britannica.com/biography/Phil-Donahue.

49. Keyssar, "Space Bridges," 249.

50. Pozner, *Proshchanie*, Chapter 7.

51. Pozner, *Proshchanie*, Chapter 1.

52. Pozner, *Proshchanie*, Chapter 5.

53. Pozner, *Proshchanie*, Chapter 7.

54. Pozner, *Proshchanie*, Chapter 7.

55. Keyssar, "Space Bridges," 249.

56. Phil Donahue, *Soviet and American Journalism* (Princeton, NJ: Films for the Humanities, 1988), VHS.

57. Donahue, *Soviet and American Journalism.*

58. Donahue, *Soviet and American Journalism.*

59. Donahue, *Soviet and American Journalism.*

60. Donahue, *Soviet and American Journalism.*

61. Donahue, *Soviet and American Journalism.*

62. Donahue, *Soviet and American Journalism.*

63. Donahue, *Soviet and American Journalism.*

64. Donahue, *Soviet and American Journalism.*

65. In my efforts to find a copy of the Soviet recording, I reached out to Vladimir Pozner, Gosteleradio, and several university libraries that hold recordings of Soviet television programs. Professor Ellen Mickiewicz, on whose analysis I am relying here, no longer has a copy of the program.

66. Quoted in Mickiewicz, *Split Signals,* 48.

67. Quoted in Mickiewicz, *Split Signals,* 48.

68. Mickiewicz, *Split Signals,* 48.

69. The spacebridge was filmed on April 8, 1987. It was produced by the Center for Communications in association with InterNews, Spacebridge Productions, and Gosteleradio SSSR by Catherine Gay, Kim Spencer, April Oliver, and Phil Martino in the US and by Galina Khomchik, Igor Menzelintsev, Elena Shmalts, and Vladimir Pozner in the USSR. It was broadcast on public television in the US and nationally in the USSR. Catherine Gay, Kim Spencer, April Oliver, Phil Martino, Galina Khomchik, Igor Menzelintsev, Elena Shmalts, and Vladimir Pozner, *Telemost Zhurnalistov: SSSR-SShA* (Moscow: Gosteleradio SSSR, First Channel), May 13, 1987. My analysis relies on the Soviet edit, which was made available on the Gosteleradiofond YouTube channel: https://www.youtube.com/watch?v=yySusHO5mbk&t =210s (last accessed August 2019). For the American version, see Catherine Gay, Phil Martino, Peter Jennings, and Vladimir Pozner, *USA/USSR Spacebridge: The Role of the Media in Current Relations* (Alexandria, VA: PBS Adult Learning Satellite Service for Center for Communication, 1987), VHS.

70. Gay and Khomchik et al., *Telemost Zhurnalistov: SSSR-SShA.*

71. Gay and Khomchik et al., *Telemost Zhurnalistov: SSSR-SShA.*

72. Gay and Khomchik et al., *Telemost Zhurnalistov: SSSR-SShA.*

73. Gay and Khomchik et al., *Telemost Zhurnalistov: SSSR-SShA.*

74. Gay and Khomchik et al., *Telemost Zhurnalistov: SSSR-SShA.*

75. Gay and Khomchik et al., *Telemost Zhurnalistov: SSSR-SShA.*

76. Gay and Khomchik et al., *Telemost Zhurnalistov: SSSR-SShA.*

77. Mickiewicz, *Split Signals,* 48.

78. Donahue, interview, May 9, 2001. In subsequent interviews Pozner and Donahue estimated that roughly 8 million viewers watched the first *Citizens Summit* in the United States. Pozner, *Proshchanie,* Chapter 7; Alexander Gasyuk, "Phil Donahue: 'We Reached Out Instead of Lashed Out,'" *Russia Beyond the Headlines,* December 7, 2012, https://www.rbth .com/articles/2012/12/06/phil_donahue_we_reached_out_instead_of_lashed_out_20867.html.

79. Peter Jennings, "Telesummitry," in Brainerd, *Spacebridges,* 8.

80. US Department of State, "Memorandum of Conversation," October 12, 1986, *The Reykjavik File. Previously Secret Documents from U.S. and Soviet Archives on the 1986 Reagan-Gorbachev Summit,* ed. Svetlana Savranskaya and Thomas Blanton (Washington, DC: National Security Archive, George Washington University), National Security Archive

Electronic Briefing Book No. 203, Document 13, http://nsarchive2.gwu.edu/NSAEBB
/NSAEBB203/index.htm. See also Matlock, *Reagan and Gorbachev*, x.

81. Pozner, *Proshchanie*, Chapter 7.

82. Donahue, interview, May 9, 2001.

83. Gay and Khomchik et al., *Telemost Zhurnalistov: SSSR-SShA*.

84. Jennings, "Telesummitry," in Brainerd, *Spacebridges*, 6.

85. Peter B. Kaufman, "The First Five Years and the Next Five," in Brainerd, *Spacebridges*, 36.

86. Christine Evans's study of Soviet Central Television has made this point more broadly. The lion's share of iconic *perestroika* shows had their roots in Brezhnev-era programming, often drawing on similar formats, "formal and visual features," and "approach to attracting their audience." See Evans, *Between Truth and Time*, Epilogue.

87. Diary entry for January 26, 1982, Washington, DC, Stanislav Kondrashov Diary of a Trip to the USA in January–February 1982, Stanislav Kondrashov Archive.

88. Two additional American books, consisting mostly of previously published materials and selected new essays, came out in 1987 and 1988. See Kondrashov, *Liudi za okeanom*; Kondrashov, *Dolgii vzgliad na Ameriku*.

89. Stanislav Kondrashov Diary of a Trip to the USA in October–December 1982, Stanislav Kondrashov Archive.

90. Kondrashov, interview, January 1999.

91. The first edition of *The Americanist's Journey* was published as a stand-alone book by Sovetskii pisatel' in 1986. The edition cited here was included in *Dolgii vzgliad na Ameriku*, a 1988 collection of Kondrashov's American writings. Kondrashov, *Puteshestvie Amerikanista*, 339–591.

92. Kondrashov, *Puteshestvie Amerikanista*, 484–485.

93. Kondrashov, *Puteshestvie Amerikanista*, 516.

94. Kondrashov, *Puteshestvie Amerikanista*, 521.

95. Kondrashov, *Puteshestvie Amerikanista*, 512.

96. Kondrashov, *Puteshestvie Amerikanista*, 390–391.

97. Kondrashov, *Puteshestvie Amerikanista*, 520.

98. Kondrashov, *Puteshestvie Amerikanista*, 525.

99. Kondrashov, *Puteshestvie Amerikanista*, 541.

100. Stanislav Kondrashov Diary of a Trip to the USA in October–December 1982, Stanislav Kondrashov Archive.

101. Smith, interview, December 11, 2008. Over the years, I have encountered people who lived in the Soviet Union and managed to get underground copies of *The Russians*. Many of these readers told me that they found Hedrick Smith's descriptions of Soviet reality compelling and accurate. One example is Mikhael' Dorfman, "Rekviem po Amerikanskoi Mechte," *Sensus Novus*, October 26, 2012, https://www.sensusnovus.ru/analytics/2012/10/26/14829.html. Another example is in this LiveJournal entry: https://izdato.livejournal.com/1687093.html (accessed August 2019). The illegal smuggling of *The Russians* into the Soviet Union is also mentioned in a 1992 spy thriller: Stanislav Garin, *Lovushka dlia Osminoga* (Moscow: Patriot, 1992), eBook edition, v.

102. Smith, interview, December 11, 2008; Smith, *The New Russians*, xxii; Hedrick Smith, interview by Stephen Hess, September 25, 2012, https://www.youtube.com/watch?v=kvjQi
-TS2As.

103. As in his previous work, Hedrick Smith often referred to the Soviet Union as "Russia" and to the Soviet people as "Russians." I use these same terms interchangeably when describing or paraphrasing his writing.

104. Smith, *The New Russians*, xvii.

105. Smith, *The New Russians*, xvii–xviii.

106. Smith, *The New Russians*, xviii.

107. Smith, *The New Russians*, xviii.

108. Smith, *The New Russians*, xviii.

109. Smith, *The New Russians*, xxi.

110. Smith, *The New Russians*, xxxi.

111. The notion of ceaseless progress toward a better society, freedom, and democracy was central to American exceptionalism and the view of national and global development it inspired. On American exceptionalism, see Lipset, *American Exceptionalism*; Dunn, *American Exceptionalism*.

112. Smith, *The New Russians*, xxvii.

113. Smith, *The New Russians*, 83–93

114. Smith, *The New Russians*, 100–101.

115. Smith, *The New Russians*, 105.

116. Smith, *The New Russians*, 116–120.

117. Smith, *The New Russians*, 97.

118. Smith, *The New Russians*, 112.

119. Smith, *The New Russians*, 182; 182–188.

120. Smith, *The New Russians*, 392, 403.

121. Smith, *The New Russians*, 427.

122. Smith, *The New Russians*, 7.

123. On Gorbachev's view of stagnation see Fainberg and Kalinovsky, *Reconsidering Stagnation*, vii-viii.

124. Schrecker, *Cold War Triumphalism*, 1–10.

125. Kondrashov, interview, January 1999.

## Conclusion · Us and Them

1. In 2017 RT consisted of four channels broadcasting from Moscow in English, French, Spanish, and Arabic; RTD (Russia Today Documentary), a documentary channel broadcasting in English and Russian; Ruptly, a news agency based in Berlin providing news and video content generated by a network of twenty-two bureaus around the world; and RT UK and RT America, individual channels broadcasting from their own studios in London and Washington, DC. The registration process itself was dogged by controversy. RT claimed that it was ordered to register under FARA by the US Justice Department, a claim that at the time was neither confirmed nor denied by the US government and for which the network itself provided no evidence. The press release announcing RT America's registration merely stated, "Americans have a right to know who is acting in the United States to influence the US government or public on behalf of foreign principals." Department of Justice, Office of Public Affairs, Press Release Number 17-1279, "Production Company Registers under the Foreign Agent Registration Act as Agent for the Russian Government Entity Responsible for Broadcasting RT," November 13, 2017, https://www.justice.gov/opa/pr/production-company-registers-under-foreign-agent-registration-act-agent-russian-government.

2. US news media invariably linked RT America's FARA registration to the allegations of Russia's interference in the presidential race, citing a report of the United States Intelligence Community titled *Assessing Russian Activities and Intentions in Recent US Elections*. The report accused RT America and RT of playing a major role in the Russian propaganda efforts to influence the 2016 presidential election. National Intelligence Council, *Assessing Russian Activities and Intentions in Recent US Elections* (Washington, DC: Office of the Director of National Intelligence, National Intelligence Council, 2017), https://www.dni .gov/files/documents/ICA_2017_01.pdf; Jack Stubbs and Ginger Gibson, "Russia's RT

America Registers as 'Foreign Agent' in U.S.," Reuters World News, November 13, 2017; Natalia Pisnaya, "Why Has RT Registered as a Foreign Agent with the US?" *BBC News*, US and Canada, November 15, 2017; Aaron Maté, "RT Was Forced to Register as a Foreign Agent—and Too Many Free-Speech Advocates and Journalists Have Been Silent about It," *Nation*, November 16, 2017. In December 2017 an official at the Justice Department confirmed that the intelligence community's assessment of RT America had indeed played a role in the decision to require that it register under FARA: Josh Gerstein, "DOJ Told RT to Register as Foreign Agent Partly because of Alleged 2016 Election Interference," *Politico*, December 21, 2017, https://www.politico.com/story/2017/12/21/russia-today-justice-department-foreign -agent-election-interference-312211.

3. Nick Shifrin, "Inside Russia's Propaganda Machine," *PBS News Hour*, July 11, 2017, https://www.pbs.org/newshour/show/inside-russias-propaganda-machine; Jim Rutenberg, "RT, Sputnik, and Russia's New Theory of War," *New York Times Magazine*, September 13, 2017, https://www.nytimes.com/2017/09/13/magazine/rt-sputnik-and-russias-new-theory -of-war.html; David Z. Morris, "Inside RT, Russia's Kremlin-Controlled Propaganda Network," *Fortune*, September 17, 2017, http://fortune.com/2017/09/17/russia-network-rt -propaganda/; James Kirchnik, "RT Wants to Spread Moscow's Propaganda Here. Let's Treat It That Way," *Washington Post*, September 20, 2017, https://www.washingtonpost.com/news /posteverything/wp/2017/09/20/rt-wants-to-spread-moscows-propaganda-here-lets-treat-it -that-way/?noredirect=on&utm_term=.8b42e2d8bfd2; Daisuke Wakabayashi and Nicholas Confessore, "Russia's Favored Outlet Is an Online News Giant. YouTube Helped," *New York Times*, October 23, 2017, https://www.nytimes.com/2017/10/23/technology/youtube-russia-rt .html.

4. Vladimir Putin's Q&A at the Valdai International Discussion Club Meeting, October 19, 2017, accessed June 2018 via *Rossiya 24*'s YouTube channel: https://www.youtube.com /watch?v=UERxWqZvgf8.

5. Gosudarstvennaia Duma Rossiiskoi Federatsii, Federal'nyi zakon No. 327-FZ ot 25.11.2017, "O vnesenii izmenenii v stat'i 10-4 i 15-3 Federal'nogo zakona 'Ob informatsii, informatsion-nykh tekhnologiiakh i o zashchite informatsii' i stat'iu 6 Zakona Rossiiskoi Federatsii 'O sredstvakh massovoi informatsii,'" [State Duma of the Russian Federation, Federal Law No. 327-FZ from 25.11.2017, "On the changes in articles 10-4 and 15-3 of Federal Law 'On information, informational technologies and information protection' and article 6 of Federal Law of the Russian Federation 'On mass media'"], http://publication.pravo.gov.ru/Document /View/0001201711250002.

6. Ministerstvo Iustitsii Rossiiskoi Federatsii, "Ob inostrannykh sredstvakh massovoi informatsii, vypolniaiushchikh funktsii inostrannogo agenta," [Ministry of Justice of the Russian Federation, "On foreign mass media fulfilling the functions of a foreign agent"], press release, December 5, 2017, http://minjust.ru/ru/novosti/ob-inostrannyh-sredstvah-massovoy -informacii-vypolnyayushchih-funkcii-inostrannogo-agenta.

7. "McCain: U.S. Must Not Shirk from Calling Russian Propaganda What It Is," *Tucson Sentinel.com*, November 15, 2017, http://www.tucsonsentinel.com/opinion/report/111517 _mccain_rt_putin/mccain-us-must-not-shirk-from-calling-russian-propaganda-what-it-is/.

8. Tsygankov, *Dark Double*, 82–89. For Russia's official denial of the accusations, see Vladimir Putin's remarks at the Meeting of the Valdai International Discussion Club, October 27, 2016, http://en.kremlin.ru/events/president/news/53151. Vladimir Putin, interview by Megyn Kelly, March 1–2, 2018, transcript published on the president's official website: http://en.kremlin.ru/events/president/news/57027; President Putin's press secretary, Dmitry Peskov, interview by George Stephanopoulos on ABC, March 31, 2017, https://abcnews.go .com/Politics/extended-transcript-george-stephanopoulos-interviews-kremlin-spokesman -dmitry/story?id=46499669.

9. Vladimir Putin's remarks at a meeting with heads of international news agencies at the St. Petersburg International Economic Forum, June 1, 2017, http://en.kremlin.ru/events /president/news/54650; Peskov, interview by Stephanopoulos, March 31, 2017; Office of Charles E. Schumer, "Schumer, McCain, Reed, Graham Joint Statement on Reports That Russia Interfered with 2016 Election," December 10, 2016, https://www.schumer.senate.gov /newsroom/press-releases/schumer-mccain-reed-graham-joint-statement-on-reports-that -russia-interfered-with-2016-election; White House, Office of the Press Secretary, "Statement by the President on Actions in Response to Russian Malicious Cyber Activity and Harass- ment," December 29, 2016, https://obamawhitehouse.archives.gov/the-press-office/2016/12/29 /statement-president-actions-response-russian-malicious-cyber-activity; National Intelligence Council, *Assessing Russian Activities*; National Intelligence Council, *Background to "Assessing Russian Activities and Intentions in Recent U.S. Elections"* (Washington, DC: Office of the Director of National Intelligence, National Intelligence Council, 2017), https://www.dni.gov /files/documents/ICA_2017_01.pdf; Rossiiskii Institut Strategicheskikh Issledovanii, "Zarubezhnye SMI v 2015g: Antirossiiskii vektor" [Russian Institute for Strategic Studies, "Foreign mass media in 2015: The anti-Russian vector"] (Moscow, 2016), https://riss.ru /bookstore/monographs/antirossijskij-vektor-zarubezhnye-smi-v-2015-g/.

10. Tsygankov, *Dark Double*, 89–93; Tsygankov, "Russia's (Limited) Information War"; Zhuravleva, "Images of the United States," 145–181; Zhuravleva, "Rossiia kak 'Drugoi.'"

11. RT was launched by a daughter company of RIA Novosti, created in 1991 as a successor to the Novosti Press Agency (APN), which has been discussed in this book. APN was established in 1961 as the direct successor of Sovinformburo—the Soviet international news agency established in 1941 to provide news reports from the Eastern Front.

12. For example, in 2018 Russia tried to ban Telegram, a popular messaging app whose "channels" feature was often used to disseminate and access content from websites blocked by Roskomnadzor, the state media watchdog. Abdujalil Abdurasulov, "Russia's Telegram Ban 'Failing,'" *BBC News*, April 20, 2018, http://www.bbc.com/news/av/world-europe-43845546 /russia-s-telegram-ban-failing; Neil MacFarquhar, "Russia Tried to Shut Down Telegram. Websites Were Collateral Damage," *New York Times*, April 18, 2018, https://www.nytimes.com /2018/04/18/world/europe/russia-telegram-shutdown.html. That same year the US Congress and the Federal Trade Commission (FTC) launched an investigation into Facebook, an American online social media and social networking service company, and its use of user data. The investigation began in conjunction with the broader probe of interference in the 2016 presidential election. David McLaughlin, Ben Brody, and Billy House, "Facebook Draws Scrutiny from FTC, Congressional Committees," *Bloomberg News*, March 20, 2018, https:// www.bloomberg.com/news/articles/2018-03-20/ftc-said-to-be-probing-facebook-for-use-of -personal-data; "Cambridge Analytica: Facebook 'Being Investigated by FTC,'" *BBC News*, March 20, 2018, https://www.bbc.co.uk/news/world-us-canada-43476594.

13. Feinberg, *Curtain of Lies*, x–xii.

14. Masuda, *Cold War Crucible*, 2–8.

15. Roudakova, *Losing Pravda*, 64.

16. Roudakova, *Losing Pravda*, 51–96.

## Archival Sources

Russian Federation

*State Archive of Russian Federation, Moscow (GARF)*

| | |
|---|---|
| Fond R-4459 | Telegraph Agency of the Soviet Union (TASS) |
| Fond R-8581 | Soviet Information Bureau (Sovinformburo) |
| Fond R-9425 | The Main Directorate for the Protection of State Secrets in the Press (Glavlit) |
| Fond R-9587 | "Novosti" Press Agency (APN) |
| Fond R-9613 | Editorial boards and publishing houses of trade union newspapers |
| Fond R-1244 | Editorial board of the newspaper *Izvestiia* |
| Fond 10124 | The Union of Soviet Journalists |

*Russian State Archive for Literature and the Arts (RGALI)*

| | |
|---|---|
| Fond 618 | Editorial board of the journal *Znamia* |
| Fond 631 | The Union of Soviet Writers |
| Fond 634 | Editorial board of the newspaper *Literaturnaia Gazeta* |
| Fond 1702 | Editorial board of the journal *Novyi Mir* |

*Russian State Archive of Contemporary History, Moscow (RGANI)*

| | |
|---|---|
| Fond 5 | Apparat of the Central Committee of the CPSU |
| Fond 11 | Commission on the Questions of Ideology, Culture, and International Party Relations of the Central Committee of the CPSU |
| Fond 72 | Ideological Commission of the Central Committee of the CPSU |
| Fond 89 | Collection of Declassified Documents |

*Russian State Archive of Social and Political History, Moscow (RGASPI)*

| | |
|---|---|
| Fond 17 | Central Committee of the CPSU |
| Fond 82 | Molotov, Vyacheslav Mikhailovich |
| Fond 629 | Pospelov, Petr Nikolaevich |
| Fond 623 | Political Literature Publishing House (Politizdat) |

*Central Archive of the City of Moscow (TsAGM)*

| | |
|---|---|
| Fond P-453 | Party organization of the newspaper *Izvestiia* |
| Fond P-3226 | Party organization of the newspaper *Pravda* |

*Stanislav Kondrashov Private Archive, Pakhra, Russian Federation*
*Tatiana Strel'nikova Private Archive, Moscow, Russian Federation*

United States

*Associated Press Corporate Archives, New York City*

| | |
|---|---|
| AP01.04B | Records of Board President Robert McLean, 1913–1973 |
| AP02.01 | Records of General Manager Kent Cooper, 1893–1955 |
| AP02A.02 | Foreign Bureau Correspondence, 1933–1967 |
| AP02A.03A | Subject Files, 1900–1950 |
| AP02A.03B | Subject Files, 1951–1967 |

Associated Press Oral History Program

*Columbia University, Rare Books and Manuscripts Library*

Harrison E. Salisbury Papers

*Library of Congress, Manuscript Division, Washington, DC*

Whitman Bassow Papers
Irving Levine Papers
Daniel Schorr Papers
Henry Shapiro Papers
Hedrick Smith Papers

*National Archives, College Park, Maryland*

Record Group 59 (RG 59)—General Record of the Department of State
  Entry 5552: Bureau of European Affairs, Office of Soviet Union Affairs, Bilateral Political Relations, Special Collection Subject Files
  Entry 5345: Bureau of European Affairs, Office of Soviet Union Affairs, Bilateral Political Relations, Bilateral Political Relations Subject Files
Record Group 84 (RG 84)—Records of the Foreign Service Posts of the Department of State
  Entry 3313: Union of Soviet Socialist Republics, US Embassy, Moscow, Classified General Records, 1941–1963
  Entry 3314: Union of Soviet Socialist Republics, US Embassy, Moscow, Top Secret General Records, 1941–1948
Record Group 306 (RG 306)—United States Information Agency
  Entry P-160: Special Reports, 1953–1997

*New York Public Library, Humanities and Social Sciences Library, Manuscripts and Archives Division*

New York Times Company Records
  Arthur Hays Sulzberger Papers, 1823–1999
  Foreign Desk Records, 1948–1993
  General Files, 1835–2001

*Tamiment Library and Robert F. Wagner Archives, New York University*

Church League of America Collection of the Research Files of *Counterattack*, the Wackenhut Corporation, and Karl Baarslag
*New Leader* Records
Newspaper Guild of New York Records
John Pittman papers

Germany

*The Research Center for East European Studies Archives and Library, the University of Bremen*
Lev Kopelev and Raisa Orlova papers

## Digital Collections

Vladimir Bukovsky Archive
http://www.bukovsky-archives.net
Wilson Center, Cold War International History Project
https://digitalarchive.wilsoncenter.org/
George Washington University, National Security Archive
https://nsarchive.gwu.edu/
John F. Kennedy Presidential Library and Museum, Digital Collections
https://www.jfklibrary.org
Ronald Reagan Presidential Library and Museum, Digital Library
https://www.reaganlibrary.gov/archives/digital-library
Franklin D. Roosevelt Presidential Library and Museum, Historic Collections:
https://www.fdrlibrary.org/historic-collections
Harry S. Truman Presidential Library and Museum, Online Documents
https://trumanlibrary.org/online-collections.htm
Alexander Yakovlev Foundation Digital Archive
http://www.alexanderyakovlev.org/db-docs

## Published Documents

Afanas'eva, E. S., Iu. V. Afiani, and Z. K. Vodop'ianova, eds. *Apparat TsK KPSS i kul'tura, 1953–1957: Dokumenty.* Moscow: ROSSPEN, 2001.

Artizov, Andrei, and Oleg V. Naumov, eds. *Vlast' i khudozhestvennaia intelligentsiia dokumenty TsK RKP(b)-VKP(b), VChK-OGPU-NKVD o kulturnoi politike: 1917–1953 gg.* Moscow: Mezhdunarodnyi Fond "Demokratiia," 2002.

Blium, Arlen, ed. *Tsenzura v Sovetskom Soiuze: 1917–1991: Dokumenty.* Moscow: ROSSPEN, 2004.

Chernyaev, A. S., A. B. Veber, V. A. Medvedev, and G. K. Shakhnazarov, eds. *V Politburo TsK KPSS . . . : Po zapisiam Anatoliia Cherniaeva, Vadima Medvedeva, Georgiia Shakhnazarova.* Moscow: Al'pina Biznes Buks, 2006.

Clark, Katerina, E. A. Dobrenko, Andrei Artizov, and Oleg V. Naumov, eds. *Soviet Culture and Power: A History in Documents, 1917–1953.* Annals of Communism. New Haven, CT: Yale University Press, 2007.

Eimermacher, Karl, Iu. V. Afiani, D. Bairau, B. Bonvech, V. P. Kozlov, and N. G. Tomilina, eds. *Doklad N.S. Khrushcheva o kul'te lichnosti Stalina na XX s'ezde KPSS: Dokumenty.* Moscow: ROSSPEN, 2002.

Goriaeva, T. M., and Z. K. Vodopianova, eds. *Istoriia sovetskoi politicheskoi tsenzury: Dokumenty i kommentarii.* Moscow: ROSSPEN, 1997.

Humphrey, David C., and Charles S. Sampson, eds. *Foreign Relations of the United States [FRUS], 1964–1968.* Vol. XIV, *Soviet Union.* Washington, DC: US Government Printing Office, 2001.

Khlevniuk, O. V., I. Gorlitskii, L. P. Kosheleva, A. I. Miniuk, M. Iu. Prozumenshchikov, L. A. Rogovaia, S. V. Somonova, eds. *Politburo TsK VKP(b) i Soviet Ministrov SSSR, 1945–1953.* Moscow: ROSSPEN, 2002.

Kozlov, Vladimir Aleksandrovich, S. V. Mironenko, Ol'ga V. Edel'man, eds. *Kramola: Inakomyslie v SSSR pri Khrushcheve i Brezhneve, 1953–1982: Rassekrechennye dokumenty Verkhovnogo suda i Prokuratury SSSR.* Moscow: Materik, 2005.

Maksimenkov, L. V., ed. *Bol'shaia tsenzura: Pisateli i zhurnalisty v Strane Sovetov: 1917–1956.* Moscow: Mezhdunarodnyi Fond "Demokratiia," 2005.

Nadzhafov, D. G., and Z. S. Belousova. *Stalin i kosmopolitizm: Dokumenty Agitpropa TsK KPSS 1945–1953.* Moscow: Materik, 2005.

Sampson, Charles S., ed. *Foreign Relations of the United States [FRUS], 1961–1963.* Vol. XV, *Berlin Crisis, 1962–1963.* Washington, DC: Government Printing Office, 1994.

Sampson, Charles S., and John Michael Joyce, eds. *Foreign Relations of the United States [FRUS], 1961–1963.* Vol. V, *Soviet Union.* Washington, DC: Government Printing Office, 1998.

Sampson, Charles S., Ronald D. Landa, James E. Miller, and David S. Patterson, eds. *Foreign Relations of the United States [FRUS], 1958–1960.* Vol. X, Part 1, *Eastern Europe Region; Soviet Union; Cyprus.* Washington, DC: Government Printing Office, 1993.

Slany, William, and Rogers P. Churchill, eds. *Foreign Relations of the United States [FRUS], 1946.* Vol. VI, *Eastern Europe, The Soviet Union.* Washington, DC: Government Printing Office, 1969.

———, eds. *Foreign Relations of the United States [FRUS], 1947.* Vol. IV, *Eastern Europe, The Soviet Union.* Washington, DC: Government Printing Office, 1972.

Tomilina, N. G., ed. *Apparat TsK KPSS i kul'tura, 1965–1972: Dokumenty.* Moscow: ROSSPEN, 2009.

———, ed. *Apparat TsK KPSS i kul'tura, 1973–1978: Dokumenty v dvukh tomakh.* Moscow: ROSSPEN, 2011.

## Oral History Interviews by the Author

Nadezhda I. Azhgikhina, October 2009
Mikhail Beglov, September 2014
Genrikh Borovik, June 2007, July 2009
Eduard Ivanian, June 2007
Susan Jacoby, December 2010
Robert G. Kaiser, December 2010
Zhores Medvedev, May 2011
Andrew Nagorski, February 2013
Jerrold Schecter, December 2008
Natan Sharansky, May 2013
Leonid Shinkarev, June 2010
Hedrick L. Smith, December 2008
Vasily Strel'nikov, June 2010
Tatiana Strel'nikova, May 2010
Melor Sturua, February 2011
Valentin Zorin, October 2009

## Books by Cold War Foreign Correspondents, 1945–1991

Adzhubei, Alexei. *"Serebriannaia koshka" ili puteshevstvie po Amerike.* Moscow: Molodaia Gvardiia, 1956.

Bonavia, David. *Fat Sasha and the Urban Guerilla: Protest and Conformism in the Soviet Union.* London: H. Hamilton, 1973.

Borovik, Genrikh Aviezerovich. *Odin god nespokoinogo solntsa.* Moscow: Sovetskii Pisatel', 1971.

———. *Prolog: Roman esse.* Moscow: Pravda, 1985.

Daniloff, Nicholas. *Two Lives, One Russia.* New York: Avon Books, 1990.

Doder, Dusko. *Shadows and Whispers: Power Politics inside the Kremlin from Brezhnev to Gorbachev.* New York: Random House, 1986.

Dornberg, John. *The New Tsars: Russia under Stalin's Heirs.* New York: Doubleday, 1972.
———. *The Soviet Union Today.* New York: Dial Press, 1976.
Fischer, Louis. *Russia Revisited.* London: Jonathan Cape, 1957.
Gilmore, Eddy. *Me and My Russian Wife.* New York: Doubleday, 1954.
Gorchakov, Ovidii Aleksandrovich. *V gostiakh u diadi Sema (reportazh).* Moscow: Molodaia Gvardiia, 1965.
Gribachev, Nikolai Matveevich. *Semero v Amerike: Zapiski korrespondenta Literaturnoi Gazety o poezdke v SShA s gruppoi sovetskikh zhurnalistov v oktiabre–noiabre 1955 g.* Moscow: Sovetskii Pisatel', 1955.
Gunther, John. *Inside Russia Today.* New York: Harper, 1958.
Higgins, Marguerite. *Red Plush and Black Bread.* Garden City: Doubleday, 1955.
Hindus, Maurice. *Crisis in the Kremlin.* New York: Doubleday, 1955.
Jacoby, Susan. *The Friendship Barrier: Ten Russian Encounters.* London: The Bodley Head, 1972.
Kaiser, Robert G. *Cold Winter, Cold War.* New York: Stein and Day, 1974.
———. *Russia: The People and the Power.* New York: Atheneum, 1976.
Kaiser, Robert G., and Hannah Jopling Kaiser. *Russia from the Inside.* London: Hutchinson, 1980.
Karev, Nikolai Nikolaevich. *Raznoetazhnaia Amerika.* Moscow: Izdatel'stvo politicheskoi literatury, 1963.
———. *Amerika posle iubileia: Reportazh.* Moscow: Izdatel'stvo politicheskoi literatury, 1978.
Klose, Kevin. *Russia and the Russians: Inside the Closed Society.* New York: Norton, 1984.
Kondrashov, Stanislav Nikolaevich. *Amerikantsy v Amerike: Ocherki i reportazhi.* Moscow: Izvestiia, 1970.
———. *Bliki N'iu Iorka.* Moscow: Sovetskii Pisatel', 1982.
———. *Dolgii vzgliad na Ameriku.* Moscow: Mezgdnarodnye otnosheniia, 1988.
———. *Liudi za okeanom: Amerikanskie ocherki raznykh let.* Moscow: Izdatel'stvo politicheskoi literatury, 1987.
———. *Perekrestki Ameriki: Zametki zhurnalista.* Moscow: Izdatel'stvo politicheskoi literatury, 1969.
———. *Puteshestvie Amerikanista.* In *Dolgii vzgliad na Ameriku,* 335–591. *Puteshestvie Amerikanista* was first published in 1986 by Sovetskii Pisatel' (Moscow). Page references are to the 1988 edition.
———. *Svidanie s Kaliforniei.* Moscow: Molodaia Gvardiia, 1975.
———. *Zhizn' i smert' Martina Lutera Kinga.* Moscow: Molodaia Gvardiia, 1970.
Korotich, Vitalii Alekseevich. *Litso nenavisti.* Moscow: Sovetskii Pisatel', 1985.
Kraminov, Daniil Fedorovich. *Amerikanskie vstrechi: Ocherki.* Moscow: Molodaia Gvardiia, 1954.
Levine, Irving R. *Main Street, U.S.S.R.* Garden City, NY: Doubleday, 1959.
Magidoff, Robert. *In Anger and Pity: A Report on Russia.* Garden City, NY: Doubleday, 1949.
Mosby, Aline. *The View from No. 13 People's Street.* New York: Random House, 1962.
Murarka, Dev. *The Soviet Union.* London: Thames and Hudson, 1971.
Nagorski, Andrew. *Reluctant Farewell: An American Reporter's Candid Look inside the Soviet Union.* New York: Holt, Rinehart and Winston, 1985.
Newman, Joseph. *Report from Russia.* New York: New York Herald Tribune, 1950.
Polevoi, Boris Nikolaevich. *Amerikanskii dnevnik.* Moscow: Izdatel'stvo politicheskoi literatury, 1957.
Pond, Elizabeth. *From the Yaroslavsky Station: Russia Perceived.* New York: Universe Books, 1988.
Salisbury, Harrison E. *American in Russia.* New York: Harper, 1955.
———. *Russia on the Way.* New York: Macmillan, 1946.
Schecter, Jerrold L., and Leona P. Schecter. *An American Family in Moscow.* Boston: Little, Brown, 1975.

————. *Back in the U.S.S.R.: An American Family Returns to Moscow.* New York: Scribner, 1988.

Shipler, David K. *Russia: Broken Idols, Solemn Dreams.* New York: Penguin, 1986.

Shub, Anatole. *An Empire Loses Hope: The Return of Stalin's Ghost.* New York: Norton, 1970.

————. *Russia Turns Back the Clock.* Washington, DC: Washington Post, 1969.

————. *The New Russian Tragedy.* New York: Norton, 1969.

Smith, Hedrick L. *The New Russians.* New York: Harper Collins, 1991.

————. *The Russians.* New York: Ballantine Books, 1980.

Steinbeck, John, and Robert Capa. *A Russian Journal.* New York: Penguin Books, 1999.

Stevens, Edmund. *This Is Russia, Uncensored.* New York: Didier, 1950.

Strel'nikov, Boris Georgievich. *Iulia, Vasia, i Prezident.* Moscow: Molodaia Gvardiia, 1966.

————. *Kak vy tam v Amerike.* Moscow: Molodaia Gvardiia, 1965.

————. *Tysiacha mil' v poiskakh dushi.* Moscow: Pravda, 1979.

Strel'nikov, Boris Georgievich, and Vasilii Mikhailovich Peskov. *Zemlia za okeanom.* Moscow: Molodaia Gvardiia, 1975.

Strel'nikov, Boris Georgievich, and Il'ia Shatunovskii. *Amerika sprava i sleva: Puteshestvie na avtomobile.* Moscow: Pravda, 1971.

Sturua, Melor Georgievich. *Brozhenie.* Moscow: Molodaia Gvardiia, 1971.

————. *Burnoe desiatiletie: Amerikanskii dnevnik 1968–1978.* Moscow: Sovetskii Pisatel', 1981.

————. *S Potomaka na Missisipi: Nesentimental'noe puteshestvie po Amerike.* Moscow: Molodaia Gvardiia, 1981.

————. *1984 and "1984": Where and How Have George Orwell's Forecasts Come True?* Moscow: Novosti Press Agency Publishing House, 1984.

————. *Ozabochennaia Amerika.* Moscow: Sovetskaia Rossiia, 1984.

————. *Amerika vos'midesiatykh: piat' let i piat' minut: pamflety.* Moscow: Izvestiia, 1986.

Vasil'ev, Sergei, and Mark Abramov. *Odinochestvo na miru: Litso i iznanka SShA.* Moscow: Sovetskaia Rossiia, 1969.

Whitney, Thomas P. *Russia in My Life.* New York: Reynal and Co., 1962.

Willis, David K. *Klass: How Russians Really Live.* New York: St. Martin's Press, 1985.

Zhukov, Yuri Aleksandrovich. *Na zapade posle voiny.* Moscow: Sovetskii Pisatel', 1948.

————. *Obshchestvo bez budushchego: Zametki publitsista.* Moscow: Izdatel'stvo politicheskoi literatury, 1978.

Zorin, Valentin Sergeevich. *Amerika semidesiatykh: Televizionnye fil'my.* Moscow: Iskusstvo, 1981.

————. *Mistetry milliardy.* Moscow: Molodaia Gvardiia, 1969.

————. *Nekoronovannye koroli Ameriki.* Moscow: Izdatel'stvo politicheskoi literatury, 1970.

————. *Vladyki bez masok.* Moscow: Detskaia literatura, 1972.

Zorin, Valentin Sergeevich, and D. Bal'termants. *Protivorechivaia Amerika: Stsenarii televizionnykh peredach i fil'mov.* Moscow: Isskustvo, 1976.

## Published Works

Adzhubei, Alexei. *Te desiat' let.* Moscow: Sovetskaia Rossiia, 1989.

Afanas'ev, Viktor G. *4–ia vlast' i 4 genseka (ot Brezhneva do Gorbacheva v "Pravde").* Moscow: Kedr, 1994.

Aksyonov, Vassily. *In a Search of Melancholy Baby.* New York: Random House, 1987.

Alekseeva, Liudmila, and Paul Goldberg. *The Thaw Generation: Coming of Age in the Post-Stalin Era.* Pittsburgh, PA: University of Pittsburgh Press, 1993.

Alterman, Eric. *Sound and Fury: The Making of the Punditocracy.* Ithaca, NY: Cornell University Press, 1999.

Alwood, Edward. *Dark Days in the Newsroom: McCarthyism Aimed at the Press.* Philadelphia: Temple University Press, 2007.

Applebaum, Rachel. "A Test of Friendship: Soviet-Czechoslovak Tourism and the Prague Spring." In *The Socialist Sixties: Crossing Borders in the Second World*, edited by Anne E. Gorsuch and Diane P. Koenker, 213–232. Bloomington: Indiana University Press, 2013.

———. *Empire of Friends: Soviet Power and Socialist Internationalism in Cold War Czechoslovakia*. Ithaca, NY: Cornell University Press, 2019.

Arbatov, Georgy A. *The Soviet Viewpoint*. New York: Dodd, Mead, and Company, 1981.

———. *Zatianuvsheesia vyzdorovlenie, 1953–1985 gg.: Svidetel'stvo sovremennika*. Moscow: Mezhdunarodnye otnosheniia, 1991.

Aronson, James. *The Press and the Cold War*. New York: Monthly Review Press, 1990.

Aucoin, James. *The Evolution of American Investigative Journalism*. Columbia: University of Missouri Press, 2005.

Bacon, Edward, and Mark Sandle, eds. *Brezhnev Reconsidered*. New York: Palgrave Macmillan, 2002.

Baldwin, Kate A. *Beyond the Color Line and the Iron Curtain: Reading Encounters between Black and Red, 1922–1963*. Durham, NC: Duke University Press, 2002.

Ball, Alan M. *Imagining America: Influence and Images in Twentieth-Century Russia*. Lanham, MD: Rowman and Littlefield, 2003.

———. *Liberty's Tears: Soviet Portraits of the "American Way of Life" during the Cold War*. New York: Oxford University Press, 2016.

Barghoorn, Frederick C. *Soviet Foreign Propaganda*. Princeton, NJ: Princeton University Press, 1966.

———. *The Soviet Cultural Offensive: The Role of Cultural Diplomacy in Soviet Foreign Policy*. Westport, CT: Greenwood Press, 1976.

———. *The Soviet Image of the United States: A Study in Distortion*. Port Washington, NY: Kennikat Press, 1969.

Bassow, Whitman. *The Moscow Correspondents: Reporting on Russia from the Revolution to Glasnost*. New York: William Morrow and Co., 1988.

Batalov, Eduard Iakovlevich. *Russkaia ideia i amerikanskaia mechta*. Moscow: Progress-Traditsiia, 2009.

Bayley, Edwin R. *Joe McCarthy and the Press*. Madison: University of Wisconsin Press, 1981.

Becker, Jonathan A. *Soviet and Russian Press Coverage of the United States: Press, Politics, and Identity in Transition*. New York: Palgrave Macmillan, 2002.

Beglova, Natalia. *Moskovskaia sem'ia riazanskogo razliva*. Moscow: Novyi Khronograf, 2012.

Bell, Daniel. "The Revolt against Modernity." *Public Interest* 81 (1985): 42–63.

Belmonte, Laura A. *Selling the American Way: U.S. Propaganda and the Cold War*. Philadelphia: University of Pennsylvania Press, 2008.

Berezhnoi, A. F., and E. M. Durygina. *Sovetskie pisateli i zhurnalisty o gazetnom trude*. Moscow: Izdatel'stvo politicheskoi literatury, 1975.

Bergman, Tony. "Soviet Dissidents and the Russian Intelligentsia, 1956–1985: The Search for a Usable Past." *Russian Review* 51, no. 1 (1992): 16–35.

Berkhoff, Karel C. *Motherland in Danger*. Cambridge, MA: Harvard University Press, 2012.

Berlin, Isaiah. *Russian Thinkers*. London: Penguin, 1988.

Berman, Marshall. *All That Is Solid Melts into Air: The Experience of Modernity*. New York: Penguin, 1988.

Bernhard, Nancy E. *U.S. Television News and Cold War Propaganda, 1947–1960*. Cambridge: Cambridge University Press, 1999.

Blium, Arlen B. *A Self-Administered Poison: The System and Functions of Soviet Censorship*. Oxford, UK: European Humanities Research Centre, 2003.

————. *Kak eto delalos' v Leningrade: Tsenzura v gody ottepeli, zastoia i perestroiki, 1953–1991.* St. Petersburg: Akademicheskii Proekt, 2005.

Borstelmann, Thomas. *The Cold War and the Color Line: American Race Relations in the Global Arena.* Cambridge, MA: Harvard University Press, 2001.

Bourdieu, Pierre, and Randal Johnson. *The Field of Cultural Production: Essays on Art and Literature.* New York: Columbia University Press, 1993.

Bourdieu, Pierre, and John B. Thompson. *Language and Symbolic Power.* Cambridge, MA: Harvard University Press, 1991.

Bovin, Alexander. *XX vek kak zhizn': Vospominaniia.* Moscow: Zakharov, 2003.

Boyer, Paul S. *By the Bomb's Early Light: American Thought and Culture at the Dawn of the Atomic Age.* Chapel Hill: University of North Carolina Press, 1994.

Brainerd, Michael, ed. *Spacebridges: Television and US-Soviet Dialogue.* Lanham, MD: University Press of America, 1989.

Brandenberger, David. *National Bolshevism: Stalinist Mass Culture and the Formation of Modern Russian National Identity, 1931–1956.* Cambridge, MA: Harvard University Press, 2002.

————. *Propaganda State in Crisis: Soviet Ideology, Indoctrination, and Terror under Stalin, 1927–1941.* New Haven, CT: Yale University Press, 2011.

————. "Stalin's Last Crime? Recent Scholarship on Postwar Soviet Antisemitism and the Doctor's Plot." *Kritika: Explorations in Russian and Eurasian History* 6, no. 1 (2005): 187–204.

Brands, H. W. *Reagan: The Life.* New York: Knopf Doubleday, 2015.

Bren, Paulina. "Mirror, Mirror, on the Wall . . . Is the West the Fairest of Them All? Czechoslovak Normalization and Its (Dis)Contents." *Kritika: Explorations in Russian and Eurasian History* 9, no. 4 (2008): 831–54.

Brennan, Elizabeth A., and Elizabeth C. Clarage. *Who's Who of Pulitzer Prize Winners.* Westport, CT: Greenwood Publishing Group, 1999.

Brezhnev, Leonid Il'ich. *Leninskim kursom: Rechi i stat'i: Sobranie sochinenii v 7 tomakh.* Vol. 1. Moscow: Izdatel'stvo politicheskoi literatury, 1979.

Brooks, Jeffrey. "Official Xenophobia and Popular Cosmopolitanism in Early Soviet Russia." *American Historical Review* 97, no. 5 (1992): 1431–48.

————. *Thank You, Comrade Stalin! Soviet Public Culture from Revolution to Cold War.* Princeton, NJ: Princeton University Press, 2000.

————. *When Russia Learned to Read: Literacy and Popular Literature, 1861–1917.* Princeton, NJ: Princeton University Press, 1985.

————. *When the Cold War Did Not End: The Soviet Peace Offensive of 1953 and the American Response.* Washington, DC: Kennan Institute for Advanced Russian Studies, 2000.

Brown, Kate. *Plutopia: Nuclear Families, Atomic Cities, and the Great Soviet and American Plutonium Disasters.* Oxford: Oxford University Press, 2013.

Burlatskii, Fedor. *Vozhdi i sovetniki: O Khrushcheve, Andropove i ne tol'ko o nikh.* Moscow: Izdatel'stvo politicheskoi literatury, 1990.

Byrne, Jeffrey James. "The Cold War in Africa." In *The Routledge Handbook of the Cold War,* edited by Artemy M. Kalinovsky and Craig Daigle, 149–162. London: Routledge, 2014.

Carew, Joy Gleason. *Blacks, Reds, and Russians: Sojourners in Search of the Soviet Promise.* New Brunswick, NJ: Rutgers University Press, 2008.

Carruthers, Susan L. *Cold War Captives: Imprisonment, Escape, and Brainwashing.* Berkeley: University of California Press, 2009.

Cassidy, Henry C. *Moscow Dateline 1941–1943.* New York: Council on Books in Wartime, 1944.

Cater, Douglass. *The Fourth Branch of Government.* Boston: Houghton Mifflin, 1959.

Caute, David. *The Dancer Defects: The Struggle for Cultural Supremacy during the Cold War.* Oxford: Oxford University Press, 2003.

Chatterjee, Choi, and Beth Holmgren, eds. *Americans Experience Russia: Encountering the Enigma, 1917 to the Present.* New York: Routledge, 2013.

Cherfas, Teresa. "Reporting Stalin's Famine: Jones and Muggeridge: A Case Study in Forgetting and Rediscovery." *Kritika: Explorations in Russian and Eurasian History* 14, no. 4 (2013): 775–804.

Chernyshova, Natalya. "Consumers as Citizens: Revisiting the Question of Public Disengagement in the Brezhnev Era." In *Reconsidering Stagnation in the Brezhnev Era*, edited by Dina Fainberg and Artemy M. Kalinovsky, 3–20. Lanham, MD: Lexington Books, 2016.

———. *Soviet Consumer Culture in the Brezhnev Era.* New York: Routledge, 2013.

Christians, Clifford G. *Normative Theories of the Media: Journalism in Democratic Societies.* Urbana: University of Illinois Press, 2009.

Clark, Katerina. *Moscow, the Fourth Rome: Stalinism, Cosmopolitanism and the Evolution of Soviet Culture, 1931–1941.* Cambridge, MA: Harvard University Press, 2011.

———. *The Soviet Novel: History as Ritual.* Chicago: University of Chicago Press, 1981.

Cohen, Lizabeth. *A Consumers' Republic: The Politics of Mass Consumption in Postwar America.* New York: Knopf, 2003.

Cohen, Stephen F. *Failed Crusade: America and the Tragedy of Post-Communist Russia.* New York: Norton, 2000.

———. *Sovieticus: American Perceptions and Soviet Realities.* New York: Norton, 1986.

Costigliola, Frank. "'Unceasing Pressure for Penetration': Gender, Pathology, and Emotion in George Kennan's Formation of the Cold War." *Journal of American History* 80, no. 4 (1997): 1309–39.

Cozma, Raluca, and John Maxwell Hamilton. "Film Portrayals of Foreign Correspondents." *Journalism Studies* 10, no. 4 (2009): 489–505.

Cronkite, Walter. *A Reporter's Life.* New York: Ballantine Books, 1997.

Cull, Nicholas J. *The Cold War and the United States Information Agency: American Propaganda and Public Diplomacy, 1945–1989.* Cambridge: Cambridge University Press, 2009.

Curran, James, Michael Gurevitch, and Janet Woollacott. *Mass Communication and Society.* London: Edward Arnold for the Open University Press, 1977.

Custine, Astolphe Louis Léonor de. *Empire of the Czar: A Journey through Eternal Russia.* Edited by Daniel J. Boorstin. New York: Doubleday, 1989.

———. *Journey for Our Time: The Russian Journals of the Marquis de Custine.* Edited and translated by Phyllis Penn Kohler. New York: Pellegrini and Cudahy, 1951.

———. *The Empire of the Czar; or, Observations on the Social, Political, and Religious State and Prospects of Russia, Made during a Journey through That Empire.* London: Longman, Brown, Green, 1843.

Daniloff, Nicholas. *Of Spies and Spokesmen: My Life as a Cold War Correspondent.* Columbia: University of Missouri Press, 2008

David-Fox, Michael. "From Illusory 'Society' to Intellectual 'Public': VOKS, International Travel and Party–Intelligentsia Relations in the Interwar Period." *Contemporary European History* 11, no. 1 (2002): 7–32.

———. "Opiate of the Intellectuals? Pilgrims, Partisans, and Political Tourists." *Kritika: Explorations in Russian and Eurasian History* 12, no. 3 (2011): 721–38.

———. *Showcasing the Great Experiment: Cultural Diplomacy and Western Visitors to the Soviet Union, 1921–1941.* Oxford: Oxford University Press, 2012.

———. "The Fellow Travelers Revisited: The 'Cultured West' through Soviet Eyes." *Journal of Modern History* 75, no. 2 (2003): 300–35.

———. "The Implications of Transnationalism." *Kritika: Explorations in Russian and Eurasian History* 12, no. 4 (2011): 885–904.

Davies, David R. *The Postwar Decline of American Newspapers, 1945–1965: The History of American Journalism.* Westport, CT: Praeger, 2006.

Davis, Donald E., and Eugene P. Trani. *Distorted Mirrors: Americans and Their Relations with Russia and China in the Twentieth Century.* Columbia: University of Missouri Press, 2009.

———. *The Reporter Who Knew Too Much: Harrison Salisbury and the New York Times.* Lanham, MD: Rowman and Littlefield Publishers, 2012.

Davison, W. Phillips, Donald R. Shanor, and Frederick T. C. Yu. *News from Abroad and the Foreign Policy Public.* New York: Foreign Policy Association, 1980.

Del Pero, Mario. "Incompatible Universalisms: The United States, the Soviet Union, and the Beginning of the Cold War." In *The Routledge Handbook of the Cold War,* edited by Artemy M. Kalinovsky and Craig Daigle, 3-16. New York: Routledge, 2014.

Dell'Orto, Giovanna. *American Journalism and International Relations: Foreign Correspondence from the Early Republic to the Digital Era.* Cambridge: Cambridge University Press, 2013.

Dennis, Everette E., George Gerbner, and Yassen N. Zassoursky. *Beyond the Cold War: Soviet and American Media Images.* Newbury Park, CA: Sage, 1991.

Divine, Robert. *The Sputnik Challenge.* New York: Oxford University Press, 1993.

Dobrenko, E. A. *The Making of the State Reader: Social and Aesthetic Contexts of the Reception of Soviet Literature.* Stanford, CA: Stanford University Press, 1997.

———. *The Making of the State Writer: Social and Aesthetic Origins of Soviet Literary Culture.* Stanford, CA: Stanford University Press, 2001.

Dobrynin, Anatoly. *In Confidence: Moscow's Ambassador to America's Six Cold War Presidents (1962–1986).* New York: Times Books, Random House, 1995.

Dobson, Miriam. "'Show the Bandit-Enemies No Mercy!' Amnesty, Criminality and Public Response in 1953." In *The Dilemmas of De-Stalinization: Negotiating Cultural and Social Changein the Khrushchev Era,* edited by Polly Jones, 21–40. London: Routledge, 2006.

Doherty, Thomas Patrick. *Cold War, Cool Medium: Television, McCarthyism, and American Culture.* New York: Columbia University Press, 2003.

Dovlatov, Sergei. *Kompromiss.* New York: Serebriannyi Vek, 1981.

Downing, John, Ali Mohammadi, and Annabelle Sreberny. *Questioning the Media: A Critical Introduction.* Newbury Park, CA: Sage, 1990.

Druzenko, Anatolii. *Pravda ob Izvestiiakh: Kniga o vtoroi drevneishei i vechno molodoi professii.* Moscow: Sterzhen', 1998.

Dunham, Vera. *In Stalin's Time: Middleclass Values in Soviet Fiction.* Cambridge: Cambridge University Press, 1976.

Dunn, Charles W., ed. *American Exceptionalism: The Origins, History, and Future of the Nation's Greatest Strength.* Lanham, MD: Rowman and Littlefield, 2013.

Eagleton, Terry. *Criticism and Ideology: A Study in Marxist Literary Theory.* London: Verso, 1991.

———. *Ideology: An Introduction.* London: Verso, 1991.

Eaton, Katherine Bliss. *Daily Life in the Soviet Union.* Westport, CT: Greenwood Press, 2004.

Ebon, Martin. *The Soviet Propaganda Machine.* New York: McGraw-Hill, 1987.

Ehrlich, Matthew C., and Joe Saltzman. *Heroes and Scoundrels: The Image of the Journalist in Popular Culture.* Urbana: University of Illinois Press, 2015.

Emery, Michael C. *On the Front Lines: Following America's Foreign Correspondents across the Twentieth Century.* Lanham, MD: American University Press, 1995.

Engerman, David C. "Ideology and the Origins of the Cold War, 1917–1962." In *Cambridge History of the Cold War,* edited by Melvyn P. Leffler and Odd Arne Westad, vol. 1, 20–43. Cambridge: Cambridge University Press, 2010.

———. *Know Your Enemy: The Rise and Fall of America's Soviet Experts.* Oxford: Oxford University Press, 2009.

———. *Modernization from the Other Shore: American Intellectuals and the Romance of Russian Development.* Cambridge, MA: Harvard University Press, 2003.

———. "Modernization from the Other Shore: American Observers and the Costs of Soviet Economic Development." *American Historical Review* 105, no. 2 (2000): 383–416.

———. "The Romance of Economic Development and New Histories of the Cold War." *Diplomatic History* 28, no. 1 (2004): 23–54.

English, Robert D. *Russia and the Idea of the West.* New York: Columbia University Press, 2000.

English, Robert D., and Jonathan J. Halperin. *The Other Side: How Soviets and Americans Perceive Each Other.* New Brunswick, NJ: Transaction Books, 1987.

Ehrenburg, Ilya Grigor'evich. *Liudi, gody, zhizn': Vospominaniia, v trekh tomakh.* Moscow: Sovetskii Pisatel', 1990.

Etkind, Alexander. *Tolkovanie puteshestvii: Rossiia i Amerika v travelogakh i intertekstakh.* Moscow: Novoe literaturnoe obozrenie, 2001.

Evans, Alfred. "The Decline of Developed Socialism? Some Trends in Recent Soviet Ideology." *Soviet Studies* 38, no. 1 (1986): 1–23.

Evans, Christine E. *Between Truth and Time: A History of Soviet Central Television.* New Haven, CT: Yale University Press, 2016.

Evtuhov, Catherine, and Stephen Kotkin. *The Cultural Gradient: The Transmission of Ideas in Europe, 1789–1991.* Lanham, MD: Rowman and Littlefield, 2003.

Fainberg, Dina. "A Portrait of a Journalist as a Cold War Expert: Harrison Salisbury." *Journalism History* 41, no. 3 (2015): 153–64.

———. "Unmasking the Wolf in Sheep's Clothing: Soviet and American Campaigns against the Enemy's Journalists, 1946–1953." *Cold War History* 15, no. 2 (2015): 155–178.

Fainberg, Dina, and Artemy M. Kalinovsky, eds. *Reconsidering Stagnation in the Brezhnev Era.* Lanham, MD: Lexington Books, 2016.

Fateev, A. V. *Obraz vraga v sovetskoi propagande: 1945–1954 gg.* Moscow: Rossiiskaia Akademiia Nauk, Institut Rossiiskoi Istorii, 1999.

Fedorova, Milla. *Yankees in Petrograd, Bolsheviks in New York: America and Americans in Russian Literary Perception.* Ithaca, NY: Cornell University Press, 2013.

Feofanov, Iurii. "Pervaia Planerka." In *Aleksei Adzhubei v Koridorakh chetvertoi vlasti*, edited by Dmitrii Mamleev. Moscow: Izvestiia, 2003.

Feinberg, Melissa. *Curtain of Lies: The Battle over Truth in Stalinist Eastern Europe.* New York: Oxford University Press, 2017.

Fiebig-von Hase, Ragnhild, and Ursula Lehmkuhl. *Enemy Images in American History.* Providence, RI: Berghahn Books, 1997.

Fielding, Raymond. *The American Newsreel: A Complete History, 1911–1967.* 2nd ed. Jefferson, NC: McFarland and Co., 2006.

Fischer, Heinz-Dietrich, and Erika J. Fischer. *International Reporting 1928–1985: From the Activities of the League of Nations to Present-Day Global Problems.* Berlin: Walter de Gruyter, 1987.

Fischer, Louis. *Soviet Journey.* New York: H. Smith and R. Haas, 1935.

Foglesong, David S. *America's Secret War against Bolshevism: U.S. Intervention in the Russian Civil War, 1917–1920.* Chapel Hill: University of North Carolina Press, 1995.

———. *The American Mission and the "Evil Empire": The Crusade for a "Free Russia" since 1881.* New York: Cambridge University Press, 2007.

Foucault, Michel. *The Archaeology of Knowledge.* New York: Pantheon Books, 1972.

Foucault, Michel, and Colin Gordon. *Power/Knowledge: Selected Interviews and Other Writings, 1972–1977.* New York: Pantheon Books, 1980.

Foucault, Michel, and Joseph Pearson. *Fearless Speech.* Los Angeles: Semiotext, 2001.

Fowler, Roger. *Language in the News: Discourse and Ideology in the Press.* London: Routledge, 1991.

Frankel, Max. *The Times of My Life and My Life with the Times.* New York: Delta, 1999.

Freidin, Gregory. "Soviet Authorship and Citizenship, Revisited." In *Sovetskoe Bogatstvo,* edited by Marina Balina, Evgenii Dobrenko, and Iurii Murashov. Saint Petersburg: Akademicheskii Proekt, 2002.

French, Mary Catherine. "Reporting Socialism: Soviet Journalism and the Journalists' Union, 1955–1966." PhD diss., University of Pennsylvania, 2014.

Fried, Richard M. *Nightmare in Red: The McCarthy Era in Perspective.* New York: Oxford University Press, 1990.

———. *The Russians Are Coming! The Russians Are Coming! Pageantry and Patriotism in Cold-War America.* New York: Oxford University Press, 1998.

Frus, Phyllis. *The Politics and Poetics of Journalistic Narrative: The Timely and the Timeless.* Cambridge: Cambridge University Press, 1994.

Fürst, Juliane A. C. *Stalin's Last Generation: Soviet Post-War Youth and the Emergence of Mature Socialism.* Oxford: Oxford University Press, 2010.

———. "'If You Are Going to Moscow, Be Sure to Wear Some Flowers in Your Hair': The Soviet Hippie 'Sistema' and Its Life in, Despite, and with 'Stagnation.'" In *Reconsidering Stagnation in the Brezhnev Era: Ideology and Exchange,* edited by Dina Fainberg and Artemy M. Kalinovsky, 123–146. Lanham, MD: Lexington Books, 2016.

Garrison, Mark, and Abbott Gleason. *Shared Destiny: Fifty Years of Soviet-American Relations.* Boston: Beacon Press, 1985.

Geertz, Clifford. *The Interpretation of Cultures: Selected Essays.* New York: Basic Books, 1973.

Geyelin, Philip L., and Douglass Cater. *American Media: Adequate or Not.* Washington, DC: American Enterprise Institute for Public Policy Research, 1970.

Gienow-Hecht, Jessica C. E. *Transmission Impossible: American Journalism as Cultural Diplomacy in Postwar Germany, 1945–1955.* Eisenhower Center Studies on War and Peace. Baton Rouge: Louisiana State University Press, 1999.

Gienow-Hecht, Jessica C. E., and Mark C. Donfried, eds. *Searching for a Cultural Diplomacy.* New York: Berghahn Books, 2010.

Gilburd, Eleonory. "Books and Borders: Sergei Obraztsov and Soviet Travelers to London in the 1950s." In *Turizm: The Russian and East European Tourist under Capitalism and Socialism,* edited by Anne E. Gorsuch and Diane P. Koenker, 227–247. Ithaca, NY: Cornell University Press, 2006.

———. "The Revival of Soviet Internationalism in the Mid to Late 1950s." In *The Thaw: Soviet Society and Culture during the 1950s and 1960s,* edited by Denis Kozlov and Eleonory Gilburd, 362–401. Toronto: University of Toronto Press, 2013.

———. *To See Paris and Die: The Soviet Lives of Western Culture.* Cambridge, MA: Belknap Press of Harvard University Press, 2018.

Gilman, Nils. *Mandarins of the Future: Modernization Theory in Cold War America.* New Studies in American Intellectual and Cultural History. Baltimore, MD: Johns Hopkins University Press, 2003.

Gleason, Abbott. "Republic of Humbug: The Russian Nativist Critique of the United States, 1830–1930." *American Quarterly* 44, no. 1 (1992): 1–23.

Goffman, Erving. *Frame Analysis: An Essay on the Organization of Experience.* New York: Harper and Row, 1974.

———. *The Presentation of Self in Everyday Life.* Woodstock, NY: Overlook Press, 1973.

Golubev, Aleksandr V. "'Tsar Kitaiu ne verit . . .' soiuzniki v predstavlenii rossiiskogo obshchevsta 1941–1945gg." In *Rossiia i mir glazami drug druga: Iz istorii vzaimovospriiatiia*, edited by Aleksandr V. Golubev, 317–50. Moscow: Institut Rossiiskoi Istorii RAN, 2000.

Gorbachev, Mikhail Sergeevich. *Zhizn' i reformy*. Moscow: Novosti, 1995.

Goriaeva, T. M. *Politicheskaia tsenzura v SSSR, 1917–1991*. Moscow: ROSSPEN, 2009.

Gorman, Lyn, and David McLean. *Media and Society in the Twentieth Century: A Historical Introduction*. Malden, MA: Blackwell Publishing, 2003.

Gorsuch, Anne E. *All This Is Your World: Soviet Tourism at Home and Abroad After Stalin*. Oxford: Oxford University Press, 2011.

———. "'Cuba, My Love': The Romance of Revolutionary Cuba in the Soviet Sixties." *American Historical Review* 120, no. 2 (2015): 497–526.

Gorsuch, Anne E., and Diane P. Koenker, eds. *The Socialist Sixties: Crossing Borders in the Second World*. Bloomington: Indiana University Press, 2013.

———, eds. *Turizm: The Russian and East European Tourist under Capitalism and Socialism*. Ithaca, NY: Cornell University Press, 2006.

Gould-Davies, Nigel. "Rethinking the Role of Ideology in International Politics during the Cold War." *Journal of Cold War Studies* 1, no. 1 (1999): 90–109.

Grabel'nikov, A. A., G. I. Zubkov, Ia. A. Lomko, Rafail Pogosovich Ovsepian, V. A. Slavina, and B. G. Iakovlev, eds. *Zhurnalisty XX veka: Liudi i sud'by*. Moscow: Ol'ma Press, 2003.

Greenberg, David. *Republic of Spin: An Inside History of the American Presidency*. New York: W. W. Norton, 2016.

Gruber, Ruth. *Ahead of Time: My Early Years as a Foreign Correspondent*. New York: Open Road Integrated Media, 2010.

Günther, Hans, and E. A Dobrenko, eds. *Sotsrealisticheskii kanon*. Saint Petersburg: Akademi-cheskii proekt, 2000.

Gurevitch, Michael, and James Curran. *Mass Media and Society*. London: Edward Arnold, 1991.

Habermas, Jürgen. *The Structural Transformation of the Public Sphere: An Inquiry into a Category of Bourgeois Society*. Cambridge, MA: MIT Press, 1989.

Halberstam, David. *The Powers That Be*. New York: Knopf, 1979.

Halfin, Igal. *From Darkness to Light: Class, Consciousness, and Salvation in Revolutionary Russia*. Pittsburgh, PA: University of Pittsburgh Press, 2000.

Hall, Stuart. *Culture, Media, Language: Working Papers in Cultural Studies, 1972–79*. London: Hutchinson, 1980.

———. "Culture, the Media and the Ideological Effect." In *Mass Communication and Society*, edited by James Curran, Michael Gurevitch, and Janet Woollacott, 315–349. London: Edward Arnold for Open University Press, 1977.

———. *Representation: Cultural Representations and Signifying Practices*. London: Sage, 1997.

———. "Signification, Representation, Ideology: Althusser and the Post-Structuralist Debates." *Critical Studies in Mass Communication* 2, no. 2 (1985): 91–114.

Hallin, Daniel C. *The "Uncensored War": The Media and Vietnam*. New York: Oxford University Press, 1986.

Hamilton, John Maxwell. *Journalism's Roving Eye: A History of American Foreign Reporting*. Baton Rouge: Louisiana State University Press, 2009.

Hammond, William M. *Reporting Vietnam: Media and Military at War*. Lawrence: University Press of Kansas, 1998.

Hannerz, Ulf. *Foreign News: Exploring the World of Foreign Correspondents*. Chicago: University of Chicago Press, 2004.

Hartsock, John C. *A History of American Literary Journalism: The Emergence of a Modern Narrative Form*. Amherst: University of Massachusetts, 2000.

Hasty, Olga Peters, and Susanne Fusso, eds. *America through Russian Eyes, 1874–1926.* New Haven, CT: Yale University Press, 1988.

Haynes, John Earl. "The Cold War Debate Continues: A Traditionalist View of Historical Writing on Domestic Communism and Anti-Communism." *Journal of Cold War Studies* 2, no. 1 (2000): 76–115.

Hellbeck, Jochen. "Everyday Ideology: Life during Stalinism." *Eurozine,* February 22, 2010. https://www.eurozine.com/everyday-ideology-life-during-stalinism/.

———. *Revolution on My Mind: Writing a Diary under Stalin.* Cambridge, MA: Harvard University Press, 2006.

———. "'The Diaries of Fritzes and the Letters of Gretchens': Personal Writings from the German-Soviet War and Their Readers." *Kritika: Explorations in Russian and Eurasian History* 10, no. 3 (2009): 571–606.

Hellbeck, Jochen, and Klaus Heller, eds. *Autobiographical Practices in Russia = Autobiographische Praktiken in Russland.* Göttingen, Germany: V&R Unipress, 2004.

Hendershot, Cyndy. *Anti-Communism and Popular Culture in Mid-Century America.* Jefferson, NC: McFarland, 2003.

Henriksen, Margot A. *Dr. Strangelove's America: Society and Culture in the Atomic Age.* Berkeley: University of California Press, 1997.

Herman, Edward S., and Noam Chomsky. *Manufacturing Consent: The Political Economy of the Mass Media.* New York: Pantheon Books, 2002.

Hertsgaard, Mark. *On Bended Knee: The Press and the Reagan Presidency.* New York: Farrar, Straus, Giroux, 1988.

Hess, Stephen. *International News and Foreign Correspondents.* Washington, DC: Brookings Institution, 1996.

———. *Through Their Eyes: Foreign Correspondents in the United States.* Washington, DC: Brookings Institution, 2005.

Hixson, Walter L. *Parting the Curtain: Propaganda, Culture, and the Cold War, 1945–1961.* New York: St. Martin's Press, 1998.

Hogan, Michael J. *The Ambiguous Legacy: U.S. Foreign Relations in the "American Century."* Cambridge: Cambridge University Press, 1999.

Hoover, John Edgar. *Masters of Deceit: The Story of Communism in America.* London: J. M. Dent and Sons, 1958.

Hough, Jerry F. "The Foreign Policy Establishment." In *Soviet Foreign Policy in a Changing World,* edited by Robbin Frederick Laird and Erik P. Hoffmann, 141–158. Hawthorne, NY: Aldine, 1986.

Hunt, Michael H. *Ideology and U.S. Foreign Policy.* New Haven, CT: Yale University Press, 2009.

Huxtable, Simon. "A Compass in the Sea of Life: Soviet Journalism, the Public, and the Limits of Reform after Stalin, 1953–1968." PhD diss., Birkbeck, University of London, 2013.

———. "Making News Soviet: Rethinking Journalistic Professionalism after Stalin, 1953–1970." *Contemporary European History* 27, no. 1 (2018): 59–84.

———. "The Life and Death of Brezhnev's Thaw: Changing Values in Soviet Journalism after Khrushchev, 1964–1968." In *Reconsidering Stagnation in the Brezhnev Era,* edited by Dina Fainberg and Artemy M. Kalinovsky, 21–42. Lanham, MD: Lexington Books, 2016.

Il'f, Il'ia, and Evgenii Petrov. *Odnoetazhnaia Amerika.* Moscow: Tekst, 2004.

Ilf, Ilya, Evgenii Petrov, and Aleksandra Ilf. *Ilf and Petrov's American Road Trip: The 1935 Travelogue of Two Soviet Writers.* Princeton, NJ: Princeton Architectural Press, 2007.

Ilic, Melanie, and Jeremy Smith. *Soviet State and Society under Nikita Khrushchev.* London: Routledge, 2009.

Ivanian, E. A. *Kogda govoriat muzy: Istoriia Rossiisko-Amerikanskikh kul'turnykh sviazei.* Moscow: Mezhdunarodnye otnosheniia, 2007.

Jansen, Sue Curry. *Censorship: The Knot That Binds Power and Knowledge*. New York: Oxford University Press, 1988.

Johnston, Timothy. *Being Soviet: Identity, Rumour, and Everyday Life under Stalin, 1939–53*. Oxford: Oxford University Press, 2011.

Jones, Polly. "From the Secret Speech to the Burial of Stalin: Real and Ideal Response to De-Stalinization." In *The Dilemmas of De-Stalinization: Negotiating Cultural and Social Change in the Khrushchev Era*, edited by Polly Jones, 41–63. London: Routledge, 2006.

———. ed. *The Dilemmas of De-Stalinization: Negotiating Cultural and Social Change in the Khrushchev Era*. London: Routledge, 2006.

Kalinovsky, Artemy M., and Craig Daigle, eds. *The Routledge Handbook of the Cold War*. London: Routledge, 2014.

Kalugin, Oleg. *Spymaster: My Thirty-Two Years in Intelligence and Espionage against the West*. New York: Basic Books, 2009.

Keeble, Richard, and Sharon Wheeler. *The Journalistic Imagination: Literary Journalists from Defoe to Capote and Carter*. New York: Routledge, 2007.

Keen, Sam. *Faces of the Enemy: Reflections of the Hostile Imagination*. San Francisco: Harper and Row, 1986.

Kellner, Douglas. *Media Spectacle*. London: Routledge, 2003.

Kelly, Catriona. "Defending Children's Rights, 'In Defense of Peace': Children and Soviet Cultural Diplomacy." *Kritika: Explorations in Russian and Eurasian History* 9, no. 4 (2008): 711–46.

———. *Refining Russia: Advice Literature, Polite Culture, and Gender from Catherine to Yeltsin*. Oxford: Oxford University Press, 2001.

Kenez, Peter. *A History of the Soviet Union from the Beginning to the End*. New York: Cambridge University Press, 2006.

———. *The Birth of the Propaganda State: Soviet Methods of Mass Mobilization, 1917–1929*. Cambridge: Cambridge University Press, 1985.

Kennan, George. *Siberia and the Exile System*. London: Osgood and McIlvaine, 1891.

Kennan, George F. *The Marquis de Custine and His Russia in 1839*. Princeton, NJ: Princeton University Press, 1971.

Keyssar, Helene. "Space Bridges: The U.S.–Soviet Space Bridge Resource Center." *PS: Political Science and Politics* 27, no. 2 (1994): 247–53.

Kharkhordin, Oleg. *The Collective and the Individual in Russia: A Study of Practices*. Berkeley: University of California Press, 1999.

Khrushchev, Nikita Sergeevich. *Vremia. Liudi. Vlast': Vospominania*. Moscow: Moskovskie Novosti, 1999.

Klehr, Harvey, John Earl Haynes, and K. M Anderson, eds. *The Soviet World of American Communism*. New Haven, CT: Yale University Press, 1998.

Knight, Amy. *How the Cold War Began: The Igor Gouzenko Affair and the Hunt for Soviet Spies*. New York: Carroll and Graf, 2007.

Koivunen, Pia. "Performing Peace and Friendship: The World Youth Festival as a Tool of Soviet Cultural Diplomacy, 1947–1957." PhD diss., University of Tampere, 2013.

———. "The Moscow 1957 Youth Festival: Propagating a New Peaceful Image of the Soviet Union." In *Soviet State and Society under Nikita Khrushchev*, edited by Melanie Ilic and Jeremy Smith, 46–65. London: Routledge, 2009.

Koltsova, Olessia. *News Media and Power in Russia*. London: Routledge, 2006.

Korolenko, Vladimir Glaktionovich. *Bez iazyka*. Moscow, 1885.

Korotich, Vitalii. *Ot pervogo litsa*. Moscow: Akt, 2005.

Kotkin, Stephen. *Armageddon Averted: The Soviet Collapse, 1970–2000*. Oxford: Oxford University Press, 2008.

———. *Magnetic Mountain: Stalinism as a Civilization.* Berkeley: University of California Press, 1995.

Kozlov, Denis. *The Readers of Novyi Mir: Coming to Terms with the Stalinist Past.* Cambridge, MA: Harvard University Press, 2013.

Kozlov, Denis, and Eleonory Gilburd, eds. *The Thaw: Soviet Society and Culture during the 1950s and 1960s.* Toronto: University of Toronto Press, 2013.

Kritika Editorial. "Passing through the Iron Curtain." *Kritika: Explorations in Russian and Eurasian History* 9, no. 4 (2008): 703–9.

Krugler, David F. *The Voice of America and the Domestic Propaganda Battles, 1945–1953.* Columbia: University of Missouri Press, 2000.

Krylova, Anna. "'Healers of the Wounded Souls': The Crisis of Private Life in Soviet Literature, 1944–1946." *Journal of Modern History* 73, no. 2 (2001): 307–31.

———. "The Tenacious Liberal Subject in Soviet Studies." *Kritika: Explorations in Russian and Eurasian History* 1, no. 1 (2000): 119–46.

Kulikova, G. B. "Pod kontrolem gosudarstva: Prebyvanie v SSSR inostrannykh pisatelei v 1920-1930-kh godakh." *Otechestvennaia istoriia* 4 (2003): 43–59.

Kurilla, Ivan. *Zakliatye druz'ia: Istoriia mnenii, kontaktov, vzaimo(ne)ponimaniia Rossii i SShA.* Moscow: Novoe literaturnoe obozrenie, 2018.

———. *Zaokeanskie partnery: Amerika i Rossiia v 1830–1850e gody.* Volgograd: Izdatel'stvo Volgogradskogo Gosudarstvennogo Universiteta, 2005.

LaFeber, Walter. *America, Russia, and the Cold War, 1945–2006.* 10th ed. Boston: McGraw-Hill, 2008.

Latham, Michael E. *Modernization as Ideology: American Social Science and "Nation Building" in the Kennedy Era.* Chapel Hill: University of North Carolina Press, 2000.

Lavrenev, Boris. *Golos Ameriki.* Moscow: Isskustvo, 1949.

Lears, T. J. Jackson. *Fables of Abundance: A Cultural History of Advertising in America.* New York: Basic Books, 1994.

———. *No Place of Grace: Antimodernism and the Transformation of American Culture, 1880–1920.* New York: Pantheon Books, 1981.

Lebovic, Sam. *Free Speech and Unfree News: The Paradox of Press Freedom in America.* Cambridge, MA: Harvard University Press, 2016.

Leffler, Melvyn P., and Odd Arne Westad. *The Cambridge History of the Cold War.* 3 vols. Cambridge: Cambridge University Press, 2010.

Lendvai, Paul. *Blacklisted: A Journalist's Life in Central Europe.* London: I. B. Tauris, 1998.

———. *The Bureaucracy of Truth: How Communist Governments Manage the News.* London: Burnett Books; Boulder, CO: Westview Press, 1981.

Leonard, Thomas C. *The Power of the Press: The Birth of American Political Reporting.* New York: Oxford University Press, 1986.

Lippmann, Walter. *Public Opinion.* The Project Gutenberg E-Book No. 6456, 2004. http://www.gutenberg.org/ebooks/6456. First published 1922 by Macmillan (New York).

Lipset, Seymour Martin. *American Exceptionalism: A Double-Edged Sword.* New York: W. W. Norton, 1997.

Losev, Lev. *On the Beneficence of Censorship: Aesopian Language in Modern Russian Literature.* Munich: O. Sagner in Kommission, 1984.

———. *Zakrytyi raspredelitel'.* Ann Arbor, MI: Hermitage, 1984.

Lovell, Stephen. *Russia in the Microphone Age: A History of Soviet Radio, 1919–1970.* Oxford: Oxford University Press, 2015.

———. *The Russian Reading Revolution: Print Culture in the Soviet and Post-Soviet Eras.* Basingstoke, UK: Macmillan, 2000.

Lucas, Scott. *Freedom's War: The American Crusade against the Soviet Union.* New York: New York University Press, 1999.

Lyons, Eugene. *Assignment in Utopia.* New Brunswick, NJ: Transaction Publishers, 1938.

Lyons, Louis Martin, ed. *Reporting the News: Selections from Nieman Reports.* Cambridge, MA: Harvard University Press, 1965.

Madsen, Deborah L. *American Exceptionalism.* Jackson: University Press of Mississippi, 1998.

Magnúsdóttir, Rósa. "'Be Careful in America, Premier Khrushchev!': Soviet Perceptions of Peaceful Coexistence with the United States in 1959." *Cahiers Du Monde Russe* 47, no. 1/2 (2006): 109–30.

———. *Enemy Number One: The United States of America in Soviet Ideology and Propaganda, 1945–1959.* New York: Oxford University Press, 2019.

Makarevich, Andrey. *Sam ovtsa.* Moscow: Zakharov, 2005.

Maltese, John Anthony. *Spin Control: The White House Office of Communications and the Management of Presidential News.* Chapel Hill: University of North Carolina Press, 2000.

Mamleev, Dmitrii, ed. *Aleksei Adzhubei v koridorakh chetvertoi vlasti.* Moscow: Izvestiia, 2003.

Manning, Martin. "Impact of Propaganda Materials in Free World Countries." In *Pressing the Fight: Print, Propaganda, and the Cold War*, edited by Greg Barnhisel and Catherine Turner, 145–68. Amherst: University of Massachusetts Press, 2010.

Masuda, Hajimu. *Cold War Crucible: The Korean Conflict and the Postwar World.* Cambridge, MA: Harvard University Press, 2015.

Matlock, Jack. *Reagan and Gorbachev: How the Cold War Ended.* New York: Random House, 2004.

Matusevich, Maxim. "'Harlem Globe-Trotters': Black Sojourners in Stalin's Soviet Union." In *The Harlem Renaissance Revisited*, edited by Jeffrey O. G. Ogbar, 211–244. Baltimore, MD: Johns Hopkins University Press, 2008.

May, Elaine Tyler. *Homeward Bound: American Families in the Cold War Era.* New York: Basic Books, 1988.

May, Lary, ed. *Recasting America: Culture and Politics in the Age of Cold War.* Chicago: University of Chicago Press, 1989.

Mayakovsky, Vladimir. *Brooklyn Bridge.* Translated by Harry Lewis. New York: Broadway Boogie Press, 1974.

McNair, Brian. *Glasnost, Perestroika, and the Soviet Media.* London: Routledge, 1991.

———. *Images of the Enemy: Reporting the New Cold War.* London: Routledge, 1988.

McPherson, James Brian. *Journalism at the End of the American Century, 1965–Present.* Westport, CT: Greenwood Publishing Group, 2006.

McReynolds, Louise. "Dateline Stalingrad: Newspaper Correspondents at the Front." In *Culture and Entertainment in Wartime Russia*, edited by Richard Stites, 28–43. Bloomington: Indiana University Press, 1995.

Mickiewicz, Ellen. *Media and the Russian Public.* New York: Praeger, 1981.

———. *Split Signals: Television and Politics in the Soviet Union.* New York: Oxford University Press, 1992.

Mikkonen, Simo. "Stealing the Monopoly of Knowledge? Soviet Reactions to U.S. Cold War Broadcasting." *Kritika: Explorations in Russian and Eurasian History* 11, no. 4 (2010): 771–805.

Mindich, David T. Z. *Just the Facts: How "Objectivity" Came to Define American Journalism.* New York: New York University Press, 2006.

Mitrokhin, Nikolai. "The Elite of 'Closed Society': MGIMO, International Departments of the Apparatus of the CPSU Central Committee, and the Prosopography of Their Cadres." *Ab Imperio*, no. 4 (2013): 145–85.

Mitrovich, Gregory. *Undermining the Kremlin: America's Strategy to Subvert the Soviet Bloc, 1947–1956*. Ithaca, NY: Cornell University Press, 2000.

Mlechin, Leonid M. *Brezhnev*. Moscow: Izdatel'svo Prospekt, 2006.

Nadel, Alan. *Containment Culture: American Narratives, Postmodernism and the Atomic Age*. Durham, NC: Duke University Press, 1995.

Nadzhafov, Dzhahangir G. "The Beginning of the Cold War between East and West: The Aggravation of Ideological Confrontation." *Cold War History* 4, no. 2 (2004): 140–74.

Narinsky, Mikhail N., and Lydia V. Pozdeeva. "Mutual Perceptions: Images, Ideas, and Illusions." In *Allies at War: The Soviet, American, and British Experience, 1939–1945*, edited by David Reynolds, Warren F. Kimball, and Alexander O. Chubarian, 307–32. New York: St. Martin's Press, 1994.

Nathans, Benjamin. "Talking Fish: On Soviet Dissident Memoirs." *Journal of Modern History* 87, no. 3 (2015): 579–614.

———. "Thawed Selves: A Commentary on the Soviet First Person." *Kritika: Explorations in Russian and Eurasian History* 13, no. 1 (2012): 177–83.

———. *To the Success of Our Hopeless Cause: A History of the Soviet Dissident Movement*. Forthcoming.

Neumann, Iver B. *Uses of the Other: The "East" in European Identity Formation*. Minneapolis: University of Minnesota Press, 1999.

Nevzhin, Vladimir A. *"Esli zavtra v pokhod . . .": Podgotovka k voine i ideologicheskaia propaganda v 30-kh–40-kh godakh*. Moscow: Eksmo, 2007.

Nikoliukin, Aleksandr Nikolaevich. *A Russian Discovery of America*. Moscow: Progress Publishers, 1986.

Nove, Alec. "Social Welfare in the USSR." *Problems of Communism* 9 (January 1960): 1–10.

Ollman, Bertell. *Alienation: Marx's Conception of Man in Capitalist Society*. Cambridge: Cambridge University Press, 1972.

Osgood, Kenneth Alan. *Total Cold War: Eisenhower's Secret Propaganda Battle at Home and Abroad*. Lawrence: University of Kansas Press, 2006.

Ovchinnikov, Vsevolod Vladimirovich. *Kaleidoskop zhizni*. Moscow: Rossiiskaia gazeta, 2003.

Ovsepian, Rafail Pogosovich. *Istoriia noveishei otechestvennoi zhurnalistiki: Fevral' 1917–nachalo 90-kh godov*. 3rd ed. Moscow: Izdatel'stvo Moskovskogo universiteta, 2005.

Panchenko, Aleksandr. "'Potemkinskie Derevni' kak kul'turnyi mif." *XVIII Vek* 14 (1983): 93–101.

Paperno, Irina. *Chernyshevsky and the Age of Realism: A Study in the Semiotics of Behavior* Stanford, CA: Stanford University Press, 1988.

Parry-Giles, Shawn J. "Militarizing America's Propaganda Program, 1945–55." In *Critical Reflections on the Cold War: Linking Rhetoric and History*, edited by Martin J. Medhurst and H. W. Brands, 95–133. College Station: Texas A&M University Press, 2000.

Patterson, James T. *Grand Expectations: The United States, 1945–1974*. New York: Oxford University Press, 1996.

———. *Restless Giant: The United States from Watergate to Bush v. Gore*. New York: Oxford University Press, 2005.

Peacock, Margaret. "Broadcasting Benevolence: Images of the Child in American, Soviet and NLF Propaganda in Vietnam, 1964–1973." *Journal of the History of Childhood and Youth* 3, no. 1 (2010): 15–38.

———. *Innocent Weapons: The Soviet and American Politics of Childhood in the Cold War*. Chapel Hill: University of North Carolina Press, 2014.

Pechatnov, Vladimir. "Exercise in Frustration: Soviet Foreign Propaganda in the Early Cold War, 1945–1947." *Cold War History* 1, no. 2 (2001): 1–27.

———. "'The Allies Are Pressing on You to Break Your Will . . .' Foreign Policy Correspondence between Stalin and Molotov and Other Politburo Members, September 1945–December 1946." Cold War International History Project. Working Paper no. 26. Washington, DC: Woodrow Wilson Center, 1999.

———. "The Big Three after World War II: New Documents on Soviet Thinking about Post-War Relations with the United States and Great Britain." Cold War International History Project. Working Paper no. 13. Washington, DC: Woodrow Wilson Center, 1995.

Peoples, Columba. "Sputnik and 'Skill Thinking' Revisited: Technological Determinism in American Responses to the Soviet Missile Threat." *Cold War History* 8, no. 1 (2008): 55–75.

Peris, Daniel. "Custiniana: The Many Histories of a Single Trip to Russia 180 Years Ago, and Why It Matters Today." Forthcoming.

Perlstein, Rick. *Nixonland: The Rise of a President and the Fracturing of America.* New York: Simon and Schuster, 2010.

———. *The Invisible Bridge: The Fall of Nixon and the Rise of Reagan.* New York: Simon and Schuster, 2014.

Pogodin, Nikolai. *Missuriiskii val's.* Moscow: Isskustvo, 1950.

Polevoi, Boris. *Ocherk v gazete.* Moscow: Izdatel'stvo vyshei partiinoi shkoly pri TsK KPSS, 1953.

Polianovskii, Eduard. "Piat' printsipov Alekseia Adzhubeia." *Izvestiia,* September 10, 2011.

Potter, David Morris. *People of Plenty: Economic Abundance and the American Character.* Chicago: University of Chicago Press, 1954.

Pozner, Vladimir. *Proshchanie s illiuziiami.* Moscow: AST, 2011.

Raleigh, Donald J. *Russia's Sputnik Generation: Soviet Baby Boomers Talk about Their Lives.* Bloomington: Indiana University Press, 2006.

———. *Soviet Baby Boomers: An Oral History of Russia's Cold War Generation.* Oxford: Oxford University Press, 2012.

Read, Christopher J. "Peeping through the Curtain: Travellers' Accounts of the Soviet Union and Russia during and after the Cold War." Paper presented at the 9th Annual Aleksanteri Conference "Cold War Interactions Reconsidered," Helsinki, October 29–31, 2009.

Reagan, Ronald. *The Reagan Diaries.* Edited by Douglas Brinkley. New York: HarperCollins, 2009.

Reed, John. *Ten Days That Shook the World.* Mineola, NY: Dover Publications, 2012.

Reid, Susan E. "Cold War in the Kitchen: Gender and the De-Stalinization of Consumer Taste in the Soviet Union under Khrushchev." *Slavic Review* 61, no. 2 (2002): 211–52.

———. "Who Will Beat Whom? Soviet Popular Receptions of the American National Exhibition in Moscow, 1959." *Kritika: Explorations in Russian and Eurasion History* 9, no. 4 (2008): 855–904.

Remington, Thomas F. *The Truth of Authority: Ideology and Communication in the Soviet Union.* Pittsburgh, PA: University of Pittsburgh Press, 1988.

Reporters of the Associated Press. *Breaking News: How the Associated Press Has Covered War, Peace, and Everything Else.* New York: Princeton Architectural Press, 2007.

Reston, James. *Deadline: A Memoir.* New York: Times Books, 1992.

Reynolds, David, Warren F. Kimball, and Alexander O. Chubarian. *Allies at War: The Soviet, American, and British Experience, 1939–1945.* New York: St. Martin's Press, 1994.

Rieder, Jonathan. "The Rise of the Silent Majority." In *The Rise and Fall of the New Deal Order,* edited by Garry Gerstle and Steve Fraser, 243–68. Princeton, NJ: Princeton University Press, 1989.

Roberts, Geoffrey. *The Soviet Union in World Politics. Co-existence, Revolution, and Cold War, 1945–1991.* London: Routledge, 1999.

Rodgers, Daniel T. *Age of Fracture*. Cambridge, MA: Belknap Press of Harvard University Press, 2012.

———. *Contested Truths: Keywords in American Politics Since Independence*. Cambridge, MA: Harvard University Press, 1998.

Rogger, Hans. "America in the Russian Mind: Or Russian Discoveries of America." *Pacific Historical Review* 47, no. 1 (1978): 27–51.

Roman, Meredith L. *Opposing Jim Crow: African Americans and the Soviet Indictment of U.S. Racism, 1928–1937.* Lincoln: University of Nebraska Press, 2012.

Rosenberg, Emily S. *Spreading the American Dream: American Economic and Cultural Expansion, 1890–1945*. New York: Hill and Wang, 1982.

Roth-Ey, Kristin. *Moscow Prime Time: How the Soviet Union Built the Media Empire That Lost the Cultural Cold War*. Ithaca, NY: Cornell University Press, 2011.

Roudakova, Natalia. *Losing Pravda: Ethics and the Press in Post-Truth Russia*. Cambridge: Cambridge University Press, 2017.

Roxburgh, Angus. *Pravda: Inside the Soviet News Machine*. New York: G. Braziller, 1987.

Rubenstein, Joshua. "Ilya Ehrenburg: Between East and West." *Journal of Cold War Studies* 4, no. 1 (2002): 44–65.

———. *Tangled Loyalties: The Life and Times of Ilya Ehrenburg*. Tuscaloosa: University of Alabama Press, 1999.

Rupprecht, Tobias. *Soviet Internationalism after Stalin: Interaction and Exchange between the USSR and Latin America during the Cold War*. Cambridge: Cambridge University Press, 2015.

Ryan, Karen L. "Imagining America: Il'f and Petrov's 'Odnoetazhnaia Amerika' and Ideological Alterity." *Canadian Slavonic Papers/Revue Canadienne des Slavistes* 44, no. 3/4 (2002): 263–77.

Sagal, Grigorii Aleksandrovich. *Dvadtsat' piat' interv'iu: Tak rabotaiut zhurnalisty*. Moscow: Izdatel'stvo politicheskoi literatury, 1978.

Sakharov, Andrei. *Vospominania v dvukh tomakh*. Moscow: Prava cheloveka, 1996.

Salinger, Pierre E. G. *With Kennedy*. New York: Doubleday, 1966.

Salisbury, Harrison E. *A Journey for Our Times: A Memoir*. New York: Harper and Row, 1983.

———. *Without Fear or Favor: The New York Times and Its Times*. New York: Times Books, 1980.

Sanders, Jerry Wayne. *Peddlers of Crisis: The Committee on the Present Danger and the Politics of Containment*. Cambridge, MA: South End Press, 1983.

Saul, Norman E. *Friends or Foes? The United States and Soviet Russia, 1921–1941*. Lawrence: University Press of Kansas, 2006.

Schorr, Daniel. *Staying Tuned: A Life in Journalism*. New York: Pocket Books, 2001.

Schrecker, Ellen, ed. *Cold War Triumphalism: The Misuse of History after the Fall of Communism*. New York: New Press, 2004.

———. *Many Are the Crimes: McCarthyism in America*. Princeton, NJ: Princeton University Press, 1999.

Schudson, Michael. *Discovering the News: A Social History of American Newspapers*. New York: Basic Books, 1978.

———. "News, Public, Nation." *American Historical Review* 107, no. 2 (2002): 481–95.

Scott, John, and Stephen Kotkin. *Behind the Urals: An American Worker in Russia's City of Steel*. Bloomington: Indiana University Press, 1989.

Seeger, Murray. *Discovering Russia: 200 Years of American Journalism*. Bloomington, IN: Author House, 2005.

Sergeev, R. A. "Na chasakh vozle krymskogo mosta (1945–1950)." *Diplomaticheskii Vestnik* 2002, no. 1.

Sergeev, Stanislav. *Izvestiia: Strana, sobytiia, sud'by*. Moscow: V. K. Mamontov, 2007.

Shanor, Donald R. *Behind the Lines: The Private War against Soviet Censorship.* New York: St. Martin's Press, 1985.

———. *News from Abroad.* New York: Columbia University Press, 2003.

Sharansky, Natan. *Ne uboius' zla.* Moscow: Sovetskii Pisatel', 1991.

Shcherbenok, Andrey. "Asymmetric Warfare: The Vision of the Enemy in American and Soviet Cold War Cinemas." *Kino-Kultura,* April 2010.

Sherry, Samantha. *Discourses of Regulation and Resistance: Censoring Translation in the Stalin and Khrushchev Era Soviet Union.* Edinburgh: Edinburgh University Press, 2015.

Shiraev, Eric, and Vladislav Zubok. *Anti-Americanism in Russia: From Stalin to Putin.* New York: Palgrave, 2000.

Shlapentokh, Dmitry, ed. *Russia between East and West: Scholarly Debates on Eurasianism.* International Studies in Sociology and Social Anthropology, vol. 102. Leiden, Netherlands: Brill, 2007.

Shultz, George P. *Turmoil and Triumph: Diplomacy, Power, and the Victory of the American Deal.* New York: Simon and Schuster, 2010.

Siebert, Frederick Seaton, Theodore Peterson, and Wilbur Lang Schramm. *Four Theories of the Press: The Authoritarian, Libertarian, Social Responsibility, and Soviet Communist Concepts of What the Press Should Be and Do.* Urbana: University of Illinois Press, 1963.

Siefert, Marsha. *Mass Culture and Perestroika in the Soviet Union.* New York: Oxford University Press, 1991.

Simonov, K., N. Virta, I. G. Ehrenburg, V. N. Bill'-Belotserkovskii, Brat'ia Tur, L. Sheinin, and S. Mikhalkov. *Za mir, za demokratiiu! Pesy.* Moscow: Sovetskii Pisatel', 1949.

Simonov, Konstantin. *Glazami cheloveka moego pokoleniia: Razmyshleniia o I.V. Staline.* Moscow: Kniga, 1990.

Simonov, Konstantin. *Sobranie sochinenii v desiati tomakh.* Moscow: Khudozhestvennaia literatura, 1980.

Sloan, W. David, ed. *American Journalism: History, Principles, Practices.* Jefferson, NC: McFarland, 2002.

Smith, Walter Bedell. *Moscow Mission, 1946–1949.* London: William Heinemann, 1950.

Solzhenitsyn, Alexander. *Bodalsia telenok s dubom: Ocherki liteaturnoi zhizni.* Paris: YMCA Press, 1975.

Sproule, J. Michael. *Propaganda and Democracy: The American Experience of Media and Mass Persuasion.* Cambridge: Cambridge University Press, 1997.

Starr, S. Frederick. "New Communications Technologies and Civil Society." In *Science and the Soviet Social Order,* edited by Loren Graham, 19–50. Cambridge, MA: Harvard University Press, 1990.

Steel, Ronald. *Walter Lippmann and the American Century.* New York: Vintage Books, 1981.

Stevens, Thomas. *Through Russia on a Mustang . . . with Illustrations from Photographs by the Author.* Boston: Educational Publishing Company, 1891.

Stites, Richard, ed. *Culture and Entertainment in Wartime Russia.* Bloomington: Indiana University Press, 1995.

Suri, Jeremi. *Power and Protest: Global Revolution and the Rise of Detente.* Cambridge, MA: Harvard University Press, 2003.

Susman, Warren. *Culture as History: The Transformation of American Society in the Twentieth Century.* New York: Pantheon Books, 1984.

Talese, Gay. *The Kingdom and the Power: Behind the Scenes at The New York Times: The Institution That Influences the World.* New York: Random House, 2013.

Taubman, William. *The View from Lenin Hills: Soviet Youth in Ferment.* London: H. Hamilton, 1968.

———. *Khrushchev: The Man and His Era.* New York: W. W. Norton, 2004.

———. *Gorbachev: His Life and Times*. New York: Simon and Schuster, 2017.

Taylor, S. J. *Stalin's Apologist: Walter Duranty, the New York Times's Man in Moscow*. New York: Oxford University Press, 1990.

Thompson, John B. *Ideology and Modern Culture: Critical Social Theory in the Era of Mass Communication*. Stanford, CA: Stanford University Press, 1990.

———. *Studies in the Theory of Ideology*. Berkeley: University of California Press, 1984.

———. *The Media and Modernity: A Social Theory of the Media*. Cambridge, UK: Polity Press, 1995.

Tolkunova, Tat'iana, ed. *Dvazhdy glavnyi: Vspominaia gazetu "Izvestiia" i L'va Tolkunova, ee redaktora s 1965 po 1976 i s 1983 po 1984 god*. Mocow: Russkaia kniga, 2002.

Tolz, Vera. *Russia: Inventing the Nation*. London: Bloomsbury Academic, 2001.

Tomoff, Kiril. *Virtuosi Abroad: Soviet Music and Imperial Competition during the Early Cold War, 1945–1958*. Ithaca, NY: Cornell University Press, 2015.

Topping, Seymour. *On the Front Lines of the Cold War: An American Correspondent's Journal from the Chinese Civil War to the Cuban Missile Crisis and Vietnam*. Baton Rouge: Louisiana State University Press, 2012.

Tsygankov, Andrei P. *Russia's Foreign Policy: Change and Continuity in National Identity*. Lanham, MD: Rowman and Littlefield, 2016.

———. "Russia's (Limited) Information War on the West." *Public Diplomacy*, June 5, 2017.

———. *The Dark Double: US Media, Russia, and the Politics of Values*. New York: Oxford University Press, 2019.

Vail', Petr, and Alexander Genis. *60-ye: Mir sovetskogo cheloveka*. Moscow: Novoe literaturnoe obozrenie, 2001.

Volkovskii, N. L. *Otechestvennaia zhurnalistika. 1950–2000*. Vol. 1. Saint Petersburg: Sankt-Peterburgskii Gosudarstvennyi Universitet, 2006.

Von Eschen, Penny M. *Satchmo Blows Up the World: Jazz Ambassadors Play the Cold War*. Cambridge, MA: Harvard University Press, 2004.

Wagnleitner, Reinhold, and Elaine Tyler May, eds. *Here, There, and Everywhere: The Foreign Politics of American Popular Culture*. Hanover, NH: University Press of New England, 2000.

Walicki, Andrzej. *A History of Russian Thought: From the Enlightenment to Marxism*. Stanford, CA: Stanford University Press, 1979.

Walker, Barbara B. "Moscow Human Rights Defenders Look West: Attitudes toward US Journalists in the 1960s and the 1970s." *Kritika: Explorations in Russian and Eurasian History* 9, no. 4 (2008): 905–27.

———. "On Reading Soviet Memoirs: A History of the 'Contemporaries' Genre as an Institution of Russian Intelligentsia Culture from the 1790s." *Russian Review* 59, no. 3 (2000): 327–52.

———. "The Moscow Correspondents, Soviet Human Rights Activists, and the Problem of the Western Gift." In *Americans Experience Russia: Encountering the Enigma, 1917 to the Present*, edited by Choi Chatterjee and Beth Holmgren, 139–57. New York: Routledge, 2013.

Wang, Jessica. *American Science in an Age of Anxiety: Scientists, Anticommunism, and the Cold War*. Chapel Hill: University of North Carolina Press, 1999.

Werth, Alexander. *Russia at War, 1941–1945: A History*. New York: Skyhorse Publishing, 2017.

Westad, Odd Arne. "The Cold War and the International History of the Twentieth Century." In *Cambridge History of the Cold War*, edited by Melvyn P. Leffler and Odd Arne Westad, vol. 1, 1–19. Cambridge: Cambridge University Press, 2010.

———. *The Global Cold War: Third World Interventions and the Making of Our Times*. Cambridge: Cambridge University Press, 2005.

White, Hayden. "The Question of Narrative in Contemporary Historical Theory." *Historical Theory* 23, no. 1 (1984): 1–33.

Whitfield, Stephen J. *The Culture of the Cold War*. Baltimore, MD: Johns Hopkins University Press, 1991.

Wolfe, Tomas C. *Governing Soviet Journalism: The Press and the Socialist Person after Stalin*. Bloomington: Indiana University Press, 2005.

Wolff, Larry. *Inventing Eastern Europe: The Map of Civilization on the Mind of the Enlightenment*. Stanford, CA: Stanford University Press, 1994.

Wyatt, Clarence R. *Paper Soldiers: The American Press and the Vietnam War*. New York: Norton, 1993.

Yurchak, Alexei. *Everything Was Forever, until It Was No More: The Last Soviet Generation*. Princeton, NJ: Princeton University Press, 2006.

Zakhar'ko, Vasilii, Leonid Ivanovich Kamynin, and Leonid Iosifovich Shinkarev, eds. *Stanislav Kondrashov v vospominaniiakh, dnevnikakh, perepiske*. Moscow: Liubimaia Rossiia, 2009.

Zassoursky, Yassen N. *Tekhnika dezinformatsii i obmana*. Moscow: Mysl', 1978.

Zelizer, Julian E. *Arsenal of Democracy: The Politics of National Security—From World War II to the War on Terrorism*. New York: Basic Books, 2010.

Zhirkov, G. V. *Istoriia sovetskoi tsenzury: Materialy k lektsionnomu kursu po istorii zhurnalistiki Rossii XX veka, spetskursam, spetsseminaram po istorii tsenzury*. Saint Petersburg: SPGU, 1994.

———. *Istoriia tsenzury v Rossii XIX–XX vv. Uchebnoe posobie*. Moscow: Aspekt Press, 2001.

Zhuravleva, Victoria Ivanovna. "Images of the United States in Putin's Russia, from Obama to Trump." *Journal of Soviet and Post-Soviet Politics and Society* 4, no. 1 (2018): 145–81.

———. *Ponimanie Rossii v S.Sh.A.: obrazy i mify, 1881–1914*. Moscow: RGGU, 2012.

———. "Rossiia kak 'drugoi' v prezidentskikh vyborakh v SShA 2016g." *Istoriia* 9, no. 8 (72) (2018), https://doi.org/10.18254/S0002446-9-1.

Zorin, Valentin Sergeevich. *Neizvestnoe ob izvestnom*. Moscow: Vagrius, 2000.

Zubkova, Elena. *Obshchestvo i reformy, 1945–1964*. Moscow: Rossiia Molodaia, 1993.

———. *Russia after the War: Hopes, Illusions, and Disappointments, 1945–1957*. Armonk, NY: M. E. Sharpe, 1998.

Zubok, Vladislav M. *A Failed Empire: The Soviet Union in the Cold War from Stalin to Gorbachev*. Chapel Hill: University of North Carolina Press, 2007.

———. *Zhivago's Children: The Last Russian Intelligentsia*. Cambridge, MA: Belknap Press of Harvard University Press, 2009.

Zubok, Vladislav M., and Konstantin Pleshakov. *Inside the Kremlin's Cold War: From Stalin to Khrushchev*. Cambridge, MA: Harvard University Press, 1996.

Page numbers in *italics* refer to figures.

Freeman, Harry, 98
Frus, Phyllis, 6
Fürst, Juliane, 172

Gagarin, Yuri, 89, 116
Galaktionov, Mikhail, *17,* 17–18, 25–26
Galanskov, Yuri, 213
Geneva Summit (1955), 82, 86, 90–91
Geneva Summit (1986), 234, 256
Gerasimov, Sergei, 81
Gilmore, Eddy, *66;* ad featuring, 112, *113;* on
  censorship, 115; on in-house experts, 66–67; on
  interpretive analysis, 65; jazz band of, 55;
  Molotov and, 48; scoops of, 56; Shapiro and, 51
Gilmore, Tamara, 53–54, 112, *113*
Ginzburg, Alexander, *209,* 213
*glasnost: Citizens Summit* and, 243; impact of,
  231–32; journalists' spacebridge and, 249–50,
  251–52, 253–54; Kondrashov and, 259; H. Smith
  on, 262
Glavlit (Main Directorate for the Protection of State
  Secrets in the Press), 49–51, 93, 127–28, 151, 256
Gorbachev, Mikhail: *Citizens Summit* and, 243;
  Daniloff case and, 237; interview of, by
  American correspondents, 227, 228–29; "new
  thinking" of, 231–32, 240, 252, 256; "peace
  offensive" of, 234–35; *perestroika* reforms of, 231,
  261, 262–64; H. Smith and, 260–61; on
  "stagnation," 264; US press on trustworthiness
  of, 236. See also *glasnost*
Goriunov, Dmitrii, 98, 149
Gorky, Maxim, 28, 148
Gosteleradio (State Committee for Television and
  Radio Broadcasting), 242, 243
Gouzenko, Igor, 31–32
government-press relations, overview of, 8–9, 12,
  79, 233
government-press relations of US: in anti-
  communist campaign, 73–74; investigative
  journalism, transformation, and, 188–93; in
  Moscow, 55–56; under Reagan, 232; Salisbury
  series and, 58–60; Soviet assumptions about,
  19–20; against Soviet information management,
  133–39; views of USSR and, 123–24
government-press relations of USSR: Adzhubei
  and, 109–10; under Gorbachev, 231–32; under
  Khrushchev, 81–82, 87, 92–94; long-form
  journalism and, 153–54; as model, 130–32; TASS
  and, 32–33, 99; US criticism of, 7. See also
  propaganda

Gribachev, Nikolai, *83,* 86
Gritsan, Vasily, *187*
Gromeka, Vasilii, 181
Grover, Preston, 136, 137
Gunther, John, *Inside Russia Today,* 121–22, 124
Gwertzman, Bernard, 218–19

Hajimu, Masuda, 269–70
Hearst, William Randolph, Jr., 23, 116–17
Hearst publications, 19, 116–17
Hedrick, Travis, 39
Helsinki Accords, 186
Herter, Christian A., 37
hippie movement: in US, 165, 168–70, 172–73; in
  USSR, 170, 172, 177
Hottelet, Richard, 52
House Foreign Affairs Committee, 37
human-interest (feature) stories, 6–7, 30, 100, 101–2
human rights: dissident movement and, 207, 208,
  212, 219, 220; NBC News feature on, 141, 142; in
  USSR, 235–36, 250
Hungarian Revolution, 95
Huxtable, Simon, 150

ideology: clarity of, as ideal, 95–96; definition of,
  283n4; at end of Cold War, 265–66; journalists
  on influence of, 245–46; news media and, in
  Cold War, 3–9, 270–73; in reports on "truth" of
  adversary's society, 142–43. See also biases in
  journalism; binary views; capitalism; socialism;
  truth
Il'f, Ilya, 27, 28, 148
Iliaschenko (TASS correspondent), 33–34
Immigration and Naturalization Service (US), 104
information management: American, 134; in
  American-Russian relations, 268–69. See also
  censorship in USSR; *glasnost;* Khrushchev
  Thaw; propaganda; restrictions on correspondents; sanctions
*Inside Russia Today* (Gunther), 121–22, 124
international commentators in USSR, 40–41
International News Service, 115
International Press Institute, *The News from Russia*
  survey of, 64–65
international reporting: American, discussion of,
  62–68; as framework for exploring USSR,
  139–40; Novosti Press Agency and, 108; Soviet,
  about US, 89–90; Soviet, new voices of, 91–96,
  100–108; Soviet, timely, 151–52; Soviet ideal for,
  81–82, 89; topics of, 78

*telemost. See* spacebridges

themes of Soviet correspondents: class conflict, 156, 158, 159–60, 165; plight of workers, 156–57; race conflict, 156, 158, 160, 165–67; soullessness of American life, 161–62

Thompson, Llewellyn, 134–35, 139

*Time* magazine, 227, 228–29

Todd, Laurence, 39

Toon, Malcolm, 103

Topping, Seymour, 140, 248, 250

Toth, Robert, 208

tourist destination, Soviet Union as, 119–20, 122, 123

travel, limits on: in US, 104–6, *105*; in USSR, 50, 211–12

Trimble, Jeff, 246

*Trud,* US bureau of, 91

Truman, Harry, and Truman administration, 32, 73, 134

truth: absolute and relative, 272; of adversary's society, 142–43; binary views of "lies" and, 4, 78, 264, 267–68, 269; Daniloff as exposing, 235–36; Kondrashov on, 264; of life in USSR, attempts to learn, 189–93; H. Smith on, 264; spacebridges and dissemination of, 253; as weapon against propaganda, 72–73

truth systems, foreign correspondents in, 2–3, 4–9, 12, 78, 270–73

Tucker, Elizabeth, 248, 250, 251

Tvardovskii, Aleksandr, 149

Twentieth Party Congress, 86–87, 149

Union of Soviet Journalists, 249

Union of Soviet Writers, 27–28, 83

United Press (UP), 51, 53, 57

United Press International (UPI), 115, 119, 121, 135–136. *See also* Shapiro, Henry

United States (US): concerns about influence of, in USSR, 94–96; consumer culture in, 161–64, 196–97, 224; events of 1968 in, 145–46; tours of, by Soviet journalists, 17–18, 82–86, *83,* 115–16. *See also* anti-communist campaign in US; capitalism; government-press relations of US; news media, US; State Department; *specific presidents*

US Embassy: Bassow expulsion and, 137; censorship and, 49; diplomatic pouches of, 50, 137–38; expansion of press corps promoted by, 139; as mediator between journalists and Soviet authorities, 138, 139, 214; Mosby incident and, 136;

relations with American journalists of, 55–56, 137–39, 212–14; relations with Soviet journalists of, 103, 178–81; Voice of America and, 59, 74

*U.S. News and World Report,* 234, 239, 244, 246

USSR. *See* Soviet Union

U-2 spy plane incident, 77, 121, 188, 240

Vietnam War: Soviet reporting on, 179–80; Tet Offensive in, 145; US citizens and, 205; US government-press relations and, 188–89. *See also* antiwar movement in US

visa wars, 139, 179, 211

Voice of America: anxieties about information and, 268–69; dissident movement and, 210; as "foreign agent," 267; R. Magidoff, Stevens, and, 56; reinvigoration of, 22; Salisbury on, 59; shortwave technology and, 151; Soviet jamming of, 132; US Embassy and, 74; Vietnam War and, 179

Vronskii, Boris, 45

Vyshinsky, Andrei, 29, 36, 38, 48–49

Wallace, George, Borovik on, 160–61

*Washington Post,* 139, 185, 237, 248. *See also* Kaiser, Robert G.

watchdog (investigative) journalism, 188–93, 206–14

welfare state: in US, Soviet critique of, 158–59, 161; in USSR, American critique of, 195–96

Whitney, Julie, 55

Whitney, Thomas, 53, 55, 58, 114

*Who Stole the American Dream?* (H. Smith), 266

Will, George, 238

Willis, David K., 164, 196, 197, 203–4

wives of US journalists in Moscow: American, 186; Soviet, 53–54, 63, 64, 65, 70, 112, 115

workers' plight theme of Soviet correspondents, 156–57

working conditions: Daniloff case and, 235–36, 238–39; diplomatic talks, cultural exchanges, and, 79; dissident movement and, 211; in Eastern Bloc, 64; foreigners' compounds in Moscow and, 186; Gilmore and Salisbury on, 65–66; intimidation of US journalists, 209–10, 211–14; Schwartz on, 62–63; Soviet information policies and, 127; Soviet outreach to American press as altering, 118–19; spacebridges and, 244; stories about, 192; in USSR, reactions to, 140. *See also* mistrust of US journalists in Moscow; restrictions on correspondents; sanctions

writers, as Soviet spokespeople, 16–20, *17,* 30